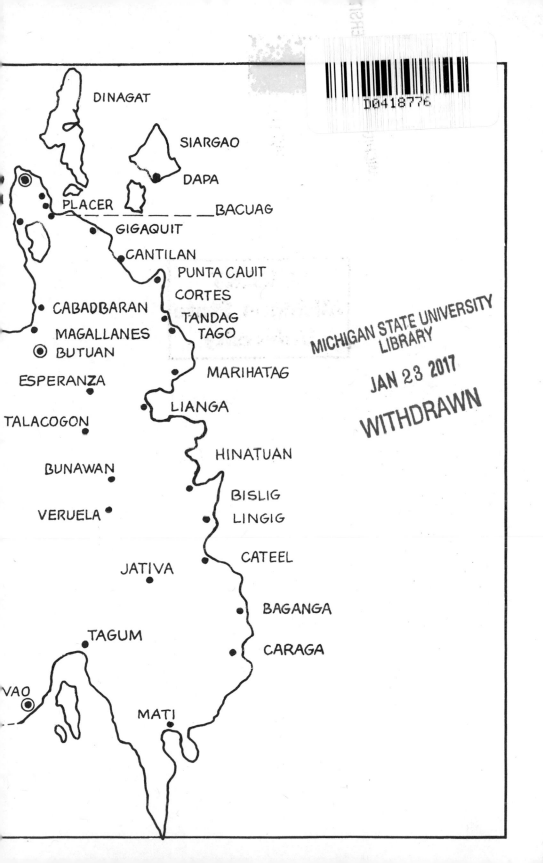

In grateful remembrance dedicated to all my former parishioners in Lingig (Surigao del Sur), Claver (Surigao del Norte), Tungao (Agusan del Norte) and Magallanes (Agusan del Norte).

Caraga Antigua 1521-1910

The Hispanization and Christianization of Agusan, Surigao and East Davao

Peter Schreurs, MSC

San Carlos Publications
University of San Carlos
Cebu City, Philippines
1989

Humanities Series No. 18
ISSN 0069-1321

ISBN 971-100-054-7 pb
ISBN 971-100-055-5 hb

SAN CARLOS PUBLICATIONS
University of San Carlos
6000 Cebu City, Philippines

Contents

Agusan about 1625. Fray Jacinto de San Fulgencio and "el padre capitan" Pedro de San Agustin. Discord between Jesuit and Recoleto missionaries about boundary line between districts.

protection. Siargao destroyed and missionary residence transferred to mainland Surigao. Missionaries killed or imprisoned. "Only the memory is left" of nearly all the former mission stations. Siege and fall of the fort of Tandag (1754) occasioned by rivalry among Spanish alcaldes and treason. Recapture of the fort by soldiers of Father Ducós, SJ of Iligan. Continuing Moro raids. The Englishman Nicolas Norton Nicols. Decline of the fort of Tandag and rise of Cantilan under Fray Valero de San Agustin.

Precarious Spanish hold on the devastated eastern seaboard and rest of Mindanao. Expulsion of the Jesuits (1768) by the Spanish Crown. Statistics. Decrease of missionaries as a result of religious persecution in Spain. Attemps at re-peopling abandoned coastal villages, especially Baganga and Caraga, and hesitancy of the dispersed Mandayas to settle there. Government and missionary reports about Cantilan, San Juan (Hinatuan), Cateel, Baganga and Caraga. Fray Joseph de Santa Orocia and his efforts to resettle Mandayas and protect them from abuse by Chinese merchants from Cebu. Alcalde Mayor Salvador Ximenez Rendon and his uneasy dealings with the Moros of Davao. The Recoletos abandon eastern Mindanao (1811) because of shortage of priests.

Repercussions in the Mindanao mission as a result of anti-clerical policies in Spain; dearth of religious. Secular priests in eastern Mindanao (1818). Reports of neglect of parishes and urgent requests by local and national government officials and people of Surigao for the return of the Recoletos. Hesitancy but eventual agreement by the Order (1831) under pressure by government and Bishop of Cebu. Campaign against the Moros of Davao Gulf by Governors Narciso Claveria and Jose Oyanguren; area under the latter's control in 1848. Administrative re-division of eastern Mindanao (1853). The Jesuits return to Mindanao; renewal of animosities with the Recoletos because of their removal from Mindanao on Government orders. Protests, but gradual take-over of the mission by the Jesuits. Antipolo and Cavite parishes given to Recoletos as compensation. Bitter reaction of Filipino clergy and prelude to the Cavite mutiny and the eventual Philippine revolution. Last Recoletos leave eastern Mindanao.

their surrender through the intervention of Urios. Butuan resists authority of Surigao under General Prudencio Garcia; finally forced to submit to him. Missionaries suspected of being "Americanistas." Clashes with local American authorities at Butuan and Cabadbaran because of the re-opening of the Catholic schools. Further troubles about ownership of church properties, especially cemeteries, and the performance of civil marriages. Protest notes by loyal Catholics at Butuan and Cabadbaran. The anti-clerical machinations of the Federal Party in Surigao and Agusan.

Benedictines taking over the Jesuit parishes of Surigao province, 1895-1902. The turbulent genesis of Aglipayanism in Cabadbaran and its anti-church activities in Agusan and Surigao. Political machinations by Governor Prudencio Garcia. Commotion around the transfer of the fiesta-date of Butuan. Aglipayan take-over in Placer, Bacuag and Dinagat. Guerilla-raid on American barracks at Surigao by Adriano Concepción. Supreme Court restores to the Catholic Church all properties taken over by the Aglipayans and local civil administrations. Increased troubles in Cabadbaran; Father Nebot abandons the parish. His extensive report to Governor-General Wright.

The Benedictines end their short stay in Surigao (1895-1908). Succeeded by the Dutch Sacred Heart Missionaries (MSC) in December 1908. Old troubles and new anxieties facing them right from the beginning. Nevertheless, a new era of stability and pastoral organization inaugurated by them.

ILLUSTRATIONS

Front Cover. View along the coastline of northern Surigao.

Introduction

In 1873 when the Spanish Jesuits of the Aragon Province were beginning to take over the Recoleto missions of Mindanao, Father Francisco Luengo, the first Jesuit parish priest of Surigao, made a reconnaissance trip by sailboat from Surigao to the south along the Pacific coast down to Sigaboy (Davao Oriental). Upon reaching the coastal village of Caraga, he wrote: *"Caraga, o que nombre este! Y cuantas ideas me despierta!"* (Caraga, what a name! And how many thoughts does it rouse in me!)

I think that I can perfectly sense the feelings behind that ebullient line. They must have been of the same kind as those that over the years have time and again gathered the momentum needed for the writing of these pages. From the earliest days of discovery till the middle of the nineteenth century, the name Caraga was not limited to only the just mentioned coastal village now belonging to Davao Oriental, but stood for the whole of east and northeast Mindanao, from Punta San Agustin (Davao) via Surigao and Butuan up to Gingoog (Misamis Oriental).

"Caraga Antigua" therefore is intended to be a contribution to the regional history of that piece of Mindanao which presently covers the province of eastern Davao, the two Surigao and the two Agusan provinces.

On p. 3 of his "Historia... (1667)" Francisco Combés speaks of "The coast of Caraga, like a wall opposing itself to the immensity of so many seas, as if to stop a wave of 3000 leagues." On p. 751 he explains the etymology of Caraga (Calagan in some sources) as deriving from "calag," the Bisaya word for "soul" or "spirit," making the territory known as a region of spirited, courageous people *(regio de gente animosa)*.

Since my arrival there in 1952, that area and its past have never ceased to cast a peculiar feeling of awe and fascination over me. That spell got all the more hold on me each time when opportunity, in the Philippines or elsewhere, brought to the surface more bits of information about its past. The urge to share such information became often a real obsession after the repeated discovery that the twentieth century development of national historiography has nearly totally relegated large parts of the nation — among them the old Caraga District — to a kind of historical non-entity. To this may be added that regional historiography — aside from its rather precarious infancy as a discipline — will soon put Filipino researchers before the added problem that its sparse primary source material is written in Spanish, a language which in our days has become a non-entity of its kind. Moreover, much of that material is deposited in places that are inaccessible to most "local" researchers.

Some years ago, a professional historian in the Philippines wrote me: "I envy you for being an amateur in the sense that you research and write out of love." Indeed, without such "amateurism" patiently nourished over the years (plus, of course, a healthy dose of natural curiosity) one would probably never have been able first to locate many of the widely scattered bits of information brought together in the following pages, and next to coax a form of writing into existence wherein to give them an acceptable ballast, shape and some relief. Perhaps — so I discovered post factum — the form chosen can be recognized in what François Furet said in "The Uses of History":

> "The 'history of events' [*histoire événementielle*] seems to me to be both a type of description of the past and a type of selection of the facts. Made with the intent to reconstitute the past "as it really happned;" and to tell it then by means of narrative, it chooses its materials according to these ambitions; that means that the latter, the famous "events," are selected and organized according to the time element in such a way as to impel the progress of a narrative" (p.57).

To which I hasten to add that often the scarce documentary material left little evidence to "select" from. At such moments, however, I found myself in the understanding company of the Spanish Recoleto cronista Pedro de S. Francisco de Asis, who in 1743 would write in the opening remarks to his "Historia General..." "We warn the reader that we shall follow no other chronological order than chance offers."

Notwithstanding the fact that there is a growing interest noticeable in regional/local history, also in east and northeast Mindanao, I am aware that this kind of writing can count on only a limited readership. But I am also convinced that nevertheless a start has to be made by somebody and in some form, even at the risk that, now or in the future, others (perhaps thanks to the information here offered) might conclude that there are better ways of dishing it up to an interested public. That risk is herewith gladly taken!

It is anyway understood that this might eventually even become necessary if ever more documentation would surface in the future. The publication in this form is itself already a further step taken after the author had previously published parts of the contents in journals such as the "Philippine Quarterly of Culture and Society" of the University of San Carlos and "Kinaadman" of Xavier University.

Throughout the hours spent on these pages, I have at all times been aware that what I was writing about was very much colonial exploits and colonial experiences in the Old Caraga. In order of appearance, Professor Resil Mojares has divided historical writing in the Philippines in two periods: 1) "Classical colonial scholarship" with its focus on the motives, actions and institutions of western imperialism; 2) Partly as a reaction hereto the "nationalist, Filipino-centric writings" of the 1950s and 1960s (Second National Conference on Local-Regional History, Silliman University, 1979).

As for my own pages, frankly, I do not know where they properly belong. On the one hand, the colonial motives, actions and institutions (including, mostly among the latter, the Church of those days), may not be those preferred by us in our "value-added" days...but time was when these were the only ones in existence and documented. In the Caraga of our context, it was nearly the whole time between 1521 and 1898 and even beyond. On the other hand it is also quite a futile experiment to saddle past generations with values and ethics that where then still in the limbo of a developing human

consciousness. At best we can ask our own times to draw appropriate
conclusions for our own and future generations. And then:

> "To accuse the Spanish, over and over again, of having
> brought us all sorts of things, mostly evil, among which we can
> usually remember nothing very valuable 'except perhaps', reli-
> gion and national unity, is equivalent to saying of a not very
> model mother that she has given her child nothing *except life....*
> The *content* of our national destiny is ours to create, but the
> basic *form*, the *temper*, the *physiognomy*, Spain has created for
> us." (Joaquin 1964:29-30).

As for colonial "experiences" then, there have of course been as
many motivations as actions... and where documented, I have tried
to bring them out with a certain option that, I hope, was not value-
free. But needless to say, they were far less documented and will at
times just have to be inferred.

In most cases, the sources used are clearly indicated as part of the
running text to save the reader as much as possible a troublesome
and interruptive recourse to separate notes or footnotes. A
bibliographic list of sources consulted over the past years is provided
at the end. It is not intended to be exhaustive.

Translations of Spanish texts, unless otherwise indicated, are my
own. On purpose I have often not aimed at "current business-
English," but kept much of the original style and flavor, which
might well be considered part of the text.

Among the many persons to whom I owe a debt of gratitude are
in the first place my superiors, who have given me sufficient freedom
and the facilities necessary for the research and writing that went into
these pages.

A very special word of appreciation goes herewith to the Prior,
archivist and the community of the Recoletos in Marcilla, Navarra,
Spain, for their boundless hospitality and the unlimited access
granted me to the holdings of their archive in May 1984.

The MSC communities in Madrid, Valladolid, Rome, Paris,
Valencia, and Barcelona offered a very welcome pied-à-terre for the
days spent on research in local archives and libraries. The same is
true for the administration and resident community of the
Universidad Pontificia de San Telmo in Sevilla and for Monica,
Maria and Julia of Poligono de San Pablo, Sevilla.

Research in the Jesuit archive at Sant Cugat del Vallés, the Benedictine archive at Montserrat and that of the Dominicans at Avila were facilitated through the great kindness and hospitality of the respective archivists and their religious communities.

With gratitude I also remember the assistance of the administrations and staff of the National Archives in Manila, the Biblioteca Nacional, Museo Naval and the Instituto Enrique Florez **in Madrid, the Archivo General del Reino in Simancas, the Archivo General de Indias in Sevilla, the Biblioteca Agustiniana in Valladolid** and the Jesuit archive in Rome.

Finally, allow me to express my great esteem to Father Joseph Baumgartner, SVD and Mrs. Lydia Colina Maldecer for all the editorial dedication they have spent on my scripta since 1977.

P. Schreurs, MSC
Tilburg, Holland
December 1987

I

On Being Discovered

There had been a slight diplomatic incident between Portugal and France in 1529. A French ship had been reported near the south coast of Sumatra, in violation of the monopoly to the Far East given by the Pope to Spain and Portugal. Part of the ensuing correspondence is a letter of protest by the Spanish government to King Francis I. Instead of apologizing, the King of France sent the following note to Charles V of Spain:

> "I would be very much interested in seeing the clause in the testament of Adam and Eve wherein it is stipulated that my brothers in Spain and Portugal are exclusively entitled to divide the world between them." (Quoted in P.A. Tiele, I, p. 28).

Notwithstanding that sarcastic response, the king was, of course, well aware that such a clause, although not written in the last will of our first parents, had been written by Pope Alexander VI in the Bulla "Inter caetera" of 1493, and in the Treaty of Tordesillas in 1494. Both had become necessary because two years earlier Christopher Columbus had performed a feat that to an astonished Europe was the fulfillment of the prophesy by Seneca: "Late in the years of the world there will be a time wherein the Ocean will release history of its shackles, and a great land will be opened; and a new seaman, like Jason's guide whose name was Tiphys, will discover a new world, and no longer will it be true that the island of Thule is the land-end of the world" (Seneca, "Medea").[1]

Indeed, a new world had been discovered in 1492, *ultramar,* overseas to the west: America. Even earlier, in 1487, Bartolome Diaz had opened the sea-route around Cape Good Hope to the East. Vazco da Gama reached Calcutta, Malabar and India. And before long it was going to be a family problem between the discoverers, Adam's children of Portugal and Spain, of who was entitled for the future to what part of the world. In the Treaty of Tordesillas the quarrel was settled (to a large extent) by Spain and Portugal agreeing to a demarcation line allotting each its own sphere of interest. The line would run 170 leagues (1000 km) west of the Azores, at the 44th degree western latitude. Future discoveries to the west of that line would become Spanish territories, everything east Portuguese property. Indeed, that was the right word: property, by virtue of the medieval *potestas directa* granted by the jurists to the Church and through her to the Christian kings over pagan territory to be discovered yet. In 1508 Pope Julius II granted to Spain the *"patronato"* rights and obligations to its colonies. The rights covered among other things the appointment of the bishops and other missionary personnel to colonial territories and the collection of taxes *(tributo)* from the natives; the obligations charged the Crown with the Christianization of the population.

But Maluku, where Portugal had entered in 1512, remained in so far contested territory that there was no clear-cut definition of its northern boundary. It is quite ironic that the companion of

---

[1] Translation of an inscription on one of the monuments at the east-side of Plaza Colon, Madrid, commemorating the voyage of Columbus.

Thule (Gr. *Thoulè*) was of old the name of the most northern point of the known world which had been discovered by Pytheas of Masalia about 330 B.C. during his voyage around Britain. It has been identified with the Shetland islands, with the west coast of Norway and with Iceland. The term "ultima Thule" has since become a general expression for a faraway country.

Alfonso de Albuquerque (who had brought the Portuguese flag to "Maluku") would seven years later be the leader of an expedition that tried to carry the Spanish banner there via the west. His name was Fernando Magallanes. Dissatisfaction with the Portuguese monarch had caused him to offer his expertise and loyalty to Charles V of Spain. The Emperor authorized him to try finding a way to Maluco by sailing westward with a fleet of five ships and 265 men. In 1519 when the fleet was ready for sailing at Sevilla, the commercial representative of Portugal stationed there to look after his country's business interests, wrote to his government: "They are a fleet of ships so worm-eaten that I would not even dare sail with them to the Azores!"

Among the sailors was a young scribe from Venice who had offered his services to Charles V as a cronista; as he said: "because you would be greatly pleased if I would write down for you all the things which I had seen and suffered during my voyage." His name was Antonio Pigafetta.

Magellan's fleet sailed out of the harbor of Sanlucar de Barrameda on September 20, 1519. On September 6, 1522 one leaky ship with tattered sails and 18 survivors of the original adventurers, most of them emaciated and sick, limped back into Sanlucar, struggled into the Guadalquivir River and anchored in the harbor of Sevilla just beyond the Torre de Oro. Writes Pigafetta at the end of his Journal:

> "From the time we left the bay [of Sanlucar] until the present day, we had sailed fourteen thousand four hundred and sixty leagues, and furthermore had completed the circumnavigation of the world from east to west. On Monday, September eight, we cast anchor near the quay of Sevilla, and discharged all our artillery. Tuesday, we all went in shirts and barefoot, each holding a candle, to visit the shrine of Santa Maria de la Victoria and that of Santa Maria de l'Antigua. Leaving Sevilla, I went to Valladolid where I presented to his sacred Majesty...a book, written by my hand, concerning all the matters that had occurred from day to day during our voyage" (Pigafetta 1969:100).

Through this Journal of Pigafetta, Mindanao, Surigao and Butuan sailed into written history for the first known time. Let us see what this adventurous cronista sailing through the Surigao Strait wrote when the fleet, having sailed too far north of an approach route to Maluku, had arrived at the coasts of the central and southern Philippines. We will take up the story at the moment when the expedition reaches the southern tip of Samar. From there they shaped their course WSW past some islands and anchored near a small one where they had seen some fire the night before. It was the morning of Holy Thursday, March 28, 1521. Eight natives approached the flagship in a *baroto*, but did not dare come aboard. Some presents were thrown down at them from the ship, and they left to call their chief, as it turned out. The latter eventually came and told some of his men to go aboard, although he himself stayed at a distance in his own boat. After thanking Magellan for the presents, he left.

In the afternoon, the Spaniards moved the ships and anchored not far from the beach at the west side of the island, close to the chief's place. Most of the communication was through sign language and some interpretation by a Malayan servant of Magellan, who hailed from Sumatra and was named Enrique. Next day, Good Friday, Magellan sent the latter ashore to see if there was some food available on the island. Coming back, he was accompanied by the chief and some of his men who this time came aboard the flagship, where they were well received by the expedition leader and given some presents. When they were going to leave, Pigafetta himself and one companion went ashore with them. On the beach they sat down under an awning of bamboo and palm leaves that sheltered a type of boat which the people called *"balanghay."* There, and again afterwards in the house of the chief, they were regaled with rice, pork and *tuba*. Pigafetta mentions that he had to eat meat on Good Friday and that his companion became even intoxicated. That night they slept in the chief's house, and next day, when they were going back to the ship, the brother of the chief came along; Pigafetta was informed that he was the ruler of "another island." Magellan invited him aboard his ship where he had dinner with the Spaniards.

> "Pieces of gold, of the size of walnuts and eggs, are found by sifting the earth in the island of that king whom I led to our ships. All the dishes of that king are of gold and also some portion of his house, as we were told by that king himself. According to their customs he was very grandly decked out, and

the finest looking man that we saw among those people. His hair was exceedingly black and hung to his shoulders. He had a covering of silk on his head, and two large golden earrings fastened in his ears. He wore a cotton cloth all embroidered with silk, which covered him from the waist to the knees. At his side hung a dagger, the haft of which was somewhat long and all of gold, and its scabbard of carved wood. He had three spots of gold on every tooth, and his teeth appeared as if bound with gold. He was perfumed with storax and benzoin. He was tawny and painted all over. That island of his was called Butuan and Calagan. [2] When those kings wished to see one another, they both went to hunt in that island where we were. The name of the first king is Raia Colambu, and the second Raia Siaui.

Early on the morning of Sunday, the last of March and Easterday, the captain-general sent the priest with some men to prepare the place where Mass was to be said; together with the interpreter to tell the king that we were not going to land in order to dine with him, but to say Mass'' (Pigafetta 1969:28-29).

---

[2]''Island of...'' A first-time reader of these and similar documents might be struck by terms as: ''the island of Butuan,'' ''the island of Caraga,'' ''the island of Bislig,'' etc. Often (like here) at the moment of the first arrival nearly all places were called ''islands,'' probably because they did not yet know how far the territory so named extended beyond what they could see of it. In fact, the expression means (for us) nothing more than the island where Butuan, Caraga or Bislig, etc., are located.

Furthermore, this might be the place to add a belated hesitant remark on the historiography dealing with ''Caraga.'' Up to the middle of the 19th century it includes Butuan in its district. Siaui, standing on Lima-sawa, pointed to a coast of Mindanao that was *visible* to him: Butuan straight southward, and the headland of Surigao with its coastline running southeast towards Cantilan, in the early reports afterwards named ''Calagan.'' Pigafetta writes: ''That island of his was called Butuan and Calagan.'' The Pigafetta sketch exhibits both as very distinct regions, indeed, and in that supposition the information given by Siaui to Pigafetta *meant:* ''On that island pointed out by him was Butuan and Calagan.'' Later geographic descriptions and maps (solely based on a literal translation of Siaui's meaning ?) have given the name ''Caraga'' to one continuous region running from appr. Gingoog and Butuan via Surigao

Later, after the Mass, a large wooden cross was put on top of a hill. The inhabitants attended both ceremonies with great reverence. They made it clear to Magellan "thay they had no other worship but raising their clasped hands and their face to the sky, and that they called their god 'Abba'."

That island, writes Pigafetta "lies in a latitude of nine and two-third degrees and in a longitude 162 degrees from the line of demarcation. It is 25 leagues from Acquada[3] and is called Mazaua."[4]

Well, that was clear and factual reporting by an eyewitness with the locality, its name and events of the First Mass clearly indicated. Or so it would seem! The stunning thing is that secondary sources have for more than 350 years located all or parts of these events at...Butuan.

Francisco Colin, SJ, in his "Labor Evangelica" on p. 144, of vol. I (1663): "On Easter Sunday, in the land of Butuan, the first Mass ever in these regions was celebrated and the first cross erected. It was taken in possession in the name of the Emperor and the Crown of Castilla."

Four years after Colin, in 1667 his confrere Francisco Combés in his "Historia de Mindanao y Jolo" separated the ceremony of the

---

down to eastern Davao. In all probability Calagan applied originally only to the eastern seaboard of Mindanao. Pigafetta never came to Butuan, but some chroniclers of Legazpi's expedition did, and they never mention Butuan in *conjunction* with Caraga. In short: the pre-Spanish Butuan was probably not a part of the district of Caraga.

After the Mactan disaster, when the remnant of the fleet was sailing off Mindanao on its way to Maluku, Pigafetta refers *three times* to Mindanao not by name, but as "the island where Butuan *and* Calagan are located." This clearly implies two *separate* regions.

[3] "Acquada": the present Homonhon, where the fleet had first anchored before proceeding to Surigao Strait. They considered it a good omen that drinking water was found there and named the place — in Pigafetta's Italian — "Acquada da li buoni segnialli" or: watering-place of good signs.

[4] "Mazaua": through all the primary and secondary documents the name of the island has been spelled in a variety of ways: Mazana, Dimasaua, Limasaua, Masava, Masaba, Macancor, Massana, Messana, Messane.

cross-raising from that of the Mass, and let only the first event happen at Limasawa, without speaking of a first Mass or its locality:

> "The first time when the Royal Standards of the Faith were seen flying over this island was when Admiral Alonso (sic) de Magallanes discovered it in this archipelago. During that very first and hazardous voyage, he had entered the Strait of Surigao, which is formed by that island and the island of Leyte, and anchored at Dimasawa (sic) which is at the mouth of that Strait. It was the first time that such a strange people had appeared there, but the barbarians made friends with them and regaled them with good food. During the time when they were resting and being well supplied at Dimasawa, they heard about the river of Butuan. Since there was a more powerful chief, what they heard enticed our men to go there, although the venture could become either a success or a failure. The fact that the place was nearby roused their curiosity. On the one hand there was the story of the barbarians, but there was also the need to get supplies for the survival of our men. Those were simple and good people, and that enhanced the hope of our men that things would turn out well. Magallanes only let them adore a cross which he had planted on a hill as a sign of their confederation in future times and as a pledge of a more propitious occasion to effect it. The solemnity of the cross-raising and the deep piety shown by the Spaniards resulted in deep feelings of reverence for the cross.
>
> Since at Butuan they did not find proper anchoring facilities for the ships, they returned to Dimasawa to deliberate further on what route to take" (Combés/Retana, Col. 77).

In this context we may point to an interesting cartographic document that is clearly based on the description of Combés (or the latter's informant): the famous map of Murillo Velarde. The edition of 1744 traces the route of Magellan in a way that clearly depicts the "shuttle-trip" from "Dimasawa" to Butuan and back to the first place described also by Combés. Also the approach route of Magellan to the strait of Surigao is depicted as running from Cape San Agustin (Davao) along the east coast of Surigao.

Gaspar de San Agustin (1696) too follows the route Limasawa to Butuan to Limasawa and from there to Cebu, but has the first Mass celebrated at Butuan.

Delgado (1751) and Zuñiga (1800) place both Mass and cross at Butuan.

And what the books had stated was boldly confirmed in stone when in 1872 a monument was put up at the mouth of the Agusan river (now Magallanes), where Butuan was then located. It had an inscription on a marble slab saying:

> To the immortal Magallanes.
> The people of Butuan with their pastor
> and the Spaniards residing there.
> To commemorate his arrival
> And the celebration of the first Mass
> on this place on April 8, 1521.
> Erected in 1872 when Don Jose Maria Carvallo
> was governor of this district.[5]

Indeed, such had always been the conviction since time immemorial of those at Butuan who bothered about giving any thoughts to the matter. But that quiet conviction was disturbed when in 1921, on the occasion of the 400th anniversary of Magellan's landing, some publications in the country disclaimed the old Butuan tradition, and even more so when an official marker was erected nearly thirty years later at Limasawa. From then on gusty winds of controversy started blowing over the waters of Surigao Strait and from Butuan to Manila. Concerned citizens of Butuan roused their Representative in the House of Congress into action, with the result that the Official Gazette, vol. 57, no. 3, January 16, 1961, p.444 can list:

---

[5] The date April 8, 1521 does indeed appear on the marble slab of the monument. Attempts have been made to explain this deviation from all written records, but it is most probably just a mistake committed when the plaque was ordered.

It is noteworthy that in 1868 such a prominent Butuano as Diego Rosales, then local gobernadorcillo (mayor), does not mention the ''first Mass'' at all when enumerating the past greatness of Butuan. (See footnote 43 of the chapter ''The odyssey of Bunawan and Talacogon.'') All *local* references to the Butuan first Mass date from after the erection of the monument (1872).

Republic Act No. 2733

An act to declare the site in Magallanes, Butuan City, and not Limasawa Island in the province of Leyte, where the first Mass in the Philippines was held, as a national shrine, to provide for the preservation of historical monuments and landmarks thereat, and for other purposes.

Be it enacted by the Senate and the House of Representatives of the Philippines in Congress assembled:

Section 1. The site in Magallanes, Butuan City, and not Limasawa Island in the province of Leyte, where the first Mass in the Philippines was held, is hereby declared a national shrine to commemorate the birth of Christianity in the Philippines.

Section 2. All historical monuments and landmarks in said site shall be preserved and/or reconstructed whenever necessary as much as possible in their original form and are hereby declared national historical monuments and landmarks.

Section 3. The National Planning Commission shall exercise supervision and control over the reconstruction and/or preservation of the aforesaid site and monuments, and shall issue rules and regulations to effectuate the preceding sections of this Act.

Section 4. Necessary funds for the purposes of this Act shall be provided for in the annual appropriations for public works, and disbursements shall be made by the National Planning Commission under such rules and regulations as the Auditor General may prescribe.

Section 5. This Act shall take effect upon its approval.

(Enacted without executive approval, June 19, 1960.)

In Butuan itself a Historical Committee was set up to organize the clamor to restore the old historical honor "to where it belonged." In 1977 a symposium of Filipino historians pitted the protagonists of the Butuan and Limasawa camps against each other in Manila to settle the controversy once and for all, or so it was hoped. The Butuan Historical Committee had prepared its representatives well and they appeared in Manila with a printed "Official Position Paper: THE FIRST MASS: LIMASAWA, LEYTE? OR MASAO, BUTUAN?" But of course, the opposing camp defending Limasawa was not unprepared either, and had in addition the support of the "general opinion" of national historians. Apart from a lot of heated discussions the symposium got nowhere. To add insult to the injured pride of the Butuanos, the First Lady of the land finally told the assembly that the discussion was only hurting the much needed national unity for solving what were presumably more important problems. As one Butuano angrily remarked afterwards: "We were practically sent home as naughty boys and told to keep our mouths shut!"

In 1980 another symposium was held in Cavite, but it too failed to convince the BHC that indeed a Magellan visit cum first Mass at Butuan was *"un suceso imaginado,"* an imaginary event, as the old Manila writer Trinidad Pardo de Tavera had said already in 1895.

The irony of the whole discussion is that both the Limasawa and the Butuan protagonists use Pigafetta as their primary, eyewitness authority. And so, most probably, had the old authors till about the turn of the century. At least, in so far as they had not just quietly followed each other, at times to near verbatim copying the texts of predecessors.

Earlier we called Pigafetta's relation about the first Mass "clear reporting by an eyewitness." It is now time to add the following: the translation used there was taken from the first complete original text, found in the Ambrosian Library of Milan, printed in 1895, and also used in vol. 33 of Blair and Robertson, as well as by the Filipiniana Book Guild, op. cit. This original manuscript was not available in the days of Colin c.s. To understand why, we must go back to where we took leave of Pigafetta the moment he handed one copy of his book to Emperor Charles V. If only at that moment he had foreseen what was going to happen to the other copy which he gave to the mother of the King of France, the Butuan vs. Limasawa controversy would never have occurred. The manuscript given to Charles V was never published and was eventually considered lost. What did, however, appear in 1550 was an abridged version, which by and by had been translated from the original Italian into French; from this (garbled) French translation it was "put back" into an Italian version, which was published by Gian Battista Ramusio. And in this latter text the mix-up can be found which led to the Butuan tradition around the site of the first Mass, because it was the very text used by Colin c.s.,

as was rightly pointed out by W.H. Scott in an article in
Kinaadman: "That Father Colin used this text is indicated by the
fact that his account is a summary of its [Ramusio's] pertinent
passages."

It is even more convincingly proven by the fact that Colin
himself, when referring to Pigafetta, notes: "vide Pigafettam, apud
Ramusium!" It might be good to put on the table what Ramusio
himself had to say (in an apologizing vein) about the quality of the
material he had to use for his "Delle Navigationi et Viaggi." (I will
quote from Scott, p. 163):

> Ramusio remarks in his introduction: "Mr. Antonio
> Pigafetta (who went on that voyage, and on his return...was
> made a Knight of Rhodes) [wrote] a long and very detailed
> book, of which he gave one copy to His Majesty, the Emperor,
> and another he sent to France to the Most Serene Mother of the
> Most Christian King, Madame the Regent, who commissioned
> an excellent and well-travelled philosopher called Mr. Iacomo
> Fabro [Jacques Antoine Fabre], who had studied in Italy, to
> translate it into the French language. This fine fellow (to avoid
> too much work, I suppose) made only a summary, leaving out
> the things that were too detailed, which [was] printed in French
> with many errors."

Because of that sloppiness, crucial mistakes (for our context) are
committed in indicating localities, persons and happenings on Holy
Saturday 1521. Let us juxtapose the two texts:

Complete Ambrosian Manuscript	*Fabre-Ramusio Text (paraphrased)*
1. The chief's *brother*, who was the chief of another island, accompanied Pigafetta from Mazaua back to the *ship* where they dined with Magellan.	1. One *son* of the chief departed and another went to the *island* where Magellan was.
2. In the island of the chief's *brother* big gold nuggets were to be found.	2. That gold was in the island where the chief came to visit the ship, ergo the island where Magellan was.

3. The island of the chief's brother is called "Butuan and Calagan."

3. "These islands" (Butuan and Calagan) are two different islands, and it is implied that Magellan was in one (Calagan) and Pigafetta in another (Butuan) and that on Easter morning Magellan had gone from Calagan to Butuan.

4. Magellan is consistently reported as being either on his ship near Mazaua or on the island itself where they stayed till April 7 and then sailed to Cebu.

4. Magellan is first at Calagan, then at Butuan (Mass), and on April 7 we find him at "Messana" from where he leaves for Cebu. See how these locations are obediently reproduced in the map of Sanson d'Abbeville.

5. The narrator (= Pigafetta) speaks in the first person when referring to himself and/or his companions: "Quando fui in terra."

5. The narrator speaks in the third person when referring to Pigafetta and/or his companions: "Quando furono giúti in terra."

Once informed about this background, one will recognize it in some early maps that unwittingly "visualize" the Fabre-Ramusio confusion in cartographic form. In the Netherlands, Ortelius and Mercator (1575) place a "Messana" close to Butuan and on the mainland of Mindanao. The most pathetic attempt to get out of the mix-up is visualized in the French map of Sanson d'Abbeville (1652), which shows a Mindanao without any Butuan, but close to Cebu (as to make up for it all) three little islands: Messane, Buthuan and Calegan!

Pastells (in 1900), already convinced that the first Mass *se dijó en la isla de Dimasaua* (sic) (Colin, I, 144, Note 2) and also that *Magallanes no tocó en Butuan* (ibid., I, 40, Note 2), still seems not to have seen the complete (translation of the) authentic Pigafetta. In his footnote 3 to Colin I, p. 144 he states that "The chief of Dimasaua was the father of the chiefs of Butuan and Caraga." This is obviously still based on the Pigafetta of Fabre-Ramusio. In the complete original Italian text Siaui of Butuan appears as the

ATORNO IL MONDO 357

A Quando furono giũti in terra, il Re leuò le mani verſo il cielo,& poi le voltò verſo li důoi pre
fati,iquali fecero il ſimile,& il medeſimo fecero tutti gli altri.Il Re preſe il prefato Antonio per la
mano,& vn ſuo huomo principale preſe il ſuo cõpagno & li cõduſſero ſotto vn luogo coperto
di paglia,oue era vna barca tirata in terra, preſa da alcuni ſuoi nimici,lunga ottanta palmi, & ſe-
dettero ſopra la poppa di quella,parlando inſieme per cenni.tutti quelli del Re ſtauano in piedi
intorno à lui,con ſpade,pugnali,lance,& targhe. Quiui fu portato vn piatto pieno di carne di
porco & vn grã vaſo di vino,& ne beueuan ciaſcuna volta vna tazza, & il reſtãte del vino ſtaua
ſempre coperto appreſſo del Re,anchor che foſſe in picciola quantità non ne beueua alcuno ſal-
uo che il Re,& auanti che il detto prendeſſe la tazza per beuere, leuaua le mani giunte verſo il
Cielo,& le voltaua poi verſo queſti duoi noſtri quando voleua beuere, & diſtẽdeua la man ſini-
ſtra verſo il detto Antonio,come ſe lo voleſſe battere, dapoi beueua il detto Antonio faceua il ſimile,& tal ſegno fanno ciaſcun l'vn verſo l'altro,& con gran cerimonie & domeſtighezza man
giarono carne il venere Santo. Donarono molte coſe,che haueano portato da parte del Capita
no al Re,& Antonio ſcriueua molte coſe,come loro le chiamano,& quãdo il Re,& li ſuoi il vid
dero ſcriuere,& che ſapeua dapoi nominare le lor coſe,ſe marauigliauano grãdemente, & quan
do fu venuta l'hora di cena,furono portati alcuni piatti grandiſſimi di porcellana pieni di riſi,&
altri piatti di carne di porco con il ſuo brodo,& cenarono con li medeſimi cenni, & cerimonie.
Poi ſi auiarono doue era il palazzo del Re,il qual era fatto come è vn tetto, doue ſi tien il fieno,
coperto di foglie di fico,& di palme, & era edificato ſopra legni alti leuati da terra:oue è neceſſa

B rio montar con ſcalini. Quiui lo fecero ſeder con le gambe incrociate, ſi come ſedeno li ſartori,
& di li à mezza hora fu portato vn peſce arroſto,& gengeuo freſco colto allhora,& del vino, &
& il figliuol maggior del Re, il qual ſi chiama il Principe,venne oue erano coſtoro, & il Re gli
diſſe,che ſedeſſe appreſſo di loro,& coſi fece. Furono dapoi portati duoi piatti l'uno di peſce col
brodo,& l'altro di riſi,accioche mangiaſſero col Principe,doue tãto fu mangiato, & beuuto che
erano imbriachi. Coſtoro vſano per far lume di notte vna gomma d'vn albore,la qual gõma ſi
chiama anima,rauolta in foglie di palma. Il Re fece cenno che voleua andar à dormire,& laſciò
con li noſtri il Principe,col qual dormirono ſopra vna ſtuora di cãne con alcuni cuſſini di foglie.
Il Principe ſubito fatto giorno ſi partì,ma come furono leuati li noſtri,li venne à trouare vn fra-
tel del detto,& gli accompagnò fino ad vna iſola,oue era il capitano,ilquale lo ritenne à deſinar
ſeco,& à lui,& à tutti li ſuoi fece aſſai preſenti.

Coperto
di foglie di
fichi & pal
me.

Anima põ
ma d'albe
ro.

In quella iſola,oue il Re venne à veder la naue delli noſtri ſi trouauano gran pezzi d'oro,co-
me ſariano noci,ouer voua,criuellando la terra.tutti li vaſi del Re ſono d'oro, & tutta la ſua caſa
è molto ordinata. Fra tutte queſte genti non viddero il piu bel huomo del Re. ha li capelli lun-
ghi fino ſopra le ſpalle,molto nerſ,con vn velo di ſeta ſopra la teſta,alle orecchie vi tiene appicca
ti duoi grandi anelli d'oro,& groſſi. Porta vn panno di cottone lauorato di ſeta,ilqual cuopre,co
minciando dalla cintura fino alle ginocchia: da vn lato ha vn pugnale col manico d'oro lungo,
& il fodro è di legno lauorato. In ciaſcun dito ha tre come anelli d'oro, vngeſi con olio di ſtorace,

Oro copio
ſo.

C & benzuin,& è di color oliuaſtro,ma dipinto tutto il corpo.Queſte iſole ſi chiamano Buthuan,
& Caleghan. Quando queſti duoi fratelli figliuoli del Re, che anchor loro ſi fanno chiamar Re,
ſi vogliono veder inſieme,vengono in queſta iſola in caſa ſua.Il maggior ſi chiama Raia Colam
bu,il ſecondo Raia Siagu.

Come li duoi Re di quei paeſi fratelli andarono col capitão ad udir meſſa,& nella ſommità d'una mon
tagna piantorono una croce.de i porti Zeilon, Zubut & Caleghan.della qualità & uſ-
ſtir di quegli huomini.del frutto detto Areca,della foglia dell'ar-
bore Bettre.dell'iſola detta Maſſana,& de gli
animali & frutti di quella.

All'ultimo di Marzo appreſſo Paſqua,il Capitan generale fece metter à ordine vn prete per
far dir meſſa,& per vn ſuo certo interprete fece dir al Re, che egli non ſmontaua già in terra per
voler andare à deſinar ſeco,ma ſolamente per voler far dir meſſa.La qual coſa come vdì il Re,ſuſ
bito gli mandò duoi porci morti,& quando fu l'hora del dir la meſſa, ſmontarono in terra circa
cinquantà huomini ſenza arme,meglio veſtiti,che poterono,& gli altri erano armati, & auanti
che li battelli giugneſſero in terra,fecero ſcaricar ſei colpi di bombarda in ſegno di pace,poi ſalta-
rono in terra,& queſti duoi fratelli Re abbracciarono il Capitan generale, & andarono in ordi-
nanza fino doue era preparato da dir la meſſa,nõ troppo lontã dalla riua,& auãti che ſi comin-
ciaſſe à dir la meſſa,il Capitano volſe ſpruciar il corpo alli detti duoi Re con acqua muſchiata.
Quãdo ſi fu à mezza meſſa,che ſi va ad offerir,li Re volſero ãchor loro andare à baciar la croce,

Viaggi. y y iiij come

Fig. 1. The page in Ramusio's version of Pigafetta's ''Viaggio atorno il
mondo'' with the garbled Fabre translation that led to the Butuan-
Limasawa controversy about the ''first Mass in the Philippines.''

brother of Colambu of Mazaua.

As for the Butuan Historical Committee, in its official Position Paper defended at the Manila symposium of 1977, the main argumentation centers around the assertion: "Pigafetta's Mazaua = Masao = Butuan" (Masao is a barrio of Butuan). The reasoning filling the Position Paper is tantamount to forcing the original Pigafetta back into the garbled Pigafetta of Fabre-Ramusio and the tradition the latter brought into existence.

It is a great pity that most of the historical self-esteem and intellectual dedication, all the years of the B.H.C. and its activity, have nearly exclusively been invested in perpetuating the Fabre-Ramusio-Colin-Combés error.

But then, it is another great pity that Butuan's most beloved dream, has, under the cold morning light of historical probing, turned out to be just that, a dream, *un suceso imaginado.*[6]

---

[6]About Enrique, the servant of Magellan, steadfastly called a "Butuanon" by some Butuan protagonists of the first Mass, because of his alleged ability to understand the local language, one author writes still in 1988: "The Butuanon dialect was understandable to Enrique, Magellan's Malay slave, who came from the same area." *(Starweek Newsmagazine,* 5 Nov. 1988).

In the same article (box, p. 8) this writer then quotes Pigafetta's *own* text, containing the very sentence: "A slave, belonging to the Captain-general, who was a native of Zamatra (Sumatra) which was formerly called Taprobana, spoke to them...."

The following comment is here called for:

1) This slave had been captured at Taprobana during a former expedition of Magellan and brought to Portugal where he was christened Enrique.

2) Pigafetta does *not* say that Enrique understood the local language at Mazaua, but that "the king" understood *his* language, as also some of the locals did. Enrique's language was not the "Butuanon dialect" as appears from the very words of Pigafetta quoted by the author referred to: "The king understood him, because in those districts the kings know more languages than the other people." Enrique spoke Malay of which many words will be recognizable in Bisaya.

3) Among the holdings of the Archivo General de Indias at Sevilla is the original of the *testament* made by Magellan before his departure. Among his beneficiaries he mentions: "my servant Enrique, born in Taprobana...."

An intriguing cartographic feature of the Pigafetta manuscript is a series of 19 small black sketches looking more like the blots of a Rorschach test than a rendition of geographic locations. They can be found in vol. 33 of "The Philippine Islands" of Blair and Robertson, and also in "Philippine Cartography" 2nd ed., p. 16 by Carlos Quirino. The latter has the following to say about them:

> "Pigafetta, the Lombardian gentleman who accompanied Magellan as an observer, was the first person in the expedition to draw the various islands they touched in the Philippines: these rough sketches accompany his manuscript at the Ambrosian Library in Milan. As he had no chance to make a real survey of the places he visited, these crude drawings have no resemblance to the originals and may be identified only by the names given them."

With a little hindsight-imagination some resemblance can be discovered in the sample which intends to show the island of Mindanao with the localities of Butuam, Calagam, Benaiam, Cippit and Mamgdanao. Note that there is no Messana near Butuan in this very first drawing of the region by an eyewitness; instead there is a separate island in another sketch of the same series, with the name "Mazzana."

Benaiam is undoubtedly the "Bisaia" indicated in the same area in the relation of the Loaisa expedition and in the map of the Dutch cartographer Peter Kaerius (1598) shown in Quirino o.c., p. 39.

Cippit is the Quipit on the west coast of Zamboanga, which the remainder of Magellan's expedition touched, after the Mactan disaster, on their way to Maluku.

Mamgdanao stands for Maguindanao.

The whole set of 19 skeleton drawings was copied by the Royal Cartographer Nuno Garcia de Toreno for the guidance of the Loaisa expedition.

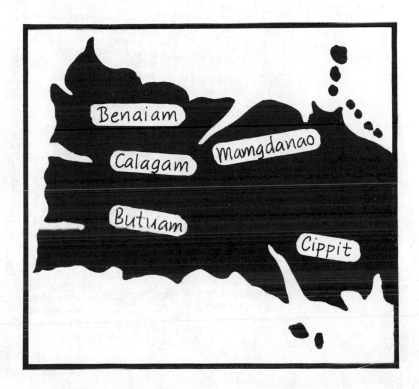

Fig. 2. Map redrawn from ''The Philippine Islands'' by Blair &
Robertson, Vol. 33, p. 230.

Fig. 3. In 1956 the Municipal Council of Sanlucar de Barrameda and the
local Ateneo initiated the placing of a commemorative tablet with
the names of the eighteen European survivors of Magellan's expedition. There were, in addition, four ''Indios'' among the
returnees. (Photo, P. Schreurs, MSC.)

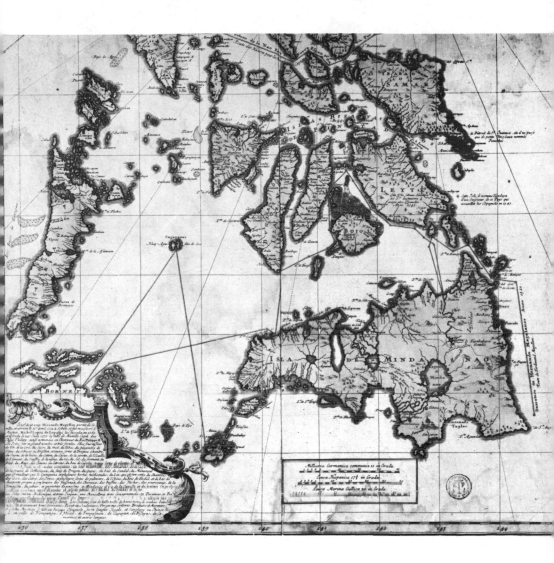

Fig. 4. Copy of the map of Murillo Velarde, by Lowitz, 1760. Note the mistaken approach route of Magellan and the ''shuttle-trip'' Mazaua-Butuan-Mazaua, inspired by Combés. (With permission of the State Archives, the Hague.)

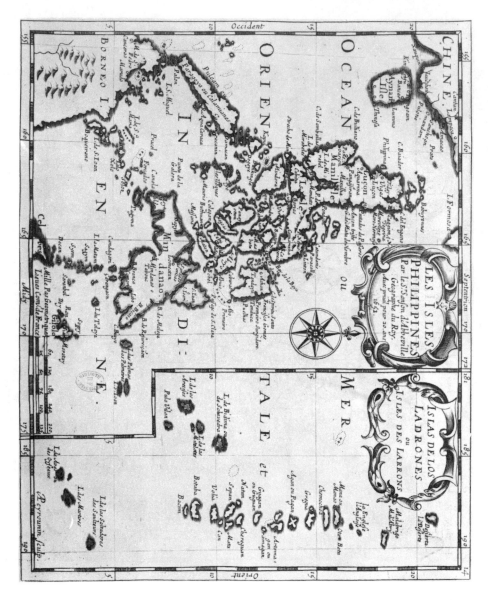

Fig. 5. Les Isles Philippines, by Sanson d'Abbeville, 1652. Obviously
based on a pathetic interpretation of Ramusio's Pigafetta. Note:
1) It has no Butuan on the northcoast of Mindanao; 2) Southwest of Cebu are three islands: Calegan (Caraga, Calagan); Buthuan, Messane (Mazaua, Limasawa); 3) Siargao = San Juan.
(With permission of the Bibliothèque Nationale, Paris.)

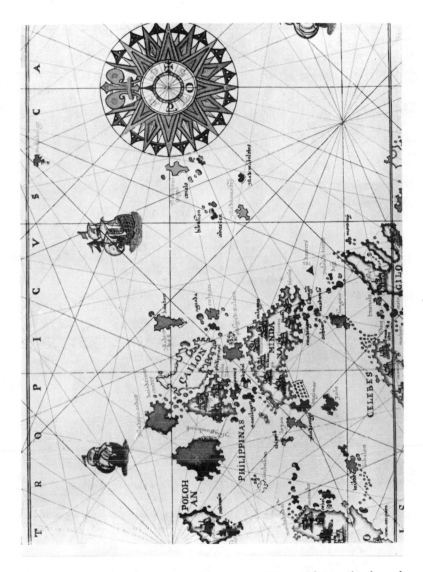

Fig. 6. Portulan map, by Joan Martinez, 1587. Obviously based on Ramusio's Pigafetta. Note: 1) Messana (Mazaua, Limasawa) is placed on Mindanao, next to Butuan; 2) Calagan (Caraga) is correctly located; 3) "Philippines" refers to the area to which Villalobos gave that name; Luzon is not yet included. Already in the 16th and 17th century Sanson d'Abbeville as well as Joan Martinez were clearly wrestling with the Butuan-Limasawa confusion. (With permission of the Biblioteca Nacional, Madrid.)

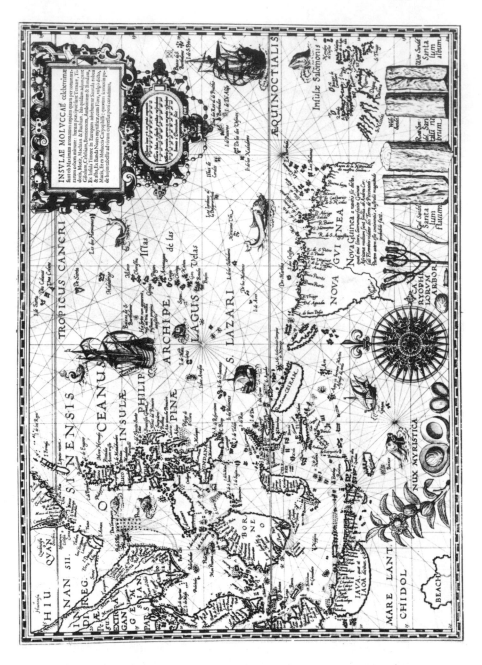

Fig. 7. "Insulae Moluccae," by P. Plancius, A'dam, 1592. (With permission of the Maritime Museum "Prins Hendrik", Rotterdam.)

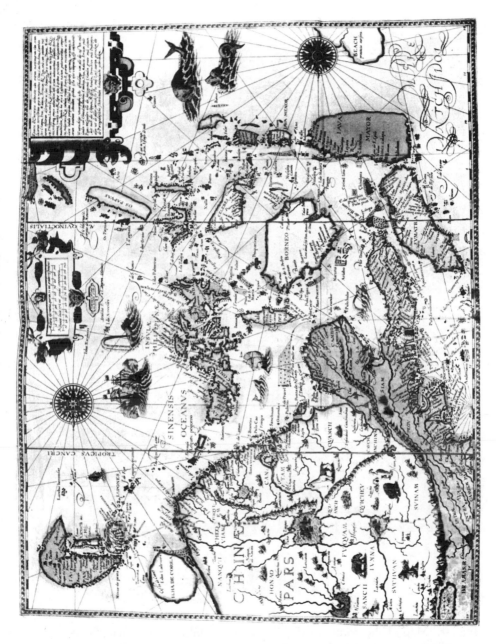

Fig. 8. ''Coasts and Lands of China'' from ''Itinerario,'' by Linschoten, 1596. (With permission of the Maritime Museum Prins Hendrik,'' Rotterdam.)

Fig. 9.   Map of the southern Philippines and Maluku, by Nuno Garcia de
          Toreno, 1523. Clearly based on the sketches of Pigafetta. See
          northern coastline of Mindanao. (With permission of the Biblioteca
          Reale, Torino.)

II

Acquaintance Attempted

"Today, January 21, 1523, the first
spices were sold here at Antwerp in the
weigh-house, cloves that had been
brought in from the new islands for our
Emperor Carolus. Three (sic) ships had
sailed out on that adventure, of which,
however, only one returned" ("Chronicle of Antwerp" - Leyden 1743-).

Those were the cloves brought by Elcano in the only surviving
ship of the Magellan expedition, the Victoria. The total receipt of the
sale is not mentioned in that market report of Antwerp, but from
other sources it was known to have reached at least 25 times the
purchase value at **Maluku**, in spite of the fact that there the price had
quadrupled because of the great hurry with which the Spaniards
wanted the commodity. After the whole transaction in Antwerp had
been entered in the books, it appeared that the proceeds were enough
to pay for all the expenses incurred by the Magellan expedition.

How anxious the Spaniards were that nobody (in Europe as well
as in **Maluku**) should learn about the enormous gain made on that
sale, appears from the following information provided by Oviedo in
his "Historia General..." II, p. 32. Among the Orientals who had

returned with the 18 Europeans in the Victoria was a man from Maluku who, once in Europe, showed too much eagerness (in Spanish eyes) to get information about the value of Spanish currency and the price at which the cloves were going to be sold there. The result was that he was not allowed to return with the other Orientals in the next expedition, because he might inform his countrymen in Maluku!

There must have been a lot that was still uncertain and unclear about the great dream of finding and taking possession of the "Islands of the West," but one thing was beyond any doubt: the spice-market could be made into the most fabulous commercial enterprise of the century. And Spain was going to have its share in that venture.

Immediately after the return of the Victoria a new Spanish fleet was readied in the port of La Coruña to sail along the route of Magellan to the east via the west. The general command was put in the hands of Garcia Jofre de Loaisa. The second in command was a very understandable choice: Sebastian de Elcano, a man exceedingly more experienced than Loaisa, of course, but as it happened, lower in social and military rank. With the expedition went along a young man of 17 years: Andres de Urdaneta. Forty years later he would sail once more to the Orient with Legazpi. Seven ships and 450 sailors departed from La Coruña on July 24, 1523.

Sailing in the track of Magellan's voyage, and after heartbreaking setbacks, Loaisa entered the Pacific in the middle of 1526. On July 30, after six of his ships had sunk or disappeared from the fleet, Garcia Jofre de Loaisa died, and the command passed into the hands of Elcano. One bad omen after another haunted the expedition: one week later also Elcano died, to be succeeded by Alonso de Salazar. On September 5, 1526 the Ladrones were sighted, and while the ship was searching for a good anchoring place, a small canoe, paddled at a furious speed came heading toward them, and to their great surprise an excited voice shouted to them in the best of Spanish: *"Buenos dias, Capitan y matelotes!"* It came from a survivor of Magellan's fleet who had deserted from the ship Trinidad during the ill-fated journey away from Maluku, which she had reached together with the Victoria in 1521 and from where she should have sailed back to Mexico. The name of the deserter was

Gonzalo de Vigo, a native of Galicia. In spite of his past, he was gladly taken aboard, since it was expected that after a stay of almost four years among the natives he could be of much use as an interpreter in the weeks to come. And indeed, to begin with, he was a great help in obtaining water and other provisions for the ship. Because a great number of the crew were sick or badly weakened, they captured 11 natives to man the bilge-pumps, and then the lone remaining ship out of the original seven set out again westward. Very soon there would be another change of command when Captain de Salazar died, and when on October 2 the Santa Maria was in sight of Mindanao at 8°4', Martin de Garquizano was her captain.

Where did they approach Mindanao? The pilot Martin de Uriarte named an island: Polo (Navarete V, 279). Burney ("History of the Discoveries of the South Sea," I-140) suggests that it could have been the (illusory) San Juan island, which is in fact Siargao. This is not totally impossible, although at variance with the given latitude of 8°4': the northern headland of Siargao is at 10°, the southern one-third degree lower.

The explanation of Mairin Mitchell ("Friar Andres de Urdaneta", p. 31) that the ship sailed around Mindanao on the west side and then made landfall "from one of the Vizayan islands" seems very improbable.

Urdaneta named the point of landfall "Vizaya," which, together with the location 8°4' seems to point to the "Benaiam" of the Pigafetta sketches, where some later cartographers (a.o. Peter Kaerius in 1598) place the name Bisaya, on the east coast of Mindanao. "We found the large island of Bendanao" Urdaneta said.[7]

---

[7] "Bisaya" ...See R.A. Skelton in Quirino's "Philippine Cartography": "In 1550 the cartographer Descelliers gives Mindanao something like its correct shape from informations gathered by two later Spanish voyages on the east coast. To the east of Mindanao Descelliers' map lays down a large triangular island, with a longer north-south axis, and with the name "Bisaya." This was the name collected by Loaisa's men for the province on the east coast of Mindanao where they anchored in 8°N. Saavedra seems to have identified it as a separate island, an error easily explained by the prominence of Mount Urdaneta when seen from the

Everything, plus the authority of such a man as Pastells taken together, we could (with the latter) conclude to the bay of Lianga (or rather Bislig?). The fact that the bay is said to go four or five leagues inland we might have to put on our "give-and-take" account as we have to do ever so often when trying to pinpoint a location with available contemporary records. There is not a single bay that deep in all of eastern Mindanao. But then, elsewhere there is none agreeing with the other indications offered to us or fitting the rest of expeditionary records, like those of the next voyage. We ought also to take into account that the report of Pilot Hernando de la Torre, from which much information has come to us, was written two years after the event, and that Urdaneta's personal journal was taken away from him by Portuguese customs officials upon his arrival in Lisbon in 1536. Reading authors who quote Urdaneta, we have therefore to keep in mind that his second report was written from memory more than ten years after the facts narrated.

Pastells' interpretation making Lianga the point of landfall seems

———————————

sea. Under the name of San Juan (perhaps by transference from a discovery of islands in 16°N by the Trinidad in 1522) this illusory island was to remain on the maps and to be described by travelers and geographers until the 19th century.''

To ''Saavedra's identification'' Skelton adds a note: ''The authority (a late one, but derived from original records of the voyages) is Herrera's ''Descripción de las Islas Indias Occidentales'' (1601). After describing the landfall of Loaisa's ship (then commanded by Martin Yñiguez de Garquizano), Herrera enumerates the provinces of Mindanao, including Vizaya (Dec. III, lib IX, cap. 9). In 1528 Saavedra *"fue a Mindanao y Vizaya y otras islas que estan en ocho grados"* (Dec. IV, lib. I. cap. 6). Later Simao de Brito and other Portuguese deserters from Saavedra's crew, sailing west from the Ladrones, came to Mindanao, *"Y llamase aquella costa Vizaya, nombre de los naturales"* (Dec. IV, lib. III. cap. 6).

Galvao also has the name Bisaya, apparently as that of an island; when Bernardo de la Torre was sent back to New Spain by Villalobos in August 1543 ''for[a] ter aa ylha de Syria, Gaonata, Bisaya & outras q. ahi muytas em onze & doze graos de parte do Norte, por onde o Magelhaes andara & (sic) Francisco de Castro...'' (Tratado, 1565, fol. 77 v.).

(About the cartographic riddle of the ''isla de San Juan,'' east of the northern tip of Surigao, see the article of Morton Netzorg in *Kinaadman.)*

(together with Bislig) not unconvincing (under the circumstances) and does not contradict further details of the ship's stay in Philippine waters prior to reaching Maluku.

> "They came in sight of the island of Mindanao and headed for an anchoring place in the bay of Lianga, which goes four or five leagues inland; they anchored between some islands where the water was about 40 fathoms deep.
>
> On October 7 the launch went to the shore to find out what kind of land it was and what people were living there, and if perhaps more landwards there might be a better anchoring place. They did indeed find one and in addition good and clear running water. The next day they moved up into the bay till the deepest landpoint. Everywhere we could use the sounding-lead up to 50 fathoms; beyond the anchoring place, about one-fourth league away, there were many good streams. While they were in that place, so related Hernando de la Torre: the chief of one of the villages came to visit us on board. He showed many signs of friendship and brought many chicken to sell to us. The captain paid for them in glass-beads. That chief and his companions were sporting golden earrings, each of which could have weighed one ducat or one and a half. They offered them to us for the price of one half arm-length of beads, but the captain did not wish to buy gold or even talk about it, to prevent that they would think that we were overly interested in it. After that, the men went away.
>
> In the morning of October 9, while we were on land and making friends with the chief, there came a man from Malaca who told the chief that he should give us nothing and should not make friends with us, because at our own good time we would kill them. This he said because he thought that we were Portuguese, and he knew the character of the latter. Because he said this, they all ran away, so that we could not talk to them anymore. Therefore we went back to the ship in our sloop without having obtained anything" (Colin, II, p. 625).

A man from Malaca... on the east coast of Mindanao would have been quite off his sailing route... but that is what the text says. He could not have been from "Malaga" (Baganga) because that name was only bestowed in 1542 by Villalobos. Did the original Ms. perhaps have "Maluku?" But we have to admit that a man from Malaca could indeed "have known the character of the Portuguese."

Fig. 10. Buddhist image, solid gold, actual size, found along the banks of the Wawa river (Central Agusan) in 1917 and brought to America by Mrs. Leonard Wood. Prof. Beyer dated the image as "probably 14th century." (With permission of the Field Museum of Natural History, Chicago.)

After much deliberation, the leaders decided to try sailing to Cebu, but once reaching the open sea of what might have been Punta Baculin and Punta Cawit (in the supposition of landfall at Lianga), strong winds and currents carried them eventually along Cape San Agustin (Davao) and Sarangani to the Portuguese in Maluco.

The reports that have come to us from this expedition, from the moment it sailed into local territory, have added only little to the written history of eastern Mindanao. But even with a relative affluence of international and national data, such little bits have to be salvaged too. Often it is out of such shapeless patchwork that a local history has initially to be brought to light.

III

The Bad and the Good Portuguese

In the preceding pages we came across "a man from Malaca" who warned the natives of Lianga against the visitors of the ill-fated expedition of Loaisa: they were "frangi" (Portuguese) he said, who at the opportune time would attack them. We made a hesitant suggestion that perhaps this man may have come from Maluku instead. Not only did foreign authors at that time more than once include the southern Philippines under a generalized terminology "Maluco" but there were even trade relations between the two territories as well as less friendly contacts. There are some possible explanations for the anti-foreign propaganda of that man; among them:

1) He had been sent by the Portuguese to play the black propaganda game, of which we will hear more during the Legazpi expedition: to upset the natives by a pre-arranged "spiel."

2) It is also possible that indeed his own experiences with the Portuguese back home in Malaca/Maluku had made him an enemy of the latter; to him, the Spaniards at Lianga were one and the same people as those in Maluku; many of the island sultans had openly or secretly turned against the spice merchants.

One shocking case of Portuguese barbarity in the southern Philippines is extensively described by the Spanish author Bartolomé

Argensola in his "La Conquista de las Islas Malucas" (1609), Bk. II, pp. 49-51. The report is about an event that happened in 1534 or 1535, because it mentions that Tristan de Atayde was Portuguese Governor of Maluku at the time in question. The anger against the Portuguese had reached such proportions that many of the Malucan island chiefs had turned to uprooting and burning the clove plantations. In addition they had blocked all possible anchoring places and saw to it that the Portuguese were deprived of badly needed food supplies. Governor Atayde decided to dispatch one of his ships under the command of Joao de Canha Pinto on a trip to forage for food along the southern coast of Mindanao. If necessary, according to Pastells (Colin II, 646), they should go as far as the southern coast of Leyte, specifically Liloan where, aside from food, also gold was easily available. From there he should sail to Palawan, Borneo and Malaca. Argensola writes that contacts with the sultan of Mindanao (the Cotabato area) were very much to the satisfaction of both parties, business-wise as well as concerns public relations.

From there they proceeded to the island of "Seriago," as Argensola spells the name of the place. Pastells (Colin I, p. 107, note 2) writes Surigao for Seriago, and indeed, in some old maps we see "Seriago" written in the area of Surigao. For some time I have followed Pastells' interpretation as to the location of that Seriago, but at present I have no difficulty admitting that "Sarangani" (Serengani in some contemporary maps) is at least as likely a location for the event related. Sarangani would, of course, have been along Pinto's sailing route to Leyte after his leaving Magindanao, as would have been Surigao.

Argensola's story is about the detestable behavior of Pinto and his men after they had been well received by the chief of "Seriago" and his people, who even concluded the *sandugo* pact of peace and friendship with them. The trust of the local population was repaid with treachery by the Portuguese. On the last day of their stay at "Seriago" Pinto tricked forty of them into the hold of the ship and locked them up as prisoners. One of them saw a chance to leap overboard at the last moment and informed the local chief of the abominable deceit perpetrated by the Portuguese. The ship was attacked by hordes of furious natives. In the middle of a fierce battle a sudden violent storm struck all the combatants, local and Portuguese. Pinto's ship finally limped back to Ternate in a disheveled condition.

At the end, Argensola vents his moral indignation on "this kind of sin that will always call for the ire of God." Not a word is spoken about the unhappy fate of the prisoners in the ship's hold!

When dealing with the Legazpi expedition, we will have a chance to speak a little more in extenso about such and similar abuses by Portuguese as well as Spanish buccaneers. Accusations about abusing the natives were often being hurled back and forth between Spaniards and Portuguese. Pinto's story has come to us through a Spanish author. I do not know if it can also be found in Portuguese sources, but from the little comparison I have been able to make between (translated) Portuguese accounts on the one hand and Spanish reports on the other, one gets the impression that more than once it is a case of the pot calling the kettle black. Less than nine years after the Pinto affair, during the Villalobos expedition, there is an acrimonious correspondence between the Portuguese Governor of Ternate and Villalobos, wherein the latter is being lambasted for pillaging native villages on the south and east coast of Mindanao, something that was *mucho contra el servicio de Dios y del Rey de Portugal nuestro Señor,* as the indignant governor put it.

But let us also listen to the deeds of a good Portuguese. He arrived in 1538, only two years after Pinto. It seems as if it was very much by accident that history finds him in Surigao in July of the mentioned year. At that time Atayde had been succeeded by Antonio Galvano as Governor of Ternate. One day two prominent merchants from Macassar (Sulawesi) came to visit him; they wanted to find out what kind of people those whites were about whom they had heard in their home island. Galvano (everywhere described as a noble and very Christian governor) acquainted them with the Christian religion; and eventually they were baptized and returned home as the first Christians of Macasar. Not much later they undertook another trip to Ternate with a load of sandal wood, some gold, bladed weapons and other commercial goods. They also brought the welcome message that many people in their homeland desired to engage in commerce and that some also wished to become Christians. Some young men had come along with them "and these immediately received the water of baptism."

Such good prospects moved Galvano to ready a ship, which was placed under the command of Captain Francisco de Castro, with orders to sail to Macasar and conclude a pact of friendship with the local chiefs, so as to prepare the ground for evangelization. In May 1538 de Castro departed from Ternate, but very soon the wind shifted and started to carry them northwards. On June 26 they reached some islands north of Maluku which were unknown to them. Joao de Barros in the chapter "Sea-voyages and Courageous Battles of Nuno Da Cunha," col. 168 (Dutch translation, 1706) relates as follows: "He got in such a heavy storm that after some days he reached a few unknown islands, more than one hundred miles north of Maluco. He got to know that the place which he had reached was called Satigano, and that the chief and the people were pagans."

The sources mentioning this voyage differ in quite a few details. Castanheda — 1561, quoted in Tiele's "Europeans in the Malayan Archipelago" — writes that one of the islands was located at 12 and 2/3 degrees, and that it was "one of the Celebes." Some early authors (among them Castanheda, according to Tiele) in using this terminology speak of an archipelago stretching from the present Sulawesi up to Cebu. What de Barros (from whom we quoted above) calls Satigano, is Chedigao in Castanheda and Setigano in Couto (apud Tiele). Where was that first landfall of de Castro?

Because of the reference 12 and 2/3 degrees and probably also because of the mentioned sailing time of at least twenty-six days, some have placed it out in the Pacific, near Guam while others refrain from mentioning a concrete locality. The correct answer was given five years later, in 1543, when the Governor of Ternate sent a protest note to Villalobos, who was then at *Sarangani,* reminding him that de Castro had been there in 1538 "and baptized many natives on *the very island where you, sir, are at the moment."* (Documentos Ineditos de Ultramar, Doc. 9, p. 73). Adding to this that Sarangani is about 100 miles from Ternate (de Barros) we may safely conclude that de Castro's landfall was there, and not out in the Pacific, or near San Bernardino Strait at 12 and 2/3 degrees. Afterwards, when dealing with the Villalobos expedition we will hear about "a native of Sarangani, who claimed to be a Christian"; there is no word of anybody baptizing there before de Castro or within the five years after him. De Barros continues: "Francisco de Castro befriended the chief, and as a confirmation hereof both opened a vein in an arm and drank from each other's blood. A few days thereafter the chief became a Christian; with him his wife, a son and three brothers plus several others, prominent and common people, were baptized."

Here the text mentions that de Castro "was engaged in this work for twenty-two days." One feels inclined to ask: Did perhaps some authors skip this twenty-two days' stay in Sarangani and included the time in de Castro's travelling time to "enable" him to reach 12 and 2/3 degrees, as mentioned above? After all, we have already met a Fabre translating Pigafetta in such a way that it necessitated one European mapmaker to "transfer" Butuan, "Messana" (Mazaua) and Calagan to near Cebu, and another to place "Messana" on the Mindanao mainland!

The travel sequence as related by de Barros seems more credible: "He departed from there in peace and friendship with everybody. While sailing on along the coast of Mindanao, he reached a river on whose banks was a village named Soligano, where the chief also became a Christian together with his wife, two daughters and many others. On that island the chief of Butuan did the same; he was given the name Juan the Great. So did the ruler of Camizino who was named Don Francisco, and also the wife and children of those chiefs with many of their people."

According to Combés ("Historia de Mindanao y Jolo," lib. II, cap. 2) the chief of Surigao (Soligano) had been given the name Don Antonio Galvano, after the Governor of Ternate.

The feat of de Castro has a very pronounced apostolic ring to it, and the question has been asked: were there priests aboard the ship? De Sousa mentions two priests, and so does de Barros. Jarricus (together with de Sousa quoted in B. Visser's "Under Portuguese Flag") says that de Castro himself could have been a priest, but that sounds very improbable: in 1543 the Governor of Ternate referred to him as a *capitan de un navio de alto bordo,* captain of a high-boarded ship. Up to quite recently the "Catholic Directory of the Philippines" in its historical note on the dioceses of Surigao and Butuan stated that those priests were the first two Jesuit missionaries to come to Butuan: Ledesma and Martinez. However, in 1538 both were not even born yet! They came to Butuan in 1596.

Of course, a priest accompanying traveling soldiers or boat crews was not unheard of during those days, but at the time in question, 1538, there was only one priest in Ternate, Fernao Vinagre, a Spanish secular, and since his territory included all of Portuguese Maluku and the Portuguese soldiers in the archipelago, it seems most unlikely that he would absent himself for so long by joining de Castro.

For that reason, the voyage has been highly rated and praised as a remarkable lay missionary feat. Perhaps it was, and perhaps that was de Castro's motivation. There is no doubt that the Governor of Ternate who sent him on that voyage was a very religious man. Naturally, both were men of their times and subject to governments that had sent them to the Orient with a double mission: to establish the Kingdom of Christ together with Portuguese presence and possession. In the daily practice one could, would, should be made subservient to the other, as required by circumstances. In 1538 those circumstances were such that an actual occupancy by Portugal of the southern Philippines (the northern Maluku?) was out of the question: too much of its fleet and manpower was invested and kept busy in the rest of Maluku. And therefore, with Spanish intentions at the back door to Maluku being obvious, there was need for Portugal to stake its claim to Mindanao with some very contemporary kind of *acte-de-présence:* the indelible imprint of Portuguese baptisms left behind on a few strategic corners (say, Sarangani, Surigao, Butuan, Camiguin) of a territory that (from a colonial viewpoint) was no man's land anyway, was the best staking activity available to Portugal under the circumstances. And the message would be all the louder if the local leaders and prominent subjects got such an impressive identity as granted by beautiful Portuguese Christian names such as Don Juan the Great, Don Francisco or Don Antonio Galvan.[8]

Although I have no sources to go by, I do not think that my surmises go beyond justified interpretations of Portuguese intentions in 1538. Intentions of this sort peep out from the lines of the protest letter already mentioned (p. 39), which the next Portuguese Governor of Ternate wrote five years later to the Spanish intruder Villalobos.

---

[8]Applying a self-styled ''jus primi baptizantis'' as a title of possession was not only standing operating procedure of Portuguese or Spaniards. Still in 1615 a Dutch Protestant minister wrote in an only slightly different vein to the home office of the Dutch East India Company: ''When territories are being occupied where the people have been baptized, then they will be under our sovereignty; if not, then they belong to the Moors; in case there is a mixed population, the Christians belong to us and the rest to the Moors'' (van Dijk 1882:217).

"On the very island (of Mindanao, the Governor mistakenly said) where you, Sir, are at the moment, with your soldiers and your fleet, many souls have been made Christians, and among them, there were some chiefs and prominent people; this happened about five years ago, when they turned Christians through the efforts *(por mano)* of a certain Francisco de Castro" (Doc. Ined. de Ultramar, Vol. I, Doc. 9).

As we mentioned earlier, this letter was delivered to Villalobos at Sarangani.

The question may very well be asked: Did de Castro indeed come to Mindanao just by accident? Of course, that is what the Portuguese reports (where the information came from) stress strongly, even to the extent of letting him first drift up to 12 and 2/3 degrees latitude. One must, however, not forget that claiming contrary winds for having sailed into an area where a ship's presence might raise questions, was a not infrequently used s.o.p. expressly ordered by higher authorities. At least so it was on the Spanish side; would it have been different with the Portuguese? Listen to the sailing order given by Philip II to Commander Legazpi:

"It could happen that you come across some Japanese ships, since we have been informed that they are great traders by sea and that their ships are big. In case you encounter them, treat them with the usual courtesy and do not permit that anyone will commit abuses against them. As for explanations, tell them that you were sent somewhere else but arrived here forced by contrary winds" (Doc. Ined. de Ultr. Doc. 21, p. 177).

"(As for the natives) you shall tell them that your real course was not for their territory, but that it was because of the wind that you arrived there" (ibid., p. 171).

The story of de Castro's missionary activity in Mindanao is also interesting for what happened towards the end:

"When de Castro wanted to depart from there to Macassar (after Camiguin and Butuan), he got caught by such strong contrary winds (!) that his ship nearly capsized. Several times he tried to take to sea, but his companions did not want him to take such a dangerous course. For that reason he returned to Ternate, bringing with him many sons of those who had become

Christians. With his own money and at great expense Antonio Galvan had established there a training school. This was the first of its kind in those regions of the Orient. The purpose was that those young flowers would be instructed with the milk of Christian doctrine, so that after some time they could serve for the upliftment of their own folk. Since that time the Holy Council of Trent for the reformation of the whole universal Church, has approved and selected this method'' (de Barros, col. 168-169).

Once more: the question of garbled meaning caused by faulty translation. The just quoted "since that time" is the English rendition of the Dutch equivalent used in the v.d.Aa translation of de Barros. The proper translation should have been "afterwards" because the Council of Trent started only in 1545. On p. 19 of his "Under Portuguese Flag," Visser writes:

"Some, also early writers say that the College of Ternate was afterwards canonically approved by the Council of Trent. In my opinion, available information does not permit such a conclusion. Jarricus is certainly more correct when saying that this seminary of Ternate was founded for the purpose afterwards intended by the Council with its prescriptions for the establishment of seminaries. The zeal and prudence of Galvano is most obvious in his establishment of a seminary wherein he brought together and accepted students from all the people whom we have enumerated, with the same purpose afterwards intended by the Council of Trent. ''

No information has come to us about what happened afterwards to these young men from Butuan, Camiguin, Surigao and Sarangani, and if and where they ever worked for the Christianization of their home folks. Were they accompanied by some Portuguese priests who have been reported as having been active in Butuan? When the first resident Jesuit missionaries arrived there in 1596, they heard that some people still remembered (having heard ?) about some Portuguese (priests) who had preached and baptized there (Colin, II, p. 159). It is not clear if that memory went back all the way to de Castro's visit in 1538, which looks quite improbable anyway; it is just possible that it concerned some Portuguese evangelization efforts after 1538 but a good many years before 1596. Those efforts, however, seem to have been made by some Portuguese priests in the service of the Bishop of Cebu who had come from Goa.

IV

Gallows on the Threshold to Maluku

In 1526 the Portuguese Governor of Ternate, Don Garcia Henriquez, had built the first stone chapel in Tidore and dedicated it to our Lady of the Rosary. Here, on July 12, 1527 Captain Martin Yñiguez de Garquizano, the fourth commander of the Santa Maria, the lone surviving ship of Loaisa's expedition, was buried after dying of poison which some Portuguese had put in his cup of wine. He had died, unknowing that just then a new fleet was being fitted out with the task to investigate what had happened to him and the mission entrusted to him. It was placed under the command of Alvaro de Saavedra and left the port of Zaguatenejo in Mexico on October 31, 1527, with three ships and a total of 110 soldiers and sailors. Two of the vessels with sixty men on board got lost and were never heard of again before they had reached the Marianas. On January 6, 1528 the remaining flagship sighted the latter islands where they stopped for eight days to load water and firewood. They were unable to obtain any victuals because the inhabitants refused to come to the ship. As a result, sickness and death soon started to break out on the next lap from the Marianas westward. Within sight of the coast of Surigao, on February 4, a third crew member, named Cansinola, died, and on that day they went ashore to bury him. The chronicler of the fleet, Vicencio de Napoles, reports that it was a little island with a good anchoring place and "located at ten degrees, only one league away from a big island called Mindanao." The island of Nonoc seems to fit this description.

They did not encounter any people, but were able to restock their supply of firewood. It may be assumed that they went foraging on the mainland of Surigao, the coast of which was clearly visible from where they were. They also surveyed the island of Bucas, and from the latter sailed southward along the east coast of Mindanao, propelled by the monsoon wind. The informations given by Pastells (Colin, Supplement to Vol. II, p. 633) based on the account of Vicencio de Napoles are not altogether exact as to the distances travelled after leaving Bucas. Since I do not possess the original text of de Napoles, I do not know if the discrepancies are his or Pastells'. The latter knew the east coast very well, having been parish priest of Caraga and Bislig and having travelled to all the other places as regional mission superior and afterwards Provincial of the Jesuits in the Philippines in the last quarter of the 19th century. It seems clear (from subsequent happenings) that Saavedra sailed from Bucas to Baganga and afterwards from Baganga to Punta San Agustin. The distances cited by Pastells are:

for the first lap: 80 leagues or 440 kms
for the second lap: 50 leagues or 275 kms

In reality the first stretch is 266 kms and the second 150. I am surprised that Pastells did not add a correcting note if the figures are not his own.

We will follow Saavedra now on the stretch that interests us here: down to Baganga and from there to Sarangani.

On the fifth day after departing from Bucas, when they were sailing off Baganga, a little boat came to meet their ship at about three leagues offshore. The occupant — who turned out to be a local village chief — stayed at a safe distance, but invited them by gestures to come ashore. Obviously, he had met Spaniards before because he shouted the Spanish words for water, rice and coconuts, indicating that these would be available on land. They followed him and in protected waters dropped two anchors, one at the bow and the other at the stern, with the ship pointing into the northwind. Most probably this was in the bay between Dapnan and Baganga, Davao Oriental. By sign language they invited the local population to come aboard the ship, but they refused to do so. Being in need of drinking water, the Spaniards let some empty earthen jars down into the sea, and made the Mandaya natives understand to fill them on land with fresh water. In this way they were able to load ten jars aboard the Florida. Next day, one of the Mandayas, named Catunao, gathering all his courage came aboard with three companions and his little son, while the rest of the village people stood watching on the beach. The guests were warmly received by Saavedra and showered with gifts. After half an hour they went back ashore, where they regaled their fellows with stories of their experiences with those strange people. It appears that the conclusion of some was that such a ship with such men and goods would make a magnificent prize! That night a small group sneaked up to the ship, cut one anchor cable and tried to pull up the anchor to load it in their *baroto;* next they attempted to pull the ship ashore. The trick did, of course, not work because the ship was moored on two anchors. Then they started cutting also the hawser of the prow anchor loose, but a guard hailed them, at which they abandoned their mischief and, so the chronicler says, "at daybreak they rowed laughingly back to shore."

The biggest surprise came the next day. From one of the rocks jutting out of the bay water they heard a man shouting for help... in Spanish. The captain sent some men out in the sloop to pick him up and bring him aboard. When the man had pulled himself together, he told his story: that his name was Sebastian, that he hailed from Oporto and had a family in Coruña. He had been with the Loaisa expedition, sailing under Captain Jorge Manrique in the Santa Maria del Parral, which had been separated from the other ships in a storm during the night of January 1, 1528. He explained that his ship had been shipwrecked on the east coast of Mindanao, and that he and two others (still being held prisoners on some unknown island) were the sole survivors; all that time he had been kept as a slave of the local chieftain. That morning, hearing about the arrival of a Spanish ship, he had seen a chance to escape and, after hiding for some time in the thickets along the beach, he had swum out to the rock where they had discovered him.

There are several reasons for busying ourselves a little further with the intriguing case of this man and the people among whom he had been living. In the first place, because he gives us some information as to the place where Saavedra was at the moment. Vicencio de Napoles mentions that Saavedra asked the straggler at what latitude they were then, and the latter answered that "while he was still with the Santa Maria del Parral, they had taken the latitude in a bay not far north from their present location, and had found that place to be at eight degrees." If correct, the ship would then have been at Lingig (Surigao del Sur), which has a small, but deep-water bay just south of the place, at the mouth of the Mandos river. If we allow for a small error — or if the man quoted only the degrees without the minutes (I tend to believe so) — he might have been referring to the bay of Bislig which is at 8°7'6" (Montano, "Voyage aux Isles Philippines," 1886, entry for January 31, 1881) or at 8°15' (Census of the Philippines," 1918). As later references by modern observers show some divergence, we may assume the same to be true for 1528. At any rate, the information seems to pinpoint Saavedra quite correctly not far south of Lingig/Bislig, near Baganga, which is at 7°30' (Census).

Another supporting detail pointing to Baganga and the southern east coast is the description which the escapee gave of the people among whom he had been staying for about half a year and which is rather typical for Mandaya country. That description has come to us through Antonio Herrera, the official *Cronista Mayor* in Spain, who made use of official archives with documents of the first discoverers and worked them into his "Historia General," the second edition of which appeared in 1609. I have taken the following account of Herrera from Agustin Santayana's "La Isla de Mindanao" (1862):

> "(Saavedra) went to Mindanao and Vizaya and other islands which are at eight degrees. There the people gave them pigs, chicken and rice-bread, and they saw signs that there was gold. The women were beautiful and the men of light complexion, and all were wearing their hair long, and they used iron cutlasses, firearms with powder as well as very long arrows and blow-pipes with which to shoot poisoned darts. They were wearing cotton vests and cuirasses of turtle-leather. The men are fighters and they conclude peace by drinking of the blood of the new friend. They also have human sacrifices. The chieftains wear a crown on their heads. The one who was then in command was named Catunao."

First a few quick notes:

1. "Mindanao and Vizaya and other islands at eight degrees" is obviously a loose way of referring to the whole Pacific coast of Mindanao.

2. The "light complexion" of the population is mentioned by all authors in the past and is still noticeable today among small Mandaya groups or families in the hinterlands of Bislig, Lingig, Cateel and Baganga as long as they have not intermarried with Manobos or coastal Visayans. This phenomenon has been explained in some chronicles by an alleged presence in earlier years of Dutch or Japanese sailors; however, the description of Herrera precedes the

arrival of the first Dutch sailors in this part of the Pacific by many years.

3. The "crown" actually refers to a headband of gold or silver (diadem).

Herrera continues, quoting Sebastian de Oporto: "Catunao had killed Jorge Manrique and his brother Diego and others of the previous expedition (Loaisa's)."

He himself and two companions had afterwards been taken prisoners by a local chieftain, who at one time had even brought him to "Cebu" where he heard that eight Spaniards of the expedition of Magellan had been taken from there to China. His two companions were still on another island named Candieta. On this island:

> "Saavedra ransomed also these other Spaniards for seventy gold pesos and an iron bar. They were brought to him naked and with their arms tied. He provided clothes for them and also made friendship with the local chief in which both drew blood from an arm and drank it.... At the end of that year Alvaro de Saavedra with his flagship was at Sarrangan and Candigan (the mentioned Candieta) at four degrees; in the latter place he had ransomed the two Spaniards."

From the straggler — who knew something of the local dialect by now — they also heard that those natives called themselves "Celebes." This fits in well with what we pointed out in connection with Loaisa's expedition: that in early times, when people did not yet think in terms of our national boundaries of today, "Celebes" stood for a large archipelago from the present Sulawesi up to Cebu.

Let us now listen to the account given by the two other rescued prisoners from Candigan. Their names were Romai and Sanchez, and according to their story the Santa Maria del Parral had reached the harbor "of the island of Vizaya" (Lianga? Bislig? Lingig?), where the captain had sent the yeoman *(bachiller)* Tarragona ashore with the sloop, together with 14 men. Their task was to make contact with the natives, conclude peace and friendship with them and barter for food. The latter promised that next day they would come back with plenty of pigs and various kinds of food. That contact was very friendly; the Spaniards returned to the ship; the morning after they went ashore again to conclude the barter deal. While they were still absent, at about ten that morning, five canoes full of armed men and foodstuff accosted the ship, but the captain forbade any transactions because he was waiting for the return of the foraging party. The

Mandayas went back to the shore, from where Tarragona and his party had not yet returned. When they had not yet appeared at night-time, the captain suspected treachery.

> "He ordered that the few remaining victuals be put away under lock. When Sebastian de Oporto saw this, he became scared, because that day the captain had threatened him with some punishment because of an insult, and he thought that he was going to mete it out any moment. Therefore he jumped ship, and went to live ashore, intending to stay with the natives, in the hope that someday another Spanish ship would pass there and pick him up, which indeed happened" Colin/Pastells II, 638).

As Romai and Sanchez continued their story, the morning after the disappearance of Sebastian, Captain Manrique had decided to go ashore to procure the return of the sloop with the landing party. When he asked the Mandayas where the latter were, they gave a very eloquent and internationally understood answer in sign language, drawing their fingers across their throats in a cutting motion. Therefore they hurried back to the ship and sailed away to another **point** about three miles away to wait there for the possible return of the shore party. When they had not appeared after four days, they prepared to move out of the area. But then three canoes appeared; the chief of another shore-village and some companions brought fruits and food for sale. Because of the scarcity on board they were allowed to come on deck — one at a time — to sell their wares. The chief told the Spaniards to remain where they were, for next day he would come back with more. And indeed, the following morning eight canoes appeared, all loaded with food. When the barter transactions were about to be concluded, the captain and his brother were suddenly jumped upon and thrown bodily into the sea where they were killed by those in the canoes. Another Spaniard, Juan de Benavides, was hit by a poisoned arrow and died that evening. The attackers fled when one of the musketeers fired twice at them. The Spanish survivors hurriedly weighed anchor and hoisted sails. Wind and current carried them to "Candigan," where they agreed to beach the ship. But then, a sudden wind-shift took care of that and threw them on the rocks. The natives stormed aboard, killed one of them, and captured the rest.

The three rescued Spaniards also informed Saavedra that on some other islands there were some seven or eight other Spaniards held as slaves by various natives.

Saavedra for sure got a lot of interesting information from the three rescued prisoners. Or so he thought! Only later would he find out the true curriculum vitae of Sebastian, Romai and Sanchez. Vicencio de Napoles, speaking about the Mandayas' fear of the Spaniards, wrote:

> "This fear to come aboard the ship had undoubtedly resulted from the previous expedition of Garquizano (Loaisa's) or from the killing of the captain of the Santa Maria del Parral, because the killers were Spaniards and were living now among them as slaves."

The killers were Spaniards? What drama then had happened somewhere at sea between Lianga and Baganga in the year 1528? The truth would come out before long. Probably over a drinking spree Romai had entrusted it "under the seal of secrecy" to one of Saavedra's Spaniards, Pedro de Raigada. Braggingly he had told him that he and nine accomplices had killed Captain Manrique, his brother Diego and the mentioned Benavides and had thrown their bodies into the sea! A shocked Pedro de Raigada — in spite of the oath of secrecy — told pilot Hernando de la Torre. Sanchez saw a chance to escape in the nick of time to the Portuguese of Ternate, but Romai was captured and condemned to death.

Two proud expeditions with a total of 450 men and ten ships had sailed for the "Islands of the West" in 1523 and 1527, one from Spain, the other from Mexico.

Their separate fates seem to have haunted each other over the Oceans, crossed near Mandaya land of Old Caraga, and finally met at the hanging-cum-quartering of Romai on the threshold to Maluku.

V

Filipinas Be Her Name

In 1529 the rivalry between Spain and Portugal about the rights to Maluku came officially to an end. Spain had to scale down its intentions in the Far East, because the two last expeditions had caused a heavy drain on the imperial coffers, and that at a time when the state finances were further strained because of the war between Spain and France. Also for another reason Charles V could ill afford to continue his hostile relations with Portugal much longer: his Lusitanian archrival was soon going to be his brother-in-law through the latter's marriage with Princess Catherine, the sister of the Emperor. What complicated matters for Charles was the embarrassing discovery that he lacked the means for a decent dowry for his sister's marriage. Therefore he decided upon a deal with his brother-in-law elect, which was confirmed at the Treaty of Zaragoza in 1529: Spain relinquished its claim on Maluku once and for all.

However, the territories to the north thereof remained very much on the list of imperial desiderata. There were, of course, nicer ways of putting it:

> "God did not want at any time to keep His Spanish children occupied with the business of buying and selling aromatic spices of Maluku. He had selected them to preach His Holy Gospel. For that task He had given them the rich countries of America, so

that, with the treasures found there, they could help other poor
countries in their spiritual needs, as for example the Philippine
Islands, which He ranked higher than Maluku, for the good of
the souls there. The Emperor in his palace had become wiser and
saw that God entrusted him with the conquest of those islands,
and that He wanted him to make an earnest effort for their
conversion'' (Gaspar de San Agustin, ''Conquistas de las Islas
Filipinas,'' 1698, p. 60 in the new edition of the Instituto
Enrique Florez, Madrid).

On November 1, 1542 a new fleet of five ships and 370 men sailed
out of La Navidad to make another attempt at an enterprise "so
pleasing to God and the Emperor." The overall commander was Ruy
Lopez de Villalobos. Four Augustinians had been assigned to the
armada as chaplains; if everything turned out as planned, they would
become the first resident missionaries in the Philippines. Gaspar de
San Agustin beautifully describes the ceremony at which they were
sent off on this important mission. The four departed on foot from
Mexico City, dressed in coarse serge-cassocks and carrying only a
walking stick, all the way to La Navidad, a distance of 120 miles.
     In Tomo I of the "Documentos Ineditos de Ultramar" we find
the instructions which had been given to the leaders of the
expedition. Among the principal injunctions for the time after
arrival in the archipelago are those about the division of profits to be
obtained from the discovery, the preaching of the Gospel and the
proper behavior of the Spaniards in their dealings with the natives in
the places where they might land.

> ''You shall send me specimens of all the products of the land
> that you can secure, and inform me of the manner of dress of the
> inhabitants, and of their mode of life, of their religion, what
> kind of faith it is, their government and their method of warfare
> with their neighbors.... You shall give very special attention to
> the preaching of our holy Catholic faith and try to convert the
> people by friendship and peace.''

In the matter of evangelization they should carefully follow the
directions of the four missionaries. In everything they should always
remember that the first aim of the expedition was indeed the spread
of religion. Also for that reason the soldiers and sailors should keep
strict discipline. None should be accepted on board the ships who did
not have a written testimony that he had confessed and received Holy

Communion. Blasphemy as well as other public sins should be severely punished.

After eighty-four sailing days they reached a small island in the Pacific Ocean, located at ten degrees. Here the inhabitants came out in canoes loaded with fruits and fish. In a way, that was not so surprising, of course. But the remarkable thing was that they greeted the Spaniards with *"Buenos días, matelotes"* (Hello, sailors), while making the sign of the Cross.

In one Dutch quotation (Tiele, o.c.) the spelling is made to appear as if the greeting had been in Portuguese. The difference between *"Bon día"* and *"Buenos días"* may have been small, but the implication is not. Could there ever have been Portuguese ships that far out of Maluku? The mentioned author explains that most probably there had been contact between the islanders and eastern Mindanao, where they might have picked up a few Portuguese words. That, of course, is not wholly impossible, but at least a little improbable. The simplest explanation is that he just quotes from a Portuguese author. It has also been pointed out that this island may be the "Chedigao" (Setigano) at twelve degrees, considered by some as the first stopping place of Francisco de Castro. As we have seen, however, that place was at or near Sarangani; most probably "Chedigao" was the "Candigan" of the Loaisa-Saavedra accounts. The unnamed island where Villalobos was greeted could have been one of the Marianas (the so-called Ladrones group), where one of Magellan's or Loaisa's ships may have stopped earlier.

At any rate, Villalobos gave it a new name: Matelotes, and then sailed on in s.w. direction, till on February 2 they reached "a large island," which according to some they did not immediately recognize as Mindanao.

Again we find certain discrepancies between the accounts of some authors. Gaspar de San Agustin, who in his "Conquistas" follows the "Cronica" of his mentor Grijalva, points to an obvious mistake made by the latter; this in spite of the fact that Grijalva's report is based on the original records of the Augustinians who were with the expedition. According to him "they were looking for a point of Mindanao which is at eleven degrees." San Agustin remarks: "At eleven degrees is located Guiguán on the island of Samar. This is the route which they should have taken in order to reach Cebu."

After sailing away from the aforementioned island "Matelotes," Antonio Conso, one of the pilots who had been with the voyage of Saavedra, strongly advised that they should sail along eleven degrees in order to avoid being carried too far south or even into Maluku.

Not everybody agreed with this, and in the case of the flagship his advice was disregarded. The result was indeed that instead of entering Surigao Strait and finding Limasawa and eventually Cebu, they were carried as far south as Baganga by the late monsoon winds. Here they found a beautiful bay which seems to have reminded them of home, because they gave it the name of Malaga. The whole island of Mindanao was named *Cesarea Caroli* in honor of Emperor Charles V. On p. 64 of San Agustin's "Conquistas" the editor of the new edition adds a footnote referring to that bay: "The bay mentioned by the author is at the island of Leyte, between Abuyog and Hinundayan" ...which is clearly wrong.

Villalobos drastically changed all existing names into new Spanish ones as a gesture of intended Spanish ownership for the future. His first intention was to make a settlement at Malaga/ Baganga. One of the fleet officers wrote afterwards: "When they named the island Cesarea Caroli, its value was as it were squared."

That may have been true in the estimate of that good Spaniard, but it clearly did not apply to Malaga, because they soon found out that the region was unsuited for a good settlement. But for this, the Portuguese author Galvao has his own explanation: according to him, in 1543 the local datus were already Christians and politically aligned with the Portuguese, and therefore they did not wish to accommodate the Spaniards in their territory! This, however, was much belated wishful thinking of that Portuguese patriot. The dispute about who was the legitimate European possessor of eastern Mindanao was far from settled. The Portuguese claimed that Mindanao was part of Maluku, which had been ceded to Portugal at Zaragoza in 1529. In addition, the Portuguese had been the first to baptize in the area (de Castro) and that gave them a kind of *jus primi possidentis,* the rights of first occupier! Spanish sources do not mention any Christians in the whole area (except one, afterwards at Sarangani), leave alone any alliance of the inhabitants with the Portuguese of Maluku, of course.

> "They spent practically the whole of Lent 1543 in Malaga and suffered a lot from hardship and disease. Nearly all the men had fallen sick with high fever, and a strange illness that was so little known that there was no cure for it. There was also another sickness that caused swelling of the gums to the extent that all their teeth were covered. The result was that they could not eat; eventually their gums rotted away, so that many of them died.
>
> Little by little the health of the men started to improve, and

a beginning was made with the construction of a launch right there in the bay. The one which they had brought from Mexico had been smashed on land by a storm and was lost. Finally, they decided to take to sea, but in spite of all their efforts, they were unable to clear the point (at Guian, to enter Surigao Strait), and in the end the only decision they could make was to sail back southwards along the great island of Mindanao, which is the first in that region to face the sea if one comes from America. All that time they went through great difficulties and storms, and it was a miracle that the wind did not carry them far away from land. Always following that course and coming close to the equinox, they discovered — among many others — a very beautiful island named Sarrangan, located near the other coast, that of Mindanao after one has sailed around Cape San Agustin, which is a little below six and one half degrees'' (Gaspar de San Agustin ''Conquistas...'' pp. 64-65).

There is a fatal irony hanging over the first four Spanish expeditions. Magellan, wishing to reach Maluku, sailed too far north and missed the logical approach to the spice islands: south of Mindanao. The next three fleets, intending to follow Magellan's track via Surigao Strait and Limasawa to Cebu and trying to avoid getting into Portuguese territory, steered too far south when approaching the Philippines, and finally were forced to go where they were not supposed to: Maluku.

Of course, being carried helplessly from the mouth of the Surigao Strait south all the way to the tip of Mindanao, and then back again and back once more...is a possible and frustrating experience.... But it could also have been done intentionally to fit the fleet's task (kept secret from the Portuguese), which was: reconnaissance in a region of which the Spaniards were not really sure if it was within the Portuguese sphere of possession. Urdaneta, in Mexico, believed it was and undoubtedly had told them so before departure. In spite of that, the sailing orders contained the tasks: *Descubrimiento... conquista...población* (discovery, taking possession, settlement). It is true that those orders also spoke about the necessity of not entering Portuguese territory, but they failed to state clearly where that territory began and no man's land ended. And as for storms and currents: it is true that a sailing ship is somewhat at the mercy of these elements...but then, these were experienced seamen!

Whatever the real truth may be, in about May or June 1543 Villalobos was stranded at Sarangani and the fleet was a tired and disheveled lot of men and ships. Also this island was renamed "Antonio," perhaps in honor of the Viceroy of Mexico, Antonio de Mendoza. The logbook of the flagship located the island at "a little below six and one half degrees" which, if referring to the main island, is about one to one and one-half degrees too high. It might lead one to suspect that a similar mistake had been made at the ship's first approach "at eleven degrees." If in reality they were then at about ten degrees, the passage to the Surigao Strait was to a large extent blocked by islands such as Dinagat, Siargao and Bucas. But, all the same, if Villalobos had managed to reach the southern tip of Samar at Guian, he would have sailed (been blown) into the Strait of Surigao and so to Limasawa and Cebu.

The island of Sarangani looked inviting, but the people were not. The man going as interpreter with a small landing party had been in Maluku for seven years with Urdaneta and the other survivors of the Loaisa and Saavedra ships; he knew the Malayan language well enough to understand the message of the natives: "Be gone!" And to make sure that it would indeed be understood that way, they underlined it with a volley of arrows. Forced by the necessity of survival, they attacked the four villages of Sarangani, which were abandoned as a consequence, with some of the inhabitants fleeing to the mainland of Mindanao. It was the latter who incited the people there not to sell any food to the Spaniards, and as a result the Spanish foraging parties soon became requisition parties. Attempts at barter contacts along the Cotabato river ended in an ambush and the death of some Spaniards. A little relief was brought by a brigantine that had landed in more hospitable country of the southern Philippines. It was one of their own fleet that had lost contact with the rest during their approach to the archipelago.

"It had followed the route indicated by Antonio Conso (higher than eleven degrees) and found it to be the right one; it had entered through the opening of the Strait of Panaon, near the point of Guiguan, and had been well received by the natives of an island Macaoa (Limasawa) which is in the middle of the Strait. They had bartered with them for plenty of victuals, which they now carried in the brigantine. They had been in the places Abuyo and Tandaya near the island of Cebu... Villalobos decided to send the vessel back in the company of another... to obtain enough food supplies from Abuyo, Tandaya and Mazaua, to increase the provisions for the flagship, so that it could start on the return voyage to Mexico. He gave this order in writing wherein he named those islands [Abuyo, Tandaya, Mazaua] for the first time Filipinas, the name they have kept till the present time. He gave that name in honor of the serene prince Philip II, the son of Emperor Charles V and his spouse, the Imperatrix Isabel, princess of Portugal. The Prince was 14 years old at that time, and they took possession of the islands in his name. Therewith, the old name of islands of the Celebes archipelago by which they were known among the people of the Orient, was wiped out" (Gaspar de San Agustin "Conquistas..." p. 68).

Again, as we see, a new Spanish name, and the old nomenclature wiped out! The obstinate refusal of Villalobos to leave the Mindanao seas, in spite of all the hardships and disappointments suffered by the expedition, seems to indicate how determined the Spaniards were to prevent the southern Philippines from becoming a Portuguese dominion. And that is obviously what also the Portuguese in Maluku understood all too well. News of the presence of Spanish ships at Sarangani and Mindanao had reached the Portuguese Governor of Ternate, Jorge de Castro. In the "Documentos Ineditos de Ultramar," I, p. 68 ff., some very spirited correspondence between him and Villalobos can be found. It opens with a letter of the Governor to Villalobos, which he received at Sarangani and which was dated July 20, 1543. De Castro calls himself in that letter *Capitan de la fortaleza de San Juan de Ternate, e islas de Maluco, Banda, Berneo* (sic), *Mindanao, con todas las islas de San Juan y Manado, Panciave, con toda la costa de los Calabres e Oanborro, con todo el Arzepielago de los Papuas!* He then implores the Spaniards not to molest any longer the inhabitants of the parts of Mindanao where they had been or were at present. It was his duty, so he said, to defend them, because all those islands were part of the Portuguese territory that stretched as far as the *Ilhas das Velas* (the Ladrones or Marianas) at 17 degrees. It was indeed the interpretation of some that by the Treaty of Zaragoza Spain had transferred to Portugal the property rights to all territories west of the Ladrones; in that case the southern Philippines fell inside the territory ceded to Portugal. And, so wrote the Governor of Ternate, not only could the King of Portugal point to that Treaty, but:

"It seems to be the will of God our Lord, because in all those islands many Moros have become Christians; out of His abundance the Lord showers His gifts over them to attract them to our holy Faith. This happened for example on the very island of Mindanao where your Lordship is at present with his troops and armed fleet; there, many people have become Christians, and among them there are some chiefs and some other elite who five years ago became Christians through the efforts of a certain Francisco de Castro, captain of a high-planked ship of His Majesty, who had departed from this fort on orders of Captain Galvao, who was then commander of Fort Antonio. Up to the present there are men and women in the fort of Ternate who hail from Mindanao, and who are Christians, married to and with children of Portuguese....And now, they have told me that it is certain that you, Sir, have landed in the island of Mindanao with five ships and one schooner, and that you have started to destroy and burn settlements in that island and to imprison many people. All this seems to be a fact, and it is very much against the service of God and the King of Portugal our Lord.

They have furthermore told me that you arrived there with the determination and purpose to proceed to these islands of Maluku, to engage here in commerce and make a settlement. For me that is hard to believe because it is against the agreement and against propriety......It makes me believe that you have been carried there by mistaken navigation, or that it is not the King of Spain who has sent that armada there....

Therefore, I beg you to, please, go back and leave immediately; do not engage in commerce in those regions and abstain from committing any outrage against the people there, and depart from Mindanao and from your camp there.''

In his answer Villalobos stated that the region in question was still far away from Maluku and within the jurisdiction of Spain. However, he assured Governor de Castro that he would not go against the instructions received in Mexico and that he intended to settle in a place that was farther away.

We have earlier mentioned that Villalobos sent two brigantines to the region of "Abuyo, Tandaya and Mazaua." For quite some time Abuyo and Tandaya were names given by cartographers to the whole of Leyte and Samar. See, e.g., the Pigafetta sketches and also the chart of Dudley's "Dell Arcano del Mare" (Florence, 1646), as well as the chart of Sanson d' Abbeville (1652) and Vingboon's (Quirino's "Philippine Cartography," p. 62).

Worried about the long absence of the two brigantines, Villalobos chartered a large native sailboat of a Tidorese merchant and sent it northwards to find the missing vessels. A resident of Sarangani who claimed to be a Christian offered to go along because he knew Mindanao and all the neighboring islands. About Mindanao he said that there were many tribes living in the interior, but less along the coasts "because of their wars"; the most important places of the island, so he said, were Mindanao (Cotabato), Butuan and "Bisaya." There was gold everywhere, especially at Butuan, and in all the places the inhabitants were very treacherous. When the latter sailboat reached Limasawa (Mazaua) in the Strait of Surigao, they encountered there a trading craft that had come from Borneo; the owner told them that he used to buy gold and slaves at Butuan.

On the island of "Abuyo" they found five Spaniards of the Cristobal, one of the two foraging vessels sent out from Sarangani. It had been well received and stocked by the natives, but some of the crew had molested the inhabitants of one village and burned their place. Consequently, they had been forced to leave Abuyo, but the natives had kept five of them as hostages to make sure that the

Fig. 11. Stretch of beach in the bay of Ambon. In the background is kampong Nusaniwe, where Villalobos died. (Photo by P. Schreurs, MSC.)

damages would be paid if another Spanish vessel were to arrive. Which was done, of course. The other sixteen were afterwards found at Tandaya.

Supplying the stranded remnant of the fleet with the necessities for bare survival was one of the difficulties of Villalobos at Sarangani. The other was sending back one ship to Mexico to inform the Viceroy of the results and the status of the expedition, as stipulated in his sailing orders. The desperate attempts of Villalobos to solve both these problems are outside the scope of interest of these pages. Suffice it therefore to say that, like the preceding fleets, also Villalobos' expedition eventually had to turn itself in and become the uninvited and unwelcome guest of the Portuguese in Maluku.

On Good Friday of 1546 Ruy Lopez de Villalobos died in Amboina, attended in his last hours by the Augustinian chaplains of his fleet and by St. Francis Xavier. The mentioned date is taken from Colin-Pastells (I, p. 150). Georg Schurhammer (in his "St. Francis Xavier and his Times," III, p. 120) prefers the date of Friday before Palm Sunday, basing himself on the writing of Escalante and Aganduru.

There is much disagreement regarding many details of the reports about the Villalobos story. In the end, however, all accounts agree that he died in *una profunda melancolia* and *consumido de tristeza.*

VI

Castilla, Castilla, Cabalian, Amigos, Amigos!

After the death of Emperor Charles V (1558) the plans to take possession of the "Islands of the West," which carried already the name of his son and successor Philip II, were taken up anew. The chances to do so still existed, given the fact that Portugal, occupied with protecting its sea routes to and from the Orient and defending its settlements in the Spice Islands, lacked the means for a definite occupation of the islands north of Maluku. Nevertheless it had never relinquished its claim to those islands by virtue of the agreement of Zaragoza (1529). Spain, on the other hand, if not guided by *de jure* argumentation then at least by *realpolitik* coveted the archipelago as a no-man's land waiting for the blessings of the Cross and of the Spanish Crown.

On November 21, 1564 another fleet left Mexico under the command of Miguel Lopez de Legazpi and the able guidance of a man who had made the voyage forty years earlier, Andres de Urdaneta, who meanwhile from idealistic adventurer had become an Augustinian monk. It is quite interesting to know that until that moment the latter was convinced that Portugal had indeed a legal claim to the southern Philippines. For that reason he had told the King that some lawful or pious reason should be used to enter that territory, like the rescue of Spaniards from earlier expeditions who might still be alive and in captivity there, or if meanwhile they had children, to save the latter from danger to their souls. How secret the

Spanish intentions were, appears from the fact that even Urdaneta, like all the other members of the expedition, was kept in the conviction that they were this time going to head for New Guinea. We can imagine his indignation when, four days after sailing from Puerto de la Navidad in Mexico, the sealed orders were opened wherein the real destination was stated: the "Islas Filipinas" up to the outer northern limits of the islands of Maluku, to be reached by sailing west on a course no lower than nine or ten degrees. In January 1565 they reached the Marianas and thereafter followed a SW course near eleven degrees, mindful of Antonio Conso's advice of 1543 to avoid drifting too far south, as had happened to Villalobos. On February 13 they were at Samar, where they anchored near a little island. Sailing along the coast in a southern direction and trying to go ashore in a few places, they were deeply disappointed at finding only hostile natives who either prevented them from landing or ran away to the forest carrying all their food supplies along. Only in Cabalian (Leyte) were they able to get a sufficient amount of much needed victuals. It was also here that the chief of some coastal village came to see Legazpi on the flagship and offered to show him the way to "Mazaua" and other islands. His name was Camotuan. It is not wholly certain that he came on his own free will as the Spanish reports make it appear, because it is also reported that when the flagship with him on board started to sail away, people ran beside it for some time along the beach, carrying a pig which they wanted to offer to the Spaniards as a ransom for Camotuan. Three of his friends had joined him on board.

> "They said that Masagua (Limasawa, Mazaua) was only three leagues away, and that the land which they could see from that place was a point of the island of "Vindanao" where much gold could be found. They also indicated in what area the places of Butuan, Surigao and Calagan were located, which are on the coast of the island of Vindanao.[9] When we asked them where

---

[9]Calagan: already so named by Pigafetta, and because of faulty translation meant to include Butuan. The information here given by eyewitnesses (Camotuan and companions) in 1565 confirms what we suggested in footnote 2 of Ch. I: that in pre-Spanish times "Caraga" did in fact *not* include Butuan, but referred only to the area of Cantilan, and perhaps to the Pacific coast southward from there. Camotuan and others

cinnamon was growing, they said on Vindanao and Camiguinin, which is a separate island. They showed us where these islands were, and also Zubu, Matan and other islands. The General asked them for all kinds of informations that he could get out of them, and made them understand that he wanted to go to Mazagua, because the people there were friends of the Spaniards whereas in other places we found no friends. He asked them to show him the way and said that he would pay them for it. He did so because he had asked the advice of the Religious and the captains, and all had agreed that we should go to Mazagua, because elsewhere we had not found friends, but in that island the Spaniards had always found a good reception; for that reason he asked the Indios what was said above.

One of the Indios who was with Camotuan said that he knew the island very well and that he would guide us there. A little later they said that Camotuan and the three Indios who were with him would all go with us, but that the people of Mazagua should not see them, so they would not be angry with them for having brought us there. The General was grateful and promised to pay them, and said that he would not anger those of Mazagua and would do no evil to them, but would do them well because the King of Spain was their friend and loved them very much, and had even sent a gift through him; therefore they would not be angry but on the contrary grateful that they had come there.

On Friday, March 9 the fleet raised sails to go from Cabalian to Mazagua; they took the four Indios along and also one canoe which they would need when going back to their place....(On Mazagua) they did not see a single house, not one Indio, nothing at all; they sailed on along the northern coast till they reached a harbor at the westside. There they saw just one Indio who shouted at them from the top of a rock. They shouted back

---

clearly name (in the proper sequence) Butuan, Surigao and ''Calagan,'' distinguishing them from one another.

In 17th and 18th century texts Cantilan is also named ''Bayoyo''or ''Calagdan.'' Presently Bayoyo and Calagdaan are still two rural barrios of Cantilan. In the early 1780s the Cantilan of our days was formed out of these two barrios which, however, afterwards resumed their separate existence. Calag(d)(a)an was originally located at the present Paniguian.

at him that they were from Castilla, and by sign language they asked him to come down to the beach to meet the sailors. But when the Indio heard that they were people from Castilla, he came down from the top of the rock lowering himself via a ladder of rattan cords. Thinking that he had descended to come to the beach to meet the sailors, they waited a long time for him, but the Indio did not do so. After coming down from the rock, he went up a hill with a hut on top; he put fire to it, and in extreme anger he climbed back to the top of the rock via the same ladder and after reaching the top, he cut the ladder, let it drop, and then, standing there high up he shouted at the landing boats. The crew came back to the galleons, and this is what they related. They said that it was the only sheltered place on that island, and for that reason they all agreed not to stay there any longer, because it would be a waste of time; it would be far better to proceed to the island of Camiguinin, which they could see from there, because it was known that there was cinnamon on it; after reaching that place they would decide what was the best thing to do'' (''Documentos Ineditos de Ultramar,'' Filipinas, Doc. 27, pp. 273-275 of Tomo I; also Tomo II, Doc. 41 and 43).

The first report has been attributed to an artillery captain, but according to others it was dictated by Legazpi.

Before leaving for Camiguin they rewarded the chief of Cabalian and his companions with some fine Spanish dresses and gave them food and water for three days. Camotuan embraced Legazpi, stepped in his sailboat, and as a last farewell shouted to the Spaniards *"Castilla, Castilla, Cabalian, amigos, amigos!"* at which he raised his hand, fore and middle fingers entwined, "indicating that they had to be like that" as the report says. And then the happy friendly chief sailed homewards dressed in a green gala uniform and wearing a Spanish hat.

On March 11, 1565 they approached Camiguin; two of the ships sailed around the island in opposite direction. They reported afterwards that they had seen houses here and there, but no people at all. They had obviously abandoned their houses in a hurry, because one landing party had found rice and other foodstuff that had been left behind.

   ''There was also no indication that there was any cinnamon,
   which they were after in the first place. In that island they took

the sun at the place where the fleet was anchored, and it was at nine and one fourth degree. The island can easily be recognized by two high mountain peaks that are on it; its whole circumference is about ten leagues. It is covered with densely forested mountain slopes.

It was clear to the General that there was nothing for him to do on the island of Camiguinin, and that there was no use in staying there any longer... They all agreed that the right thing to do for the Armada was to go to Butuan, which was east of that island. There they could get information about many things, since it was known that it was a place with much commerce, and there might be somebody who would understand the Malayan language; up to now we had not found any, and we did not know the language to understand the natives'' (loc. cit., Tomo I, Doc. 27, pp. 278-279).

On March 14 the ships raised sails in the afternoon and attempted to set out eastwards for Butuan. But after spending the whole night battling contrary winds and currents, they found themselves near the coast of Bohol at daybreak. Here they anchored and started reconnoitering that island instead. Also here the people had deserted their houses and villages. The plan to proceed to Butuan was postponed for the time being, but it was decided that when it was to be realized, not the whole fleet should go there, but only the small patache "San Juan," because it was a light vessel and therefore more suited for tacking against the wind and entering shallow waters. The rest of the fleet would wait at Bohol for the return of the "San Juan," and depending on the information which it would bring back from Butuan, they would afterwards decide whether or not the other ships should go there. The information that would interest them most was the presence and quantity of cinnamon and gold at Butuan.

"They would also have to conclude peace and friendship with the chief of Butuan and inform him how much His Majesty the king of Spain loved them. They should offer him all favors and help from the fleet. With his permission we would go to his place and put up a trading post for commerce in the name of His Majesty, with the result that he and his territory would benefit very much.

In case they found any trading vessels from China or Borneo, they should make peace with them and not inflict any harm on them, because such is our foremost intention here. They should ask them informations about neighboring islands, what kind of people are living there and what their commerce is; what things they import or export, where and at what price they buy and sell. In everything they should take care not to give occasion for irritation or friction, and even if the natives were to cause such, they should not mind it, just as if they had not noticed it.

The General ordered that Geronimo Pacheco, the interpreter of the Malayan language, should go with them, because he believed that in Butuan — since it was a place of commerce — it was impossible that there would not be somebody who understood it. After all, in these regions the Malayan language is so generally used that in any place there are people who understand and speak it.

If they found no cinnamon at Butuan, they should sail on along the coast of Vindanao southwest till they would reach the province of Cabit [Quipit, Zamboanga]," (loc. cit.).

While the ships were at Bohol, a sailboat from Borneo was captured in the neighboring waters. After a skirmish it was brought peacefully to the anchoring place of the Spaniards where its pilot became the friend of the Spaniards. He turned out to be well informed about Mindanao, Cebu and other places of the archipelago and also spoke the local languages. From him they heard about commercial conditions at Butuan.

"There was much gold in its rivers, as, e.g., in the area called Surigao, and another named Calagan. This Moro told Legazpi that there were two junks from Luzon in Butuan to buy gold, wax and slaves. The things carried by those junks were practically the same as those carried by the Borneans, and because their merchandize consists of articles from China, people in these islands call the Bornean ships and those from Luzon by the name "junks from China."

In their dealings with the local people the Borneans call themselves also Chinese, but in fact Chinese junks do not come here because they are very large ships that are not suited for sailing between these islands. They do, however, go every year to Borneo and Luzon, where the merchants buy from the Chinese the things which they afterwards bring to these islands.

He pointed out that the island of Luzon is much farther to the north, unlike Borneo. He also said that at present the Borneans do not come to Butuan because of existing hostility caused by some raids and killings committed by the Borneans at Butuan in past years." (loc. cit., pp. 291-292. See also: "Conquistas de las Islas Filipinas" by Gaspar de San Agustin (1696), Capitulo XXI in the new edition of the Instituto Enrique Florez, Madrid, 1975).

In the party that sailed to Butuan in April 1565 were Guido de Lavezares, the treasurer of the fleet (afterwards to become the second Governor General — after Legazpi — of the Philippines), also Andres de Mirandaola, the "factor" or administrator of the royal properties, Juan de la Isla, the captain of the patache, his brother Rodrigo, who was the pilot, and the Augustinian Fray Martin de Rada, a learned cosmographer and afterwards a protector of the rights of the natives.[10]

Aside from barter goods for trading purposes, they took along a special set of vestments to serve as a gift to the chief of Butuan. Originally these clothes had been intended for the ruler of Limasawa.

Upon reaching Butuan the local chief informed them that they would be permitted to enter the river, provided they came with only one vessel. From the details of the report we have to conclude that at that time Butuan was not located along the main Agusan river but along one of its tributaries: the "San Juan could not enter because the river was only one fathom deep." The Agusan river was certainly navigable by a thirty-ton patache like the "San Juan"; even our present-day interisland vessels can enter it up to at least ten kilometers, the site of the present Butuan. It may be presumed that the Butuan of 1565 was somewhere beside the Banza or Baug rivers; archaeological findings in those areas clearly point to pre-Spanish settlements.

As the trader from Borneo had told them in Bohol, there were indeed two junks in Butuan owned by "Moros of Luzon," who came out in small *barotos* to visit the Spanish ship. They showed a keen interest in the *"tostones de plata"* (silver from Peru and Mexico melted into coins or small bars) which the Spaniards carried for trading purposes. They offered gold in exchange and also wax, which they had bought from the inhabitants. The exchange rate of gold to silver was one to six by weight.

---

[10]See Pedro de Galende, OSA: "Apologia pro Filipinos" (Manila, 1980).

''We went to the town called Butuan to speak to the king. As soon as we got there we went to the house of the king, and the first thing they did to us in the house of the king was to make us sit down, after which there came out to us seven or eight women, pretty ones. I mention this because they were certainly pretty, and some of them were dressed in Indian silk. They told us that it was a custom of the country for the women to make their appearance first. I asked the Moor for the names of the king and queen, and he said that the king was called Lumanpaon and the queen Bucaynin and the king's son Lian and the king's brother Sigoan. Then the king appeared and sat down. I told the interpreter to tell the king that I was the pilot of the ship out there and that I had come at the captain's orders to bring him a present. He took it and put it on immediately. I then told him that the captain had come at the behest of the King of Castile in order that his treasury officials might bring merchandise to sell to the natives; and I asked him if it was his pleasure that the cloth (we brought) be sold to his subjects. He said yes, adding that some of the natives had much gold and others little, and so each will buy what he can... (After the royal audience) the Moor took me to see his ship, which was a big *parao* with a foremast and a mainmast. He showed me a swivel gun of bronze and asked me if we brought many rials. I said yes. He said that he had three quintals of gold which he would trade for rials. He asked me if we want beeswax. I said yes. He said that there was much beeswax in that country. I asked him if it came from China. He said no, on the contrary; the Chinese came to his country with porcelain, iron tips for spears, swords, and jars, which they sold throughout these islands for gold to bring back to their country, and also beeswax, because it was for these things they came'' (De la Costa 1973, 13).

According to the report, the Luzon Moros wanted to prevent the inhabitants from trading directly with the Spaniards, or if they did, oblige them to accept only silver *tostones* in payment. By their own trading with the Spaniards and the natives they hoped to get hold of all the silver of the Spaniards. But the problem was that the natives did not know anything about the value of the *tostones* because they were totally new to them. Another point of friction arose when the Spaniards discovered that the Luzon traders were cheating them: inside the big blocks *(panes)* of wax which they offered for sale, a good amount of earth was found. For that (and probably some other) reason some of the Spanish soldiers started planning to pillage the Moro junks, especially after they had heard that they were carrying a lot of gold. It came to a near mutiny when Fray de Rada and some officers strictly prohibited them from doing so. The author of the report remarks that gold was the principal object of greed of the soldiers, and that even Captain de la Isla would have loved to attack the junks and ransack them.

Because of the unruly and tense atmosphere among the Spaniards, it was decided to return to Bohol earlier than initially planned and without making the reconnaissance trip along the coast up to Zamboanga as they had been ordered to do. In another document (39, Tomo II, p. 140ff.) we read that some months later, when the fleet had moved from Bohol to Cebu, a conspiracy developed among a group of malcontents (most of them non-Spaniards, especially Frenchmen) who planned to hijack the "San Juan," sail it back to Butuan, raid and ransack the place and as many coastal villages as possible, and then sail the ship to Guatemala or Peru and return to Spain from where they would disappear to France. As an alternative they could also turn to the Portuguese in Maluku, who would gladly help them to escape to Portugal for having run away from the Spanish camp. However, at the last moment (November 27, 1565) the plot was betrayed. The leader was executed on the galleys and then decapitated, his head being exposed on a stake as a public warning to the soldiers and sailors. The report itself says: there was a large number of scoundrels and disloyal non-Spaniards in the expedition. The investigation brought to light that the conspiracy and other evil plans were not just a sudden temptation of the moment: many of the culprits involved in the escape-to-Butuan plot had already in Mexico agreed to hijack the "San Lucas" a few days after the departure from the port of La Navidad.

Looking back at about forty years of occasional western arrivals on the coasts of the southern Philippines, one cannot help noticing the following: With very few exceptions, sooner or later the contemporary reports of the post-Magellan expeditions mention cases of fear and hostility on the part of the inhabitants. The Legazpi expedition, being more extensively documented than those of Loaisa, Saavedra and Villalobos, has (consequently?) more references than the latter concerning conflict situations on the beaches of the Visayas and Mindanao, encountered or caused by itself or betraying delayed reactions by the natives to the misdeeds of earlier ones. As for its own experiences, the story of the natives disappearing at the sight of the Spanish ships or resisting landings, runs like an accusing line of wrong and injury from Samar to most of Leyte, Limasawa, Camiguin and Bohol and even Butuan. At

Limasawa, where things had been so different forty-four years earlier (as the reports mention repeatedly), that wrong was pathetically illustrated by the fury of the lonely man on the hill shouting at the Spaniards to be gone. What had gone wrong? That was also one of the foremost questions which Legazpi and Urdaneta asked themselves.

In fairness, or at least for the sake of completeness, it must be said that there were fear and wrongdoing in the primitive settlements *before* the arrival of the Spaniards or Portuguese. In the Villalobos report we met a man from Sarangani, who knew Mindanao well, telling that the coastal areas of the island were then rather depopulated "because of the people's wars." We heard about slave trading at Butuan in the relation of Villalobos as well as in those of Legazpi. Presumably, those slaves had not been bought or caught in China! The original inhabitants of northern Surigao, the Mamanuas, as well as those of the eastern coastal region of Caraga were not driven to remote mountain districts by the Spaniards. And the tree houses of the Mandayas and the inhabitants of early Siargao were not built as a protection against any four-legged enemies. The primitive inhabitants were most probably not exactly peaceful, unspoilt lambs living in a tropical paradise and then suddenly jumped upon by Caucasian wolves!

But what concerns us here is that there had been Caucasians around. And it is interesting to compare Spanish with Portuguese reports and listen to who is calling wolf across the demarcation line.

Let us first listen to a sworn statement by expedition member Geronimo Monzon before the *escribano* Fernando Riquel on March 25, 1565 at Cebu:

> "The armada came in sight of the island of Mazaua where people were very old friends of the Spaniards; each time when they had come to their island, they had met and received them in peace and took very good care of them. But this time, seeing that the ships were coming, one Indio put fire to a house and then climbed to the top of a high rock, cut the ladder, and with shouts gave to understand that he did not like the Spaniards to come there. That makes this witness believe for sure that they did so because they were very much afraid of the Portuguese. In the island of Botuma (sic, Butuan), when the *patache* "San Juan," which his lordship the Governor had sent there, had arrived there alone for trading purposes, this witness saw an Indio who said that he was the son of the chief of Mazaua and who was wearing signs of mourning in his dress. He said that

the *Franguez*, that means the Portuguese, had destroyed his island, and that for that reason he was now staying in Butuan among his relatives.[11] This witness knows this because he had asked about it in the dialect. Also, because afterwards when the *patache* returned from the port of Butuan to the island of Bohol where the fleet was waiting for it, he heard the Moros of Borneo say through the interpreter for the language of the Bornean Moros, that also the inhabitants of the island of Bohol were complaining about the Portuguese from Maluco who, accompanied by some inhabitants of those islands, had come to the island of Bohol; they had said that they wanted to do business with them, but afterwards when the people of the island of Bohol were indeed engaging in business and feeling safe because of the pact of friendship which had been made according to custom, the Portuguese and the Malucans had suddenly attacked them, killing and wounding many Indios, and taking many of them away as captives; they had ransacked the whole island and perpetrated other damages in it.

For that reason the natives were upset and scared, and from then on they did not dare trust anybody, not even their friends. The witness saw that the natives of Bohol were so scared to come aboard the ships that even when the Bornean Moros, their friends, who knew the Portuguese, would come with them, they did not trust the Spaniards at all" ("Documentos Ineditos de Ultramar", Tomo II, Doc. 43, pp. 303-304).

Elsewhere in his statement the witness says that when the Spaniards had arrived at Cabalian, "the inhabitants had asked them if they were 'Franguez' which means Portuguese, because that is how the Indios call them, and that when the sailors said that they were not Portuguese but Spaniards... they came on board the flagship and made friends with the Governor."

That was 1565 and the expedition of Legazpi. Earlier, in the reports of Villalobos (1543) we heard about the angry letters of the Portuguese Governor of Ternate imploring the Spaniards (then marooned at Sarangani) to stop raiding villages and killing people on the south and east coast of Mindanao. From the same reports it is known that the crew of a brigantine which Villalobos had sent to "Abuyo y Tandaya" (Leyte) had burned one village in that province. Again, still earlier, in 1525 when in Lianga Bay, the natives there

---

[11]When Magellan was in Limasawa in 1521, he met there two datus who were brothers; one was the chief of the island, the other of Butuan.

were warned by a man from Malacca (?) not to trust the foreign arrivals "because he thought that we were Portuguese."

Pastells, in his edition of Colin's "Labor Evangelica" (II, pp. 625-626) explains that the word actually used here for Portuguese was "Foranguis" (Pranguis in Concepción's "Historia General" and Herrera's "Decada III"), a word that in Malacca stood for Portuguese. But according to Pastells, for people on the east coast of Mindanao that term primarily referred to "people from the "Polangui" river of Cotabato (river populated by strangers), ergo Moros, who had been raiding the coastal towns of eastern Mindanao previously; only in an indirect sense the word would apply to the Portuguese. Pastells' reasoning is rather roundabout but the long and short of the etymology of "f(o)rangi" is that it stands for "stranger" and that in the 16th century Asian context it would in fact mostly refer to Portuguese.

Anyway, if prior to 1525 those "frangi" from Cotabato had raided Mindanao's east coast, it would disprove the theory of some that the notorious Moro raids on that stretch of the Pacific and elsewhere in Mindanao or the rest of the country, could only have been a reaction against Spanish intrusions. (Which, however, became afterwards an important, perhaps the chief motivation.)

Some Spanish reports make it appear that the Portuguese abuses were actually committed as a kind of black propaganda or psycho-warfare. Those Portuguese would have told the pillaged inhabitants that they were Spaniards, so that if and when real Spaniards should show up, they would find the name Castilla thoroughly hated and feared. But it seems more probable (and simple) that the poor victims, seeing no difference between Portuguese and Spanish features, would anyway have mixed up the two nationalities. Like any white man, even if he were Dutch or Russian, would now be called "Americano."

Pastells (loc. cit., p. 626) rightly notes, however, that the historian Juan de la Concepción — following Herrera — is definitely mistaken when suggesting that the alleged Portuguese mentioned in the Loaisa report at Lianga had been the sailors on board the ship of Francisco de Castro, of whom we have spoken earlier. De Castro arrived ten years after Loaisa, and of his voyage only good has been reported. Which is more than can be said about the Spaniards of the Villalobos expedition who had been at Mazaua in 1543.

All in all, the gist of all these sad stories is that both Portuguese and Spanish arrivals misbehaved more than once in their contacts with the natives. We have already seen that not a few of the first discoverers were an ugly lot of adventurers. Keeping them in check was clearly and recurrently one big problem for the officers of Legazpi's expedition. And it can definitely be said that as a rule it was the four missionaries of that expedition who took up the cause of the natives.

In the story of the intended mutiny at Cebu we mentioned that the leaders had already one year earlier, back in Mexico, plotted to hijack the *patache* "San Lucas" early in the Pacific voyage of the fleet. This plan did not materialize, but the little vessel just named would nevertheless sail into the pages of history with another story that linked her in a very remarkable — although controversial — way with the past of Surigao.

On December 1, 1564, ten days after leaving Mexico, this *patache* had become separated from the fleet in a storm. Indeed, separated, and "by an act of God," that is what its captain, Don Alfonso de Arellano, would stress in his report afterwards. That report fills the whole Document 37 in Tomo II of the "Documentos Ineditos de Ultramar." Subsequent investigations in Mexico and Spain after the return of the "San Lucas" strongly hint at an intended *(preconcebida)* separation from the convoy. That investigation was spurred when Urdaneta had returned to Mexico, where he heard that the earlier arrival, Captain de Arellano, had been praised and feted for a courageous venture: the first trip with only one light vessel all the way to the Philippines and back.

Let us first listen to the report which Legazpi himself gives of the events surrounding the disappearance at sea of the "San Lucas."

> "For five days [after leaving Mexico] the fleet sailed south-west, but on the sixth we directed our course due westward until we reached the ninth degree. We sailed on this latitude in search of the island of Los Reyes in order that we might go from that point to the Filipinas. A week after we had taken this course, we awoke in the morning and missed the *patache* "San Lucas" with Captain Don Alonso Arellano in command. There had been no stormy weather to make it lose sight of us;[12] nor could it have been Don Alonso's fault, for he was a gallant man as he had

---

[12] The report of the chief pilot of the fleet, Esteban de Rodriguez, reads: "December 1: this night the *patache* San Lucas became separated from the fleet. Afterwards, early in the night, we had a rain squall *(aquacero)*."

shown. It is believed that it was due to the malicious intent of
the pilot. And as he [Don Alonso] had already been informed
about the expedition we were making, and the course we were
to sail, and as he was fully instructed as to what he must do in
case he should lose sight of us — as actually happened — and
whither he must proceed to await us, we expected all the time
that we would find the vessel in some of these islands. But up to
this time we have heard nothing of it, which gives me not a little
uneasiness'' (Blair & Robertson 2, pp. 196-197).

A court case was filed against de Arellano and pilot Lope Martin,
but the Spanish Audiencia (court) never let it come to a verdict and
let de Arellano enter history with the benefit of the doubt hanging
over his intentions and over the question if he ever really reached the
Philippines. Unlike some commentators who have passed off his
story as a big hoax, we believe that he did. As to the quality of his
voyage and his courage, the compiler of the "Documentos Ineditos"
has the following to say in his introduction to Tomo II: "We have to
admit that the voyage of the "San Lucas" is one of the most
audacious that has been registered in the history of navigation."

Arellano's report about that feat has been translated into English
in the collection "The Christianization of the Philippines," jointly
published by the Historical Conservation Society and the University
of San Agustin in Iloilo. It is a pity, however, that the translation
into "current English" does more than one injustice to the factual
contents of the report and is a few times downright wrong, albeit not
in essential facts. Therefore I prefer to translate from the original
Spanish text in Tomo II of the "Documentos Ineditos." It may be
true that it is rather difficult to trace the exact course of much of
the route taken by de Arellano to and around Mindanao and the
Visayas — personally we consider it to be an intended
(preconcibida) difficulty — but it is very well possible that the "San
Lucas" did reach the Philippines at the coast of Surigao at 9
degrees on January 29, 1565. Let us give the table to Captain
Alonso de Arellano.

"(Steering west to northwest) we sailed along nine degrees
till the 29th of the said month. That was a Monday, and at
midday, while the pilot and I were sitting on the stern, he saw
some land and pointed it out to me, saying that it was
Mindanao, because we were sailing at its altitude; Mindanao
was a land different from what we had seen up to here, very
high and one of the principal islands of the Philippines. When

we came close to it, it was already late. The wind had suddenly calmed, but there was still a strong sea-swell caused by the breeze. It certainly would have thrown us on land within one hour, and therefore we had to lower the sloop. This, however, took quite some effort, because the ship was heaving so much that when the sloop was in the water there was danger that it would be smashed to pieces... While we were still struggling, the wind started blowing from the land, undoubtedly sent by our Lady of Guadalupe and of Consolación, because the wind came with a most sweet smell. The result was that it looked as if we had been in no trouble at all. We swung around seaward again and kept following the coast which runs north to south. The sea current is from northeast to southwest, and therefore the only way to make headway was by tacking first to a higher altitude (away) from the island where it forms the cape which is the land end of the northeast coast. The chart indicated that the principal port of that island is located where that coast begins to run northeast to southwest. We found that port indeed, entered it, and dropped an anchor; that was the thirtieth of the said month. We fired a gun three times as a sign of peaceful intentions. From some members of earlier fleets I had heard that such was the custom in those islands'' (Documentos Ineditos de Ultramar, Doc. 37, pp. 27-29).

These details show that the place where the "San Lucas" was nearly tossed on the east coast of Mindanao must have been somewhere in the Tandag-Cantilan stretch. Those who know the area will be reminded of Punta Cawit and the danger of approaching the mainland under the monsoon conditions of January. The description of the coastal direction to the "principal port" leads to the general area of Surigao City, all the more evident if we connect it with a later reference to a more important port that undoubtedly was Butuan, as we will indicate in the proper place.

Of course, one misses any reference to the various islands near the headland of Surigao, but then, there is so much one will miss in most of the navigation reports of those days, because we, now, read those reports with our knowledge born of experience or exact modern maps in the back of our minds. The two primitive sketches made in Surigao Strait on board of ships of the Legazpi expedition illustrate what I mean. In addition: the "San Lucas" sailed that stretch at night. We must also not lose sight of the fact that de Arellano was definitely not writing guidelines for captains or pilots of future ships! On the contrary: in his particular situation it might even have been advisable for him not to give away too many pinpointing details about the places where he had been. The less his accusers in Mexico knew, the less chances they would have to prove that while in Mindanao and the Visayas, he had intentionally avoided meeting the main fleet. At any rate, subsequent events after his return to Mexico make clear that in spite of his possible desertion in mid-ocean, Legazpi did not lose faith in his capabilities. We can read this in the latter's report about the "San Lucas" case, and it was confirmed again two years later when de Arellano was already back in Spain, by the fact that Legazpi invited him to come back to the Philippines.

Let us rejoin the Spanish soldiers and sailors at Surigao. A detachment of seven men under the first officer Pedro de Rivero landed in a sloop, and to their great joy found good drinking water, of which they filled eight barrels. De Arellano remarks that apparently it was a good country. The people were not like in the islands previously touched, where often they swarmed over the ship even before it had anchored. As a matter of fact, initially none of them showed up. Only the next day three men came to look at the ship, but they stayed at a safe distance, half hidden in the bushes on top of an elevation, from where they shouted at the sailors who shouted back and signaled them to come down.

> "Seeing that they did not want to come to the beach, the pilot with three or four men got into the sloop. When the Indios saw that they were near land, they came down to the water and by sign language told them to jump on land, but the pilot told them to come to the sloop. One of them started to tuck up his dress to get into the sloop, but the others did not allow him. Then they threw a colored cap to them on land; they took it and raised their hands to heaven as a sign of peace. They were wearing cotton dresses and carried daggers in their belts and had also shields and lances. By these things we knew that we were in the Philippines and would be well treated by them. By gestures they made the sailors understand that they should wait there because they would come back afterwards. They took leave and ran away, and the pilot returned to the ship.
>
> Later in the afternoon about 30 or 40 Indios with lances and shields appeared on the beach. In front was one who was the leader because they all showed respect to him. They signaled us to come on land, and therefore the pilot and I with some men of

the ship went down and came as far as the water-edge; the chief told us to jump on land, and just when we jumped, he stepped into the water, took some of the water in the cup of his hand, and started to make the sign of the Cross like one of us; by sign language he said that we should do the same, because such is the customary way to indicate peace or welcome among them. Then I did what he had done, and when he saw that, he was very happy. We went on land and embraced him and he us with much friendliness. In order to make the peace bond stronger, the chief took his dagger and indicated by signs that he wanted to make a cut in the skin of his stomach or arm, to draw some blood to confirm his friendship with us, because such is the custom among those islanders.[13] But I took his dagger away so he would not cut himself and told him also by signs that even without that we would be very good friends. At that he was satisfied; he sat down and told us to do the same, which we did. They started to pour some wine from a very large and thick cane filled with wine, and started to give it to us to drink, but before we were going to drink, he drank once from it in front of all of us, so as to make us understand that it was something good and did not contain any poison. So we drank from it, each once, and the wine was sweet and had a tangy taste, somewhat like ginger; it had the color of cinnamon water, and I think they put cinnamon in it, because of the color which it has. Seeing that we drank their wine without showing repugnance, they gave us a number of sweet canes and cooked yams. We also gave them of the things that we had; to the chief we gave among others a piece of iron which he liked very much. In their own language they call it a nail. We asked him by signs if there were cows or goats on that land, and they said yes, indicating (the form of) big horns. They said that next morning they would bring us some things to eat. Because it was getting late, we took leave of them and went back to the ship. They went to their village, much contented for having made friendship with us. We, on the other hand, were even more happy because of the mercy which Our Lady had bestowed upon us by letting us find such intelligent people and because we had found a source for water and firewood and a port where we could wait for the fleet" (loc.cit., pp. 30-32).

---

[13] In Spanish sources named *pacto de sangre*; locally *"sandugo."*

It would appear from this report that there had been earlier arrivals of Spaniards or Portuguese in Surigao. There is, e.g., the pilot's chart which "indicated," according to the text, where the principal port was located. More intriguing is the remark about the local chief "making the sign of the Cross." The times when they could have learned to identify the sign of the Cross with Caucasians could have been 1528 (Saavedra) or more probably 1538 (arrival and performance of baptisms by Francisco de Castro), or 1543 (Villalobos). The ceremony of taking water in a cupped hand might be an indication that they had indeed witnessed the ritual of baptism. It seems doubtful, however, that the combination of scooping water with making the sign of the Cross was the "customary way" to indicate peace and friendship, as de Arellano saw it. No other contemporary reports about similar encounters speak about it. Nevertheless, that combination could have been witnessed in a baptismal ceremony.

The report goes on to mention that next day about two hundred of the natives came back with all kinds of fruits and foodstuffs to barter for pieces of iron. They also told the Spaniards that initially they had been afraid because in the past some people "looking like us had treated them badly." (See our earlier remarks on the misbehavior of Portuguese and Spanish sailors in eastern Mindanao and the Visayas.)

De Arellano mentions also that the name of the locality was Atocco and that the local chief was called Buian, in the rest of the text spelled Viban.

All through his report de Arellano keeps repeating that what he and his pilot wanted most was to be reunited with the rest of the fleet. The accusation raised against him in Mexico, however, stated that on the contrary he must have studiously avoided rejoining Legazpi's ships "although he had seen their sails from the look-out post on the mast of the 'San Lucas'." This cannot have been the case when the "San Lucas" was in Surigao because she left there on March 4, 1565, while Legazpi sailed through the Strait of Surigao not earlier than March 9 on his way to Limasawa. The accusation must therefore refer to one or two days after that night when the "San Lucas" had become separated from the main fleet.

Eventually the stay at Surigao was marred by an ugly happening, which we are going to deal with here not just for its own (negative) significance, but more for some of its intriguing ramifications that run from Surigao to Butuan to Cebu and even as far back as the predeparture days of the fleet in Mexico. The story is about the attempted desertion by four of the sailors around the third week of their stay at Surigao. Some of the men had been complaining about the increasingly frustrating state of affairs they found themselves in. One day, when de Arellano had put them to work on the cutting of timber for the repair of the "San Lucas," they grumbled that

> "they had not come to China[14] to cut timber for the ship, but at their return they wanted to be loaded with gold." In addition they said that this was not the real port, which was located more to the south, where they would find many junks loaded with precious things, and that they knew this for sure, and that this had been their foremost interest for joining the expedition. As a result they had incited some men to mutiny. The pilot became aware of this when being told that when he was with me on the shore attending to his business, some men who had stayed behind on the ship (that were the mutineers) had opened his map chest and consulted the chart to see where Maluco was located, because that is where they wanted to go."

Four of the schemers were eventually able to get hold of some of the muskets, and after stealing the small sloop they went to hide in a nearby creek to wait for the others who were in on the plot. After one

---

[14] "China..." The first document to circulate in Spain about the results of the Legazpi expedition was printed by Pau Cortey at Barcelona in 1566. (See Blair & Robertson 2, p. 220). The opening sentence has the following: "Desto de la China." The author probably thought, like many contemporaries, that the general area of the (western) Pacific islands was the outskirts of the "Reino de la China." (Primitivas relaciones..., edited by the Director General de Archivos y Bibliotecas, 1958, p. xxiii.)

The author of the Cortey document writes about "two reports" having been received "from China" about that expedition: one by the captain of the San Lucas (de Arellano) and the other by Legazpi.

Sixty years earlier, the young Hernando Cortés, later to become the conquistador of Mexico, reached the island of Hispaniola under the same treacherous circumstances as related here about de Arellano: the captain of his ship had deserted the main convoy at midsea. The treachery was still a secret at the moment of their arrival. Also Cortés voiced his disdain of manual labor in this phraseology: "I came to get gold, not to till the soil like a peasant."

day, however, they were jumped upon by a search party that had stalked them over land. Brought back to the ship, they were sentenced to death. Four pulleys were prepared to hang them, but "when they were sitting with the ropes already around their necks and waiting to be kicked overboard, the pilot and Pedro de Rivero came to me and argued that it would be impossible for us to sail the ship out of the port if those four men were to die, because we were already so few in the ship, and most were even sick."

It was then decided to spare their lives and that once the "San Lucas" should rejoin the main fleet they would be handed over to Legazpi for proper punishment. The chronicler reports that from then on they behaved decently in order to atone for their past misdeeds.

Putting all these informations together, and in addition remembering the happenings at Butuan and Cebu which we related earlier, one cannot help being intrigued by the following:

1. They said that "south of where we were" there was a more important port....This would seem to point to Butuan. Or, looking at it another way, one may see here a confirmation of what we had concluded earlier for other reasons: the "San Lucas" was indeed in the Surigao area.

2. For the mutineers, that bigger port in the south had a connotation of commerce with the outside world, more specifically through "junks" "loaded with all kinds of good things." We will remember the information given to Legazpi by the Bornean trader at Bohol about Butuan, and the subsequent findings when the "San Juan" had been dispatched from Bohol to Butuan.

3. The mutineers at Surigao had identical aims with those of the "French connection" at Cebu mentioned before: getting hold of the merchandize of the junks at Butuan and then escape to, e.g., Maluco.

4. The Surigao rogues "knew for sure" about the opportunities for robbery at Butuan; in addition that knowledge dated back to the pre-departure days in Mexico, and furthermore it had been "their foremost interest for joining the expedition" (Surigao mutineers); "gold was the principal object of the greed of the soldiers" (near mutiny at Butuan). In 1550 the Ramusio edition of Pigafetta's diary about Magellan's expedition had appeared in Europe and it had found avid readers among circles interested in further discoveries in the *islas del Poniente*. Pigafetta has a clear report about the ample presence of gold at Butuan. It may be assumed that his description was known among those who joined the Legazpi expedition. This throws some telling light on the "greed of the soldiers" and their

urgency to proceed to that Butuan!

5. Our former friends, the culprits involved in the escape-to-Butuan conspiracy at Cebu as well as those at Surigao, had jointly and already at an earlier date entertained another perverse aim: to hijack our very same "San Lucas" a few days after its departure from Mexico:

> "It was discovered (in Cebu) that some of those who were
> in the plot, had already in La Navidad conspired to desert the
> fleet with the San Lucas" (loc. cit. Doc. 39, pp. 149-150).

Shortly before the disappearance of the "San Lucas," the Maestre de Campo of the expedition had indeed discovered suspicious sail and ship maneuvers within the convoy, irregular enough to be noticed and put down in the logbook.

6. Notwithstanding all the obligatory confessions and communions prior to departure from Mexico, the atmosphere among a considerable number of the expedition members seems hardly to have been one of holy peace and harmony. In his report about the mutiny at Surigao, de Arellano states that when questioned about their motivation, the deserters "gave such an angry reply to the pilot that even a Protestant *(Luterano)* would not have used the kind of language they had used. What it came down to was this: as their first plan had not succeeded they would now rather die among the Indios than return to the ship. Because of that answer he asked them what was really on their mind for deserting, since nobody had done them any wrong? They answered that they were under no obligation to explain, and that it was their own decision. After all, so they said, they had been deceived when they departed from La Navidad, and now it was their turn to do as much harm as possible."

"They had been deceived." Would this refer to the fact that in Mexico the whole fleet had been kept in the conviction that the expedition was destined for New Guinea? Only four days after departure the true destination had been divulged, a (security?) trick that also Urdaneta and many others had deeply resented.

In spite of all his daily problems at Surigao, de Arellano regularly took out time to gather some interesting information concerning the inhabitants who came to the nearby beach nearly every day to trade with the Spaniards. Many were wearing elegant cotton dresses and carried beautiful, sharp cutlasses and daggers. They wore earrings of very fine gold, and often their teeth were pierced and skillfully inlaid with gold in a way no goldsmith would have been capable of.

When asked if there was gold in their own territory, they affirmed it and pointed inland. One day a man came down with a bamboo tube full of gold nuggets, but de Arellano says that the Spaniards did not wish to trade for it "to show that we did not care for it" (perhaps so as not to drive the price up ?).

Among the game hunted in the locality was deer "which they call *usa* in their language."

Nevertheless, if some Spaniards (in spite of their avowed Christianity and devotion to Our Lady) were not beyond coveting the junks loaded with good things at Butuan, neither were some natives at Surigao (in spite of their avowed friendliness) beyond a more than superficial interest in the Spanish ship and its contents. Thinking that the Spaniards would soon leave, the local chief — under the pretext of going on a hunting trip — went to see some other chiefs and to recruit manpower for a surprise attack over land and sea. The first attempt on March 2nd was beaten off, but the natives withdrew to prepare for a second attack. The Spaniards thought it prudent not to wait for it to happen, and on Sunday morning, March 5, 1565, after having been part of the "current events" at Surigao for 33 days, the wayward ship "San Lucas" sailed away, this time on the homeward lap of its controversial odyssey to and from the "Islands of the West." On July 31 they reached the coast of California.

> "That night the westwind calmed down and we were left without even a breeze. But the wind from the southwest started blowing gently at dawn. Since only a little bit of our sails was still left, and we did not even have two handpalms of canvas available on board, the pilot ordered that we make bonnets out of our sleeping blankets so we could catch the sea breeze at noon. With the help of Our Lord and with our own efforts we reached Puerto de La Navidad on the 9th of August of 1565....All said under oath that this is the truth, and Don Alonso de Arellano, the captain, and Lope Martin, the pilot, signed the statement with their names, and the others said that they did not know how to sign"...Puerto de La Navidad, before me, Alonso de Segura, His Majesty's Clerk.

Fig. 12 is taken from a drawing showing the northern coastline of Mindanao, from the headland of Surigao up to appr. Gingoog Bay. In the original this coast is indicated as *"tira de Baguindanao"* (1). Butuan (2), and Camiguin(in) (3), are indicated by name. Immediately to the north of the Surigao headland is Dinagat (4). From there to the west runs the Strait of Surigao and the sea of Mindanao. Bohol (5) is north of Camiguin and Sequior (6) to the left of Bohol. At the outer west is "Zubu" (7) with "Matan" (8) moved to its northern tip. In the original, *Asiento de los Españoles* (camp of the Spaniards) is written at the northern headland of Cebu. Immediately east of Mactan is the west coast of "Abuyo" (Leyte) (9) — in many old maps Abuyo is the name for Leyte; from there northeast is the northern tip of Samar (10), at its Pacific side of the inscription "Isleta del Primer surgidero" (11): the place where Legazpi made the first landfall in the Philippines.

For the sake of more clarity the sketch has been redrawn from a photograph of the original; unclear written indications have been replaced by the digits used above.

This sketch can also be found in Pastells' edition of Colin's "Labor Evangelica".

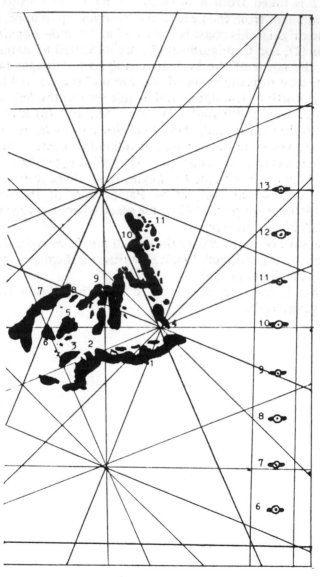

Fig. 12. This sketch of the Surigao strait was made on board of one of
Legazpi's ships. For a proper understanding the viewer should
realize that the blots are *not* islands, but merely the coastal outline
of islands as seen (for the first time) from a passing ship. One
should therefore, not expect too much geodetical exactness in the
locations indicated.

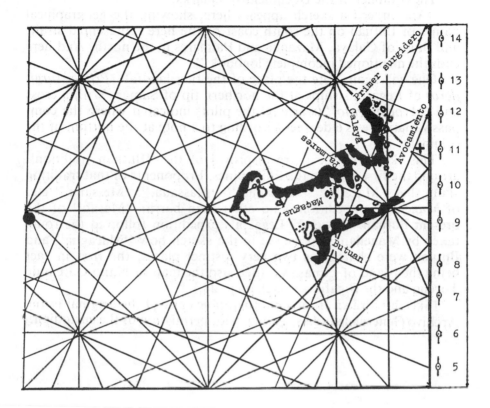

Fig. 13. Also this sketch was made by pilots of Legazpi's fleet while sailing through the Strait of Surigao; it is taken from the logbook of the pilots Jaimes Martinez Fortun and Diego Martin. In vol. I, pp. 352-353 of the "Documentos Ineditos de Ultramar" we read:

"Tuesday, February 13 we saw land at 12 degrees, which was of the Philippine Islands. That day we anchored in the protection of a small island in water of 40 fathoms. This land and all the rest that we, the pilots Jaimes Martinez Fortun and Diego Martin have seen of these Philippine Islands, we indicated with a sketch, complete with route and altitude, as God Our Lord made us understand it."

The compiler of the Documentos remarks:

"And indeed a sketch appears here, showing the geographical names of Butuan on the south coast of the here represented strait, and those of Calaya, Mazagua and Palmares in the north. And here ends the mentioned incomplete logbook."

One will again note the place of the first landfall *(Primer surgidero)* of Legaspi's ships at the northern tip of Samar. With a cross and *"Avocamiento"* (warning) the pilots indicated where the compass variation was 6 degrees according to a note at the bottom of the original.

This sketch is one more disproval of the "Butuan tradition" around the first Mass in the Philippines. Proponents of that tradition claim that "Mazaua," "Masagua," "Massana," "Messana," etc. of Magellan's expedition is no other than barrio "Masao" of the present Butuan. However, Legazpi's expedition followed the route taken by Magellan, and we see in the sketch how "Macagua" and Butuan were charted as two very distinct places, the first in fact being the island of Limasawa. (See also the map of Nuno Garcia de Toreno and the Pigafetta sketch on p. 28.)

(Sketch redrawn from a photographic copy of the original in the Archivo General de Indias, Sevilla, with permission of the custodian.)

VII

Possessed But Not Pacified

> "I have to admit that to politicians it must seem that nobody would come from so far just to earn a morsel of bread! But it is a fact that if one wishes to serve your Majesty punctually and at the same time lead a Christian life, it is difficult to acquire much property" (Governor Juan Niño de Tavora to the King, July 8, 1632).

After making landfall at the northeast coast of Samar, Legazpi sent his ensign-general Andres de Ibarra ashore with a landing party "to take possession, in the name of His Majesty, of the part and place where he went...and of all the other areas subject and contiguous thereto" (Documentos Ineditos de Ultramar, Vol. I, Doc. 28).

The act and the fact of the takeover were duly notarized. It can be assumed that once the Spaniards had established themselves fairly in Cebu, the northern and eastern coasts of Mindanao were similarly visited and declared property of the Royal Crown of Spain.

But how does one just take possession of another man's country?

> "As a token of true possession he (Ibarra) passed from one end of the land to the other, cut branches of trees, plucked grass,

threw stones and performed such other acts and ceremonies as are usual in such cases; all of which took place quietly and peaceably, with the common consent of those who were present, without opposition of anyone'' (loc. cit.)

On May 27, 1565 Legazpi informed Philip II that he was in need of more men for settlement, more soldiers for pacification and more money and material for an undertaking so vast and of such great importance, spiritual as well as temporal, which will result in great blessings in the service of God and of your Majesty, which will increase your royal income and add to the universal good of your kingdoms (Blair & Robertson 2, p. 175). Two days later, the officers of the King's "Camp in the Islands of the West" (Cebu) wrote to Philip II:

"We supplicate your Majesty, with all humility, to grant the usual favors to your Majesty's faithful servants and vassals, in consideration of the faith, fidelity and zeal shown by us in the service of your Majesty" (loc. cit., 177).

That the new arrivals were going ahead with the Hispanization of the newly appropriated territories, appears from the following request which the *capitanes conquistadores oficiales* addressed to the King in 1566; therein they urgently asked:

1. To send religious and secular priests for the preaching of the Gospel and the conversion of the natives. Presently there were only three left, not even enough to take care of the spiritual needs of the Spaniards.

2. To send at least 500 men with sufficient arms, and as soon as possible additional arms for those already here, because the natives were "vicious and a bad lot," and in case they would refuse to accept the Faith voluntarily, they should be forced by arms.

3. That Legazpi should be properly rewarded for his services to the King.

4. That all those who had served the King in this expedition should be confirmed in their present position as a reward for all their labor, sacrifices and other services.

5. That one of the rewards to those who had done their share in this new discovery, should be exempted — to be extended also to their children — from any kind of personal taxes or duties.

6. That they should be given a share of the land, in perpetuity and transferable to any person of their choice.

7. That meanwhile, till the land grants were realized, the Crown take care of the families of the discoverers; they had invested so much in this enterprise that now they and their relatives were impoverished; also that the Crown take care of the families of those who had died in this expedition.

8. That nobody, except the Crown and the discoverers, be permitted to engage in business in this country.

9. That the Moros, who were trading in gold, wax, cinnamon and other articles and were preventing the natives from trading with the Spaniards and converting to the Faith, should be turned into slaves and that all their properties should be confiscated.

10. That all government officials, the royal treasurer, the paymaster, the administrator and the inspector, as well as one inheritant of each should be perpetuated in office. Aside from that office they should also be given a share in the division of the land.

11. That a considerable salary increase be granted to all to meet the increased cost of livelihood.

In a separate request the *primeros conquistadores y descubridores* asked to be permitted "to buy slaves who are being sold in this country and employ them in mines or any other kind of work, like the native chiefs do also" (Documentos Ineditos de Ultramar, II, Doc. 45).

With the occupation of Luzon and the rest of the archipelago in 1570-1571, attention was drawn away from Mindanao for a while, and consequently very little documentation about Agusan, Surigao and Davao is to be found for the period 1570-1596. What little there is, however, forms very much part of the accounts dealing with developments that would exert a farreaching influence on the future of the whole country: the repartition of land and people of the islands into the so-called *encomiendas,* and the concomitant institution of the tax form called *tributo.*

The *encomienda* was not granted with the right of ownership of the territory and people in question. As the verb *encomendar* means "to entrust to," the proper translation of *encomienda* would be "trust territory"; mostly it would be granted only "for two lives," i.e., it could be inherited only once. In his territory the *encomendero* was given the right to collect a certain amount in taxes payable in

goods or gold and to require certain labor services to be rendered by
the inhabitants. For his part the *encomendero* obliged himself to
attend to the defense of the population and to their temporal and
spiritual welfare. In the pertinent accounts the latter obligation is
called *"instruction."* By applying for and accepting an *encomienda,*
the grantee relieved the Crown of the obligation to provide him with
a salary; he was supposed to be self-supporting. It takes little
imagination to understand how many doors to how many abuses
were opened this way.

For those who selected the Old Caraga district as their *encomienda,* the interest in gold — reportedly very much present in
the area — must have been one of the foremost motivations. It is
therefore most probably no coincidence that in 1573 Guido de
Lavezares was accused before Philip II of "having appropriated for
himself the inhabitants along the Butuan river which is on the island
of Mindanao." De Lavezares was the official treasurer of the
Legazpi expedition and would succeed Legazpi as Governor General
after the latter's death in 1572. As we know, he had been a member
of the reconnaissance party to Butuan in 1565, when he must have
been impressed by the easy and ample availability of gold.

In 1571 Legazpi himself had allotted choice pieces of territory as
encomiendas to the first fifty married Spaniards with whom he had
founded the Spanish settlement of Cebu. On that occasion Pedro
Navarro and García Sierras Chacon became the beneficiaries of the
"rivers and villages of Surigao and Parasao (Cantilan) with their
hills and hill tribes" (List of *encomiendas,* 1521, Blair & Robertson
34, p. 307).

Already one year later a survey had been made of the district; on
January 8, 1573 the findings were included in a report which the *real
factor* (administrator of royal properties) Andres de Mirandaola sent
to the King:

> "Much gold is found in the island of Vendanao, in the
> districts of Butuan, Curigao and Parasao" (Blair & Robertson 3,
> p. 223).

There is a curious portion in that report which could tempt one
to believe that gold mining, already before Spanish times, had
produced a kind of terminology of its own, understood in Luzon
and in Mindanao, and that there is some relation (what?) between
its terminology and the names of two villages on the coast of
southern Surigao.

> "The kinds of gold that are found among the natives of the city and vicinity of Manila are: "Bizlin," which is worth two pesos a tael; the weight of a tael is one and one eighth ounces. The second kind is "Malubay" and the third is "Linguingin." These are the kinds of gold which the natives trade and barter. The Malubay gold is worth the same as the Bizlin. The Linguingin gold is worth four pesos. For the goods for which they trade and barter, the natives use Malubay and Bizlin and Linguingin" (loc. cit., p. 224).

Of course, this is a report about gold mined in Luzon, but those familiar with Surigao will not fail to be struck by the remarkable similarity between *Bizlin* and *Linguinguin* and the names of the two neighboring southern Surigao towns of Bislig and Lingig, all the more so because in the oldest reports of the 17th and 18th century the spelling of their names is indeed Bizlin and Linguin with only slight variations like Bezlin, Beslin and Linguib, Linguid, Lunguib.

Another account, the so-called "Augustinian Memoranda" of about 1580 could refer to one of the little offshore islands near Placer, Surigao, now called Masapilid:

> "The chief mines...are...in the island that the Spaniards call Vermeja, about two leagues from Curigao, where, according to a report of the Indios, was the greatest wealth of all. However, that island is now deserted because of a certain superstition having to do with the death of the children of the man who was its ruler once. Also in many other parts of the island of Mindanao, especially in the river of Curigao, in that of Parasao and that of Butuan" (Blair & Robertson 34, p. 284).

Although the initial results of the gold rush were not very encouraging, the Old Caraga district was obviously enticing enough to be given as *encomienda* to successive families of the early Spanish conquerors. Some of their names can be found in the reports compiled in Blair & Robertson, whereas others are slumbering in the Archivo General de Indias at Sevilla (Filipinas, Ramo Secular, Legajos 47-57) and at least one in the National Archives at Manila.

In Blair & Robertson 4, pp. 295-296 we find a report of 1579 which concerns Butuan and is probably quite illustrative of contemporary methods employed to bring an area under administrative control. It is worth noticing how soon after 1565 the terminology *toma de posesión* has been replaced by *pacificación*, which seems to indicate conflict situations, resistance, the need for force and the right to use it.

> I, Gabriel de Ribera, captain of infantry and of the fleet and the men who come to pacify the islands of Jolo and Bindanao (sic), at the order of the very illustrious Governor and Captain General in the service of His Majesty for these islands; Inasmuch as the instructions of the said Governor ordered me to send someone from the town of Santisimo Nombre de Jesus (Cebu) to pacify the river and the tingues (hills, upland) of Butuan; and considering how much we may shorten the long voyage by going from this district of Cavite (= Quipit, Cuavit, Cauit of Zamboanga) instead of from the said town, and that we have here ships and rowers suited for this undertaking; therefore I entrust the said expedition to **Sergeant** Lope de Catalinaga. I order him to go as leader for the said pacification with fifteen soldiers beside himself. I order him to go with those soldiers to the mentioned river and tingues of Butuan to pacify the said people in the tingues. He shall try to render them obedient to **His Majesty, making the best possible terms of peace by means** of interpreters whom he will take along. From the natives of the said tingues, when they are pacified, he shall have the power to collect such tribute as in all•fairness can be collected from them. As he has the matter in hand, he shall do what is most convenient in this. Having collected the tribute, he shall keep one half very carefully, as it belongs to His Majesty. The other half, in compliance with the order of his Lordship, shall be divided among his soldiers, according to custom. Everything that shall be done in this expedition shall be attested to by notary; and I authorize him to appoint one, before whom shall be transacted all the proceedings necessary, so that an account may be rendered of everything. I order all his soldiers to regard, consider and obey him as their leader, and observe all his orders, under such penalties as he may inflict.

Given in Cavite, on the fourteenth of April, 1579.

Gabriel de Ribera.

(By order of the Captain: Benito de Mendiola
                            Notary of the fleet).

There seems to be some contradiction here with other accounts: Ribera's report makes it appear as if Butuan was not a private but a so-called "King's *encomienda*" with its own provisions for the disposal of tributes. Still, six years earlier Butuan was reported as belonging to Guido de Lavezares (1573), and the same is stated in 1582 by Loarca, as we will see. The explanation is that the Manobos living in the interior, from a certain point along the Agusan river belonged to "His Majesty's *encomienda,*" the rest and also Jabonga to private *encomenderos* (see Colin/Pastells, III, 722).

A good source for information about the state of affairs during the Hispanization process in the last quarter of the 16th century is the "Relación de las Yslas Filipinas" (1582) by Miguel de Loarca. The author was a resident and *encomendero* of Oton, the settlement on Panay, which had been founded right after Cebu.

> "*Island of Siargao*. Twelve leagues from the island of Panaon, and next to the island of Mindanao, is the island of Siargao, which is about fifteen leagues in circumference and six leagues wide. It may have about four hundred inhabitants and its villages are built around rough and dangerous estuaries. There is only one *encomendero*. The people are poor because of their indolence; for although there are numerous small islets near this island which contain many goldplacers, they do not work them. They give as reason that if the corsairs should discover that they are working these mines, they would come hither to take them captive; but even now, when no one can molest them, they do not work these mines, and hence we may infer that their poverty is mainly due to sloth.
>
> *Island of Macagua.* West of the island of Baybay is a small island called Macagua, about which Father Fray Andres de Urdaneta related so many wonders. It is four leagues in circumference and one league wide; it has about sixty inhabitants as well as an *encomendero*. The people are poor and wretched, possessing nothing but salt and fish.
>
> *Island of Mindanao.* Of all the islands discovered up to the present time, Mindanao is supposed to be the largest, although but few of its inhabitants are friendly, almost none in fact, and those dwell along the coast. The Spaniards have explored only about one hundred and fifty leagues of this island, namely, from the river of Cateel up to the principal river, which is called Mindanao. From the city of Cubu one has to sail southwest to

reach the nearest point of Mindanao which is called Dapitan.

Rivers. Paniguian, Ydac, Matanda, Ytanda, Tago, Ono, Beslin, all of which have together about three thousand men, for the most part hostile. Around the river Butuan which belongs to Guido de Lavezares, dwell about six hundred Indios who are in this island. Farther on are to be found the rivers of Surigao, of Parasao and others, ... all of which have a population of about three thousand, mostly hostile'' (Blair & Robertson 5, p. 51).

Another survey of the archipelago can be found in the "Account of Encomiendas in the Philippine Islands" (June 30, 1591) by Governor General Gomez Perez Dasmariñas. From it we quote the following:

"Butuan: Doña Lucia de Loarca owns the *encomienda* of the river of Butuan. She collects there one thousand two hundred tributes. It has justice, but no instruction. Two religious are necessary to take care of it, for it has four thousand and eight hundred persons.''

(Lucia de Loarca was the daughter of the previously mentioned Don Miguel, author of the "Relación" of 1582. Note that the relation between the number of tribute payers and the total number of inhabitants is put at one to four. At other times also the rule-of-thumb one to five was in use.)

Zampojar: (Sampongan = Jabonga) Diego de Carvajal collects along this river of Zampojar fifty-eight tributes. They are not all well pacified, and have neither instruction nor justice.

Caraga (here perhaps Calagan = Cantilan district): Juan Gutierrez del Real and Francisco de Santa Cruz collect eight hundred and ninety-two tributes in Caraga. This represents three thousand five hundred and sixty-eight persons. They have no instruction and are not pacified, but when that will be effected, it will need two ministers.

In the Philippine National Archives (Reales Cedulas) the following document, dated June 4, 1598, exists:

"In the name of His Majesty, I grant in *encomienda* to you, the said Captain Toribio de la Miranda and Captain Antonio

Freyle the natives of the towns and *encomiendas* which Juan
Gutierrez del Real, deceased, held on the coast of Caraga.''

Combés (Lib. II, Ch. V Col. 99) mentions as *encomendero* of
Butuan for 1602 a certain Francisco de Poso, who was eventually
killed together with the Portuguese priest Alonso de Campos, then
working in Agusan.

In the Archivo General de Indias of Sevilla ("Confirmaciones de
Encomiendas, 1616-1700") under Ramo secular, Legajos 47-57,
appears under the year 1616:

> "Given to Alferez Juan de Represa, resident of Manila, one
> fourth of the *encomienda* of Caraga, in the province of
> Pintados" (Leg. 47).

> "1619: given to Alferez Juan de las Mariñas, the
> inhabitants of the rivers of Bislin and Cateel which are in the
> province of Caraga" (Ibid.).

De las Mariñas had come to the Philippines in 1602, and fought
here against *los enemigos naturales y olandeses*. At that time (1619)
the inhabitants of Bislig and Cateel had been without an
encomendero for some time *(estan vacos)* because the former
encomendero had abandoned them.

1622: the district of Butuan, Sampongan (Jabonga) and Caraga
are reported being *encomiendas* of Francisco de Santa Cruz (see
1591), Doña Maria de Vega and Doña Ines de Bolaños; Bislig and
Cateel of Juan de las Mariñas.

1623: "To Sergeant Joseph Ginete de Heredia, husband of Doña
Ines de Bolaños, is given in *encomienda* one half of the inhabitants
of Caraga" (Arch. Gen. de Ind., l.c. Leg. 48).

1626: July 30, the ad interim Governor General Fernando de
Silva writes to the King:

> "I likewise requested your Majesty last year to prevent that
> my wife will lose the *encomienda* which she inherited from her
> father and grandfather who served so long in these islands, and
> that you would order a decree to be dispatched, so that she
> might enjoy them wherever she and her daughter would live, as
> the latter is the last heir" (Blair & Robertson 22, p. 103).

Elsewhere it appears that de Silva's wife was the daughter of Lucia de Loarca, ergo the granddaughter of Miguel de Loarca. The Loarcas were *encomenderos* of Oton and Butuan. De Silva had requested the King to be transferred to Panama or Guatemala; the favor which he asked was that his wife, once she joined him there, would be allowed to keep her *encomienda*. In Colin's "Labor Evangelica" I, p. 52 we read:

> "When Don Fernando de Silva possessed the *encomienda* of Butuan, I heard him say that in order to pay the tribute, his Indios had to work only one week, because there was so much gold along the river of Butuan, that any Indio who put himself to it, could find a quantity as heavy as a real, which is worth at least eight pesos."

We will notice that at the same time when Colin calls Butuan an *encomienda* of de Silva, the latter calls it his wife's. So does King Philip IV in his response to the aforementioned request of de Silva (October 1627):

> "You [de Silva] were married in those islands to Doña Maria de Salazar, granddaughter of one of the earliest and most prominent conquistadores and settlers of the islands, and your father-in-law was the first Spaniard born in the said islands; and in commemoration of the services which the aforesaid performed, the *encomienda* of Butuan and Oton was given to them, which they enjoyed.
>
> I conceded the favor of prolonging to the said Doña Maria de Salazar, your wife, the same *encomienda* for one generation more, by a decree of February 24 [one thousand] six hundred and twenty two; and to it shall succeed the person to whom it shall belong and pertain according to the law of succession" (Blair & Robertson 23, p. 80).

In the documents used for the chapter "The Revolt of Caraga" we find Juan de Chavez as *encomendero* of Bacuag in 1631. De Chavez belonged to one of the earliest Spanish families in Cebu and would afterwards distinguish himself in the sea battles against the Dutch in Philippine waters together with Don Agustin de Cepeda.

In 1650 Agustin de Cepeda is reported as *encomendero*.[15] Again there is a discrepancy in the accounts of 1622 when Philip IV speaks about Butuan as *encomienda* of the de Silva/Loarca family, whereas Bishop Arce of Cebu, when assigning the Recoleto Order to Caraga, names Butuan as *encomienda* of Francisco de Santa Cruz; in 1591 the latter was reported *encomendero* of a part of Caraga.

What were the proceeds from such *encomiendas?* From a letter of Governor Juan Niño de Tavora to the King, dated August 1, 1629, it appears that the de Silva-Loarcas received 4000 pesos per year from their territory, but it is not clear if this refers to Butuan alone or to Oton and Butuan taken together.

And how did the primitive inhabitants of Agusan, Surigao and Davao fare under the various *encomenderos* to whom they had been entrusted. Of course, very little documentation has come to us about the years between 1566 and 1596. This, however, changed considerably when the first resident missionaries had established themselves at Butuan (1596) and in Surigao province (1622). From their accounts we know about a general uprising at Butuan about 1602 (Colin, II, p. 280), in which also one of the two Portuguese priests working there was killed. In 1609 a fortress with a garrison was established at Tandag, Surigao, of which contemporary sources say that initially its function was not to curtail the Moros, but the very coastal tribes, who "were fierce and warlike and could ill endure to be subjected to Spain" (Luis de Jesus, 1681, Dec. Quinta). In 1631 all of Caraga revolted, except Butuan, and there is more than one bitter complaint by contemporary Recoleto missionaries on the spot about the behavior of Spanish officials and soldiers.

Perhaps even a priori it could be assumed that by establishing the feudal *encomienda* system "in regions so remote and far away from the possibility of appeal to His Majesty" (Governor Dasmariñas) and entrusting it to people who — in spite of the Christian vocabulary of the day — were often plain military conquerors and

---

[15] Combés dedicated his "Historia de Mindanao y Jolo" to General Agustin de Cepeda, a nephew of Saint Teresa of Avila. He was a good *encomendero* and an outstanding Christian. Later he became the last but one Spanish Governor of Ternate. When the Dutch were about to take over the island, he took a great number of Christians with him to the Philippines, where they eventually founded "Ternate" of Cavite and enriched the local dialect with the "Chabacano."

adventurers, the Spanish Crown had created a Frankenstein in its colony. I am perfectly aware of the many noble intentions of many of the great decision makers of those days. But it does not have to be mere hindsight painstakingly granted to us by colonial centuries that makes one shudder when meeting certain clausules of the Cebu petition of 1566, which was quoted above (p. 88). Shortly before that year there was a Spaniard who once, in 1511, had been granted an *encomienda* in Cuba, but who returned it to the Crown three years afterwards, deeply disgusted when seeing the deplorable conditions in the *encomiendas* all over the country. He went back to Spain and started a campaign for the enactment of new laws to abolish the *encomienda* system. Of course, we cannot, by a simple anachronism of a few years, let Bartolome de las Casas act as spokesman for Philippine conditions. There are even reasons to believe that these conditions were never as bad as they had been in South America just thanks to the warnings shouted in Spain by de las Casas. But, for sure, we are entitled to listen to some other voices, very involved, very concerned and very contemporaneous in Spain and in the Philippines.

Instructions of Philip II to Governor General
Gomez Perez Dasmariñas, August 9, 1589

"I have been informed that, in collecting the tributes from the Indios, there has been in the past, and is at present, great disorder, because the former Governors of the said islands have done things very confusedly and haphazardly.... This disorder has consisted in each one collecting whatever he wished, to the great offense and injury of the said Indios. I have also been told...that many other *encomiendas* pay tribute by pure force of soldiers and arms, that people rebel and revolt because of the oppression and severity with which they are treated...." (Blair & Robertson, 7, p. 169).

Conclusions of Bishop Salazar of Manila
and His Theologians, January 8, 1591

"His Majesty is bound to give orders and to make all possible efforts for the conversion of the infidels...and this should not be accomplished in the manner hitherto employed, namely, by the perversion of all laws, divine and human; by murders, robberies, captivities, conflagrations and depopulation of villages, estates and houses" (ibid., pp. 287-288).

Very little information from Agusan, Surigao and Davao before the year 1596, as we said. But would the happenings elsewhere in the archipelago that worried the King in Spain and evoked the anger of Bishop Salazar in Manila not also have been representative for what occurred in the Old Caraga district?

Aside from the abuses and suppression which the Bishop denounced, he pointed to a typical injustice being committed in the collection of the tribute in a great number of *encomiendas*. By Royal decree it had been stipulated that one fourth of the amount collected should be put aside as a fund for the expenses of the ministers of the gospel, or where they were absent, for the efforts towards religious instruction in each *encomienda*. In most cases there was no minister nor was any attention at all given to the indoctrination of the *encomendees*. In other words, the natives were forced to pay for services which they did not receive. This should be considered a matter that burdened the conscience of the *encomenderos* concerned, so the Bishop publicly announced. He even threatened to deny absolution and holy communion to those who refused to pay restitution for the amounts already collected in the described way. On February 15, 1591 the *encomenderos, pobladores y descubridores de todas estas Islas Filipinas* brought a petition to Governor Dasmariñas reminding him how many of them had arrived 27 years ago and had since "spent the years in the propagation of Our Holy Catholic Faith, the defense of the preaching of the Gospel and the service of the King Our Lord." The King and the Governor, so they went on, had rewarded them with the allotment of "a certain number of natives." These grants, however, had allowed them only a scant subsistence, but they had been content with that for the service of God and the King. And now, so they bitterly complained, the Bishop would forbid them to collect such tributes anymore and even order restitution of what had been paid in the years past. Four months later Dasmariñas forwarded that complaint to Philip II:

> "Now the *encomenderos* come to me sorely troubled, saying that in the pulpits, sermons and confessionals they were being greatly harassed, and many obstacles were being imposed on the collections in their *encomiendas*. They say that they are being ruined, since they were prohibited from collecting more than the third or the half of their tributes. Furthermore, they were being pressed to make restitution of past payments. If this continues, they will have to be allowed to leave their *encomiendas*" (loc. cit., 8, p. 143ff.).

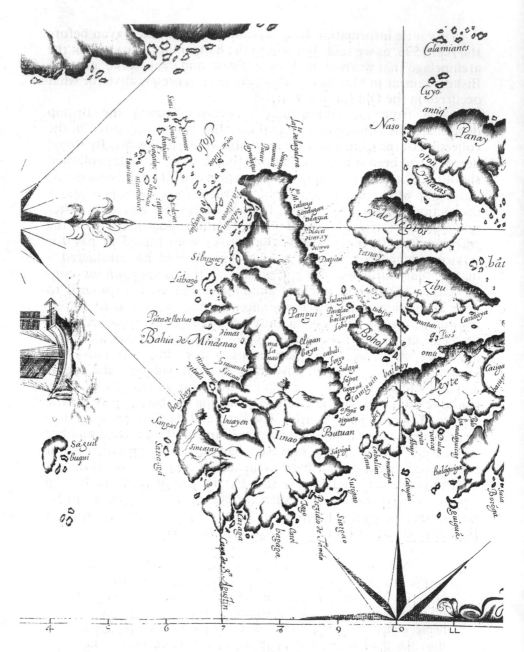

Fig. 14. From the map: ''Planta de las Islas Filipinas dedicada al Rey N.
Señor D. Phelipe Quarto'' by Marcos de Orozco, Madrid, 1659
(in Colin, Ed. Pastells).

VIII

Crusade for Silongan's Soul

"But we see more. We see the beginnings of an historic transformation. An indigenous society, vaguely recognizable as ancestral to our own, is under the catalytic and cohesive influences of a new faith and a different culture being transmuted, for better or for worse, into something we can unhesitatingly recognize as Filipino. Values are being refashioned, age-old institutions are being exchanged. A new way of life is evolving, and scattered and independent tribal communities are being unified into a nation. Dimly but unmistakably we are in the presence of the beginnings of our history" (Echevarría 1969:xv-xvi).

On p. 680 of his "Conquistas de las Islas Filipinas" Gaspar de San Agustin, OSA has a remark that would intrigue anyone trying to patch together the past of the Old Caraga from the often scarce and unrelated bits of information:

"At that time (1598) Fray Jeronimo de Ocampo, together with another religious priest, was assigned to administer the holy

> Sacraments on the island of Mindanao, to the soldiers of the
> *presidio* of Caldera and also those of Tampacán, where there
> were some Christian natives, although very few. The Governor
> had recommended that mission to us with much insistence, and
> therefore it was fitting not to object to such an undertaking. Out
> of this originated the ministries of the province of Caraga,
> Tandag, Butuan and Siargao, which afterwards were under the
> secular priests and were finally, in 1621, entrusted to the
> discalced Recoletos.''

What is intriguing about these lines is the suggestion that the
Augustinians were the ones to make a start or to prepare the way
for the first systematical evangelization of, e.g., Butuan. Which is
rather far from the truth, as we are going to see very soon. Unless,
of course, we understand "originated from" in a very loose sense.
Moreover, the author omits the ministry of the Jesuits at Butuan
prior to 1621.

What is true, however, is that in the 1590s, when the Hispanization of Luzon had just begun to take concrete form and a fair
beginning had been made with the Christianization of Luzon and
some regions of the Visayas, Spanish attention was drawn back
very soon to the southernmost island of the *conquista*. It did that
presumably for a threefold reason. In the first place, because the
second biggest island of the archipelago was beginning to give the
colonial government a great deal of concern due to the pressure of a
considerable number of unpacified and impatient tribesmen such as
the Moros and the Caragans. The repeated raids of the latter into
Visayan territory were becoming an increasing bother for Spaniards
and Indios alike.

In the second place, there was the troubling possibility that the
Portuguese, Borneans and Ternatans would team up with the
bellicose Mindanao tribes to render any Spanish foothold on the
island more and more precarious. Several times corsairs from
Borneo and Ternate had already joined Caragans and Moros on
plundering raids in the Visayas and even beyond.

Thirdly, under these conditions, the ever pressing need for
evangelization — already so entwined with Spanish colonial designs
— was accentuated even more. Up to 1580 Augustinians,
Dominicans and Franciscans plus some secular priests had been
available for that purpose. In 1581 Philip II sent the first Jesuits to
Manila, and in 1583 Bishop Salazar wrote to him:

"Those Fathers came to this land to examine and consider
the opportunity that may exist here for the Society to settle and
send religious here...(but) their resolution was that they would
go away unless...they could busy themselves in the things they
are used to do in other places where they work, namely, the
teaching of the letters and religious instruction... But their
establishment in this city and these islands is so necessary that
not only should Your Majesty not permit those who are here to
go away, but it is necessary that you order their general and
provincial of Mexico to send others, so they may start with the
work of their order and inaugurate a college where they may
have persons to teach the children of the inhabitants of this city
and those of the hamlets of these islands as well as the mestizos
and the sons of the chief Indians....

Your Majesty must not neglect to send ministers every year,
either secular or religious, or some of both, for the satisfaction of
your royal conscience, so they may work at the conversion and
perseverance of these natives" (Colin I, p. 351, Note 1).

Obviously, the wish of the Bishop and the will of the King
prevailed, and after Manila and a few other places in Luzon, we find
Jesuits engaged in Cebu, Leyte, Samar and Bohol, and eventually
Butuan.

The arrival of those missionaries was important not only for what
they came for: the systematic efforts at evangelization, but also
because of the information which they have left behind about the
areas and the people entrusted to them. To which, however, we may
have to add again and again:

"But only to a certain extent. Aside from the fact that their
letters are relatively few, they also give us only incomplete
insight. The readers of those days liked to hear picturesque
particulars of faraway countries and their peculiar populations
touched by the faith for the first time. What they asked for in
the first place was more edification and instruction than
accounts full of deep-going details. In those days there was
only little interest in the important missionary questions of
today. The title of the French collection of (Jesuit) missionary
letters to appear later reflects very well the contemporary
attitude: "Lettres Edifiantes et Curieuses." For that reason it
could happen that important portions of the letters were left out
or shortened" (C.J. Wessels, SJ: "History of the Roman

Catholic Mission of Amboina, 1546-1605'').

And of course, they were written in the literary style of the day, not seldom by authors more pious than accomplished writers. To a modern reader insufficiently aware of this, many accounts might for that reason have the ring of irritating, pious cant.

In November of 1596 the first two Jesuit missionaries, Valerio de Ledesma and an unnamed lay brother arrived at Butuan, to be joined early in 1597 by Manuel Martinez. From that moment on we are quite well informed about developments at Butuan by a few letters written by the missionaries, which are included in the so-called *Cartas Anuales* or yearly reports of the Jesuit missions in various parts of the world, and from there they found their way into the "Relación de las Islas Filipinas" (1604) by Father Pedro Chirino SJ and/or Colin's "Labor Evangelica" (1663) and Combés "Historia de Mindanao y Jolo" (1667).

Chirino, Colin and Combés themselves belonged to the earlier Jesuits to arrive in the Philippines. Chirino had arrived in Manila in May 1590. After working for some time in Luzon, he founded the first Jesuit mission of Leyte at Carigara; in 1595 he was appointed to the Jesuit college of Cebu. In his official capacity of "visitor" to various mission stations of his order, he gathered a lot of interesting information about the whole country and its population, from which he drew up a long report *(Relación)* for the superior general of the Society in Rome, which was printed in 1604. It served as the main source of the first part of Colin's "Labor Evangelica" (1663). Francisco Combés, SJ has his own informations about the Mindanao and Butuan of the end of the 16th and the first half of the 17th century in his "Historia de Mindanao y Jolo" (1667).

The mission of Butuan was accepted because of the repeated requests of the *encomenderos,* who seem to have had a hard time to keep the Agusanons pacified. That Butuan was an unruly vassal up to 1595 appears from a reference in Combés, wherein he states that the first Jesuit assigned to Dapitan,

> "Francisco de Otazo, traveled with the expedition which Captain Salgado undertook to pacify Butuan; ... they proceeded to that place which, once surrendered to Spanish arms, surrendered with even more ease to the love of the ministry. From the very onset, each time when force was used, they found comfort and protection with the Fathers, and as a result they put their trust in them; this protection made it easier for them to

overcome their natural fear and primitive shyness'' (Lib II, Cap. II, Col. 97).

Combés also points out that the Spaniards considered it very important to have a foothold in Butuan and Dapitan. Butuan gave easy access to other coastal settlements in the region and could serve as a jump-off point for operations along the east coast of Mindanao.

It seems that the arrival of the first resident missionaries had been preceded by passing visits of the Fathers Juan de San Lucar, Juan Bautista Vilancio and the aforementioned Francisco Otazo, who had been able to win the goodwill and trust of the inhabitants. At first it had looked as if the missionaries were going to encounter the same hostility as the other Spaniards. After all, until then the inhabitants had only met with soldiers and tax collectors. Chirino/Colin do not mention anything about abuses by the latter, which had created much aversion along the borders of the Agusan river; if initially the inhabitants did not show much inclination to listen to the Gospel message, Chirino explains it by pointing to the vicious and depraved life they were leading. Combés seems more honest about local tensions in Butuan in 1596. All in all it is somewhat difficult to see how the two accounts tally at times with regard to persons and moments mentioned. There is no reason to doubt the correctness of the Chirino/Colin informations: Father Chirino was the superior of the Jesuit community in Cebu, from where the Butuan and Dapitan mission was directed at the time in question. Combés became a missionary at Dapitan about 50 years later, in 1645; even in his report about Butuan, one seems to feel his Dapitan sympathies seeping a little through the lines. There were indeed connections between some happenings in the Dapitan mission and those of Butuan between 1595 and ca 1605; also between one or more leading families of each place, who might have known each other via Bohol from where Dapitan had been founded. After one has grown a little accustomed to the murky style of Combés, one may find that his account can be used as a supplement to Chirino's contemporary data about Butuan; the latter covers more exclusively the first few years (1596 till c. 1602); Combés the subsequent years before 1620.

About the first resident missionaries, Valerio de Ledesma and his unnamed companion, Chirino tells us that in the beginning they encountered still some aloofness among the people; the first night even the devil himself loudly manifested his disgust by poltergeisting noisily in and around the house where they were staying. After some exorcisms and after the first mass next morning, however, *el gran demonio de Mindanao* seemed to have folded his tent and left Butuan. Also the initial coldness and fear of the people soon melted away when they experienced the gentleness and unselfishness of the two missionaries. Combés could relate in 1667:

> "Chief Silongan, who belonged to the leading elite of those islands, came to them every day and with increasing insistence said to them: "Please, tell me, Father, what you want. Do you want gold? or civet? or wax?" And because the Fathers always said no in the midst of so many offerings inspired by love and noble hospitality, the people did not know what to do" (Lib. II, Cap. V, Col. 99).

Some related to them that they still remembered how long ago some whites had come to Butuan to preach about Jesus Christ and had baptized some residents, but of all that no visible traces were left in 1596. Early in 1597 de Ledesma was joined by Manuel Martinez. With the help of two resident Spaniards, the regional Governor Juan Langub and Miguel de Mora, a beginning was made with the formation of a very basic Christian community, which was considerably strengthened in its newfound faith with the conversion of one of the two local tribal chiefs, named Elian.

In the following pages I will give ample space to the original accounts as they have come to us. These reports seem to wear something of a nimbus, because time and again they sound like echoes of the pristine accounts found in the Acts of the Apostles about the first Christian communities founded by them. Each Christian community was once a first. I have therefore no difficulty treating the Butuan reports with respect.

Let us begin with a letter dated June 26, 1597 at Manila, from the hand of Father Diego Sanchez, the Jesuit superior, found in Colin II, pp. 160-161:

> "Butuan is situated on the mainland, on the coast of Mindanao facing Leyte. It is fertile and rich in food. It also has plenty of gold, which is much sought after. There is furthermore musk and cinnamon. The natives are warlike and courageous, which to us is not a very good sign. We find proof of the Lord's hand in this work of conversion in the turning to Christ of many chieftains, particularly one chief whose conversion was the least expected, as he was cruel, a constant fighter, and very much feared in the district. His conversion was very edifying

and happened as follows:

The missionaries invited the people to attend Sunday services, and urged them never to forget this. The people were very faithful and would come in large numbers. At such a service the children would walk in front with the priest, who carried the Cross. They went in procession to the place where the holy mysteries were going to be explained. Once, while the people were together in the church, Father Martinez stepped forward to begin a sermon, and Our Lord made his words so convincing that this hardened pagan was touched. Without any further delay he knelt down in the middle of the sermon. It caused the Spaniards great consolation, and many of them were unable to keep back their tears. The natives too were witnesses of this important conversion. This impression increased when Father Ledesma went to fetch a Cross and continued the service. Finally, Elian went to the front of the church, and with the greatest humility, kissed the feet of the crucifix, in which he was followed by Osol, another chief and many more.

Not content with this, Elian sent all his wives back to their families, after giving each one of them the gold to which she was entitled. He also declared that anyone who had a claim on him, could obtain it. To be baptized as soon as possible, he remained in our house, for he now only cared about the salvation of his soul. His conversion was followed by that of another datu, a chief of a barrio, who said: "If the father of all the people becomes a Christian, what else could the others do?"

An incident that contributed to the conversion of Elian was his sorrow over the tragic death of his son, whom he liked very much. This son had a quarrel with a servant and both became so angry that it cost them their lives. The son, enraged by the servant's answer, grabbed a small spear and pierced his chest. The servant forthwith pulled it out and stabbed his attacker in the chest too; as a result, both of them collapsed, mortally wounded by the same spear.

We also heard of the conversion of another very influential chief, Silongan, about whom we have the following report of Father Ledesma:

Thanks be to God, all along the river people are asking for baptism. In the villages, in the houses, at work, while rowing on the river, while walking, one hears only the songs of the religion classes. I visited all the houses where they should gather. They meet at the chiefs' houses, and even the adults answer the songs of the children. Our songs are heard in the houses of the chiefs all day and night. This has all been arranged by Our Lord, who first influenced the hearts of the chiefs, especially that of Silongan, who was bound by the chains of his six wives, and the huge dowries he had given for them. He, however, found the courage to free himself, and after sending away five of his wives, he stayed with the first one. One day Silongan came to have one of his children baptized; he was clothed with silk and gold. He will be baptized as soon as he is instructed.''

A very important day in the evangelization story of Butuan is that of the solemn blessing of the first church on September 8, 1597. Father Martinez wrote a letter about this event to Father Chirino in Cebu:

"We went in procession to the church; leading were the cross and candle bearers, then the children singing songs, and finally the Spaniards with the priests, one of whom carried the relics. The two of us sang. The women followed us. At regular intervals triumphal arches had been put up. Near the house of the *Corregidor* there was a beautifully decorated altar, where we stopped and said two prayers. In front of this altar there was a tower, decorated with small flags; as we passed, guns were fired and bells rang out. Between the tower and the altar was a fountain. Near the church there was a high tower containing guns and bells. Near the houses of two Spaniards there were also guns. The High Mass with sermon was celebrated in front of the church.

This is Butuan today. I may mention here also: this is the place where three fishermen found a golden headband. Shortly after having received baptism, the man who found it first, was called by the Lord unto Himself. I consider him happier now because he is in possession of the true wealth of heaven.''

Also from the inland along the far reaches of the river people had come to ask for instruction and baptism. In the letter which Father Martinez wrote about this on April 30, 1598, he names the place "Calilaya" and locates it "about 10 leagues (ca 57 kms) upstream''; that would mean in the general area of Talacogon.

"I came back from Calilaya, about ten leagues upstream, where I had gone to preach and to administer baptism. I did not succeed, for upon my arrival I found the whole village deserted. A month earlier there had been a murder; the murderer had fled and the whole population as well. I was not able to bring the people to the village and hoped that I would have more success later on. I had been there for about six days, and on the feast of St. Mark I went up the river to remind the people that the next day was Sunday and that I would give religious instruction in the church. Suddenly an arrow flew by me from among the houses; it hit neither myself nor the servants, but fell close to the *baroto* in the water. The three boys dove into the water and swam away. Because I could not swim, I waited in the *baroto* to see if another arrow would come. Nothing happened, which may be considered a miracle. I then returned to Butuan, thanking Our Lord for having escaped a great danger.''

It seems that less than four years after the opening of the Butuan mission the Jesuit superiors decided on a drastic retrenchment on account of their scarce manpower. One result was that they informed the Bishop of Cebu about returning Butuan to him to be cared for by secular clergy. For the moment, one priest, Cristobal Jimenez, would go to Butuan until he could be replaced by a secular. He arrived there on March 24, 1600, and shortly afterwards sent a letter to his predecessor, Father Martinez, who was then in Tinagon, Leyte.

"I do not know where to begin to sing the praises of the good people of Butuan. Since my arrival here I have been greatly edified and comforted by the zeal, the order and discipline with which youngsters and old people come for instruction. I arrived on the eve of Our Lady's Annunciation, and the people, thinking it was you, came from both sides of the river and went to the church to welcome their missionary. The next morning I addressed them and told them not to be afraid and come to me like they used to come to you; that even if I were not as pleasing as my predecessor, I would do my very best to attract them. The following Sunday when we were together, I spoke to them again, and it looks as if they had no fear at all and are happy to come.

The children continue to say their prayers. Your idea of giving the people a piece of string with knots to count the fast days and feastdays has been very successful. They make no mistakes. They go to confession very religiously. On Holy Thursday there was a public penance. The children following behind the cross and chanting the prayers, led the procession. Miguel de Mora and the other Spaniards sang the Litany. At the rear was Governor Juan Langub; at intervals he knelt down, asking God for forgiveness. I was content seeing the sincerity with which it all was done. I had explained to them beforehand what the discipline meant, and what those carrying the *ceriales* should meditate on, and how and why they should discipline themselves. There was a big attendance at Mass on Easter and afterwards the children performed dances.''

In 1602 Father Jimenez left Butuan. For the continuation of the Butuan chronicle we must now shift to Combés, Lib. II, Cap. V, Col. 99:

"A Portuguese secular took over the care for Butuan, at the request of the *encomendero*, Don Francisco de Poso. But his greed was no less than that of the latter, and it fitted in well with that of the *Corregidor*, so that both started abusing their authority. Piety was used as an instrument of absolute tyranny. This forced the people to withhold their obedience, because there was nobody to have recourse to, as they had had in the zeal and unselfishness of our Fathers at moments of affliction.

The fury of their revenge was more than Silongan would have wished, but who can with his reason control all the pain and anger that has turned into despair? Driven by their fury, they killed the priest, the *Corregidor* and all the Spaniards.... They joined their strength with the rebellion of the bellicose Caragans, their neighbors, those bloodthirsty corsairs.''

At this point of the story we will need Chirino (II, 388) and Colin (III, 28). Here we discover that the year must have been 1603-1604 when the "Caragas Moros" had been rampaging along the coastal villages of Leyte and up to the Camotes islands. In Dulag (Leyte) the resident Jesuit missionary Melchor Hurtado had been taken prisoner and brought to Cotabato. A punitive expedition under General Juan Manuel de la Vega was dispatched to the east coast of Mindanao to subdue the Caragas, but the latter avoided all battle and absconded in the jungle.

The account in Colin mentions only the viciousness of the Caragas, which called for Spanish military action. Combés is again honest enough to inform us that (at least in Butuan) some of it had been provoked by abusive Spanish behavior.

Returning once more to Combés and Butuan, we are informed that as along the coast of Surigao and Davao, also along the borders of the Agusan river people went into hiding in the forests, including Silongan. According to Combés, it really pained the Jesuits in Cebu that such a promising mission as Butuan was in danger of totally falling away. They prevailed on local authorities not to use force to re-pacify Butuan, but to let one of them, Fabrico Sarsali, go there and try to win Silongan back.

The Governor of Cebu asked him to join an armed party of soldiers and sailors that was going to be dispatched to Butuan. After they had entered the river, they found that the whole place was abandoned; in spite of some extensive scouting, it was impossible to make contact with Silongan. They were afraid to penetrate too deeply into his guerilla country, because that would have been suicide for the soldiers, so Combés writes:

> "For many days they remained in that desperate situation, until finally Father Fabricio Sarsali realized that by arms nothing could be obtained.... The whole difficulty was to get into contact with Silongan, because he knew that due to the respect and veneration which his people had for him, it would depend on him whether they would surrender or not....then some solution occurred to him, inspired by heaven, namely to make use of a noble woman of Dapitan, Doña Madalena Baluyot, because he knew how much weight the word of such an important woman would have with Silongan. It was believed that with the help of her influence, we could assuage the fear which the chief had about dealing with us, especially if he knew about our preparedness and heard the noises of war in his territory. We mentioned already the special gift which heaven had given to this noble lady to win over people with rebellious intentions and hostile feelings.
>
> Through her he sent a message to ask him to come out in the open, proposing that they talk things over among the two of them, and that he would intercede for him with the Spaniards, so he could put himself under their friendship again in a very honorable way."

This *manang Madalena* must have been like one of the *mulieres fortes* of the Bible, or we might as well say, of local church history in action in the Philippines ever since. In a tiny *baroto* she paddled upstream from the river mouth and slipped into the mangrove swamps and mudflats of the riverine delta near Banza; and, of course, she found Silongan and could afterwards inform Father Sarsali of his willingness to meet him — all alone, just the two of them — on a little river islet. The result of that encounter was much to the satisfaction of both parties: Silongan, with all his people, came out of their hiding place to settle again in the old village, where "in less than six hours the houses were put up again, and the streets laid out. To anybody who knows those natives, that is a miracle, because with their slowness and laziness it takes them an eternity to construct even a little miserable hut; just watching an Indio work makes the patience of the most restrained Spaniard turn into despair."

For Father Sarsali it was a very welcome opportunity to give the Spaniards a good piece of his mind: he told them how all the efforts of patient and difficult missioneering could be undone in the shortest possible time by the "stupid behavior of a few Spaniards" lacking the most elementary respect for native sensibilities, and how difficult it was, and how costly, to win their estranged feelings back.

> "From then on Silongan was much respected and was given the title of Camp-master of Butuan and Governor of his people. And that tribe, being the fruit of the labor of the Society, was fully entrusted to its care, not in the sense that it was given a resident missionary, but that all its affairs were put in the hands of our ministers for arrangement" (loc. cit., Col. 103).

We owe this Doña Madalena Baluyot a few more lines, all the more so because they will lead us back to the origin of Dapitan and some past history of Butuan itself.

The genealogy of her family can be traced from Combés, Lib. I, Cap. IX. In 1565 (1566?) Datu Pagbuaya of Dapitan pledged loyalty to the Spaniards of Legazpi's expedition. He had a son Manooc, who after his baptism became Pedro Manuel Manooc, and a daughter, who was our Doña Madalena. A daughter of Pedro Manooc was Maria Uray; he had a cousin, Captain Laria, whose son, Gonzalo Maglenti — obviously knowing a good woman when he saw one — married Maria Uray. Their son was Pedro Cabelin. Doña Maria became very well known for her pious life. Although unrecorded time has afterwards obscured much knowledge about these families, we will recognize each of the names in the Who's Who of some areas in the present Philippines.

About 25 years later we find her under the name Magdalena "Bacuyo" in the "Historia..." of Luis de Jesus (Decada IV, Ch. 10, p.38ff.). This author mentions that at the time when the Recoletos were going to establish themselves in Cagayan (1622-1623) she was the grandmother of the local chief Salansang, who through her intervention allowed the missionaries to live and work in his territory; eventually Salansang became the first convert of his people.

In the same chapter Combés mentions:

> "The rulers and nobility of the islands of Jolo and Basilan
> call the village of Butuan their place of origin; although it is
> located on this island, it is actually part of the Visayan tribe. It
> is on the northern coast, in sight of the island of Bool and only
> a few leagues away from Leyte and Bool; the latter islands are at
> the same stage of civilization. Therefore, that village of Butuan
> can boast of having given chiefs and nobility to these tribes."

Around 1660 older people in Basilan, Jolo and Butuan still remembered, says Combés, the historical background of such family pride. One can appreciate so well the gesture of Combés: "It will be well to relate its beginning, before time will obscure it." Obviously, those beginnings must have taken place at Butuan during the incumbency of the grandson of Siagu (see Pigafetta), at least if the same dynasty had remained in power in Butuan. It is just possible that part of the genealogy of the Butuan rulers, taken from the years when the names are mentioned in historical accounts, runs roughly as follows:

1521: Siagu
1567: Limampas
1596: Silongan.

In 1667 Combés writes that "the old sultan of Jolo who is still alive" had personally known a brother of the chief of Butuan, who after a quarrel had left his native soil (perhaps refusing to follow the baptism and subjugation of Silongan?) and established himself in Basilan island. This settlement soon split in two parties, of which one group migrated to Jolo under the leadership of datu Paguian Tindig. From Jolo the latter married off his cousin Adasaolan (probably also a Butuanon) to a daughter of Dimasancay (Limasangcay) of Cotabato. Adasaolan converted to Islam.

Up to the present there is a remarkable similarity between the real Butuano Bisaya and the language of the Joloanons, as I have been assured by residents of both places. [16]

The next Jesuit to stay for about two years (1609-1611) in Butuan was Francisco Vicente Puig. In the "Carta Anua 1611-12" (Colin, III, p. 329) the Jesuit superior, Father Gregorio Lopez wrote:

"The request of Silongan and the inhabitants of Butuan to have again priests in their midst, was repeated many times. The encomendero of Butuan, the civil and ecclesiastical authorities have been urging me, this year even with the more insistence. Since these people had been evangelized and baptized, and need our protection even more in these troubled times, we felt obliged to agree to their request. In order to protect Butuan from attacks of the Mindanao (= Cotabato) natives, the Governor has decided to put a garrison in the place, and he had assigned a captain and some soldiers of Cebu to the place. Because of the rumors about the natives of Mindanao, these men were not at all happy with this assignment, but when they heard that the Jesuits, among them Father Francisco Vicente, would accompany them, they took heart. The journey was uneventful. People came out in *barotos* to meet them; the oars struck the water at the rhythm and the sound of the sweet names of Jesus and Mary. From that invocation the church and the convent got from then on their names....

Although peace and submission to Spain is not yet stable enough to give ensurance for the future, for them the important thing is to have the Fathers with them. They respect and esteem them highly, especially Father Vicente, who is with them now, and who treats them with prudence, love and generous zeal. Should there be talk of fear or rebellion because of the misbehavior of the Spanish soldiers, the Governor is willing to

---

[16] In Dutch documentary sources of the VOC (United East India Company) one will repeatedly find a Butuan, Botuan, Boutuan located in the area of the Davao Gulf. I have not been able to find out if the name of that locality came somehow into existence as an aftermath of the wandering into exile by the scion of the leading family of the Butuan in northern Mindanao (see Combés), or if the name existed fully independently thereof and in its own right. (Cfr.: *R. Laarhoven* "From Ship to Shore: Magindanao in the 17th century, from Dutch sources," Manila, 1985 and: "*Chronicle* of the Fort Batavia," anno 1663, p. 246.)

suppress the garrison, because he knows very well that peace in
this village is better ensured by the Society than by a garrison.''

It was this missionary who also made the first contacts with the
Hadgaguans, who were feared, even in Butuan, for their cruelty.
They finally asked him what they should do to become peaceful
vassals of Spain, and if a priest could be assigned to their territory.
The same happened with the people of Linao (near Bunawan) and
the Mamanuas of the mountains in the direction of Surigao.

The last Jesuit to stay (with a lay-brother) at Butuan was Father
Juan Lopez, but within less than one year the Butuan mission of the
Jesuits was definitely closed. For a while there were two secular
priests, whose names are mentioned as Alonso de Campos and
Lorenzo Perez in the assignment letter of Msgr. Pedro de Arce, the
Bishop of Cebu, appointing the Recoletos to Butuan in 1621. One of
them died (it is not clear whether in Butuan or Cebu) and the other
abandoned the station. Shortly before the assignment of the
Recoletos, one secular had still received an appointment for Butuan:
Domingo de Soto. Another went to Siargao; he also served the
Spanish garrison at Tandag. In 1621 the archbishop of Manila wrote
to the Spanish king: In Caraga are fifty Spanish soldiers who,
together with four hundred Indian natives, are ministered to by one
secular priest'' (Colin/Pastells, II, pp. 688-689).

From Combés we also learn that during the stay of the last Jesuit
in Butuan, the only son whom Silongan had with his legitimate wife
Maria Payo was sent to the Jesuit school in Cebu, together with
some other local boys. It can be assumed that out of these young
boys a new political leadership of Christian Butuan grew, which
one generation later, when in 1631 the whole rest of Caraga rose up
in revolt, would remain loyal to Spain. — We will come to that
eventually.

Aside from Madalena Baluyot and Maria Uray in Dapitan,
another zealous convert is mentioned in the accounts of those days:
Diego Inongan of Butuan. He had been a disciple and convert of
Father de Ledesma. In 1603, after a raid on Dulag, Leyte (where
Father Melchor Hurtado had been captured) the Caragans and
Moros had plundered also Butuan on their way home.

Among the captives there was also Diego Inongan. All prisoners
were brought to Cotabato, where Father Hurtado was deeply
impressed by the exemplary faith of the prisoner of Butuan. While
many of the other captives renounced their faith under pressure, he
courageously refused to do so, and he became the right hand man of

Father Hurtado. Another Jesuit missionary, Pascual de Acuña, had at the same time been a prisoner of the Caragans, writes Diego de Bobadilla in 1638).

The first decade of the 1600s was marked by two punitive expeditions sent to Caraga from Cebu, the first in 1605 and the second in 1609.

> "An ordinance had been passed (in 1605) that of those Christian soldiers some would be recruited and others would be withdrawn from fortifications elsewhere, or selected from local inhabitants; out of these a flotilla of armed rowboats would be formed, strong enough to go to Mindanao and castigate the enemies who shortly before had come to the villages of Dulag and Ormoc and had perpetrated there the destruction which we have mentioned before. They should mete out a special punishment to that wild tribe to which we referred there.
>
> That flotilla set out, and with it went as chaplain one of our priests with a companion. Upon their arrival they jumped on land with the courage to which the Spaniards are used, but in the villages they found nobody to take prisoner, because the natives did not dare show up, but had retired to the vastness of the forests. They captured only a few who fell into their hands by chance" (Colin, III, p. 28).

Then, in 1606 there was another danger threatening the southern half of the archipelago, which concerned Spanish presence in a different way: the Moros of Mindanao had hatched a conspiracy with some chiefs of Leyte, and (according to Colin) there was a great danger that it would spread to other islands and totally undo the progress that had been made in the last ten years. A few Moro sultans had promised the said chiefs that within one year they would come back; meanwhile the Leyteños should already begin to rise up everywhere against the Spaniards, make life impossible for the priests and burn the churches. After a short time the Moros would come and join forces with them to exterminate all the Spaniards. Initially it was discovered that here and there settlements absconded from the villages to the mountains. They said that they did so to be safe from the Moros, which does sound believable under contemporary circumstances. It was the Jesuit missionaries who eventually discovered what was really at stake. They informed the caretaker governor of Cebu, Diego Garcia, about it, who alerted the commander of the Cebu garrison, the Bishop and the Governor General of Manila. An armada of soldiers was rushed to Leyte where the rebellion was crushed before it had erupted into the open.

Less than one year later a wave of Moro and Caraga pirates swooped down on the coastal villages of southern Leyte again. This time the Manila government decided that Spanish occupancy of Mindanao was in need of some drastic action for its self-preservation. A strong fleet under Captain Juan de la Vega sailed to the east coast of Mindanao in 1609. On that occasion a stone fort was put up at Tandag and garrisoned with one company of Spanish infantry and one of Pampangos. This is the first time that we find accounts pinpointing a center of Caraga power in one locality. The second place mentioned as such is Marihatag, which was then the domain of a Mandaya chief feared by Spaniards and natives alike: Datu Hinoc (Inuc). About events there Colin writes:

> "An armada of sailboats with rowers was sent from Cebu against a chief named Hinoc, who was steeped in treachery, robbery, burning of villages and churches, who had made captives of many Indios of our mission stations among the *Pintados*. Father Juan Lopez went with it in the flagship with the title of fleet chaplain. Without being discovered they reached the village of the chief, but he escaped with all his people and also the prisoners of our (Leyte) missions. The latter had been thinking that the new arrivals were Sulas, another enemy tribe so barbarous that on their sea travels they take no food along for the crew. It was known that they just eat the prisoners whom they have taken."

They found one woman who had remained behind in the village. Since she had been sentenced to death, she had decided to stay, hoping that in this way she would escape that lot. She had already been tied to a stake, and in accordance with custom was to be slowly killed by spears thrown at her by the women.

The report of Father Lopez mentions that at the same time another human sacrifice had been in preparation near the beach: a new canoe was about to be launched into the water, sliding with its sharp keel over the prostrate body of a prisoner, so that his blood would splatter it as a promise of successful commission.

When news reached the prisoners in the forest that the newly arrived warriors were Spaniards, many escaped and came to the camp. The Jesuit letters of those days have some very shining examples of Christian strength shown by imprisoned women from the Visayan missions. The remarkable thing is that these were all first generation Christians.

In 1613 the Tandag fort was attacked and surrounded by more than 300 Caragans, who put the inhabitants in extreme danger. Only after some fierce battles were the attackers driven away (Luis de Jesus, "Historia..." Decada IV, Ch. 2, p. 31).

In retaliation, in 1614 the Spaniards swooped down on coastal villages and riverside settlements of Caragan pirates, burning their houses, destroying crops in the fields and liberating a great number of Visayan prisoners.

In many of these accounts it is not possible to see where traditional piracy and tribal conflicts end and opposition against Spanish presence and abuses begins. However, it can easily be imagined how precarious the existence must have been of such a Christian outpost as Butuan. At the closure of the Jesuit mission, Butuan counted more than 800 Christians, while most of the rest of the population were in various stages of catechumenization. The departing Jesuit Juan Lopez took a considerable number of these Butuan Christians with him and settled them in Bohol.

It is noteworthy that the Recoleto *cronista* Diego de Santa Theresa, commenting on alleged distortions committed by Father Combés in his "Historia de Mindanao y Jolo...," drastically lowers the just mentioned number of converts at Butuan to "hardly 300 in the whole Jesuit territory!" (Decada VII, Ch. 7, p. 295ff.).

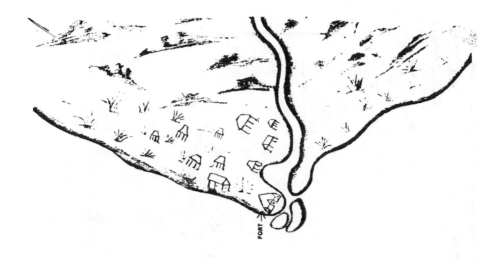

PACIFIC   OCEAN

Fig. 15. Location of the old Fort of Tandag. (Original in the National
Archives, Legajo 118 Pte. I, 1796.)

Description of the Tandag Fort by Fray Juan Francisco de San Antonio,
OFM (1738).

This fort has been built on the seashore, and it dominates a bay in such
a way that it blocks the passage of any vessel if it gets close to the beach.

It is made of stone, but the warehouses, chapel and barracks are roofed
with nipa.

Its shape is triangular with three bastions at three points.

It has enough cannons of various calibers and other weapons and
soldiers for its defense.

This fort was built to prevent the Moros from passing through and to
contain the Bisayas, a people who have been very warlike, and were it not
for this and the other forts, would continue revolting as they have been used
to ("Cronicas," translated by D. Pedro Picornell, p. 125, no. 377.)

It should be noted here that the fort had originally solely been
constructed as a defense against the local tribes, not against the Moros. Of
course, it did afterwards also serve against Moro incursions.

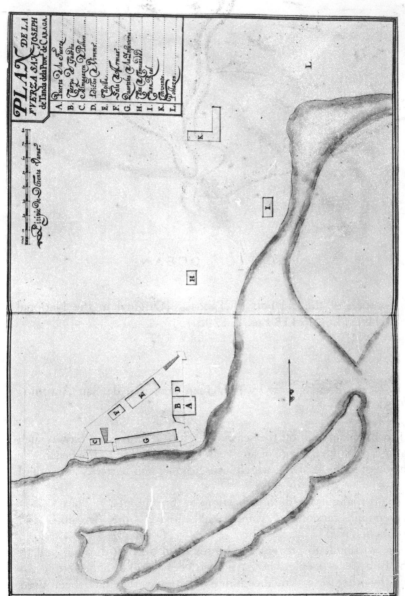

Fig. 16. Sketch of the fort of Tandag (1739) from the book: "Relación en que .... las Yslas Filipinas" by Fernando Valdés de Tamón. Ms. 19.217. (Courtesy of the Biblioteca Nacional Madrid.)

Description of the Fort by Governor Fernando Valdés de Tamón in 1739.

This fort is located at the seashore, at 8 degrees and 33 minutes latitude and 164 degrees eastern longitude, at a distance of 147 leagues southeast of Manila.

Its shape is that of an inequilateral triangle; it has two uneven bulwarks and one semi-bulwark. It is constructed of lime and stone and the total length of its walls is 762 feet. The entrance at the westside has a palisade which contains it and also the lookout post. (Note: The entrance was on the eastside.) The fort lodges a protective garrison and it has the necessary quarters, powder magazines and food stores as well as other rooms.

This description (like that of all other military establishments in the Philippines) can be found in a survey ordered by Governor General Fernando Valdés de Tamón. For Tandag, see p. 99. Title of the work: "Relación en que de orden de su Magestad Catolica... se declaran las plazas, castillos, fuerzos y presidios de las provincias sugetas a su Real dominio en las Yslas Philippinas" (1739).

A beautiful manuscript copy (209 pages) is in the Biblioteca Nacional in Madrid (Ms. 19.217).

That survey had been ordered because all documents about the Philippines stored in the royal palace of Madrid were lost in a fire that consumed the palace on Christmas 1734.

The manuscript has an Appendix with an extensive description of the ecclesiastical situation in the archipelago.

About Caraga it says: "Nowadays, because of the Christian religion their natural fierceness is well-disciplined. In the past they were a tribe much feared in all the districts."

IX

With A Spirit Apostolically Bold

"Modern detractors have seen only the destruction and the misery in those places (of Caraga) where, if only the stones could speak, they would answer them with stories of heroic deeds of abnegation and self-sacrifice, of love and dedication, of endeavors for progress and greatness, and above all of the labor of giants.

Have not the *frailes* been here for three centuries? What then, have they done?

But since the stones do not speak, we will ask: What would Mindanao have been without the Recoletos?

Only with the Recoletos can the history of Mindanao be written'' (Jose Garcia de S. Lorenzo OAR, 1940).

The above quotation is from an 18-page typewritten pamphlet entitled "Apuntes Historicos sobre la Conquista de la región de Caraga." It was written at the request of the superior of the Sacred Heart Missionaries of Surigao in 1940 on the occasion of the consecration of the first Bishop of Surigao-Agusan, Msgr. J. Vrakking; it was published in a domestic Recoleto Bulletin, in the

Cebu daily "La Nación" and the Surigao weekly "Ang Cabugason."

"Habent sua fata libelli," Terence said long ago: a lot of things can happen to a pamphlet. For some years after hearing about its existence, I possessed only the lines quoted above. Neither Recoleto nor MSC archives in the Philippines could produce the complete text. I finally found it in the Recoleto archives at Marcilla, Navarra, Spain, in Legajo 63. A surprise, of course...and in more than one sense! The typescript copy had a note attached to it, dated 1959, from the hand of the man who wrote it in 1940:

> "This work was written upon request of the Dutch Religious of the Sacred Hearts of Jesus and Mary (sic, Missionaries of the Sacred Heart) who have been missioneering in the region of Caraga since 1905 (sic, 1908). The reason was the creation, in 1940, of the new diocese comprising the provinces of Surigao and Agusan....It should be noted that those Dutchmen, after taking over the care for that region, which had been abandoned for some years (?) as a result of the revolution, had been speaking and writing in a derogatory way about the Recoletos. And the choirboys of the revolution took over the tune: "What have the frailes done in three centuries?"

I am afraid that either Fray Jose Garcia de S. Lorenzo was suffering from some complex or knew very little about those early Dutch missionaries of Surigao; not improbably both explanations are true. As far as I am aware, not a single one of the latter has ever written in the vein imputed to them above; in fact none of them had ever written anything about the Recoletos in Caraga, with one exception, and he offered a stirring defense, which no Recoleto could have improved on (see "Biblioteca Hispana Missionum," Tomo I, 1930). The present author, a Dutch Sacred Heart Missionary of a later generation, and the Recoleto Fathers at Marcilla, also of a later generation, had a good laugh about that disapproving finger belatedly wagging from between the documents of Legajo 63!

At any rate, the following pages are going to be about those Recoletos of Caraga, partly indeed also because "the stones don't speak," and many who were not stones also failed to do so.

After the withdrawal of the Jesuits from Butuan, the history of the Old Caraga district, from 1622 till the third quarter of the 1800s (with an interruption of about 20 years) was going to be a history written by the Recoletos. It is quite possible that these missionaries would have set foot on the shores of Surigao and Agusan one decade earlier, if it had not been for some internal corporate problems affecting the Order in Spain as well as in the Philippines. The on-and-off presence of the Jesuits at Butuan after they had officially already turned over the district to the Bishop of Cebu, could mean that they were, so to say, just watching the store till their successors solved those organizational difficulties. Already in July 1606 the first Recoletos, eight priests and five laybrothers, had arrived in Manila. At that time the Order had about 400 members in Spain, and 40 more of these had been requested for the Philippines. That some of the latter, soon to be expected, might be destined for Caraga, can be deduced from a letter of the Bishop of Cebu, dated May 20, 1607, which exists in the Archivo General de Indias at Sevilla (Filipinas, Legajo 79, Ramo IV, pp. 142-220). In that letter the Bishop expresses his joy over the arrival of the Recoletos in the Philippines and invites them to his Diocese. Against the background of an abandoned Caraga, one understands the Bishop's reaction.

The Recoletos were a young Order, which in 1588 had branched off from the Augustinians as a result of the "Reform" movement that gripped some major religious institutes at that time. In 1602 the several reform communities in Spain were joined into a separate province, which in 1621 was officially consolidated under the name Recollect or Discalced Augustinians. The first 13 Recoletos mentioned had left for the Philippines at a time when the dismembering and organizational process was still painfully going on at home. Soon that pain would be felt in the Philippines as well, as appears from the following complaint which the little group addressed to Philip III in 1610:

> "The Visitor of the Augustinians in the Philippines has forced the Recoletos to reunite with the Augustinians. This is not only a great disappointment to them, but also an obstacle to their religious observance" (AGI, Legajo 79).

Indeed, that Visitor, the (Augustinian) Bishop Diego de Guevara of Nueva Caceres, had informed the King that in the Philippines there was no need for an additional Order. The existing four, so he stated, were sufficient to take care of the evangelical needs of the archipelago. It would be better to send the Recoletos to Ternate and the other islands of Maluku!

Obviously, it was hardly apostolic motivation or information of the first order that inspired the opinion of Bishop de Guevara. As long as matters were not cleared up in Spain and Rome, the little flock of Recoletos already in the Philippines was going to be a lonely group, because under those conditions the superiors in Spain were not going to send reenforcements. In 1610 the Archbishop of Manila warned Philip III that their number was decreasing and that their mission would come to an end unless Spain sent additional personnel to join them. On July 15, 1611 they sent the following plaintive letter to the King:

> "It is only natural that a son will resort to his father and a vassal to his King in their necessities, so that by their appeal to him they may find comfort and help. Therefore, this little congregation of Discalced Augustinians which six years ago, on orders of Your Majesty, came to these Philippine Islands, and now bereft of all consolation, seeing how instead of increasing, it is decreasing in number, because no religious of our Order are forthcoming from the Kingdom to these islands, in the first place humbly kiss the feet of Your Majesty, and beg you to, please, comfort us by telling our Order to send some religious to increase the number of those who are here. It was through your Royal Majesty that our Order came to these islands, and was planted here; it is therefore befitting that Your Majesty see to its upliftment and increase" (AGI, loc. cit.; see also Colin III, 405, n.).

In 1610 Pope Paul V, who two years earlier had ordered the Recoletos to reunite with the Augustinians, revoked his decision and allowed them a separate existence, but this turnabout became known in the Philippines only two years later. The way was now open for the Order to send an increasing number of missionaries to the Philippines, so that eventually

> "they decided to extend their apostolic field and to augment the interests of the Lord by opening a mission in the province of Caraga, which was then a very important district of the big island of Mindanao. Already in 1596 and 99 evangelical workers of another Order had penetrated there, but because of the ferocity of the inhabitants, the voice of those was stilled and their daring zeal stopped" ("Labor Evangelica de los Padres

Agustinos Recoletos'' by Gregorio Fidel de Blas OAR, 1882, p. 58).[17]

Few Jesuit authors would wholly agree with that comment on the reasons for the closure of the Butuan mission! It sounds like a late naughty undertone, an echo from the clerical controversy that for many years ran loud and bitter between the Mindanao missions of the Jesuits and Recoletos, to which we will have to listen at the proper time.

---

[17] Letter of Bishop Pedro de Arce of Cebu entrusting the Caraga mission to the Recoletos.

''We, Fray Pedro de Arce, through the grace of God, ... Since we have been requested in the name of Fray Rodrigo de San Miguel, Provincial of the Order of the Discalced of our Father Saint Augustin in the Philippines, through Fray Miguel de Santa Maria, of the same Order, and because of the holy Catholic zeal for the conversion of the pagan natives and the increase of our holy faith, which they have shown in the service of God our Lord, and for the good of the souls which they have kept before their eyes, and with which they strive to occupy themselves in the apostolic work of gaining souls for heaven, for these reasons we adjudicate to them and put them in charge of some missions of our diocese....We take hereby into account the good fruits which will result hereof for the service of both the divine and the human Majesties. Therefore, by these presents, we adjudicate and give to the said Order...the *encomiendas* and villages of Butuan, Sampongan and Caraga, with all the rivers and hills located in the *encomiendas* of Alférez Francisco de Santa Cruz and Doña Inés de Bolaños, plus the islands of Siargao up to Tandag where the garrison of the Spaniards is located. Also the *encomienda* of Bislin and Cateel that belong to Juan de las Mariñas, with all the upland rivers and villages and the hinterlands of Butuan.

All these places have been abandoned for many years because of the departure of Archdeacon Alonso de Campos and the death of Lorenzo de Perez, the last owners, and some of them never had any catechization or minister, like in the *encomienda* of Juan de las Mariñas, and some villages of Caraga because they are not yet fully under control and pacified.

We give them all the powers required by law, with the instruction to ask before anything else the permission and approval of Señor Alonso Fajardo de Tenza, Governor and Captain General of these islands and President of the Royal Court, so that, in the name of His Majesty and in virtue of his Royal Patronate, he may concede and approve it. After that, the Order may send Religious there, dutiful and with knowledge, to

From the records of the Order, kept by *cronistas* and afterwards digested into some volumes of a "Historia General," a good deal of information about Caraga and the endeavors of the Recoletos for its evangelization has been preserved for us. For the subsequent pages about the Caraga mission we are much indebted to the *cronistas* Luis de Jesus, Pedro de San Francisco de Asis and Diego de Santa Theresa. Later volumes of the "Historia General" used by me are those compiled by Gregorio Ochoa del Carmen (Tomo VIII-IX) and Manuel Carceller (X-XII). All of these I consulted in the Recoleto archives at Marcilla. Some use is also made of the "Labor Evangelica..." of Gregorio Fidel de Blas, 1882. Of great importance were also the many manuscript accounts (in various stages of legibility) kept at Marcilla, at the Biblioteca Nacional of Madrid, some at Simancas and Sevilla, and one (1751) kept in the British Library, London. The latter is one of the many historical records stolen during the British Occupation of Manila in 1762. Repeated searches at the National Archives in Manila also produced some interesting information helpful to attempts to draw a vague picture of the Old Caraga and its Hispanization and evangelization.

In Decada Quarta, Ch.II, p.24ff. Luis de Jesus opens his account of the Caraga mission with descriptions given by his confreres on the spot about the strange new country and the people entrusted to them. The district had some nice settlements, especially along the many rivers. The land was good for rice farming, and various kinds of fruit could be found everywhere. After describing some pecularities of the fauna of Caraga, de Jesus turns to those of the human inha-

---

catechize and instruct the natives and the Spaniards living in the village and in the garrison, and administer the sacraments to them, in conformity with their duty and office....

We order the *encomenderos*, the collectors and other persons in charge of the *encomiendas* there to support the Religious that will be sent there by the Order for the said ministry, by paying and giving to them the customary stipends and alms. '' (''Bullarium OAR'', for 1622; see also Licinio Ruiz: ''Sinopsis'' I, p. 327).

Capitulo IV. §. I. 285

Año 1674

CAPITULO IV.

Cobra nuevos adelantamientos la Fè Catholica, por la predicacion de nueſtros Religioſos en Philipinas; y mueren algunos con grande opinion en Eſpaña.

§. I.

Por la predicacion de nueſtros incanſables Operarios ſe convierte en la Iſla de Mindanào una gran multitud de infieles Tagabalòyes, que tenian ſu habitacion en los montes contiguos al partido de Biſlig.

Joſue, cap. 6.

600

Ara llegar el Divino poder à derribar los muros de Jericò, diò la orden ſu Mageſtad, de que por ſiete dias, y el ultimo dia ſiete veces, rodeaſſe el Exercito à la Ciudad, llevando la Arca del Teſtamento, y reſonando en las bocas de los Sacerdotes las buccinas; à cuya diligencia ſe arruinaron las murallas, y, quedando deſtruida la gentilidad, ſe enarbolaron en Jericò los eſtandartes de la eſcrita Ley. Tan poderoſo era Dios para triunfar de aquella Poblacion rebelde en la primera buelta, como en la ultima; pero quiſo, que ſe repitieſſen las diligencias del Exercito, y el clamor de los Sacerdotes; para darnos à entender, que en la conquiſta de las Almas, no debemos deſmayar, ſi à los principios parecen infructuoſos nueſtros clamores, y trabajos: ſirviendonos de conſuelo, que

en llegando el tiempo del beneplácito Divino, ſi noſotros no ceſſamos de dar voces con la tuba Sacerdotal, y Evangelica, caheran por sì miſmos los muros mas fuertes de la idolatria. Eſta maxima ha ſeguido nueſtra Philipina Reforma, y la ha viſto muchas veces comprobada. Pues, combatiendo caſi de continuo à la gentilidad, encaſtillada en los montes contiguos à los Partidos reducidos de ſu adminiſtracion; aunque malogrò no pocas fatigas, ſin poder cantar la victoria, al fin ſe coronò de triunfos, quando le pareciò congruente à la Divina providencia. Varias expediciones hemos viſto, y verèmos, comprobativas de eſta verdad; y al preſente nos ocurre la que ſe hizo en los montes de Biſlig.

601 El partido de Biſlig, que es el ultimo, y mas diſtante de Manila, entre los que poſſehe alli nueſtra Reforma, ſe halla en Caràhga,

llla

Fig. 17. Two pages from "Historia General de los Padres Agustinos Descalzos" by Diego de S. Theresa, 1743.

286 Decada IX.

Isla de Mindanào, y consta de cinco Pueblos; conviene à saber, Bislìg, que es el principal, Hinatòan, Catèl, Bagàngan, y Carhàga; de quien se denominò en sus principios la Provincia, por ser entonces la Poblacion de mayor monta. Para la administracion espiritual de este Partido suele haver destinados solos dos Religiosos, que en su exercicio tienen demasiado trabajo. Porque los Pueblos estàn muy distantes entre sì; la gente es sumamente belicosa; confinan con los Moros, enemigos irreconciliables; y el Mar de aquellos parages, por donde precisamente se ha de viajar de unos Pueblos à otros, es con extremo borrascoso, bravo, è impenetrable en algunos tiempos: à cuyos escollos de los mencionados peligros han perdido varios Religiosos la vida, segun harà patente en adelante esta Historia. Mas, no obstante, que los dos Ministros assignados à estos Pueblos, apenas pueden atender llenamente à la direccion de los Indios Christianos; y aunque por la penuria, que padece casi siempre de Religiosos nuestra Reforma en aquellas Islas, rara vez pudo emplear allì mas sujetos: siguiendo estos pocos la maxima, usada allì, de trabajar uno por muchos, no dexaron de solicitar siempre la conversion de los Gentiles confinantes, de que hay gran numero por aquellos montes.

602. Especialmente en unas Serranias, que corren à lo largo de la playa, desde enfrente de Carhàga, hasta cerca de Bislìg, (en distancia de veinte y cinco leguas à lo largo, sin que se sepa lo que se estienden à lo ancho tierra à dentro) hay tanta multitud de Indios infieles, y Naciones barbaras, que ni aun los Indios Christianos las conocen todas. La Nacion mas cercana à nuestros Pueblos, es la de los Tagabalòyes, los quales toman el nombre de unos montes, que ellos llaman Baloòy; y

habitan entre sus malezas, sin sujecion à la Fè Catholica, ni à la Monarquia de España. Son estos Indios domesticos, apacibles, tratables, y aliados siempre con los Christianos; à quienes imitan en ser enemigos irreconciliables de los Moros. Son gente muy corpulenta, bien dispuesta, y de mucho valor, y fuerzas, à que les acompaña buen entendimiento, y mas que mediana industria. Es Nacion en sus tratos fiel, y en sus palabras constante, como descendientes; que se precian ser de Japones, à quienes se assemejan en el color, semblante, y costumbres. Su vida es bastantemente politica, sin mostrar aversion à la sociabilidad humana. Toda una parentela, por dilatada que sea, suele vivir en una Casa, con separacion de viviendas, segun las familias. Hacen estas Casas muy elevadas, de modo, que desde tierra al primer piso es comun tener dos picas de altura; y usan para toda la habitacion de una escalera sola, con tal artificio, que la quitan desde arriba, recogidos yà todos; y assi, se hallan seguros de sus enemigos. Viven cerca de los Christianos muchos de estos Tagabalòyes, à quienes tratan, visitan, y se ayudan mutuamente. De nuestros Religiosos no huyen, antes gustan de comunicarlos, mostrandoles suma, amor, y respeto; de manera, que qualquiera Ministro pudiera vivir entre ellos, tan seguro, como en un Pueblo Christiano.

603 Todas estas partidas, yà se vè quàn à proposito son para que Nacion tan docil reciba nuestra Santa Fè; pero con todo esto, hasta el año 1671. se adelantò muy poco en su reduccion; siendo assi, que el cuydado, y la predicacion de los nuestros la procurò sin cessar. A mas de la voluntad de Dios, cuyas resoluciones son investigables, huvo varios motivos de texas abaxo, que bolvieron infructuosos los conatos de

los

bitants. He makes it very obvious that Caraga was a tough mission territory. The autochthonous population were Negritos who now, however, had been pushed back by pre-Spanish "colonizers" from their coastal and river dwellings, and were living a nomadic life in the jungles away from the shore. Their weapons consisted of bow and arrow and machetes so sharp that in one stroke they could cut off a man's head. Their favorite victims were the present sea and riverside dwellers, whom they hated furiously for having forced them out of their original habitat.

And if such parishioners did not scare them enough, they could look forward to meeting even worse ones:

> "From serious and trustworthy people it was known that deep in the jungle giant and very ugly men had been seen who walked with their feet backward; they did not work but supported themselves with the flesh of wild animals, tree roots and fish. The sight of them was so horrifying that he who had the misfortune of seeing one, kept afterwards a permanent cast in his eyes and squinted like those whom we call cross-eyed. This information was confirmed by an eyewitness who said that he had seen and known some Indios who were almost squinting as a result of having looked at those monstrous men. They related that those beings could sprint with such a speed that just by running they could catch the swiftest deer, and that if they caught one of the Indios, those men just talked very confusedly among themselves; afterwards they left the captives hanging from some trees, from where they descended with great risk; after that they were squinteyed from having looked at those horrible monsters. A few years afterwards, another witness, well acquainted with what went on in that island, said furthermore that such monsters, called Tecmas, had been spotted whose ears were totally out of shape because of their size, and who had a snout like that of a dog; they had such horrible faces and teeth that they caused great fright" (Luis de Jesus, loc. cit., Ch III, pp. 25-26).

I suppose that even the most dull-witted *capre* ("ogre") would recognize himself in that description!

The creatures mentioned here seem to have stepped straight out of the travelogues of Sir John Mandeville (14th century), who populated many (imaginary) regions with the kind of monsters described here by de Jesus. De Mandeville's stories captivated European imagination up to the 16th and 17th centuries.

Understandably, the new missionaries had a more than passing interest in the religious beliefs and practices prevailing among the Caragans. Although the term "animism" was unknown to them — it was coined only in the midst of the 19th century — the account given by de Jesus clearly point to the presence of a set of myths, cults and forms of behavior attributed by anthropologists under the term "animism" to certain primitive populations. It reflects a view that populates the cosmos with a great number of invisible but active beings such as divine spirits or the spirits of the dead. The animist believer lives with a faith in water, fire and sky spirits, nightmares, werevolves, ancestral veneration and totemism. The *capre* mentioned above clearly looks like a barely acculturated cousin of the werewolf (who, so it would seem, was even still spooking in the unspoken mental background of our Spanish informants!). The symptoms related by de Jesus are, until today, often stealthily tiptoeing through the cosmic views and psychic anxieties all over the Philippine archipelago. De Jesus tells us that for some

> "religion consisted in adoring the sky, for others the moon, or their deceased ancestors, the mountains or the forest where, so they believed, their foreparents lived in the company of some deities and enjoying perpetual rest. They took it for certain that those who in life had been most courageous and tyrannical would turn into divine beings; also, that for some there was eternal punishment" (loc. cit.).

The presence of stone or wooden idols (*diwata*) is also mentioned, each with a peculiar function, to be implored for victory in war, health in sickness, or fertility for their fields. Very intriguing is the information that they thundered back, so to say, at a thunderstorm by loud and furious shouts at the deity who had caused it. If that failed to impress the thundergod, they even threatened him with brandished arms.

Islam had tried to get a foothold on the east coast of Surigao and Davao, but the requirements of the Koran were too exacting for a people given to a stiff drink or two and a good bite of pork.

There were no specific days for religious ceremonies or sacrifices; these were rather occasioned by important events such as preparations for war raids or slave hunting, in sickness, the beginning of the planting season or the building of a house. Sacerdotal functions were exercised by men as well as women, carrying the name *"baylan."* Animals as well as human prisoners served as sacrificial victims. Fortune telling and sorcery were the specialties of the *bailanes,* and the rites were adapted to the occasion. In all ceremonies intoxicating drink and trance dancing were used to excite *bailanes* and bystanders alike.

In their daily lives, activities and decision making, especially on their hunting or war treks through the jungle, they let themselves carefully be guided by the sound of the turtle-dove *(limocón),* a practice still existing today among some simple mountain dwellers.

After a death, mourning ceremonies with plaintive songs punctuated by fearful cries were held for more or fewer days depending on the social standing of the departed, which also determined the number of slaves to be killed and buried with the deceased, a practice of which de Jesus says: "so the dead went hand in hand with the living, without dispensation."

During their whole lives the Caragans preserved a deep reverence for their ancestors *(humalagar).* For the rest:

> "The vices of those people were enormous. Love for peace was something unknown among them; what they were after was continual warfare; the slightest pretext was enough for them. They were obsessed by the desire to rob others or to make captives on land and sea, although in ancient times they had condemned stealing severely.
>
> Their arms consisted of a lance, a long narrow shield covering the entire body, and a dagger looking like a broad knife. Herewith they could easily cut off the head of a victim, something that gave them much delight.... They also used arrows with poison extracted from the teeth of venomous snakes. They wounded and killed by shooting these from a blow-pipe which they cleverly concealed between the fingers of their hands; they blew the arrows so that they hit the flesh of their opponents" (loc. cit., Ch. V).

Clearly, a lot of hazardous work was awaiting the eight missionaries assigned to Caraga. In the act of appointment signed by Bishop Pedro Arce of Cebu, it was specified that the Recoletos were going to be entrusted with

> "the districts of Butuan, Sampongan (Jabonga) and Caraga (here Calagan = Cantilan ?) with all the villages, rivers and mountains which are *encomiendas* of Francisco de Santa Cruz, Doña Maria de Vega, and Doña Ines de Bolaños; also all the

islands of Sidargao up to Tandag inclusive, where there is a Spanish garrison; also the district of Bislig and Cateel, governed by Juan de Lasmariñas, with all its farmlands, rivers and villages; also the hinterland of Butuan'' (Licinio Ruiz, ''Breve Enseña...'' p. 327).

The chronicler mentions that the first group of eight Recoletos, six of them priests and two laybrothers, left Manila among the general holy envy of their confreres there "who would also have liked to spend their lives in such a holy endeavor." In Cebu they went to visit Bishop de Arce to ask for his blessing and to receive his last instructions for a missionary undertaking of such heroic proportions. From Cebu they sailed very soon for Mindanao and arrived at Tandag, the Spanish *presidio* with a garrison and a stronghold named "Royal Fort of Saint Joseph of Tandag," which had been established thirteen years before. "This was the beginning of the most blissful event ever to happen to that land," so wrote Luis de Jesus.

We can easily imagine that once in Tandag they were extensively briefed about the east coast of Mindanao up to Butuan, which was going to be their missionary territory, and about the kind of people and their leaders now entrusted to them to be made into vassals of Christ and of the King of Spain. Within a few days they had decided how to divide for the time being the Evangelical Labor among the eight of them. The superior of that "spiritual squadron," as the chronicler calls them, Miguel de Santa Maria, obviously was a man with the proper evangelical motivation and a feeling for apostolic realities in the locality. Disregarding his personal safety offered by the fort, he decided to build his own church and convent along the river, about five kilometers inland, because he had noticed that the natives were afraid to come near the fort. Under the circumstances this was truly a gesture of missionary courage, because to the fierce inhabitants (and especially to the local datus, who had been deprived of much of their old influence and authority) he was just another Spaniard, queerly dressed perhaps and engaging in queer activities from time to time, but ultimately one of "them" and having come to tell the inhabitants what to do and not to do anymore. Not many years later it was indeed deemed necessary for safety reasons to build another residence and church closer to the protection of the fort.

One priest was assigned for the Spanish and Filipino soldiers inside the fort and to assist the first resident parish priest of Tandag in the church along the Tandag river. The other six swarmed out, first to Gigaquit, where they split up in two groups, one for the headland of Surigao and the neighboring islands, and the other for Butuan, where "with a spirit apostolically bold Fray Juan de San Nicolas planted the Standard of the Cross in the village close to the shore." If we were to believe the author of "Labor Evangelica de los Pp. Agustinos Recoletos" (1882) they founded nine mission stations in that same year 1622, but it should be noted here that the *"cuadros estadisticos"* of the author are (here) very sloppy or murky, which is perhaps partly explained by the fact that those statistics were published in 1882 during a heated controversy with the Jesuits to prove the heroic efforts of the Recoletos in Mindanao, at a time when they were forced to give way to the Jesuits of the restored Society. In another statistics (Bullarium ORSA, Appendix II, p. 464) an obvious correction is made when it is stated that those nine stations were founded *non omnes hoc anno* ("not all in that year").

In fact, Bislig, which in the first mentioned statistics is included in 1622, was founded only in 1642.

It is anyway rather risky to accommodate all stations in statistics under a heading "founded." This would seem to imply their permanent existence as an independent station afterwards, when in reality some were just temporarily visited or tried out, to become soon a dependency of a more permanent station.

A good thing for later historiography was that already in 1624 the group of Recoletos in the Philippines became a "province" of its own. As a consequence they had to convene a "Chapter" every three years to evaluate the condition of its corporate existence and the requirements of its apostolic mission. The "Acts" of those Chapters, in so far as they have survived, give a relatively fair insight (in absence of much other information) into how the various mission stations developed in about 250 years. The first Chapter of 1624 mentions as priors (local superiors):

> in Bacuag: Jacinto de San Fulgencio
> in Gigaquit: Juan de San Antonio

In the Chapter of 1626 we find the following appointments:

> Tandag: Juan de San Nicolas
> Gigaquit: Jacinto de San Fulgencio
> Butuan: Juan de Santo Tomas
> Calagdan (Cantilan): Juan de San Antonio
> Dinagat: Francisco de San Agustin

This points to six actual stations in 1626. In 1629 Calagdan had disappeared from the list of residential stations, and so did Tago in 1632, Gigaquit in 1635, Dinagat in 1641 and Linao (Bunawan area, Agusan) in 1650. Calagdan, Gigaquit and Dinagat became dependencies of Siargao, each at its own time, Tago of Tandag in 1632 and Linao of Butuan in 1650. Cateel, Baganga and Caraga (the settlement at the extreme southern end of the district) remained dependencies *(visitas)* of Bislig till August 1671, when a resident missionary was also assigned to Baganga and Caraga. However, the occupancy of the last two places did not last very long.

As for the deployment of personnel, it seems that in 1638 this had reached a more or less settled stage. In that year the Provincial in Manila reported to the Governor General that in the Caraga district Tandag and Butuan were the main stations and that the *"vicariatos"* were Siargao, Linao and Bislig. Except for the vacancy of Linao, the same setup is found in a similar report to the government dated June 29, 1655 listing "all the ministries paid for by His Majesty in these islands." The Recoletos reported eight priests in four residencies in Caraga: Tandag, Butuan, Siargao and Bislig. During all the time of the Recoleto mission, till their (second) departure in the last quarter of the 19th century, the number of personnel listed in statistics will hardly change, as can be gleaned from various Recoleto documents in Marcilla. The following enumerations show the number of priests in the main stations for the years indicated.

1740	*1752*	*1758*	*1771*	*1774*
Butuan 3	Tandag 1	Tandag 3	Tandag 2	Tandag 2
Siargao 3	Butuan 2	Butuan 2	Butuan 2	Butuan 2
Tandag 3	Siargao 3	Surigao 2	Surigao 2	Surigao 2
Bislig 2	Bislig 1	Siargao 2	Bislig 1	Bislig 1
		Bislig 2	Jabonga 1	Jabonga 1
		Jabonga 1		

1776	*1779*
Tandag 2	Tandag 2
Bislig 1	Bislig 1
Surigao 1	Surigao 1
Butuan 1	Butuan 1

Lack of personnel has always hampered the Caraga mission and would cause considerable dissatisfaction in government circles in

Manila. It also encouraged the Jesuits to suggest to the government
that the Society take over Caraga.

Let us now take a preliminary look at the first acts of these
apostles at the opposite ends of the Caraga mission, Tandag and
Butuan. Like today, just south of Tandag there was a place with the
beautiful name Marihatag. Some have explained that name by
deriving it from Visayan *"hatag ni Maria"* (Mary's gift). That
etymology is, however, more pious than historically probable,
because the name existed already (also spelled Marieta) before
Mary's name had ever been preached on the coast of Caraga. In the
previous chapter we have mentioned an expedition against the
notorious Datu Inuc in the hinterlands of Marihatag. That fierce and
feared chief had not mended his ways after the lesson meted out to
him on that occasion; in 1622 he was still the foremost problem
parishioner for the priests of Tandag and the commander of the fort
there. Or putting it another way, we might say: the Inuc question
became the first major challenge for the pastor of Tandag. Luis de
Jesus gathered the following report for us:

> "We should, by all means, mention a very outstanding
> conversion that took place in the province of Caraga. There was
> a chief named Inuc, who was so notorious and feared that by his
> power and cunning he had become absolute lord over a large
> territory and along the banks of a river that afterwards took his
> name. This barbarian was not satisfied with tyrannizing his own
> territory, but he invaded also those of others by sailing through
> the bays and along the coasts, looking for opportunities to rob,
> capture and kill. It was said of that man that he kept more than
> 2000 slaves and that with his own hand he had killed
> numberless people. As a consequence, he was much feared in the
> neighboring islands, and no vessel dared to go to his domain,
> especially not one of Spaniards, whom he despised in the
> extreme......Fray Juan de la Madre de Dios, after preparing
> himself by fasting and praying, decided to subdue him with no
> other help than his confidence in God. He went to see him, all
> alone. Even Inuc himself was astonished at the boldness of this
> Religious who dared to come in his presence. Fray Juan talked to
> him so beautifully and with such fervor...that the tyrant started
> to like him very much" (loc. cit., p. 33).

The result was that Inuc promised to come to terms with the
Spaniards of the Tandag fort and to allow them to enter his territory

for trading and to preach the gospel. Before long he complied with all the requirements for baptism by freeing all his slaves and keeping only one of his many wives. Diego de Santa Theresa, another chronicler of this period remarks about that event: "Fray Juan alone, with no other forces nor arms than those of his virtues, went out to meet Inuc; with only the power of God's word he conquered a man who had whole squadrons around him. The religious conquered a fighter, the lamb a lion" (Decada VII, nr. 232).

There was great rejoicing in the fort and the convent of Tandag when Inuc came down from his lair to take the oath of loyalty to the King of Spain; as his witnesses for that solemn moment he had chosen the commander of the fort and Fray Juan.

At the Butuan end, the reports of those days seem to indicate that in the mid 1620s the village had moved from some tributary river where it was in 1565 to the banks of the mainstream, probably at Lilo (Banza), where a few remnants of an old stone church with cemetery annex still exist. This structure dates from the second half of the previous century, but artifacts robbed from graves in the old burial site betray a much older Christian cemetery.

> "Butuan is named after the river of that name which flows along the village before rendering the tribute of its waters to the sea" (loc. cit., Ch. VIII).

The new missionaries found that the natives of Agusan had the same customs and religious practices as the Caragans of the east coast; only their social behavior was a little less wild,

> "probably because their manners had been refined by the law of the Gospel which they had enjoyed for some time. Although afterwards they had abandoned it because the ministers had abandoned them" (de Jesus, loc. cit.).

I am not sure that no clerical barb is intended here!

The greatest obstacles to conversion were polygamy, the keeping of slaves, and, of course, adherence to primitive religious practices and idols. For the latter, the missionaries showed little mercy. In spite of possible hostile reaction of the river tribes, the gospel message together with King's greetings were brought to the inland reaches of the river as far as Linao, forty leagues distant from Butuan, where soon a wooden fortification would be put up named Fort San Juan Bautista, annexed to a church cum convent under the patronage of Santa Clara de Montefalco.

It is interesting to note that already then on their river trips the missionaries took some Christians of Butuan along as apostolic helpers.

In Gigaquit, at the eastern end of the Caraga mission, the riverboat companions of the missionaries seem to have been of a lesser apostolic mettle. There was Fray Juan de San Nicolas, who one day in 1624 "asked some Indios to bring him in their *baroto* from the village of Gigaquit to join the other Fathers who were then missioneering upstream." He never reached them, because his boat companions made the *baroto* capsize on purpose so that he drowned (Hist. Gen de Ph., Pastells, T. 7, pte. 1).

He was the second Recoleto to be killed in about one year in the new mission of Caraga. The other was our former acquaintance, Fray Juan de la Madre de Dios, who had converted Inuc. He had gone up the Tandag river one day because a local woman had asked him to intercede for her with Datu Suba, who had made her a slave for an unpaid debt. Obviously, this datu was not yet ripe for the kind of admonitions dealt out by the missionary: poor Fray Juan was first pierced by Suba's lance on the doorsteps of his house and then killed off by the datu when still trying to run away. He was 34 years old.

Suba himself found a similar end not long afterwards when the fort commander of Tandag sent one of his Indio soldiers, Dacsa, after him with 50 armed men.

About the island of Siargao Luis de Jesus mentions in 1681 that there were 2000 Christian families (presumably at the time stated, when he wrote his chronicle). Aside from these: "According to trustworthy people, on a certain occasion some short men had been seen, tiny but beautiful, having the looks and the size of pygmies. They are very lightfooted and hide in the vast forests. In spite of some attempts, none have been caught thus far. Nevertheless, people remember that in the past some had been captured but in a few hours' time they had died of fear."

On one of their reconnaissance trips on the island, the missionaries found an indication of some earlier Spanish visit. On top of a rock on the beach of Sapao was a stone-cross which obviously had been fashioned by some sailors of an early Spanish expedition. However, its size had been much reduced and the inscription had become illegible having been eroded by the waves.

For the rest, the island was fertile and had many springs of good drinking water; people called them "bito." It was noticed that their water level always remained the same and was not affected by the change of seasons.

Another peculiarity of the island was that, unlike on the coast of mainland Caraga, monkeys did not survive on Siargao. From time to time people had brought some from the forests of Surigao, but they died very soon. "There is a peculiar kind of tree called Nono. It springs from the root of some other large and leafy tree and while growing, it embraces the latter and absorbs its substance; in this way it fattens itself, and once it is sturdy and can stand alone, it dismisses the other and discards its previous support, maltreating it till it dries out. A living image of the children of this world!"

On the island of Siargao they also noted big houses built high up in huge trees. They found out that the inhabitants were mostly runaways who were in hiding because they refused to pay tribute. The Spaniards had a hard time dislodging them from those lofty strongholds, from which men, women and children furiously fought back at the soldiers. One of the lay brothers related that when he was still a soldier in the fort of Tandag, he had been in one such house which had sheltered sixty people. In another he had found a gruesome scene: a woman had hanged her two daughters and then herself to avoid being caught alive by the soldiers, which may be even more telling about those soldiers themselves!

The fort of Linao was constructed about 1625. The chronicles of Diego de S. Theresa and Pedro de S. Francisco de Asis give the following information about its genesis:

> "Fray Jacinto de S. Fulgencio and Agustin de S. Pedro (*el Padre Capitan*) decided to put up their residence in Linao...All the Indios there received the faith, and for that reason they became the target of attacks by their pagan neighbors in the forests...Fray Agustin started training his parishioners in the art of military tactics. He convinced them that for their protection it would be very useful to construct a stronghold. Since it was impossible to build it of stone, he let them cut many trees... and out of the trunks hereof he made a palisade strong enough to resist any attack...This stronghold is still in existence today (1743) and manned by a competent garrison of soldiers for the protection of those Indios" (op. cit., p. 287-288). [18]

---

[18] About 1850 the garrison of Linao was moved to the mouth of the Hijo river in Davao. In 1861 the village of Linao was completely destroyed by flood and the inhabitants were made to join those of "San Jose de Bunawan." The documents of this disaster and of the transfer can still be found in the National Archives at Manila (Caraga; Erección de Pueblos).

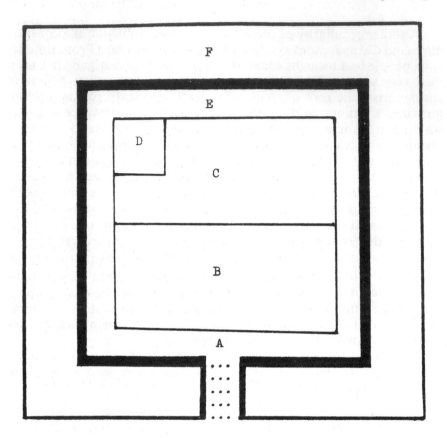

A : Entrance

B : Quarters of troops   E : Earth-wall and palisade.

C : House of the Captain.   F : Moat

D : Store-room.

Fig. 18. Ground plan of the fort "San Juan Bautista" at Linao (near the present Bunawan, Agusan del Sur) as it was in 1739. It was a square redoubt of palisades with an earthen wall, each side 8 meters long, surrounded by a moat with a width of 2 meters. It was a small-sized stronghold *(fuertecito)* identical to the one at Cateel (Davao Oriental).

Redrawn with permission of the Biblioteca Nacional, Madrid, from Ms. 19.217: *"Relación en que...las Yslas Philipinas"* by Fernando Valdés Tamón, 1739, p. 106. Enlargement (1.5x) of the original Ms.

Before Linao, *El P. Capitan* had served for some time as assistant in Butuan from where he attended to Jabonga and Gingoog. Later (1626) he was transferred to Cagayan, where he became famous for leading troops against Sultan Corralat near Lake Lanao. From 1638-1641 he was back again as parish priest in Butuan. During that time he and the commander of Tandag led a detachment of soldiers over land to Lake Lanao to help the troops of Iligan and Zamboanga (on request of Father Belin, SJ) repel the forces of Corralat. This event deserves some closer attention, not only because of its colorful principal actor, but also for another, say clerical, reason involving a dispute running through the Recoleto and Jesuit missionary presence in Mindanao all the way to the last quarter of the 19th century.

During his incumbency as parish priest of Cagayan (1626-1638) and his military forages against the Moros, he had — in the opinion of the Jesuits — not only planted the Spanish flag in some sections of Moroland, but also unfurled the Recoleto banner in Jesuit territory. The Bishop of Cebu, however, had already in 1625 adjudicated the disputed territory to the Recoletos. Governor Juan Niño de Tavora (1626-1632), to prevent future disputes, had ordered a demarcation line to be drawn from Punta Sulawan (Macajalar bay, Cagayan) to Punta San Agustin (Davao), allotting the area east thereof to the Recoletos and the western side to the Jesuits. This line is clearly indicated in some 17th century maps. With that boundary line, the area around Lake Lanao falls indeed inside the Jesuit half of Mindanao. This was also confirmed by Governor Hurtado de Corcuera in 1637. In 1638 el Padre Capitan was transferred to Butuan, deeply disgusted because of — what he considered — the shrinking of Recoleto missionary territory for which he had fought so hard. When in 1640 news reached him in Butuan about renewed Moro hostilities near Lake Lanao, he blamed it on misadministration by the Jesuits and the unheeded clamor of the inhabitants to be restored to the Recoleto jurisdiction. When the military situation in the lake area became quite desperate for the Spanish troops, the Jesuit chaplain, Gregorio Belin, wrote a very urgent letter to the Padre Capitan at Butuan, to, please, come to their aid as quickly as possible. Fray Agustin's confrere Diego de S. Theresa quotes the letter in full, presumably with much relish:

> Dear Father Prior of Butuan,
>
> It is not possible that the heart of your Reverence would be able to acquiesce to the idea that we, here at this lake, are

perishing. Your Reverence, for the love of God for whom you
have suffered so much in pacifying and subjecting this area, come
to our aid with all the forces you can muster (op. cit., p. 292)!

The letter goes on describing the despair of the Spaniards in the
war-zone and begging the addressee to forget his past grievances and
think only about the honor of God and of Spain. Which Fray
Agustin did, as appears from a letter of the Recoleto Provincial to
the King of Spain in 1654:

> "I should not withhold from you the great service which my
> Order has done to your Majesty through Fray Agustin de San
> Pedro, a member of my Order, who, together with Don
> Francisco de Atienza, Alcalde Mayor of Caraga, came very
> timely to help subdue all the villages of Lake Lanao. He himself
> paid for the sustenance of a great number of Indios whom he
> took along on that expedition from the village of Butuan where
> he was prior at that time. He made them take along boats which
> they dismantled and dragged over land. Upon arrival at the lake
> they assembled them again, and in this way they were so
> successful in their endeavors that the number of tribute payers
> was increased by more than 12 thousand" (Colin/Pastells, III,
> 714).

He paddled personally with two disguised soldiers into the
interior to contact the local chiefs and convince them to surrender,
after which he brought them to Iligan, where they swore obedience to
Spain again before the local commander.

To *El Padre Capitan* it must have appeared that he was not just
conquering Moro territory for Spain, but also recovering Jesuit-
held mission land for his order![19]

---

[19]Up to a point there is truth in what Wenceslao Retana says about the
antagonism between the two Orders: *era hija del mas laudable celo
religioso*, it was "the product of an otherwise praiseworthy religious zeal"
(*Prologo* to the Combés/Retana "Historia de Mindanao y Jolo y sus
adyacentes," p. xxix).

Fig. 19. *El Padre Capitan.* Painting in the Recollect Monastery at Marcilla, Navarra, Spain. The inscription reads:

"The venerable Father Agustin de San Pedro, Augustinian Recollect. He went to the Philippines in 1623, where he was assigned to preach the Gospel in the province of Mindanao. Here he made the missions prosper in a very short time. He founded more than 100 villages, and distinguished himself in a special way by dominating the Moro pirates who had surrounded them, so that they were much afraid of him. For that reason he earned the nickname of El Padre Capitan, under which he is known in the history of the Philippines.

To him is due the construction of the forts of Linao, Cagayan and Romblon. He died a holy death in 1653.

Fig. 20. Anonymous Map of Mindanao (1683).
Note: 1) ''La fuerza de Tada'' (the fort of Tandag); 2) The ''demarcation line'' between the mission territory of the Recoletos and of the Jesuits; 3) ''Laguna de Sapogan'' (Jabonga) = lake Mainit. (With permission of the Archivo General de Indias, Sevilla.)

X

The Revolt of Caraga, 1631

In the "Historia General..." (1681) of Luís de Jesús, Decada Quinta, p. 163ff. a relation is found of some shocking events that happened in east Davao, Surigao and Agusan in 1631. Juan de la Concepción has the same report in Vol. V of "Historia General de Philippinas" (1784) and it is also contained in the historical collection of Blair and Robertson (vol. 35).

While researching in the Recoleto archives at Marcilla, Spain, I came across a manuscript account that clearly was about the same events and had been written in Manila in 1632. The paper, however, was so damaged by age and termites and consequently the text so mutilated that hardly one fully legible sentence was left. With a bleeding heart I put it back into the Legajo from which it had come. But since it is undoubtedly the oldest existing written document exclusively dealing with eastern Mindanao, its existence and condition kept haunting me. Later, in the Augustinian library in Valladolid I came across an article in an old issue of "Archivo Historico Hispano Agustino" that according to the author was based on a manuscript with similar contents existing in the Biblioteca Nacional at Madrid. Indeed, I found there the manuscript to which the author refers (Codice 3-828). It was written, in an infuriatingly unclear hand, probably by a 19th century copyist, who took it from some original and crowded it on ten very closely spaced pages of A4 size. This text is far more detailed than any of the above-mentioned sources. There is at least one indication (as we will point out afterwards) that at the time of Luis de Jesus one more account existed of the same happenings. A comparison with the Marcilla document shows that the latter actually contains the text of the sworn and attested hearings to which we will refer at the end.[20]

For a proper understanding of the genesis and historical context of what happened in eastern Mindanao between 1629 and 1631 we must know that in 1609 the Spanish presence on the east coast (then named District of Caraga) had started with the construction of a stone-fortification at Tandag. In 1622 the Recoletos had started their systematic evangelization of the district, and in 1631 there were mission stations at Tago, Tandag, Siargao, Bacuag/Gigaquit, Jabonga, Butuan, and Linao in upper Agusan. For the subjugation of the Moros in southern and western Mindanao, the Spaniards made use of native soldiers recruited from, a.o., the Caragans of Surigao. The latter, after seeing that the Spaniards were unable to subdue the Muslim rebels although these were rather few, lost their respect for Spanish might. If such a limited number of people like the Moros could resist Castillian domination, why not they? Combés ("Historia de Mindanao y Jolo," Col. 217) puts it this way:

> "About 300 Caragans under Captain Lorenzo de Olazo had taken part in that campaign, and upon returning to their territory, they also decided to resist Spanish domination from then on. They had been the most outstanding fighters in that campaign."

---

[20] The manuscript used here is far more detailed than any other account, as we said. There are two obvious reasons for this. The first is that it was for a great deal (wholly?) written by a very involved eyewitness: Fray Lorenzo de San Facundo. The meticulous details, the abundance of names mentioned ("the new boat built by Tagpito"), the official notarization at Manila, the signatures of five witnesses from Caraga (Marcilla document) can also be explained by the fact that the purpose of the report was to prove in an intended ecclesiastical process that the four murdered Recoletos were martyrs, killed *in odium fidei* (out of hatred against the faith). For such purposes Rome has always insisted on accuracy and a great amount of informative details. See Licinio Ruiz, OAR "Sinopsis Historica" p. 329ff. To us it seems rather clear that the four were not really killed for that reason but out of hatred for contemporary Spaniards as such. It seems that such was also the final verdict of Rome (if the case ever reached there) because the four do not appear in the "Martyrologium" of the Church.

Once back home on the east coast, they took up contact with the Moros of Cotabato and Jolo to ask for their help; they promised to become their vassals and pay tribute to them. For this purpose they sent a man from Tago, Manaral, to Sultan Corralat in 1630. An agreement was reached between the two that in June 1631 the Moros would come to Caraga with a strong armada. In the meantime the Caragans themselves should already make a start with the rebellion by killing all Spaniards, including the missionaries. Above all, the fort of Tandag was to be eliminated at the proper time. Some of Corralat's spies went along to Caraga when Manaral returned home. They started surveying the territory, the harbors and rivers, and also working on the feelings of people. They paid special interest to the condition and strength of the fort of Tandag. From some Dutch records it appears that in 1630 the Dutch Governor of the Moluccas recommended to the Governor General at Batavia to give some naval assistance to the sultan of Sarangani to help the latter dislodge the Spaniards from the fort of Tandag (see R. Laarhoven: "From Ship to Shore" Manila 1985, p. 90 in the MS). At the same time the Caragans began secretly building a great number of boats all over the district. However, since this activity was going on in so many rivers and creeks, it came to the attention of the Spaniards and aroused their suspicion. Roaming soldiers of the Tandag garrison noticed shortly afterwards that all the people along the Tago river had disappeared. In the end, news was also received from some Spaniards at Cotabato about the pact which had been concluded between Corralat and the leaders of Caraga.

The first preventive steps taken were some punitive raids on individual coastal and river settlements where the Caragans had started to keep their end of the bargain with Corralat by killing or assaulting Spanish soldiers. These sorties were stepped up in 1631 when the fort commander Felipe de Lezcano, a veteran of the battlefields of Flanders, had been replaced by Captain Pedro Bautista. This new commander decided to put the garrison of Tandag on war footing. However, his raiding parties to suspected trouble spots were often so cruel and oppressive that the hostility of the natives only increased.

The hottest hearth of trouble was Baganga. On July 4, 1631 Bautista with a selected group of soldiers (in the document of the Biblioteca Nacional their names are all mentioned) set out southward to punish the troublemakers of Baganga. The parish priest of Tago, Jacinto de Jesus, went along as chaplain. All in all there were ten boats, each manned by at least one of the Spaniards, and a group of native soldiers who were in the company of their local chiefs and fighters: Mangabo, nicknamed the "crocodile of Tago" because of his size and fierceness, Adie, Osor, Pixin, Dumblag, Balintos, Samal, Dana, Dolocan, Bicoy, Gumban, and Banuy; the last mentioned was a relative of Inuc, the datu of Marihatag, who had been pacified and baptized a few years earlier.[21] Next day, upon reaching Marihatag, one of the Spanish soldiers had to be sent back to Tandag because he had become seriously ill. The trip to Baganga ("Bapangano" in the text) took eight days. Probably because the local troublemakers had meanwhile been warned, there was only a limited engagement, and in the end not more than 16 prisoners were taken to be brought to Tandag as slaves. But before the *flotilla* sailed away from Baganga, Dumblag had released seven of them without the knowledge of Captain Bautista. Upon reaching "Cheta" (Cateel) on the way back to Tandag, the captain, Fray Jacinto and three soldiers went ashore, and here the insubordination of Dumblag became known to Bautista. The latter had him put in leg-irons and court-martialed, also because there were some other complaints pending against him. The rest of the boats arrived not much later, and among the native soldiers who came ashore was Balintos, a relative of Dumblag. The prisoner complained bitterly that his tribesmen and friends permitted the Spaniards to treat him that way, and he begged Balintos to organize a group of trusted men to free him. In a subsequent surprise attack the captain, Fray Jacinto and the other Spaniards were all killed on the beach of Cateel and in the boats. This happened on July 13.

After that feat they could, of course, not return anymore to Tandag, and therefore they sneaked into the Tago river at night. There they spent three days feasting in one grand drunken orgy. They even performed a mock-mass wherein a local Christian woman, Maria Campan, acted the role of Fray Jacinto by sprinkling the attendants with "holy water." The church and the convent of Tago were ransacked and burned on July 18.

Here at Tago final plans were made to put a definite end to the Spanish occupation by killing all soldiers and priests; the places

---

[21] Inuc: not long after the construction of the fort of Tandag (1609) the Spaniards had attacked Inuc in the hinterland of Marihatag, which was his territory. He was later converted and baptized by the very first Recoletos of Tandag (see above, p. 136f.).

where this was going to be done were selected as well as the leaders and soldiers to do the job in each locality. It was agreed that everywhere they would present themselves to the people as acting on orders of Corralat, the sultan of Magindanao.

There were few inmates in the fort at the time. Somebody from Tago had warned them and they had locked themselves in. They had fired one of the mortars as a pre-arranged signal for the convent that there was danger of an attack but the missionaries were soundly asleep and did not hear it. Mangabo with his followers killed them; next the convent and church of Tandag underwent the same fate as in Tago.

Meanwhile another group under the command of Balintos sailed to Siargao in 11 boats. First they attacked Cabuntog and burned the place. Sapao escaped destruction because a local resident who happened to be the brother-in-law of Mangabo vigorously objected and told the attackers that only over his dead body could they advance against the place.

In Cabuntog they had hoped to find the local missionary, Lorenzo de San Facundo, and at least one other Spaniard, but the priest had sailed to Bacuag only two days before. The other Spaniard, however, was caught in one of the mangrove swamps where he was hiding with a boatload of rice intended for the fort of Tandag. They killed him in his boat.

Fray Lorenzo who had left the island on July 18 "in a new boat that had been made by Tagpito," arrived in Bacuag on the 19th. On the 21st the other priest, Fray Pedro de San Antonio, "the parish priest of Abucay," left in the same boat for Cebu to get provisions for the convent, and Fray Lorenzo took his place for the time being. The following Spaniards were then in Bacuag: Fray Lorenzo plus the laybrother Francisco, the tax collector Gaspar de los Reyes and his son, Sergeant Antonio Garcia del Valle, Diego del Castillo and Diego de Mesa. The sergeant and de Mesa were preparing to depart for the fort of Tandag and took leave of the rest on the bank of the "river Cayawan flowing next to Bacuag."

The son of Mangabo named Zancalan had sailed from Tago directly to Parasao (Cantilan), where all the people surrendered to him and joined the rebellion; only a few sympathizers of the Spaniards (*unos cuantos Fernandillos*) went into hiding in the mountains. Two soldiers of the fort of Tandag were stationed at Parasao and Calagdan at that time: Antonio Garcia and Cristobal Moreno. The author mentions that up to the day of his writing they had not been heard from and he presumed that they were killed. In

Cantilan, Zancalan ordered that two additional sailboats be readied and manned with some of his fighters who were to accompany him to Bacuag. They got under way to that place but after one day of traveling they went ashore somewhere near Punta Tugas, probably to spend the night. Here they were informed that the two Spaniards who were traveling from Bacuag to the fort of Tandag were in the neighborhood. They caught them unaware and attacked them with lances; after a short fight both were killed. They had been transporting quite a load in their sailboat: 50 baskets of rice, which the author of the report explains by saying "because this was the *encomienda* of Juan de Chaves."[22]

All in all 16 Spaniards had been killed thus far, of whom three were missionaries; two native servants of the latter shared their fate.

From here on we are going to listen to the text as it is found in the document of the Biblioteca Nacional, from which we obtained much of the previous information. The text was written by a man directly involved: Fray Lorenzo of Siargao, who, as we heard already, had sailed away from the island to Bacuag just before the arrival of Balintos and his raiders. We left him in Bacuag after Fray Pedro de San Antonio had departed for Cebu. This Fray Pedro is named "parish priest of Abucay" in the text. The story does not indicate where this village was located. From the context analysis it becomes clear that it cannot have been far from Bacuag. This is not much of a help in itself, however, because it is certain that in the 17th and 18th centuries Bacuag was not located where it is now, but at the site of the present Pahuntungan. To keep a long story short: It can safely be assumed that the Abucay of 1631 was located where

---

[22]From the whole story it is clear that the events took place (in Siargao, Bacuag, Cantilan, upper Agusan) at a time when the *"tributo"* in natura was being collected in the *encomiendas*. It seems not farfetched to imagine that the natives were already in a far from happy mood with so much of their rice collected and taken away, as indicated by the *"boatloads of rice"* mentioned three times in the report. We might perhaps say that the fury of the Caraga revolt was increased by previous experiences of people with the *encomenderos* during a period of about 30 years. It should also be noted that often the local parish priest was the official tribute collector: in Linao also the boat of the parish priest which was captured by the rebels, was loaded with rice.

now Placer is.[23] We give the word now to Fray Lorenzo, a very involved eyewitness.

"When hearing that the priest of Abucay, Fray Pedro de San Antonio had left two days earlier for Cebu, chief Manangalan ordered to go after him. Not sufficiently provisioned for the trip, Fray Pedro had to enter the Surigao river. Manangalan himself entered there shortly after him and sent two Indios ahead to kill him.

They went upstream and discovered the priest at the river dock[24] and said that they had come to inform him that there were

---

[23] The terminology "prior of Abucay" indicates that at the time in question it was a place with a resident parish priest. We should, however, not forget that in 1631 the Recoletos were still experimenting to find the best places for some permanent mission centers. Elsewhere we find that shortly before our story, Fray Pedro de San Antonio was "parish priest of Dinagat" for one year (1629).

Where was this Abucay located? It was not Gigaquit, which is known by its own name in the earliest Recoleto reports since 1622. Neither was it the present Surigao, because "the river of Surigao" is, in our document, mentioned as distinct from Abucay. The map of Murillo Velarde has an Abucay near the outlet of the present Lake Mainit. The first Manila edition of this map was printed in 1734; I do not know if Abucay was then already on it; it is in the 1744 Manila edition and also in an undated French copy presently in the State Archives in The Hague, Holland. Also a map by Francisco Alegre (1751), which is in the British Library in London, places an Abucay in the same location, but then as an islet in the mouth of that outlet (which makes one suspect that Alegre had the situation at the mouth of the Agusan river in mind). The Abucay in both maps cannot have been our place in question, because the river outlet (Sampongan, Jabonga) is afterwards again mentioned in opposition to "our" Abucay. At present there is an Abucay about halfway between Placer and Bacuag, but it cannot have been the location of 1631 because it is not near the seashore. There is one Recoleto report mentioning a "bay of Abucay" in the general area, which would seem, after all, to point to the present Placer, a conclusion that fits all written reports.

[24] "'the river dock'"; Luis de Jesus, op. cit., p. 166 specifies: "the river dock of Diego Amian" and also gives the additional information that the name of the killer was Malagoy. This shows that at his time of writing (1681) there were more original reports about these events.

enemies in Abucay. While talking to him, they pierced him with
a lance and took away everything he had with him and returned
to Abucay.

Meanwhile the traitor Zancalan, who was traveling with
two boatloads of his people, had made up his mind to proceed to
the village (= Bacuag) with twelve Indios and his wife
Geronima Moag.

On the feastday of St. Magdalene, July 22, I said Mass,
which was attended by all the Spaniards. Afterwards, I was
surprised that there were so many people in the village, and I
asked who they were. They told me that those were the son and
the daughter-in-law of Mangabo, who had come to visit their
relatives, and that put me at ease. Next, during a drinking spree
Zancalan told them what he had come for on orders of his father
Mangabo. They listened with much approval to his proposals,
but during their deliberations it was remarked that we were
many, namely two friars and three other Spaniards; therefore it
was decided that they should take utmost care in killing us.

At ten o'clock two fighters threw themselves on Diego del
Castillo and stabbed him four times with their daggers (*iguas*).
Next, during siesta time they killed the collector Gaspar de los
Reyes and his son while they were sleeping. In spite of the fact
that everybody in the village, big and small, knew about that
treachery, there was nobody who warned us.

At about two o'oclock I had the bell rung for the Vespers.
Then the *cantores* brought a woman for burial and I performed
the ceremonies, after which I sat down under the house where
11 *pandais* (carpenters) were working. Zancalan arrived with
seven of his men; he kissed my hand and asked how I was, after
which he went upstairs to see the house. While they were going
up, one of the *pandais* said: "Father, look what a big group of
people, what do they want upstairs?" I told them that they just
wanted to see the house. After that I also went upstairs to talk to
them, and I said: "Well, datu, what about it? What do you
think of this house?" "It is very good" he answered. Then
he turned around and said something to one of the servants
which I did not understand. At the same moment one of them
attacked me from behind and said, "Stab him!" The boy,
whose name was Nicolas, shouted: "You rogues, you will kill
the priest?" They stabbed him twice in the stomach so that his
intestines came out; however, he lived long enough to make
his confession afterwards. Aware of their treachery, I was able

to shake off the Indio who was holding me by banging him against a post. Then I ran to the window of the room to jump from there into a ditch, but while I jumped, one of them pushed me and I landed on the ground hitting a rough piece of wood and sprained my back. There was a real riot in the house, and they came out with lances and shields. In spite of my pain I stood up, got into the sacristy, sprinted through the church and started to run to the landing place at the river. My plan was to go hiding in the woods, but then I saw that three men armed with lances were coming after me. A Chinese carpenter named Aingo was running ahead of me together with a Ginbano Indio (= from Jolo) who had a machete; he gave it to me and said: ''Take it, Father, and see to it that they will not kill you.'' I saw that one of the three who ran after me, came near; the other two had stayed behind, one to kill the Indio, the other the Chinese. I turned upon the lone man, but he threw a lance at me which passed through my cassock and cut the right leg of my trousers, but because I had jumped aside, I escaped being hurt. With that lance and the machete I ran back to the house, where brother Francisco was defending himself with a lance which they had thrown at him. When I was about to enter the house, Zancalan came outside with his lance and shield to finish me off, and because he was at the point of striking out at me, I wanted to flee, but then I saw that two out of a group of three men came at me. I aimed my lance at Zancalan, and he took to flight, after which I got inside the house. The Indios, although they were more than one hundred, seeing that we fought with determination, turned around and started to run to the boathouse where they stayed together. When I noticed that the Spaniards had not come to our defense, it dawned on me that they had killed them.

So, there we were, with the whole population of the village against us, notably Manangalan, Alindahao and Cagaom with us inside the house were only a sea gypsy, who was our houseboy and whose name was Reyes, and a little *cantor* from Caolo (Siargao) named Olandos. It was clear to me that if they attacked a second time, they would certainly kill us, because the house was completely open, or they might set the house on fire and let us be burned inside. For that reason we decided to send the houseboy to ask them what they had in mind, and tell them that, if necessary, we would die fighting; we also told them that if they wanted to plunder, they should give us a boat so that we could get away to safety. They told us that we should surrender our weapons, and that they would absolutely not kill us, but would give us a boat so that we could get away. We had decided that we would not hand over our weapons, but then we saw that they had three firearms, which they had stolen from the Spaniards whom they had killed. That discouraged us, and we notified them that we would surrender our weapons, provided they would not kill us and give us a boat. They swore to do so, and told us to go to the beach where a boat would come in which we could get away. But that was a lie; they even took away the clothes which we had put on when leaving the convent. On the advice of the villagers we retired to a small hut, scantily dressed. Then they started to plunder the house of the collector and the convent; in all there were 1,200 baskets of rice and more than 600 gold and silver pesos, not to mention the clothes. The statues were submitted to numberless outrages; they even challenged them saying that, since they were the gods of the Spaniards, they should fight with them. They dismembered the bigger ones, cutting off the arms, hands, feet and heads, especially of Our Lord Crucified, after which they threw the holy relics on a garbage heap. In the end, everything had been profaned and plundered. Finally, I decided to call chief Zancalan, and asked him why he had not done what he had promised, namely, to give us a boat wherein we could get away. He answered that undoubtedly the others would kill him if he let us free; therefore he really could not do it. In the two days while we remained in that situation, we did not even see a single Indio from the village who did not come to curse or ridicule us or scoff at us, foremost among them those to whom we had done most good. Time and again I had to hear: ''Those men there, why do they keep them alive? Why don't they kill them?'' Since we knew that already three priests and one servant had been killed, we were sure they would kill us too; therefore my companion and I used our time to thank God who had delivered us up to that fate.

On Friday, July 25, on the feast of St. James, they told us to get into a boat, and we left for Tago. Under way some very dangerous things happened to us, but the worst was what occurred on Sunday night near Punta Cawit. There we saw 11 boats, which were those that had come from the island of Siargao, coming at us like arrows. Zancalan told us to hide under the stern-awning of the sailboat. When they were close, they started greeting each other exuberantly, invoking their *diwatas*, and their leaders went inside the bow-awning to talk with our boss. He informed them that he had us on board still alive. At that Dumblag started to shout with happiness, because now he had somebody to kill. ''Quick, give me my lance,'' said one; ''my dagger,'' said another. What a hand clapping and shouting ensued then! ''Bring us one, so we can let him feel a dagger,'' some said; ''no,'' our boss answered, ''because then the whole boat will be spattered with blood; let us bring them on land and do it there.'' ''No,'' again another said, ''we are so many of us, let us make food out of them.'' There was one who asked: ''Let us offer at least one now to the *diwata!*''

O, what turmoil gripped my soul when I heard all that! I did not know how to compose myself before God, and have to admit that I lost my mind for a while, but then I pulled myself together with such vigor that I could ask the Divine Spirit for love and strength and my patron San Lorenzo to let me share the deep aversion for false gods which he had known; and then I felt that my fear, sweat and agony had disappeared, and I experienced such a new joy and comfort that it seemed to me they could not call us soon enough. Brother Francisco afterwards confessed that he had felt the same.

The result of their deliberation was that we should first go to Tago; there they would have a big celebration to their *diwata*, and then they would sacrifice both of us. With that they returned all to their own boats and we were told to come out of our hiding place, which we did. They gave us so much food that we had never eaten with so much gusto until then. Opon and his son Adie stayed with us; on my part I felt sad when seeing myself deprived of the hope for the chance of serving and praising God in a death which I thought already so sure. But at the same time I denounced such enormous sins and asked God to enlighten them and forgive them. One thing was sure: the fruit was not yet ripe and worthy for God's table.

So we sailed on to Tago, traveling with high spirits because we hoped that upon our arrival we would see ourselves in prison, and that, as they had decided a while ago, we would then go to rejoice in God.

Finally, we arrived in the afternoon of Monday, which was the 28th. Zancalan stepped on land and went to talk to his father Mangabo to tell him that he had brought us alive.

But God had changed Mangabo's hatred into love! He

stepped immediately in a *baroto* and came to our boat, where he told me to sit down. Then he fell on his kness, kissed my feet much against my will, and then my hands; he did the same to the brother, to the great astonishment of the others. He embraced us and told us to listen to him. Then he told us the reason for the killing of the captain and other Spaniards and the priests. He had only very flimsy reasons, exonerating himself and carefully putting the blame on others. Then he asked for a knife, lowered his trousers which had been made from an altar-cloth of colored and embroidered damask, which he had stolen in Tandag. He made two cuts in the skin of his lower stomach; he drew some blood and told his son to gather it with his finger and put it in a kind of hat filled with wine. Then he began to swear and invoke his *diwata* with such an extreme shouting that even the river got scared. He called all kinds of curses upon himself if he failed to be our friend and protector, even if it cost him his life. After drinking from the wine, he put the hat on, shouted with an extremely loud voice "*tigbabagna*," embraced me and put his red turban on my head. That was the conclusion of the "*sandugo*" oath, which they consider inviolable.

Nevertheless, a serious quarrel developed about the matter, because Dumblag and some others asked for at least one of the religious to be killed. However, Mangabo said that he was not going to do so, as he had sworn to protect them; if they liked to fight about it, they could do so! It still took a lot of debating before they decided to go to sleep.

Then came the morning of the 29th, and they started to quarrel again. But then Mangabo took his dagger and wanted to start a fight, telling them to get into a boat and disappear from the river. Dumblag did so, but he was spitting fire.

Mangabo brought us to his house, took some Spanish wine for us — to the others who were more than 100 he just gave some *tuba*. We asked for two cups to drink from, and they brought us two chalices, one from Tandag and the other from Bacuag. When I saw them, I threw myself on them and covered them again with the cloth in which they had come. I told him "My father Mangabo, for the love which you have for me and I for you, I beg you not to use these chalices, not to touch them and not allow them to be touched by a woman in labor." Tears came out of my eyes, and everybody was astonished.

"Well, it shall be as you say, son" he said. He stood up,

fetched a Christ-image of gold-plated bronze, which his son Zancalan had taken away from me because he thought that it was of gold, and said: "Here you have that God which I kept to bring it to Manila when we will go there together." But I answered him: "Keep it, may it help you when you honor it, but if you don't, it will put you to shame; remember, it is the God of heaven and earth, my Lord Jesus Christ."

Later came also the aforementioned Maria Campan, and she brought me a Japanese wooden box with some holy oil stocks in it, which she said came from Tago. I opened it and saw that nothing had been taken out. I tore a piece from the cloth that I was wearing around my neck, wrapping them inside and knotting it; I told her not to open it and not to take anything out; I would give her six pesos to get it back, although the metal was not even worth four. She promised to keep it well. But of course, I could not get back any of those items because I did not have even one cent.

Later, after all these things had happened, Mangabo came to see me again and said: "Son, I have seen that you are sick; if you like to go to the fort of the Spaniards, I will have you brought there, on condition that the Brother will stay here to help us if the Spaniards come. Remember your father Mangabo and help him as much as possible." I answered him that I appreciated very much what he had done. He kept his word, and they put me in a boat in which they brought me to the fort where I am now. I have the church ornaments and the chalice of Tandag, but no Mass wine or hosts to say Mass as a first thank-offering to God's goodness for such a great benefit as having given me life among so many deaths and delivering me from such great dangers."

The Brother was afterwards ransomed for money, as the author mentions; he also says that there were still many other things that had happened and were presently going on, but not wishing to be longwinded, he would rather omit them.

The Surigao rebels understood only too well that even if their revolt had been successful on the east coast, without the support of the Agusan tribes theirs would be no more than a precarious and narrow foothold. In case of a Spanish counter-attack, which was to be expected, they would have very little friendly hinterland to escape into; and if the Spaniards should succeed in gaining active sympathy and support in the Butuan area and in the Agusan valley, the free Caragans would soon find themselves between two fires. Of course, they did have the sympathy of Sultan Corralat, but Cotabato was far away, in the first place. In the second, it seems that the cunning sultan would rather let Caraga first fight for its territory before spending his own men and material for their benefit and expose himself to another Spanish attack from Zamboanga. After all, his territorial interests did not really go beyond Cateel.[25]   In short, for the Tandag-Tago rebels it was at least as important to have a good neighbor in Agusan as a sympathizing friend in Cotabato.

In 1631 there were Recoleto churches and convents at Butuan, Jabonga and Linao. The latter place was far up the river in the interior. Balintos, the man who had killed Captain Bautista, decided to go to this place first. Upon reaching the Agusan river over land, he also sent some messengers with letters downstream to Butuan to rouse the sympathy of the leaders there. He himself went upstream to Linao with the intention of killing the local missionary, Fray Juan de San Agustin. In the river-villages which he passed, many people joined him when told that Corralat with three hundred boats was standing by near the coast ready to attack all those who did not

---

[25] See the letter of Father Pedro Gutierrez, SJ (Zamboanga, September 30, 1638): "He [Corralat] does not wish to fight with the Spaniards; on the other hand he makes impertinent demands, namely, that the country from Sibuguei to near Cateel and the lake of Malanao, be left to him" (Blair & Robertson 29, p. 147).

As late as 1700 a similar "demand" can be found in a document of the Dutch VOC (United East India Company: "Logbook of Captain Paulus de Brievings and Ensign Jacob Cloeck about their voyage from Ternate to Mindanao..." June 15, 1700 till January 14, 1701). The document is in the State Archives at The Hague, Holland. It contains a.o. a list of Maguindanao settlements and the number of able-bodied men living there plus the names of their rulers. For "Caragan" we find: the king is named Maninkabu; there are 1000 able-bodied men. A note adds: "At Caragan ends the domain of the Maguindanao *keyser* (chief) at this side of the island, and that of the Spaniards begins."

For "Samboangan" a note is added: "Here ends the domain of the Maguindanao *keyser* and starts that of the Spaniards."

See: R. Laarhoven: "From Ship to Shore: Maguindanao in the 17th century, from Dutch sources," (Manila, 1985) pp. 467-468 of the manuscript.

declare themselves in rebellion against the Spaniards. *Hic et nunc*, that revolt would mean: killing the Spanish missionaries.

Once in Linao, they told the priest that they had come on orders of the captain of the Tandag fort to help thwart an attack which Corralat was going to launch via the river from Cotabato. But in secret he told the local leaders what were his real intentions. For two days he worked on their feelings, cajoling and threatening, but he was unable to convince any of them to be his accomplices in the killing of their priest. Finally, fearing for his own safety, he angrily started downriver again, northward to Butuan. Not far away from Linao they met the river boat of the priest, which was loaded with rice. They stole it and took the four servants of the priest prisoners. This news reached Linao that same day and roused the deep anger of the local leaders. Fearing for the safety of the missionary, they brought him to Butuan under armed protection. Let us again follow the text of the Madrid document.

> "The letters of Balintos for the leaders of Butuan had arrived there on the feastday of St. James, July 25. They were read in the presence of the people. Once informed about what had happened on the east coast and what Balintos expected from them, they all unanimously declared that they would rather die than consent that the Fathers be harmed or even the very cloth of their dresses damaged. While the Fathers were at table, they all came to the convent in a dense crowd, bringing the letters along and also the messengers. The letters were read, and after the Fathers had heard the contents, they said: Children, here we are, do with us what you like, since it is the will of God Our Lord. They all started shouting and crying that the Fathers should take courage, because they would rather die than permit that anyone harm them. This they did with so many oaths and so insistently that nobody would believe it who had not seen it.
>
> From that day on, none of the local leaders, their wives, and children included, left the convent. In this way, the Fathers felt quite safe, but nevertheless, one of them proceeded to Cebu to report the happenings in Surigao and the worrisome situation in the whole district....
>
> The loyalty of the Butuanos became known to the rebellious villages, and their leaders started making plans of their own to kill the priests of Butuan and force the people to join them. The biggest instigator of all was Manangalan, the chief of Abucay. He came to Sampongan (Jabonga) to talk the matter over with

the people there, many of whom found it a good plan. For the execution of it they selected an Indio who was well acquainted with the Fathers; they gave him careful instructions about what he had to do, and promised him a big reward. The name of this Indio was Sumalay, and he came to Butuan with the intention of killing the Fathers there. Upon his arrival he started spreading the news that the sultan of Mindanao was at the east coast and had already put up a stronghold in Surigao for the defense of the district. He thought that now the people of Butuan would feel obliged to kill the Fathers. But they swore unanimously that they were prepared to withstand any enemy who might come to their village. To make sure that the Fathers would be safe, they fetched them and brought them to a hiding place in the forest, while they themselves manned the stronghold which they had built in their village.

The scheming Indio of Jabonga seeing that his cunning and lies did not have the desired effect, decided to execute the plan himself. And so he went to the place where the missionaries were hiding, with the intention of killing them. But they discovered him, and because he was behaving so nervously and was found to be armed with a dagger, they suspected him of evil intentions. They stayed away from him and informed the village leaders. These got hold of him and put him under guard in the stockade. There they forced him to divulge the truth of the matter, that he had come to kill the priests on order of Manangalan and his companions. In spite of what he had done, they spared his life. One thing is very sure: if the Butuanos had not been so faithful and loyal, all the Religious would have been killed.

Thanks to the example of Butuan, some villages have remained friendly to us.

To the Butuanos is due the conservation of what is still intact.''

After the arrival of Fray Jacinto de San Fulgencio, who had gone to Cebu to inform the authorities there about the developments in Caraga, an attack fleet was mustered. On August 1 it sailed from Cebu to the rebellious district, with Fray Jacinto coming along as chaplain. The fleet consisted of four ships and was under the command of Captain Juan de Chaves, the *encomendero* of the district of Bacuag. This puts some aduitional light on the information given by Luis de Jesus in his "Historia General"; "they anchored first before Bacuag." We can imagine the feelings of Fray Jacinto who nine years earlier had started his missionary career at this very spot.

From Bacuag they sailed southward to Tandag, and while rounding Punta Cawit at night, they were spotted by a flotilla of enemy boats that were on their way for a raiding visit to Leyte. Recognizing the Spanish ships, they returned to the various rivers from which they had sailed out.

> "This became known through a servant of those who had wanted to capture the missionary of Linao, Fray Juan de San Agustin. They had taken him along as a spy on the planned Leyte raid. Upon their forced return he saw a chance to escape and is now in Butuan.
>
> Many of the rebels died of hunger in the forests where they had fled after hearing that a punitive fleet had arrived. Others, who also would have perished of want because of lack of food, surrendered voluntarily to the Spaniards. The most guilty ones were punished, others were made slaves, and the rest were given a general amnesty.
>
> After that, the district settled back into the peaceful existence wherein it had been before, and the churches and convents were rebuilt.
>
> Of all these happenings an authentic report was made before Bishop Pedro de Arce of Cebu, with five witnesses who had come to Manila from Caraga, and were present to prove that it had happened *in odium fidei*, ("out of hatred of the faith") and said that the people were settling to a peaceful life again as it had been before, and that the Religious were ministering to it as usual.
>
> Done in Manila on July 3, 1632, and attested to by Andres de Zarate, Secretary and Apostolic Notary of this city, and certified by Alonzo Gomez, Royal Scribe, and Alonso Baeza del Rio, Public Secretary, and Sebastian Zambrano, Secretary of His Majesty, residing in the said city of Manila, *sede vacante.*"

About this notarization Luis de Jesus says in 1681 ("Historia...," Decada V, Ch. 7, p. 173) that of the original report two authorized copies were made. One was sent to the Royal Council of the Indies in 1635; the other was kept in the archive of the Order in the convent of Madrid. The latter is most probably the copy presently in the

Marcilla archive.

As we said in the beginning, the document at Marcilla consists of this sworn statement of the hearings just mentioned.

Five days after the date of this account, on July 8, 1632, Governor General Juan Niño de Tavora wrote the following letter to Philip IV in Spain:

> ''The inhabitants of Caraga revolted, as I mentioned in my former report, after killing the captain commander with twenty soldiers in an expedition that he made. Thinking that they could gain the fort by force, they came to it, but it did not fall out as they imagined. The greater part of the province rose, and they killed four Discalced Religious of the Recoletos. A severe punishment was inflicted upon them in the month of September, and recently, in the month of May just passed, another fleet went there to punish and resettle them. I trust that, with the help of Our Lord, they will remain quiet, although they are not Christians; there is little confidence to be placed in them'' (Blair & Robertson 24, p. 216).

I was not able to locate the "former report" to which de Tavora refers in the Sevilla archives where the just quoted letter is found. There is, however, one more letter, wherein the Governor General complains about his weakness and worsening health. He died two weeks after signing the previous letter, on July 22nd, 1632.

From the biography of a great missionary of those days and places, Fray Jacinto de San Fulgencio, it appears that even after the expedition of Captain de Chaves had ended its punitive mission, the east coast of Mindanao was far from quiet. Fray Jacinto was assigned to Tandag in 1635 *"a tiempo que la quietud era nulla"*: at a time when there was trouble everywhere in the district, as Luis de Jesus says. The atmosphere had become very tense again after the Mandayas had killed another fort commander of Tandag, Captain Juan de Heredia. Especially the southern end of Caraga was a trouble spot for the Spaniards. The village chiefs in the Baganga area misled the new commander Gonzalo Portillo into believing that the killers of de Heredia were from the Tagabalooy Mandayas in the hinterlands of Hinatuan, Bislig and Lingig. They proposed to join the Spanish soldiers to penetrate with them the rivers and forests of the Tagabalooyes, but their secret intention was to ambush the Spanish detachments one by one. However, when Commander Portillo was ready with his own soldiers, the Baganga warriors failed to show up. The captain therefore decided to send a good friend of the Spaniards to Baganga: Dacsa, who already in 1623 had helped them to avenge the killing of a Recoleto by Datu Suba. It was Dacsa who found out the plot hatched at Baganga. Warned by him, Portillo played the same game with the chiefs of Baganga, whom he was able to disarm and bring to Tandag as prisoners. Four of them were hanged and the rest condemned to become galley slaves or go into exile outside the district.

As could be expected, the result was a continuous spiral of violence. Upon his arrival, Fray Jacinto de San Fulgencio found that on the east coast *"todo era un desorden tumultuoso"*: it was one great upheaval everywhere. Nearly all the village chiefs had absconded to the mountains and forests, and in the settlements the atmosphere was edgy and loaded with fear. The same was true in the fort of Tandag, according to *cronista* de Jesus. This can also be gleaned from a letter written in 1637 by Father Juan Lopez, the superior of the Jesuit residence at Cavite. In this letter Lopez writes a.o. about some events that had occurred in Caraga "last year in the month of September." It appears that the fort commander of Tandag, Gonzalo Portillo, had been succeeded by Juan Nicolas Godino. In September 1636 he went on another punitive expedition against "tributaries of Cachil Corralat." This seems to point to the Caraga-Baganga area, which Corralat considered part of his dominion, up to Cateel. Obviously, some remnants of the 1631 revolt were still active in the southern Caraga region. There was an encounter with six of their war boats close to the shore; the vessels were sunk or captured but most of the occupants escaped to land, where subsequently one village was ransacked and put to the torch. Upon his return to Tandag, Godino's boats were filled with captured loot and 120 prisoners. Among the dead left behind was Dumblag, whom we have met at the outbreak of the 1631 rebellion on the beach of Cateel. Balintos, who had killed Captain Pedro Bautista on that occasion, was now one of the prisoners brought to the fort of Tandag.

Peace returned only very slowly to southern Caraga, not through soldiers, arms and punishment, but through the missionary methods of Fray Jacinto and his companions.

XI

Help! The Dutch Are Coming!

"The years passed by, entwined with many events, some friendly, some adverse. This world, being the vale of tears which it is, gave its favors with a stingy hand, and its burdens with prodigal liberality, especially in the years 1646 and 1647, when the Dutch were the rulers of the seas" (Diego de S. Theresa "Historia General..." Decada 7, p. 135).

At the time when the Spanish hegemony in the Philippines was becoming a reality, Holland was fighting its so called "Eighty Years War" (1568-1648) to shake off Spanish domination in the Low Countries of Europe. While they were imposing their own occupational rights on large areas of Indonesia and preparing to drive the Spaniards out of the rest of that archipelago, an important part of the Dutch-Spanish conflict was being fought in Malucan and Philippine waters. Already in 1621 the archbishop of Manila could write to the King in Spain:

"The most powerful cause, then, that destroys and consumes the Indians of Philipinas is the same one that has destroyed and consumed the Spaniards. All have been ruined by the continual and large fleets with which the Dutch enemy persecutes us; and our forces are too few to oppose them, as I have stated in other letters that I have been writing to Your Majesty. It is impossible to prevent us all from suffering and even perishing very speedily, if Your Majesty's most powerful hand does not help and defend us. Consequently, Sire, I consider as inexcusable the vexations that have come and are coming upon the Indians in the building of ships and the making of other preparations to defend us. For these would be very much less if the Indians were paid for their work as Your Majesty orders, if they were placed in charge of disinterested persons, and if compassion were shown them'' (Blair & Robertson 20, p. 245).

It was the time of the battles between Dutch and Spanish naval forces, of which the yearly *La Naval* procession in Manila reminds us till today. The seas around the archipelago had become so unsafe that most of the ships stayed inside harbors and rivers. Inter-island commerce came practically to a standstill. What traveled from island to island were rumors and fear. Aside from harassing Spanish ships on the seas between Aparri and Jolo, the Dutch made secret contacts through local emissaries with many tribal chiefs all over the islands. They promised to free them from the Spaniards if they rose against them in their respective areas. Out of fear of a Dutch invasion — which indeed had been blueprinted — Don Diego Fajardo de Tenza, the Governor-General, started gathering information about the condition of harbors, ships, rivers and military strongholds, ordering that suspected sympathizers of the Dutch be rounded up to suppress any real or imagined local attempts at uprising. Feverish shipbuilding activity was started in Cavite and Oton, and for this purpose all over the country forced labor — especially carpenters — was being recruited and brought to the shipyards of Iloilo and Cavite. With all that force used on people and the resulting local disruption and dislocation, the promises of the Dutch became of course more and more enticing.

In the district of Caraga the Alcalde Mayor of Tandag started his own reign of terror. The superior of the Recoleto convent at Tandag, Fray Pedro Roxas, took up the cudgels for the oppressed natives. Let us listen to the poetical language of Diego de Santa Theresa:

   ''As a teacher, he had to aid the Indios with the doctrine, and as a Father he had to look after their protection. Seeing his faithful persecuted by injustice and oppression, he felt obliged to go against the excesses of the Alcalde. Fray Pedro looked at his people in Tandag and the *visitas,* burdened by impossible obligations, and he saw that they were suffering such deep sorrow that their weeping did not even dare rise from the heart to the eyes, and their bosoms could not thrust their respiration to the lips. He noticed that the more they had to sacrifice for the greed of others, the less zealous they became to live in accordance with Catholic principles. Since there was nobody who would speak up for the Indios if his zealous minister did not open his mouth, he decided to take some effective steps for them'' (op. cit., p. 135).

Seeing all his admonitions and petitions unheeded at Tandag, he decided to take the matter to the highest authority in Manila. At that time the church and convent of Tandag were located very near the fort, obviously to prevent such disasters as had happened in 1631. Now it was going to be this proximity that would cause a tragicomical state versus church conflict. The Alcalde, peeved because of Fray Pedro's report to Manila, wished to avenge himself and sent a communication of his own to Governor General Fajardo de Tenza. Therein he stressed that the fort of Tandag in itself was strong enough to withstand any Dutch attack. But the trouble — so he stated — was that its strength was weakened, strategically speaking, by the proximity of a church and a convent made of strong materials. If these buildings were ever occupied by an enemy, the latter could entrench himself there and have a stronghold of his own right next to the ramparts of the fort. Therefore, so the Alcalde informed Manila, the church and convent should be demolished. Let us give the word to chronicler Fray Diego again:

"In Manila the Governor called a meeting of the auditors, judges and other officials of the Royal Treasury, and on the 19th of December (1647) they passed a general order to all the Alcaldes Mayor that stone churches and convents along the seashores should be demolished. The reason given was that if the Dutch succeeded in capturing them in their invasions, they could use them as strongholds enabling them to continue their raids with greater persistency. By that time, the mentioned captain — whose name is omitted for a special reason — had been withdrawn from Tandag; in his place had been appointed Don Juan Garcia; his appointment fell at the same time when the order from the Royal Audiencia in Manila was received. The

latter called a meeting of the captains Juan de Sabata and
Marcos de Resines, also summoning Sargento-mayor Don
Andres Curto and the former Alcalde Mayor of Tandag;
nobody knew yet that he had sent the aforementioned report''
(loc. cit., p. 136).

The consensus of that meeting was that in case of necessity (if the
Dutch really came) it would take only about six hours to burn the
church and convent and tear them down, because the walls were of a
very soft kind of stone and the roof was of nipa. So, why destroy
them already now, while the possibility of a Dutch attack was just
that: a possibility? It was also feared in Tandag that the native
population of the village would run away to the mountains to avoid
being forced afterwards to work in the construction of a new church
and convent. Therefore, so the meeting decided, the demolition
should be postponed for the time being. (This could well be an
indirect indication of just how spontaneously the Tandaganons had
assisted at the first construction!)

The minutes of that meeting were sent to Manila. Governor
General Fajardo was struck by the contradiction between the two
reports from Tandag, the former Alcalde saying that it was very
important to demolish the church and convent because they were
very strong and located too close to the fort, while the second said
that it was not really necessary to destroy them, because they were
not much of a hazard, and also because there was the possibility of a
revolt by the natives.

Obviously, fear of a Dutch invasion was more keen in Manila
than in Tandag. Therefore, the first report of the unnamed Alcalde
prevailed, and a decree was sent to Tandag to demolish the church
and the convent.

''This was done right away but everybody was very sad
about it; the religious as well as the Indios hung their heads over
such a dictatorial decree. That was how malice had its way and
vengeance its satisfaction, but also an Order so meritorious was
being disregarded. Nevertheless, although its members had
reason enough to be angry, they never said a word about it. In
their conversations with the natives they persuaded them not to
run away to the mountains'' (loc. cit.).

We will do well to remember that a demolition like this one did
not only happen at Tandag, but also elsewhere. It may therefore

be doubted that the resentment of the local commander had such a strong bearing on the developments as the account makes it appear. One place where the parish buildings had to disappear for being strategic hazards was Abucay; this was not the Abucay of the previous chapter but an identically named village in the present province of Bataan.

Although fear of a Dutch invasion was all-pervading in the Philippines, the missionaries of Tandag proceeded with the rebuilding of their church and convent. Years ago it had been built five kilometers away from the fort, for pastoral reasons. Then it was moved close to the fort, for reasons of safety. This time, for reasons of safety of a different kind, it was again located at some distance from the fort!

Fray Pedro, after all his attempts to protect the Indios and after losing the battle against Spanish attitudes at Tandag and Manila, left for re-assignment in Luzon, but he died in Manila one year later. He was 39 years old. If he had stayed alive for two more years, he might have died of shock and anger in 1653 when the provincial superior of the Recoletos received a letter from the Royal Court of Spain, from which it appeared that certain people had given the King a false picture of the reaction of the Tandag missionaries against the demolition of their parish buildings. That Royal letter deserves to be quoted in full.

> "Venerable and devout Father Provincial of the Augustinian Recollects of the Philippine Islands,
>
> It has been learned in my Royal Council of the Indies from letters of the Royal Audiencia in the city of Manila, that, in virtue of a resolution taken by the Council of War and Treasury of those islands certain strong churches in the islands were ordered to be demolished, such as those of Abucay, Marinduque and Caragha, so that they would not be seized by the enemy, as those edifices were a notorious menace and peril to the islands after the Dutch had attacked Cavite.
>
> It was learned that, although the church of Caragha was indeed demolished, it was only done after the greatest opposition from the Religious of Your Order who are established in those missions. The Father Instructor of the Indios there threatened that the Indios would revolt, as happened later. For the villages did rise in revolt and the Indios took to the mountains, thereby occasioning the many and serious troubles that demand attention. The matter having been examined by my

Royal Council of the Indies, it has been deemed best to warn you how severely those proceedings by the Religious of the said Order have been censored, so that, being warned thereof, you may correct them and improve them, in order that the Religious may restrain themselves in the future and not give occasion to the natives to become restless. For they are under the strictest obligation to do the contrary, and they ought to have taken active part in calming the Indios and restraining them if they believed that they were attempting any unwanted movement. The care and watchfulness of the officials cannot suffice if the Religious of the missions fail to aid them in their dealing with the natives.

I trust that you will pay attention to correct this matter from now on. For besides the fact that this is in harmony with your obligation and with the example that the Religious ought to give to others because of their rules, I shall consider myself well served by you.

Madrid, May 27, 1651
I, the King''

To which our chronicler caustically remarks: "It cannot be denied that the terms of that Royal letter could serve even the most austere man for no mean amount of exercise in mortification!" (op. cit., p. 137). [26]

---

[26] In 1642 Governor Sebastian Hurtado de Corcuera had ordered all the buildings in Bagumbayan (just outside the Walled City) to be torn down for fear of the Dutch who might garrison them in case of an invasion. Among those buildings were the convent and the church of the Recoletos. In spite of the efforts of the Religious to save them, they were demolished and a fort was built on the same lot! The Order refused the 4000 pesos offered by the Governor, saying that their possessions were worth more than 50 thousand pesos. This action of the Governor was part of the packages of charges raised against Corcuera when Governor Diego Fajardo filed a case against him and had him imprisoned for five years. He had to pay the Order 25 thousand pesos in damages. The fort was then demolished and a new church and convent erected on the lot.

The unhappy fate of the Bagumbayan church was shared by those of Ermita, Malate, Parañaque, Dilao, Binondo and Santa Cruz.

It is remarkable how many lines were written by Recoleto chronicles of that time to prove the innocence of the ministers in the matter of local uprisings in Caraga, and on illustrating how, on the contrary, they had acted as very obedient and loyal servants of the

---

The Dutch did not invade either Manila or Tandag, but Abucay in Bataan was less lucky. After a fierce battle by 600 Pampango troops in Spanish service, the Spanish commander decided to surrender inside the stone convent, instead of retreating to the hinterland and take a new stand there, as the two missionaries of Abucay wanted him to do. A large number of the surrendering Pampangos were cruelly massacred by the invaders; the commander and the two missionaries were shipped off to imprisonment in Batavia (Jakarta). The Dutch stayed for some months in the coastal villages of Bataan, practically in sight of Manila. Like the Recoletos, the Provincial of the Dominicans received a reprimanding letter from the King concerning the behavior of the missionaries of Abucay on that occasion. (See: Ferrando's "Historia de los Pp. Dominicos," 1870, Vol. II, p. 494ff.).

It looks as if the King was very one-sidedly informed about the complete background of the events at Tandag, Bagumbayan and Abucay, and obviously the informers were not friends of the Dominicans or the Recoletos either. These complications had a lot to do with the unpleasant relations between some Governors and (some) religious Orders. Consequently, often when reading certain interpretations given by (religious) authors about decisions made by Governors, we should remember that their reports might be slanted because of their sympathies or antipathies. On more than one occasion we will also have to keep in mind the particular religious affiliation of the author, or of the feelings of the Governor for a particular Order. The Jesuit Murillo Velarde writes with high esteem about a man such as Governor Corcuera...who was very partial towards the Jesuits. Velarde's sympathies were definitely not shared by the Dominican Ferrando!

The same unfriendly atmosphere existed between Corcuera's successor Diego Fajardo and at least the Recoletos and Dominicans; the evil right hand man of Fajardo, Venegas, made the relations even worse. Fajardo was Governor at the time of the Abucay disaster.

As for Mindanao and Caraga, to understand much of what went on in the middle of the 1700s at both sides of the missionary demarcation line, we must take into account the sympathies and antipathies of Governors Obando and Arandia in addition to the strained relations between Recoletos and Jesuits. All in all it must be said that this animosity does not belong to the better pages of the Church history of Mindanao up to the end of the previous century.

King and of the Spanish cause in Caraga and elsewhere in the archipelago. The King's reproach had obviously hurt, not only because it was undeserved; there was also the fear that their yearly rations of rice, wine and oil plus, of course, the King's stipends might be endangered, which seems to have played a not insignificant part in their extensive self-defense! Much attention is given to how in 1654 the Recoletos of Tandag were vindicated with regard to their behavior at the time of the demolition: no less than the captain of the fort of Tandag at that time, Don Juan Garcia, confirmed in Manila that the Recoletos had not lost their composure, that the natives had not fled to the mountains and that there had been no insurrection that could be attributed to the demolition order.

In 1648, at the peace treaty of Münster, eighty years of war between Holland and Spain came officially to an end. It could from now on be expected that at least some reprieve would be given also to Caraga and the fort of Tandag. However, even important news such as this travelled to the Orient at the slow speed of sailboats. And so it could happen that still in 1649 a disaster hit the Philippine economy as an indirect result of the mentioned war and the slow communications of those days. In this "Historia General de Filipinas," Tomo 9, p. XCIII, Pastells reproduces the official report of that disaster which he introduces as follows: "The calamities of the Filipino archipelago reached the limit with the loss of the galleon Encarnación."

Because of Dutch threats in the seas around the Philippines, the economy had already suffered badly. The life-line of that economy was the yearly galleon voyage between Manila and Acapulco and vv, and that life-line had been cut more than once by Dutch corsairs. In 1649 the proud trading-galleon "Encarnación" under Captain Lopez Colindrico had set out on the return voyage from Mexico to Manila. Perhaps to await confirmation about the rumored impending peace between Spain and Holland — which would make the voyage considerably safer — Colindrico had left Acapulco late, and consequently had lost the better part of the season of the *"brisas,"* the favorable winds. One morning in early 1649 the inhabitants of Baganga were watching a spectacular sight: a huge galleon had run aground at the entrance to the bay. Undoubtedly, the Mandayas whose ancestors knew what to do in such cases, were nostalgically licking their lips! But most of the voluminous cargo of the Encarnación was unloaded and safely brought to Tandag in available native vessels. On board were also six Franciscan missionaries, who stayed with the Recoletos of Tandag and afterwards traveled from there to Cebu and Manila, where they also testified that there was no truth whatsoever in the accusation that the missionaries of Tandag had instigated the natives to rebel against the demolition orders.

The galleon had been damaged when hitting the reefs off Baganga, but after some provisional repair, the captain nevertheless decided to sail her to Cavite. Caught in a typhoon she perished near Bulan, Sorsogon.

On August 4, 1650 Governor Diego Fajardo de Tenza wrote to the King that the galleon instead of sailing straight to Manila, had coursed towards the southern Philippines "so as to avoid an encounter with the Dutch enemy" near Manila. It seems not too farfetched to assume that Colindrico had had to perform some hurried emergency maneuvers to put his ship into the bay of Baganga, because beyond that point there was only unconquered Moro territory and finally the unfriendly Dutch in the Indonesian archipelago.

It has been believed on the east coast that the Encarnación sank near the coast of Caraga (Bislig, says one author in "Kinaadman" vol. IV, p. 63) and that part of the crew went to live among the Mandayas, which would have contributed to the fair complexion of many members of that tribe (evolving the Mandaya race, the author calls it). This contradicts the official version of the disaster, which speaks of reaching Baganga, being damaged and unloaded and perishing near Bulan, Sorsogon, with the crew being saved *("que fue gran misericordia de Dios que se salvase plata y gente,")* as stated in the report of Governor Fajardo de Tenza.

> "The Dutch did not appear at Tandag, and nothing was heard about them anywhere on the coast of Caraga. Therefore, Fray Pedro exhorted the faithful to help rebuild the church and the convent, and they did so, with the assistance of Bernabe de la Plaza, who then was commander of the fort. It took two years to rebuild that holy temple of God" (op. cit., p. 141).[27]

But how did the Dutch propaganda and threats affect the Spanish presence in Agusan? We have seen that, to speed up emergency shipbuilding to counteract the Dutch navy, the insular government

---

[27]For a historical outline of Dutch activities against Spain in Philippine waters, see Fernando Blumentritt's "Ataques de los Holandeses" (Madrid, 1882).

had deported laborers, especially carpenters, from all over the
country. The decree ordering them to report for work in Oton and
Cavite had not been promulgated on the east coast because the
situation was already uneasy enough there. But it did reach Agusan,
and the parish priest of Butuan had a very hard time to prevent even
the loyal Butuanos from rebelling against it. In Linao the missionary
did not succeed in quieting the agitated Manobos ruled by Datu
Dabao. Until lately, relations between the two had been quite
cordial, although it had taken Fray Agustin de Santa Maria a lot of
effort and bribery to create that entente. Dabao had even entrusted
his son to the priest to give him an education. The chronicle says that
it had always been a precarious and opportunistic kind of loyalty.
When informed about the forced-labor decree, Dabao secretly
started instigating his tribe against the Spaniards and enticing them
with promises made by the Dutch to free them from the Spaniards
and allow them to practice their old religion again. Like Balintos 20
years earlier, he told them that a whole fleet of Dutch ships was
standing by to send troops ashore who would come to their aid as
soon as they revolted and killed all the Spaniards around. Dabao was
able to assure himself of the sympathy of many Manobos and with a
clever trick he succeeded in ambushing and killing the missionary
and many of the Spanish and native soldiers of fort San Juan
Bautista. Those who survived the massacre, many of them badly
wounded, came out of their hiding places and assembled a bamboo
raft to start the torturous trip downstream to Butuan. All along the
river they were repeatedly attacked with arrows, so about halfway
they entered the Ojot, a tributary of the Agusan river, to seek the
assistance of a friendly datu named Palan. He provided them with
barotos and a protective escort all the way to Butuan.

The reaction of the Manila government was as one would expect.
A detachment of Spanish infantry under the command of Captain
Gregorio Dicastillo was directed to Butuan, where a garrison was put
up to direct the military operations against the Manobos of the
interior. They were joined very soon by the troops of Tandag under
the fort commander Bernabe de la Plaza. The chronicles speak with
considerable indignation about the subsequent pacification campaign. First, a general pardon was promised, accompanied by a
warning that those who did not surrender, would experience the full
force of the military. But of those Indios who did surrender, many
were treacherously hanged; of those who came down from the
mountains, a great many were made slaves. Some from Linao who
returned some stolen church property, hoping to save themselves this

way from punishment, were kept as slaves just the same. The account states that the oppressive manners of the Spaniards did put a halt to the uprising, but the final upshot was a deep hatred of the Manobos against them. Undoubtedly, aside from other factors, this may have been the reason why for more than 200 years no resident priest would be assigned anymore to the lonely region of upper Agusan. Only the threat of the military outpost of Linao could assure a semblance of safety for Spanish presence in the area.

> "The city of Manila and the surrounding districts were flooded with those slaves. Even the chiefs of Butuan who had been mirrors of loyalty suffered persecution, exile and imprisonment. Eventually they were able to regain their honor, but only after all their property was lost" (op. cit., p. 148-149).

It was the Recoletos of Manila who brought the plight of the many Manobo slaves to the attention of the insular government. In 1650 slavery was officially abolished. If Spanish military oppression is very much part of the history of Caraga, so is the missionary protection by the Recoletos. Even after authentic reports have been shorn of all the contemporary devotional wool in which they have been wrapped, they convey the same clear message which we heard in Tandag in 1648: "There was nobody to speak for the Indios if the missionary did not open his mouth."

The anti-slavery decree of 1650 required some court procedure for each individual slave to become a freeman. The Manobos of Caraga enslaved in Manila and environment were overjoyed at the decree,

> "but their great worry was that they had nobody to bring the matter of their freedom before the Court and pay for the expenses involved. Consequently they thought that the day of their freedom was an impossible dream. They were afraid to seek the help of the Recoletos in Manila, because they thought that the latter were angry at them for having murdered one Religious during their insurrection. But the Recoletos considered this as one of the vicissitudes of life. Therefore they took up the cudgels for the Manobos and did the utmost for their protection.
>
> Fray Agustin de San Pedro was at that time the Secretary of the Order in the Philippines. He was known under the name of Padre Capitan for his military feats and he had brought the light of the Gospel to those Manobos; for that reason they still

had much affection for him. He started to make a list of all the slaves in and around Manila with their names and surnames plus the villages where they lived. Into that list he smuggled the names of many who did not fall under the provisions of the decree of 1650. He put this list before the Governor with the request to pass an order that they should be freed. That order was promptly signed, and accompanied by the notary, Fray Agustin went to all the houses to have it put into effect.

It was very tiresome work, and it resulted in violent objections. There was hardly a house where he was not received with insults by people who had bought their slaves and were now being deprived of them. It cost him a lot of effort, but he obtained what he wanted.

All the slaves were freed, and the Order took care of them and provided them with all the necessities of life, until they could be taken to their native places. One Religious accompanied them, because it was considered necessary that there be a person to defend them in case anyone should try to do them harm'' (p. 149).

Shortly thereafter the Provincial of the Recoletos went on an inspection trip to all of Caraga, and on that occasion he also visited Linao. People had many complaints about the behavior of the soldiers, but everywhere he encountered the greatest sympathy for the missionaries. "That race is not so rude that it can not be conquered by kind acts," the author states.

It is sad to note that such protection by the missionaries was obviously still much needed in the years to come. In the Recoleto archives at Marcilla, among the documents exchanged between the civil government and the Provincial of the Recoletos, there is one of 1657:

"Order by the higher government to the Alcalde of Caraga to abstain from imposing pecuniary punishment on the natives because they are already poor and wretched. Instead, where necessary, they should apply more appropriate punishment'' (Legajo 61-1).

And in 1658:

''Instruction by Governor Sabiano Manrique de Lara to the Alcalde Mayor of Caraga against the tribute collectors of the

King's *encomiendas*, in connection with outrages committed against the Indios'' (ibid.).

It is again noteworthy that those instructions had been passed on request of the Recoleto Procurator in Manila.

XII

Baptize Now, Evangelize Later?

> "They, however, went out to preach everywhere, and the Lord worked with them, and gave strength to their word by the signs that accompanied it" (Mk. 16: 20).

The phenomenon that has been termed "instant acculturation" at the dawn of the hispanization of the Philippines, is undeniable: the sudden, often very individual but at times rather large-scale conversion to Christianity and acculturation with Spain. It is a phenomenon that will not fail to instill wonder and curiosity when one reads the early reports about the colonization of the Philippines. And the more he reads, the less he will be convinced by the often simplistic explanations stating that people were "converted by force of arms" facilitating a copious flood of baptismal water, even if he be aware of documentation like the hot-headed Cebu-declaration of 1566 which we came across in the chapter "Possessed but not Pacified." Such unorthodox "praeambula fidei" may a few times have been forced on the working of the Spirit (as in the case of the Cebu baptisms of Magellan and Legazpi) under the pressing momentary need of establishing a Spanish claim to the archipelago. But even if at times baptismal water may have flowed too quickly

and abundantly, we might perhaps — and some authors should — do
some thinking on the words of Edward Gaylord Bourne:

> "That was the way in which Christianity had been
> propagated in what are the ruling Christian nations of today.
> The wholesale baptisms have their real signification in the frame
> of the mind receptive for the patient nurture that follows.
> Christianity has made its real conquests and is kept alive by the
> Christian training, and its progress is the improvement which
> one generation makes upon another in the observance of its
> precepts" ("Historic introduction" to Blair and Robertson).

Even the great apostle of Agusan, Father Saturnino Urios (in the
1870s and 1880s), was at one time reprimanded for his "baptize now,
evangelize later" attitude. Obviously (from the results which we
witness today) the defense was in good hands.

The early Christian communities of the Thessalonians, Philip-
pians, Corinthians, Ephesians and Galatians were established by St.
Paul and a few companions in less than ten years (47-57 AD). In the
year 58 Paul considered them sufficiently Christianized to write to
Rome: "I have no more work to do here...." (Rom. 15:23), and he
moved on to other regions! Some modern missiologists (starting with
the Lutheran Roland Allen) are convinced that the later missionary
church in her first-time dealing with non-Christian peoples and
cultures has rather erred by too much than by too little missioneering. (See a.o. *Vincent J. Donovan:* Christianity Rediscovered" -
1982 - p. 32ff.) Perhaps the essential substance of the Christian
message was initially less cumbersome and complicated than it has
become in the "institutionalized" Church of later ages?

After all the allowances and qualifications, and admitting that
not a little amount of syncretism must have prevailed even long after
the baptismal water had dried up, the early years show a remarkable
number of conversions that could very well hold their own in
comparison with those appearing in European Christianity under
similar circumstances.

Historical exactness and honesty command us not to be blind to
the often tarnished image presented by the Church/State Missionary
and the Church Sedentary of the Philippines in later years when
Spain's great age of Faith had declined. But that same exactness and
honesty shall also make us acknowledge the orthodox apostolic labor
of the early missionaries who set that evangelical acculturation into
motion. And not to forget, of course, the inner makeup of so many,

enabling them to come to terms in a remarkable way and in so short a time with new demands that cannot but have been profoundly disturbing to their old humanity and ethics.

Let us first call to mind a few facts about working conditions in Caraga. In the 1600s (and much later) a very small number of missionaries (between eight or less to not more than 12 at any time) took care of the coastal stretch from Punta San Agustin, Davao up to Gingoog, Misamis Oriental, or roughly 550 kilometers; in addition to a small group of off-shore islands (Siargao and Dinagat) plus a river stretch of about 40 miles into the heart of Agusan.

The coastal waters, especially the Pacific littoral between Surigao and Davao, belong to the most dangerous seaboards of the archipelago: much of it is unnavigable for sail- and rowboats between November and April.

Initially, most of the mission district was still "unpacified" territory, as we have seen; it could, with relative ease, still turn against foreign control, even after its people had become vassals of sorts of Church and King. (See the chapter: "The Revolt of Caraga, 1631"). Truly, any of those missionary pioneers could in all honesty make some words of St. Paul (2 Cor. 11:26-28) his own, adapting them to his condition:

> Being shipwrecked and tossed by the waves in the open sea, always on the go, in spite of danger from rivers and robbers and half-baked Christians, plodding and toiling, with many sleepless nights, in hunger and thirst, burdened day in and out by anxiety for their farflung Christian communities.

To these, more or less 'normal' problems inherent in much pioneering missionary work, should be added another: For quite some time it must have been impossible for the inhabitants to distinguish between the Spanish missionary and the Spanish *encomendero,* soldier or tribute-collector. Consequently, hatred not seldom incurred by the latter must often have extended to the foreign missionary as well. Nevertheless, after twenty-eight years of apostolate in Caraga, the following statistics were submitted to the Manila Chapter of the Recoletos in 1650:

1. *Convent of Tandag,* capital of the province of Caraga; it has a Spanish garrison and is 150 leagues from Manila. Under its care are 700 Christian families. Initially located more than one league upriver, it was later transferred to the seashore for reasons of convenience. It has a pious confraternity of the Blessed Virgin and

another of St. Augustin. [28]

2. *The convent of Butuan,* located along the river. It was founded by Fray Francisco de San Nicolas.[29] The village counts 1500 Christians.

3. The *convent of Sidargao,* on an island at 10 leagues distance from the fort of Tandag. There are 2000 Christian families.

4. *The convent of Bislig* with 2000 families.

5. *The convent of Gigaquit* has 800 Christian families. It was founded by Fray Juan de San Nicolas along a river on the coast of Caraga.

6. *The convent of Laylaya* (Ilaya?), which means "up river," located at 40 leagues distance from Butuan. (Here was a Spanish garrison, and from indications it must have been at Linao.) It ministers to 1600 souls.

7. *In Calagdan* (= Cantilan) another convent was reported by Fray Felipe de la Madre de Dios in a manuscript with historical notes which he left behind. He reported that there were 700 Christian families.

8. *The convent of Tago,* named after the river that flows along the village. It ministers to 900 Christian families.

Not all the mentioned "convents" should be considered as referring to as many stations with a resident priest. This is clear from a.o. a letter by the Provincial to the Governor, dated June 29, 1655, ergo five years after the report given above:

> "*Tandag* is the capital of the province of Caraga. It has two priests; there are 600 tribute payers in the capital and the outstations. The latter are: Parasao [= Cantilan], Tago, Marihatag, and Lianga. The Tandag garrison is also served by our Religious."

Butuan, the *encomienda* of General Agustin de Cepeda, and part of the province of Caraga, has two priests and 400 tribute payers. Its stations are Jabonga, Amongan, Gibong, Linao (40 leagues up

---

[28] The text has "the girdle *(correa)* of St. Augustin": an association of so called "Tertians," or lay extension of the Order intended for men. The pious association for women was that of the "Mantelatas" or "Beatas."

[29] Perhaps this should be Juan de San Nicolas, the man who "with a spirit apostolically bold planted the Standard of the Cross at Butuan." In 1622 Francisco de San Nicolas was at Calamianas, Palawan.

river), Argawan, Odyongan and the Manobos who belong to his Majesty's *encomienda*.

Sidargao, also belonging to Caraga, is the *encomienda* of Sergeant Martin Sanchez de la Cuesta. It has two priests and 600 tribute payers. Its stations are Sapao, Cabuntog, Bacuag, Gigaquit, Bolor, and Surigao.

Bislig, part of Caraga and *encomienda* of Sergeant Juan Camacho de la Peña, has two priests and 300 tribute payers. It has the following stations: Hinatuan, Cateel and Baganga (Colin/ Pastells, III, p. 722).

We will notice how little helpful the data of the 1650 report still are for one who wants to know: how many baptized inhabitants were there, or: what is the approximate surveyed population, how many are "pacified," or tribute payers, or living outside controled areas. The account lumps together such items as "Christian families" (for Tandag, Siargao and Gigaquit), "Christians" (for Butuan), "families" (for Bislig) and "souls" (for Linao).

The report of 1655 is in so far an improvement that it works exclusively with the number of tax payers. By applying a rule-of-thumb of one to four or one to five, one could, in wholly controled areas infer an approximate number of 7,600 or 9,500 inhabitants. However, it can safely be assumed that in 1655 (and more so in 1650) an even larger number were still living in the jungles between the Pacific coast and the Agusan river outside the control of church and government. Perhaps, without too much haphazard guessing and pointless speculation, we might conclude to a total of about 30,000 inhabitants for Caraga in 1655. This number could also be accommodated under the report of 1650.[30]

Speaking about those numbers of baptized, numbers of missionary centers and priests residing there after roughly 50 years of missionary presence in Caraga, one feels asking oneself time and

---

[30] About 80 years later Juan Francisco de San Antonio OFM, obviously using Recoleto sources, writes about Caraga that it had 5,221 tribute payers in the *encomiendas* of the King and 3,042 belonging to private *encomiendas*. Combining the figures and applying the factor one to five then in use, this would point to a population of 41,320; to this number should again be added unregistered tribals living in the jungles, whose number, however, was probably quite reduced by then ("Cronicas," 1738, Picornell translation).

again: what kind of mental picture ought one to form of the process of ethical and spiritual transformation undergone by those thousands? How, and by what pastoral methods, was it effected? How much real acceptance or resistance did it encounter? But such is a kind of vocabulary that came into existence only in the 19th century together with the development of the social sciences of modern times. Out of the Caraga mission not enough data have come to us to warrant acceptable answers to such and other analytical questions. The source material with which one has to work when groping for at least a glimpse of the answers, consists as a rule of condensations and interpretations or condensed interpretations of reports by the "change-agents" and their superiors or chroniclers. The authenticity, is, so to say, second-hand. Seldom will one come across accounts like that of the Caraga revolt of 1631.

Nevertheless, also in Caraga the truism will apply that profound change, in order to be humanly possible, should not place individuals before too many and too deeply disturbing dilemmas. In addition, the new human condition demanded from people should offer the "change-patients" at least a number of new gratifications for old ones being renounced. This will all the more be true where the environment remained untouched by or even hostile to change.

Needless to say, such preambles apply a fortiori to a change as profound as a religious conversion. Herein, however, there is always the hidden mystery between God and the convert of where, and at what wrenching moment of his or her primitive humanity God intervened and "in His goodwill towards them begot in them any measure of desire or achievement" (Phil. 2:13). Speaking from hindsight knowledge of what developed from the early days till the days one has seen with one's own eyes, we may safely conclude with St. Paul that for the primitive animists of Old Caraga "God had set limits to their epochs and fixed the boundaries of their regions in such ways so that they could seek God, yes grope for Him and eventually find Him, because He was not really far from any of them" (Acts 17·27).

Of course, if one wishes to look for "tongue-in-cheek" Christians, he can find them personified in Caragans such as Maria Campan and Geronima Moag in 1631, during the Caraga revolt, who are on record; no doubt, many more have remained unrecorded. But we possess records, no less, of a Diego Inongan (1604) of Butuan, Madalena Baluyot and Maria Uray of Dapitan, Miguel Ayatumo of Bohol (1609). And on p. 217 of his "Historia General" Fray Pedro de San Francisco writes about

> "a woman of Siargao, endowed with much Christian perfection whose name was Rosa de la Cruz. Ever since she was a young girl, she had been one of our Mantelatas and had walked the ways of a most heroic sanctity." (The account is of about 1647.)

When she was about twenty years old, a notorious local man wanted to marry her, but she had promised to devote her whole life to the service of God in virginity. In order to enable her to do so, the parish priest Fray Miguel sent her to Manila. Here she died while in the last stage of her preparation for profession as a Tertiary.

These Tertiaries (or Mantelatas: invested with the veil) were also called "Beatas." Although not religious in the canonical sense and not necessarily living in community, they devoutly dedicated their lives to Christian perfection, service to the local church and other forms of apostolate. Naturally, their spirituality and devotional practices were closely patterned after those of the local religious Order of which they became some kind of an extension.

Also the chronicles of Butuan have extensive accounts of two converts whose lives clearly indicate a commitment not just to "plain" Christian living but to Christian perfection. In the biography of a great Recoleto apostle of the Old Caraga, Fray Jacinto de San Fulgencio, it is stated that

> "in 1624 he was appointed prior of the convent of Saint Joseph in Butuan. Here, among many others, he made two important conversions: that of the famous Ramera Caliman, who after her baptism took the name Clara and lived an exemplary life, and that of the Hermana Isabel. Both belonged to our Mantelatas and they were the firstlings of his apostolic zeal" (Pedro de S. Francisco, Decada 7, Libr. 2, p. 360).

Clara Ramera[31] Caliman and Isabel were born during the Jesuit era of Butuan (Clara perhaps a little earlier) and were baptized as adults by the earliest Recoletos, Clara in 1623 (she died in 1639 "sixteen years after her conversion"). Most probably the baptismal names of Clara and Isabel had been given to these two Butuanas in honor of the Spanish Infanta Isabel Clara Eugenia (1566-1633), daughter of Philip II and Governess of the Netherlands. Luis de

---

[31] "Ramera" is Spanish for prostitute.

Jesus mentions that they were given the veil of the Mantelatas by Fray Jacinto de San Fulgencio; Clara when he was "prior of the convent at Butuan" and Isabel "when he was Vicar-Provincial of that province." Fray Jacinto was prior at Butuan from 1629 till 1631, and that places Clara's investiture between those years. He was Vicar-Provincial from 1638 till 1641, between which years Isabel received the veil. Both had been married, because the accounts say that Fray Jacinto invested them "after their husbands had died." Clara, as said, died in 1639 and Isabel in 1646. Both were buried near the old church site of Butuan (at Banza), and probably their bones have already been scattered by the ghouls who (with public knowledge) have for quite some time professionally engaged in the crime of grave robbing. The thought of this possibility may leave one with one comfort: the treasures which these two Butuanas took with them into their graves are beyond the reach of dirty claws.

Luis de Jesus devotes one whole chapter to Clara and Isabel each. We will quote the text in full, not merely out of curiosity for what it can tell us about Clara and Isabel, but also because implicitly it reveals the spirituality, devotional and pastoral practices in vogue at that time.

About the Life and Holy Death of Hermana Clara Caliman, Beata or Mantelata of the Recoletos of Our Father Saint Augustin. 1639.

"In the village of Butuan lived an India named Clara Caliman, very beautiful and very rich. It was during the time when our Religious were trekking through the settlements along the river to preach the word of God to the inhabitants to tear them away from their idolatry and blindness. They were given to a life of vices, unrestrained, because they were in the bondage of satan, who by his enticements entrapped many souls in his net.

But like another Magdalene, wounded by the arrows of Christ's words, Caliman changed her heart and escaped the net, after listening to our Religious preaching against their vicious customs, and explaining that worldly delights last only a very short time and are unbecoming to people endowed with reason; that they are a serious offense against God and result in eternal torment as punishment.

The Lord put fire into the words of His minister, and this India responded to it with faith. Like Saint Augustin — whom she took as her spiritual father — she could say: "You have called for me, Lord, cried for me, and destroyed the locks that kept my ears closed" (Confessions, Book 10).

The Lord gave her a deep understanding of her sinful life; He warned her that true happiness can only be found in following Jesus Christ. Like a thirsting deer she ran for the waters of baptism, after preparing herself with copious tears and deep contrition resulting from the horror caused by her guilt.

With solemn publicity she decided what day she was going to be baptized, so as to give an example to the rest of the people who were also waiting to hear a doctrine that was wholly new to them. On the day before her baptismal day Caliman distributed large amounts as alms, and she freed many slaves whom she had held in tyrannical possession. To the church she gave a generous donation for beautification and vestments. With such disposition she came to the fount of grace.

The Religious baptized her in the admiring presence of many people who came to witness a rare example of penance in her who before had been notorious for her scandalous and shameless life. Caliman took the name of Clara, a name that pointed to the fruit of the sacrament which she had received. From a somber cesspool of darkness she was transformed into clarity and into a resplendent Temple of the Holy Spirit.

Since she was spiritually reborn, Clara began to take good care of her life from that moment. She read devotional books that had been translated into her mother tongue. With deep fervor she cared for the Temple. She wished to be instructed very extensively in the mysteries of our holy Faith. She meditated on them, and for this reason God filled her abundantly with great consolations in order to attract her. For such is the manner used by the Divine Majesty to bring souls close to Him.

Clara went on growing in virtue and wished to become still closer to the Lord Whom she had come to know. She asked that they accept her as a Beata or Mantelata, since her husband had already died. This was not easily granted to her, and it cost her many supplications, pleas and tears. By the delay which it took, she proved her spirit and constancy.

This was a wise procedure of our Religious, and it should be followed by all in the matter of the newly converted. St. Paul indicated this already in his letter to the disciple Timothy. St. Gregory the Great explains his words, pointing to the caution that should be taken with novices in the Faith, so as to make them climb the state of perfection.

> We know, he says, that no load should be placed on the
> walls of buildings before they have dried; when standing
> without load, they will not collapse due to a burden they were
> unable to carry. Trees that have recently been cut are not good
> for construction purposes; being still green, they will warp, with
> considerable damage to the building.

For this reason Clara's request to be given the habit of Beata was postponed till her perseverance should be obvious. But after finding that every day she became more studious in self-correction and virtue, the Father Provincial of the province of San Nicolas in the Philippines gave permission to accept her.

On the appointed day Fray Jacinto de San Fulgencio, prior of the convent at Butuan, gave her the habit in the presence of a large number of people. Clara was crying with happiness. The devout Christians praised the Lord; the pagans, astonished at such great change in that woman, became contrite, and this disposed them to receive the Faith of Jesus Christ.

From then on she dressed in coarse cloth instead of the fineries which she used previously after her fashion; she put on a tunic of thick serge instead of soft skirts. She mortified herself with a penitential chain covered with sharp points; the sight of it was already horrifying. Daily she flagellated herself intensively. She fasted regularly till her death, eating only some kind of vegetables. She used to tell her confessor that God had been so merciful to her that she did not feel hunger or thirst, although these must have affected her much. Aware of her previous bad and licentious life, all the penance which she inflicted upon herself at present seemed insignificant to her. Such were the effects of the heavenly light that was reflected in her soul.

She was very devoted to prayer and contemplation. At sunrise she was already in the convent church. Everyday she stayed motionless and in kneeling position in front of the main altar during four hours, absorbed in the meditation of Christ's passion. Aside from that she attended the complete divine Office with unusual devotion. She was given permission to receive Communion three times a week, and her eyes were filled with tears when she received the divine Bread. From this her spirit drew great upliftment and radiated with the fire of love.

Unceasingly she engaged in works of charity by helping the poor in their needs. She visited the sick, comforted them with pious words, served them food with her own hands, and although she was a woman of high standing, she did not wish that her servants would do the cooking. She herself performed all the most humble work because she believed that she served Christ in the poor. While she was still engaged in those works of charity, the time to eat her meal of vegetables would come; after that she would return to the convent church for Vespers. She remained there till sunset engrossed in fervent prayer. Thereafter she went out to attend to the sick and the poor. If she came across somebody who was dying, she assisted and strengthened him with Christian thoughts. For this purpose she had some prayers written in a book and these she read with great tenderness to imprint them in the soul of the one in agony, so as to enkindle his spirit with the love of God and contrition for his sins. In this way she prepared the dying for certain salvation. When finding a dead person, she took care of enshrouding the body while she herself donated the shroud as an alms. Personally she prepared the body, without granting herself reprieve from any kind of work, because she desired by all means to engage in acts of charity to please her Spouse Jesus Christ.

Clara was a rare example of virtue, however deep satan had made her fall before. She became so much respected that everybody behaved well in her presence. When our Religious discovered this, they told her to go to the places where the Indios came together for their games, so that at the sight of her there would be no disturbance or misbehavior.

She had her land divided in three parts (as has been said also of St. Joachim and St. Anne). One part she used for the benefit of the church and convent; another part to help the poor, and the third part she designated for the support of her household.

For sixteen years after her conversion, with holy and unwavering perseverance, she lived this kind of life; then, strongly founded in perfection and already well prepared, God wished to take her to Himself. Gravely ill, she asked for the Sacraments of the church and received them all with singular devotion and happiness. And while uttering sweet words to Jesus her Spouse, she gave up her spirit.

May the Lord be praised for all ages, because the immensity of His mercy embraces all and because he knows how to make faithful servants out of great sinners, for the honor of His holy Name and for the edification of those who dwell in this miserable life." (Luis de Jesus, "Historia General," Ch. 9, p. 196).

Capitulo 6. §. Vnico.   371   Año
1646

CAPITVLO SEXTO.

MVERE SANTAMENTE EN LA
Provincia de Butuan la Venerable Hermana Iſabel, Beata.

§. Vnico.

Año
1646.

STE Año paſ-
ſò à mejor
vida , en el.
Pueblo de
Butuan de
Filipinas vna
Beata nueſ-
tra , llamada
Iſabel , de
quien no ſabèmos mas, que a verſe có-
vertido à la Fè por la Predicacion
de los nueſtros, quando entraron en
aquella Provincia. Alumbròla el Señor, para que dexaſſe las tinieblas de
ſus idolatrias, bautizandola, ponien-
dole nombre de Iſabel. Hizo grande
fruto en breve , que la mano de Dios
no ſe ata à duraciones de tiempos ; y
viendola tan aprovechada en los
Miſterios de la Catolica Religion, la
mandaron nueſtros Religioſos fueſſe
Coadjutora , y Madre Eſpiritual de
muchas Almas , à quienes reduxo à
la Fè, y catequizò , ganandolas para
la Igleſia.

Embiaronla à los Pueblos donde
el Demonio hazia mayor guerra, en-
gañando con ſus embuſtes, para que
ſe opuſieſſe con ſu exemplar vida, y
ſuavidad de Doctrina. Sentava ſu Eſ-
cuela en vna caſa del Pueblo, adonde
concurrian las Donzellas , y con ad-
mirable eloquencia les dava à entender el camino errado de ſus vanas
ſuperſticiones, y explicava los rudi-
mentos, y principios de la Doctrina

Chriſtiana. A ſus horas determina-
das iba à la Igleſia cada dia , y con-
curriendo la Gente , enſeñava à los
rudos; confirmava à los converti-
dos; alumbrava à los ignorantes; y
eſto con tanta gracia , y ſuavidad de
palabras , que prendia los coraçones
de los Oyentes ; juntando à eſto vna
modeſtia, y compoſtura, ſuavemente
grave , con que hizo gran provecho
en aquellos Barbaros.

Como ſe experimentaſſen tan co-
pioſos frutos por medio de Iſabel,
afsi en la reformacion de las coſtum-
bres, como en los muchos que ſe con-
vertian del ciego Gentiliſmo ; la
mandaron los Padres, que predicaſſe
en las Calles, y Plaças; donde concurrian à oìrla , vnos por curioſidad,
otros llevados de la buena gracia en
el dezir ; y con eſte medio quedavan
preſas muchas Almas , y pedian el
Bautiſmo, ſiendo vna zeloſa Obrera,
y Apoſtolica Coadjutora en aquel
Rebaño del Señor. Entravaſe tambien en las caſas de los que tercos no
ſalian à oìrla en las Calles ; y alli, con
Platicas ſuaves, y llenas de Caridad,
ablandava los coraçones, y los incli-
nava à recibir la Fè.

Aviendo empleado algunos años
en eſte genero de vida Apoſtolica,
muriò ſu Marido ; y viendoſe libre
del yugo matrimonial , quiſo ſujetar
el cuello al de la Religion. Diòle el
Abito nueſtro de Mantelata, ò Beata
el Padre Fray Iacinto de San Fulgencio, que à la ſaçon era Vicario Provincial de aquella Provincia. Reco-

Aaa 2   no-

Fig. 21. Two pages from "Historia General ..." by Luis de Jesus OAR:
"Muere Santamente en la Provincia de Butuan la Venerable
Hermana Isabel, Beata."

372 ## Decada Sexta,

noció, como bien entendida , y fabia en el camino de la Perfeccion, que le corrian mas eftrechas obligaciones de aprovecharfe à fi mifma , mejorando vida ,y de emplear el talento, que avia recibido de Dios,en beneficio del Proximo. Afsi lo executò.No fe puede facilmente ponderar la diligencia con que bufcava las Almas; los medios que arbitrava para facarlas de las tinieblas de la Gentilidad. Què caminos no hizo! Què trabajos no pafsò! Andava de vnas partes en otras , difcurriendo con Efpiritu , y fuerças, no de Muger flaca, fino de Varon fuerte. Ayudavala el Señor, cuya caufa hazia; pues el folicitar Almas para Dios , es fervicio tan de fu gufto.

Llegò à ver toda aquella Provincia de Butuan convertida à la Fè de Iefu-Chrifto, de que muy gozofa le dava gracias. Retiròfe, para darfe à la contemplacion Divina , pareciendola , que debia difponerfe para la partida defte Mundo, la que tanto tiempo fe avia dedicado al bien del Proximo. Acompañofe con la Hermana Clara Calimàn (cuya Vida efcrivimos arriba:) Imitò fus penitencias, ayunos, y modo de vida ; con que era vn exemplo de Virtudes.

Decada 3. cap. 9.

Orava devotamente largas horas; vifitava los Enfermos ; fervialos ; exortavalos à dolor de fus pecados, y que llevaffen con paciencia fus dolores. Efmeròfe tanto en eftas obras de Mifericordia, que pareciò à nueftros Religiofos (que governavan aquel Partido) no dexarla defcanfar, y que viuieffe folamente para fi. Erigieron vn Hofpital, para curar los Pobres, y mádaronla cuidaffe dellos. Bufcava los necefsitados ; traialos muchas vezes fobre fus ombros:Tanta era fu Caridad! Guidavales del Alma , haziendo, fe les miniftraffen los Sacramentos;y del cuerpo, aplicando las medicinas convenientes. Solicitava regalos, y limofnas ; y ella tenia horas diputadas para falir à pedir para fus Pobres enfermos. Todo lo executava con femblante alegre , y apacible, que indicava el Amor de Dios con que tenia encendido fu pecho. En eftas ocupaciones llegò fu hora; enfermò gravemente ; conociò fer llamamiento de Dios ; pidiò los Sacramentos de la Iglefia Catolica ; y aviendolos recibido con alegria, entregò fu Alma al Señor ; dexando, con el dolor de fu falta, grandes prendas, de que defcanfa eternamente.

The saintly death of the Venerable Sister Isabel, a Beata,
in the Province of Butuan. 1646.

"One of our Beatas, named Isabel, passed to the better life this year in the village of Butuan in the Philippines. We know nothing else about her (early years) except that she was converted to the Faith by the preaching of our Religious when they entered that province. The Lord enlightened her and as a result she was baptized and given the name Isabel. She produced great fruit in a short time, because the hand of God is not restricted to time limits. Seeing of how much use she could be in the spreading of the Mysteries of the Catholic religion, our Religious sent her to become a lay worker and mother of many souls whom she brought to the Faith and taught the catechism, thus gaining them for the Church.

She was sent to the villages where the devil was waging his fiercest war and deceiving people by his tricks, so that she might oppose herself to him by her exemplary life and the gentleness of her teaching. She established her school in a house in the village, and there the young girls came together. With wonderful eloquence she made them understand that the path of their false superstitions would lead them astray, and she explained the rudiments and principles of the Christian doctrine. At fixed hours she went to the church every day and after the people had gathered she instructed the foolish, strengthened the converted and enlightened the ignorant. She did all this with so much gentleness of words that she captured the hearts of her hearers. To this she joined a modesty and bearing so sweet and grave that she made great gains among those barbarians.

Since such great results were made through the help of Isabel, in the reformation of morals as well as in the many who were converted from their blind paganism, the Religious sent her to preach in streets and open places where the people would gather to hear her, some from curiosity and others carried away by her wonderful grace in speaking. By that means many souls were captured and asked to be baptized; she was a truly zealous worker and an apostolic helper in that flock of the Lord. She also entered the houses of the obstinate ones who had not come to hear her in the streets. There, with mild conversations and full of charity, she softened their hearts and inclined them to receive the Faith.

After she had worked for some years in that apostolic life, her husband died. Free from the yoke of matrimony, she decided to submit herself to that of religious life. Fray Jacinto de San Fulgencio, at that time Vicar-Provincial of that province, gave her our habit of Mantelata or Beata. She was aware, since she was very intelligent and experienced in the road to perfection, that now she was even more obliged to make herself useful, that she must lead a better life and employ the talents which she had received from God for the benefit of her fellow men, and that is what she did. One cannot easily imagine with how much diligence she went to look for souls, and the means she employed to draw them from the darkness of paganism. What roads she did not travel! She went from one place to another, always discussing with a spirit and strength that was not that of a weak woman but of a strong man. The Lord whose cause she was promoting, aided her, for to gain souls for God is a service that pleases Him very much.

She finally saw how that whole province of Butuan was converted to the Faith of Jesus Christ, and full of joy she thanked God for that. Then she retired to give herself to divine contemplation; she thought that she should prepare to leave the world after having given so much time to the welfare of her fellow men. She went to ask instruction from Clara Caliman (whose life we have described earlier) and imitated her in her penitence, fasting and mode of life, so that she became an example of virtue. Isabel prayed for long hours and very devoutly; she visited the sick and took care of them; she exhorted them to repent their sins and to bear their sorrows with patience. She devoted herself so entirely to those works of charity that our Religious (who were in charge of that district) thought that she should not withdraw from it to live exclusively for herself. They put up a hospital to cure the poor and put her in charge to care for them. She went to look for the needy and often carried them on her shoulders, so great was her charity. She cared for their souls by seeing to it that they would receive the Sacraments; also for their bodies by having the proper medicines administered to them. At regular hours she went out to beg for gifts and alms for her poor patients. She did all this with a cheerful and calm expression which reflected the love of God which burned in her heart.

While she was still engaged in this work, her hour came. She fell seriously ill and understood that God was calling her; she therefore asked for the Sacraments of the Church. After having received them with joy, she surrendered her soul to the Lord. In spite of the sorrow for her loss, she has left us with the certainty that she has eternal rest'' (op. cit., Ch. 6, p. 371).

17th century descriptions of contemporary spirituality and devotionality often are somewhat unpalatable to the modern reader. Still, the two biographies reflect clear characteristics of authentic

conversion followed by high-grade Christian living that could
without effort be translated and written in terms of the best of
essential Christian witnessing and desiderata of a Church for today.

Without wishing to engage in illfounded analyses of the limited
number of accounts available, one gets the impression that in the last
quarter of the 1600s a semblance of Christian villages were emerging
along the shores of Caraga. The chronicler Pedro de San Francisco
de Asis offers us a few glimpses into their situation and development.

Since 1642 the parish of Bislig had been the southernmost
Recoleto outpost along the east coast of Caraga. It was staffed by
only two missionaries to take care of the littoral villages of
Hinatuan, Cateel, Baganga and Caraga plus the scattered pagan
settlements that could be reached along the inland rivers and in the
rainforests facing the Pacific Ocean.

> "There, such a big number of pagan Indios and wild tribes
> are living that even the Christian natives do not know them all.
> The tribe that lives closest to our villages is that of the
> Tagabaloyes, named after some mountains which they call
> Baloy."

The Tagabaloyes are described as living in the inland jungle back
of Hinatuan, Bislig, and Cateel outside the control of government
and church. They were a peaceful and sociable people, who had
regular contact with the Christians of the coastal settlements. Like
these, they had a deep hatred for the Moros, probably because the
latter, on their periodical raids had gone up the various rivers and
ransacked also their jungle abodes.

They were a sharp-witted lot and more industrious than most
other tribals encountered by the Spaniards thus far. It looks as if the
Tagabaloyes possessed what 300 years later would become known as
a "blue-seal" ego, because they claimed to be descendants of
Japanese and were proud of it. Indeed, so the account mentions, the
color of their skin and their customs were very much like those of the
latter. From all indications it seems that the author is referring to a
group generally known as the Mandayas.

Often, many related families shared one big house wherein each
family had its own compartment. Sometimes those houses were
constructed high up in the trees as a defense against an attack by
enemies. They were not afraid of the missionaries and even liked to
associate with them. The priests said that among them they felt as

safe as in a Christian village.

Up to 1671 only little progress had been made in the conversion of this sympathetic tribe.

"In the first place because of the continuous wars with the Moros which hardly allowed Christians and Tagabaloyes alike to put their weapons out of hand. In such a turbulent situation the Catholic religion, which loves quiet and peace, can hardly progress.

The second reason was that the governors of Caraga and the military commanders of Cateel extended only little or no help to such an undertaking. The same is true of some leading Christian Indios in the settled villages. In their trading contacts with the Tagabaloyes they stood more to gain if those Indios remained pagans than if they became Christians. It is known of old that human depravity spends its efforts firstly in the pernicious pursuits of greed, without regard for the advancement of the Faith if the latter is considered an obstacle to the former. (Elsewhere the chronicler complained about the military commander of Cateel 'whose shadow is more powerful here than in other parts of the world').

But it was foremost because of a third reason that the hoped-for results were not obtained. As we suggested already, this consisted in the fact that mostly there were only two Religious in that area. Neither of them could stay for a long time in the villages of Cateel or Caraga, which are closest to the jungles of the Tagabaloyes. They could go there only two or three times every year" (op. cit., p. 287).

During those sporadic visits the missionary could stay only two or three weeks in the coastal villages of Cateel, Baganga or Caraga, where he was kept fully occupied ministering to the local Christians. The little time he was able to spend for the pagans in the interior was practically wasted. The author remarks that at his time of writing (about 70 years afterwards) it was sometimes said in Spain (but wrongly so) that the reason why so many pagans remained unreached in the Philippines was that the missionaries were not working anymore with the same vigor as in the beginning.

It was only at the Recoleto Chapter of 1671 that the area south of Bislig was given more importance in the appointment policy of the superiors. This change was spurred by the new Provincial who, prior to his promotion, had been working for some years along the southern part of the east coast. Aside from Bislig, he assigned one resident priest to Cateel and another to Caraga. During his visitation of 1673 he found that in Cateel and Caraga the number of baptized adults had reached over 800. In 1674 the parish priest of Bislig mentions to the Chapter of that year that in Cateel, Baganga, Caraga area about 800 jungle dwellers had been resettled in existing littoral villages. He stated that with these developments the number of tribute payers had been increased by 200, indicating herewith that the rule-of-thumb of one to four was still in use in the area. With the possible exception of an earlier report about Linao at the time of "el Padre Capitan," this is the first time that the process of "reduction" or resettlement of scattered jungle residents is mentioned in the Caraga district. Two centuries later, the Jesuits of the restored Society would make the reduction system one of the principal instruments of Christianization, second only to moral attraction by preaching.

In the few accounts that have come to us about the southern end of the Caraga mission in the second half of the 1600s, we are told how the conversion of the Tagabaloyes was greatly enhanced by a series of miracles performed through an adventurous statue of Our Lady which became locally known as "La Virgen de la Costa de Cateel." We could also call her "Our Lady who came in from Ternate." The history of this statue from Maluku is intimately linked with that of the still existing Santo Niño in the present Ternate of Cavite.

In 1662-1663 (not 1666 as Pastells states) the Spaniards had started to abandon Maluku (except Siao) and the Governor, a pious man, took great care that all church ornaments and statues were timely evacuated. The principal statue of Our Lady of the Rosary went to Siao; the Santo Niño plus another statue of Our Lady was brought to Manila by the Malucan soldiers who accompanied the Governor.[32]

---

[32] This information is connected with another related in "Documenta Malucensia" by H. Jacobs SJ, vol. III, pp. 616-617:

1) List signed by Father Francisco de Miedes, SJ wherein are written down the properties and ornaments belonging to the Confraternity of the Name of Jesus (= Santo Niño).

2) Another list containing the ornaments and the jewels of the Confraternity of Our Lady of the Rosary of Ternate which were sent to this city of Manila, to be put in the custody of the Archbishop. Ternate, May 18, 1663.

This Governor probably did not get his piety from strangers. His name was General Agustin de Cepeda, and back home in Spain, one of his aunts had died about fifteen years before he was born in Talavera de la Reina of Toledo. Her name had been Teresa de Cepeda y Ahumada; in 1622, when Don Agustin was about twenty-four years old, she was canonized as a saint: Teresa of Avila or Teresa de Jesus. Her nephew Agustin came to the Philippines as a soldier not long afterwards. He would eventually become one of the *encomenderos* of northern Agusan. In the famous letters of St. Teresa there are quite a few about and to her uncles who once were prominent Spanish officials in Quito, Peru. In the Philippines Don Agustin had played an important part in chasing the Dutch away from Abucay and Cavite in 1642-1643, and in 1660 he was confronting them again as the penultimate Governor of Ternate. Most of his native Malucan troops accompanied him to the Philippines and were eventually settled in Ternate of Cavite.[33]

---

[33] Together with Spaniards, Pampangos, Cebuanos, Boholanos and Caragans they would be mustered against the expected forces of the Chinese pirate Kue-sing (Cog-sen or Koxinga), who had plans to attack Manila. The Malucans were named "Mardicas" or "free people" (from the Malay merdeka = free). Colin, in his "Labor Evangelica," vol. III, p. 266 and 812, has the following information about them; "They are the Malays who accompanied the Spaniards from Ternate where they had formed a village. Their name means "free people.""

Juan de la Concepción (Historia de Philipinas, 1784, vol. VII, p. 102) writes: "Under this name are included natives of Ternate, Tidore, Siao and also Manado, Cauripo, Celebes and Macassar. They were allotted a place of residence at Marigondon, on the great bay of Manila. Theirs is also the island of Corregidor, from where, by signal fires, they give warning of the ships being spotted."

He also mentions that they spoke three languages: Spanish, Tagalog and their own dialect. De la Concepción wrote this in 1784, about 120 years after the arrival of the Mardicas in the Philippines. A mixture of these three languages eventually became the "Chabacano" of Cavite. The same author also writes: "They regard themselves as the spiritual sons of St. Francis Xavier, to whom they are singularly devoted, a feeling inspired by their forefathers who had known him and had witnessed his marvelous work."

Ferrando ("Historia de los Pp. Dominicos," 1870, Vol. III, p. 94)

The saga of the statue of Our Lady that was brought to the Philippines and given to the Governor of Caraga is described as follows in the Recoleto chronicles of Pedro de San Francisco de Asis:

"Among the sacred images evacuated from Ternate was one of Our Lady; it was extremely gracefully made and was very beautiful. The Governor of Ternate gave it to the Alcalde Mayor of Caraga, and the latter sent it to the garrison of Cateel, so that it could become an object of devotion in the chapel of the fort there. The statue was then named "La Virgen de la Costa" after the place where it was enthroned, because "costa" in the local vernacular is the same as "castillo."[34]

mentions: "These people have preserved their own dialect, usages and customs. Up to recent times they had not intermarried with Filipinos of neighboring villages. They had brought with them a statue of the Santo Niño, which they hold in high veneration. Their village is now independent from Marigondon."

Originally they had been allotted a place near the "Estacada," a fortified barrio not far from Binondo, Manila. The place "independent from Marigondon" is the present Ternate, where the mentioned Santo Niño statue is still seen and venerated as patron of the town.

[34] Probably "cota." Long after the fort of Tandag has disappeared, the inhabitants still keep referring to its former location as "ang cota." Kota derives from the Sanskrit "koeta," which means a fortified place.

I have not been able to ascertain who was that Alcalde Mayor of Caraga in 1662-1663. What is sure, however, is that Don Francisco Atienza y Bañes (Vañes, Ibañes, Ybañes), the very last Governor of the Spanish-held part of Ternate in Maluku (1663), had been Alcalde of Caraga in 1639 when he subdued the Moros of Lake Lanao with the help of "el padre Capitan" Agustin de San Pedro. (See Chapter IX "With a spirit apostolically bold.") Atienza had also been commander of the Spanish forts of Iligan and Zamboanga. He was well acquainted with Don Agustin de Cepeda, his predecessor in Ternate and *encomendero* of Butuan in 1650. Obviously, both had still personal relations with the unknown incumbent Alcalde of Caraga who received the mentioned statue of Our Lady from Ternate in 1663. Both de Cepeda and Atienza belonged to the most involved officials in Spain's 17th century colonial and military affairs in the Philippines and its conflicts with the Dutch in the seas of the Philippines and Maluku.

From the first moment when her veneration had started in the mentioned village, she extended her goodness in a magnificent and magnanimous way not only to the Christians but also to the pagans of the vicinity. When troubled by a shortage of rain, or by an invasion of locusts or by epidemic diseases, they took recourse to this beautiful statue, and immediately they were given relief. It looked as if through this statue the Virgin was the loving mother of the Tagabaloyes. The sight of such large groups of pagans coming to Cateel, walking in very orderly processions and praying for relief of their problems, was something that caused no little admiration... The miracles performed by Mary, so visible and palpable, were the main reason why so many pagans in that region embraced the religion that taught them to venerate, with humble and loving prayers, such a beneficent and generous Princess... This... was of great help for the strengthening and expansion of the Catholic Faith in those regions which still need the watering of miracles, so that their rational plants may bear the kind of fruit that correspond to the sweat and cultivation of the Evangelical workers'' (op. cit., p. 289).

During those same years Bislig is reported as having its own miracle worker in the form of a crucifix, of which the author mentions a few extremely mysterious events.

"This miraculous cross was afterwards placed in an artistically made niche above the tabernacle of the chapel of Jesus Nazareno in our church of Manila. When I was there, it was, still in the same niche, put above the lectern of the choir; when I left for Spain, it was still there, highly revered by the Religious'' (op. cit., p. 294)

In the other corner of Caraga, Agusan, the evangelization was much speeded up after the conversion of a notorious datu in the upper regions of Agusan, whose name was Putig Matanda. That event is included in a chronicle dated 1677 "when Fray Miguel de Santo Tomas made that river shine with his presence." If Matanda's conversion really happened in that year, it could not have been the result of Fray Miguel's labor; he was in Surigao in 1647, in Butuan in 1648, in Bislig in 1654 and died in 1671. It is more probable that the datu was converted by resident missionaries of Butuan and not of Linao because at the time indicated Linao seems to have been just an

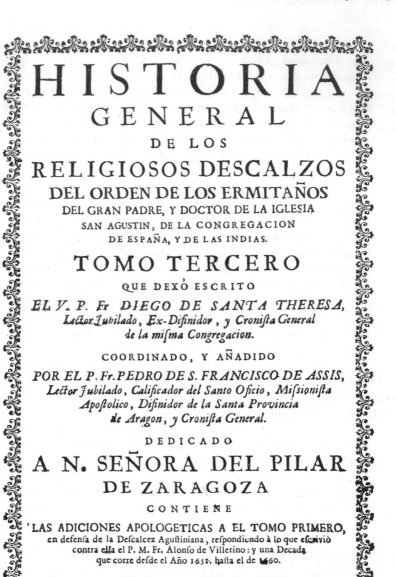

HISTORIA
GENERAL
DE LOS
RELIGIOSOS DESCALZOS
DEL ORDEN DE LOS ERMITAÑOS
DEL GRAN PADRE, Y DOCTOR DE LA IGLESIA
SAN AGUSTIN, DE LA CONGREGACION
DE ESPAÑA, Y DE LAS INDIAS.

TOMO TERCERO
QUE DEXÓ ESCRITO
EL V. P. Fr DIEGO DE SANTA THERESA,
Lector Jubilado, Ex-Difinidor, y Cronista General
de la misma Congregacion.

COORDINADO, Y AÑADIDO

POR EL P. Fr. PEDRO DE S. FRANCISCO DE ASSIS,
Lector Jubilado, Calificador del Santo Oficio, Missionista
Apostolico, Difinidor de la Santa Provincia
de Aragon, y Cronista General.

DEDICADO

A N. SEÑORA DEL PILAR
DE ZARAGOZA
CONTIENE

'LAS ADICIONES APOLOGETICAS A EL TOMO PRIMERO,
en defensa de la Descalcez Agustiniana, respondiendo à lo que escrivió
contra ella el P. M. Fr. Alonso de Villerino: y una Decada
que corre desde el Año 1651. hasta el de 1660.

Con licencia. En Barcelona : En la Imprenta de los Herederos de Juan Pablo,
y Maria Martí, administrada por Mauro Martí, Año 1743.

Fig. 22. Title page of the book, ''Historia General de los Religiosos
Descalzos...1743.''

outstation of Butuan. Another indication of mixed-up reporting is the name given to Matanda's district: "Hothibon," which is a garbled rendition of either Ojot or Hibong.

Anyway, what really counts in the report is that as a result of Matanda's conversion "more than 300 adults were reborn in the salutiferous water that made them children of God and heirs of eternal glory."

In order to convince the doubting reader that indeed the Lord showered some choice blessings on the Manobos of upper Agusan, he might be assisted by the following account of Linao:

> "In Linao a tall cross had been placed that had been made of two big pieces of wood. This cross was seen to incline successively from north to south and from east to west. It did so three or four times, after which it stood erect again, as if it had been giving its benediction to that land."

As has been said before, the arsenal of available documentation from the 1600s and 1700s dealing with the hispanization and Christianization process of east Mindanao is so limited that it hardly permits the drawing-up of a responsible running account of its development. Working with such a drawback, one will find little help but nevertheless some comfort in one Recoleto chronicle complaining long ago:

> "How qualified soever the artists (of accounts available to him) may have been at drawing up a true picture of that past, there are only few existing works clearly depicting things and persons so worthy of being preserved from oblivion. The reason is no doubt that there was too little color to work with, i.e., information which is a prerequisite for drawing images on the canvas of history." (*Pedro de S. Francisco,* "Historia General ...").

Elsewhere another, referring to the scarcity of documentation which was either lost or never composed, sadly speaks of "time, the destroyer of all things, and our neglect in leaving advisory news thereof." What we have to work with, so he sighs, are just "some confused memorials which time excused."

If 250 years ago such could be justified complaints of Recoleto chroniclers who had at least immediate access to a certain number of documents "which time had excused" up to then, how much more will it be true for us, doomed to work more than once with only shreds of references of the latter?

Evangelization, in its daily reality, was and is not only a matter of teaching Christian doctrine, worship and the administration of the Sacraments. In addition to these, it has always very much consisted of the mode of presence of the missionary among local pagans, catechumens, or the Christian community formed out of them. About this daily presence there is, in Marcilla, one document (Legajo 61-2-1) dated 1729, the contents of which, however, seem to be of an earlier date. Time has been rather merciless to the paper and ink, so that much of its contents has become illegible. From its precarious remains one can, nevertheless, still decipher that once it must have offered the reader a kind of information that nowadays would gladden the heart of any researcher:

> "Modo de administrar...?... estos nuevos
> pueblos de Mindanao''

The first chapter is about "The exemplary way of life to be observed by the Religious in our ministries.'' The salient points that can be reconstructed are the following:

1. All our behavior should be guided by the rule of St. Augustin: to avoid doing anything that would offend others (in...omnibus... nihil fiat quod cuidam offendat).

2. While this is already important in our dealings with anyone, it is even more so before "estos Indios,'' and it will be more effective than many sermons or pious words.

3. They shall never enter the houses of the natives, except for the administration of the Sacraments.

4. Women shall not be allowed inside the living quarters of the convent. The priest will talk to them at the door of the church or on the groundfloor of the convent near the first landing of the staircase.

5. Every day the Religious shall spend at least one hour for mental prayer in the church; he shall also say his Breviary there.

6. Foremost among the acts of devotion and worship which the parish priest should promote, are:

— Observance of the Angelus every late afternoon.

— Praying of the Rosary in all houses "en voz alta y de rodillas'' (aloud and in kneeling position).

— Obligatory attendance at Sunday Mass.

— Wearing of the Rosary around the neck.

Chapter 2 contains rules "Concerning those who have to serve in the convent and the care that should be taken of them."

1. There should only be as many servants as are really necessary.

2. They should be well trained *"en buenas y santas costumbres"* but only for the service to the priests, not for others.

3. They should be properly dressed, but without vanity.

4. In the convent, they too shall pray the Angelus, followed by the Rosary, in the way indicated before.

5. No payment is to be given for their services. (The author adds here a note of his own, from which can be deduced that the original text was of an earlier date: "This has been changed *much later,* when it was decided that the *mayor-domo,* the cook and the fiscal should be paid a decent salary, and this in time.)

6. Care should be taken that they go to confession, and that those who have permission to do so, receive Holy Communion. Chapter 3 still has some legible notes and instructions about the parish schools.

1. In all *pueblos* and *visitas* there should be a school for boys and another for girls.

2. It should be constructed by the community, because it is for the good of their children. (We may note here that, in conformity with the "Recopilación de las Leyes de Indias," the Spanish *encomendero* was to reserve a certain part of the *tributo* for salaries of the teachers and for other expenses involved in the "instrucción" within his territory.)

3. School attendance is obligatory from seven years of age.

4. The subjects to be taught are "reading, writing, arithmetic *(contar)* and Christian doctrine."

5. From among the leading locals some should be taught Gregorian chant and organ playing.

6. The parish priest or his assistant should visit the school at least once every week, examine the pupils and give some reward to the best ones.

7. The parish priest should help the children *(estos pobres)* by providing them with paper, pens and ink.

The following chapters are about:

—Rules for the pupils.

— When to ring the church bells.

— Duties of teachers and cantores

— Processions

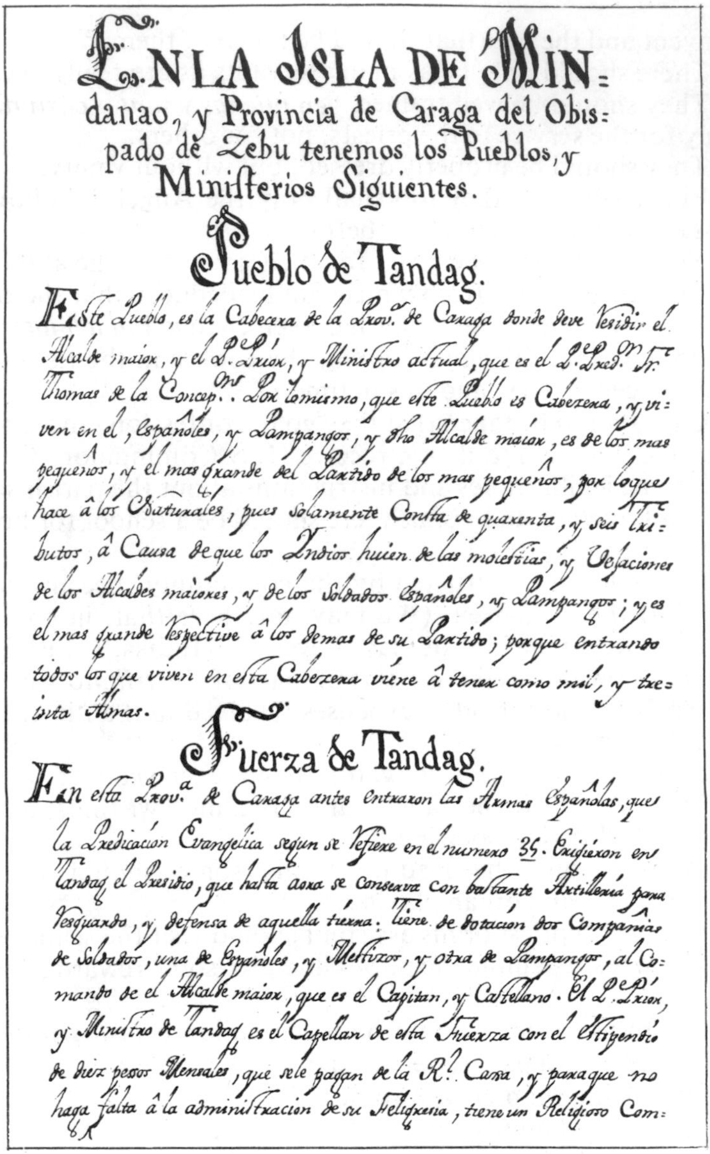

En la Isla de Min-danao, y Provincia de Caraga del Obis-pado de Zebu tenemos los Pueblos, y Ministerios Siguientes.

Pueblo de Tandag.

Este Pueblo, es la Cabecera de la Prov.a de Caraga donde deve residir el Alcalde maior, y el R. P. Prior, y Ministro actual, que es el R. P. Pred.or Fr. Thomas de la Concep.on Por lo mismo, que este Pueblo es Cabecera, y vi-ven en el, Españoles, y Pampangos, y dho Alcalde maior, es de los mas pequeños, y el mas grande del Partido de los mas pequeños, por lo que hace â los Naturales, pues solamente Consta de quarenta, y seis Tri-butos, â Causa de que los Indios huien de las molestias, y Vejaciones de los Alcaldes maiores, y de los Soldados Españoles, y Pampangos; y es el mas grande respectivo â los demas de su Partido; porque entrando todos los que viven en esta Cabecera viene â tener como mil, y tre-inta Almas.

Fuerza de Tandag.

En esta Prov.a de Caraga antes entraron las Armas Españolas, que la Predicacion Evangelica segun se refiere en el numero 35. Erigieron en Tandag el Presidio, que hasta aora se conserva con bastante Artilleria para resguardo, y defensa de aquella tierra. Tiene de dotacion dos Compañias de Soldados, una de Españoles, y Mestizos, y otra de Pampangos, al Co-mando de el Alcalde maior, que es el Capitan, y Castellano. El R. P. Prior, y Ministro de Tandag es el Capellan de esta Fuerza con el Estipendio de diez pesos Mensales, que se le pagan de la R.l Caxa, y paraque no haga falta â la administracion de su Feligresia, tiene un Religioso Com-

Fig. 23. Seven pages of complete statistical data of the District of Caraga, compiled in 1750. This is one of the many documents stolen during the British Occupation of Manila in 1762, at present in the British Library in London (Ms. 13973, Add.) (With permission of the British Library, London.)

panero asignado, que es el P. Pred.r Fr. Rodrigo de los Dolores, para que exensa la Plaza de Capellan Real. En otra Cabezera de Tandag à mas de los Soldados otros, y Officiales Correspondientes, que muchos de ellos son Cassados, así muchos Reformados Españoles, Mestizos, y Indios de las misma Calidad, y con todos se forma un buen Pueblo. Y este Ministerio de Tandag, tiene à su Cargo Cinco Visitas, ó Pueblos Anexos, que son los Siguientes.

Pueblo de Tago.

El primero es el Pueblo de Tago distante como legua, y media de la Cabezera, por Mar, y por tierra. Consta de Ciento, y treinta Tributos, y seis cientas Almas.

Pueblo de Marihatac.

El Segundo es Marihatac, distante de Tago, quatro leguas, por Mar, y tierra. Consta de treinta, y seis Tributos, y Ciento, y Cinquenta Almas.

Pueblo de Liangan.

El tercero es Liangan, distante de Marihatac, cinco leguas. Consta de Ochenta Tributos, y trescientas, y Cinquenta Almas.

Pueblo de Calagdàn.

El quarto es Calagdàn, distante siete leguas de la Cabezera. Consta de trescientos Tributos, y de mil, y dos cientas Almas.

Pueblo de Bayuyo.

El quinto es Bayuyo, distante como media legua de Calagdàn, Consta de dos cientos Tributos, y como mil Almas. Necessita este Partido à lo menos de otro Religioso, para la administracion de dichos Pueblos.

Pueblo, y Ministerio de Bislig.

Este Pueblo es Cabezera de Partido, y le administra, el P. Pred.or, y Prior actual, Nr. Fran.co de la Virgen de Magallon. Consta de Cinquenta Tributos, y doscientas, y Cinquenta Almas. Tiene à su Cargo el P. Prior de este Pueblo, quatro Visitas, ô Anexos, que son los siguientes.

Pueblo de Ginatoan

Necesita el P. Prior de Bislig para administrar este Pueblo medio dia de Navegacion, y buena voga. Consta de cien Tributos, y de quatrocientas, y Cinquenta Almas.

Pueblo de Catèl.

Este Pueblo, dista de Ginatoan, como seis leguas. Consta de doscientos Tributos, los Ciento, y Cinquenta de Christianos, y los Cinquenta de Infieles Cathecumenos, y de mil Almas, poco mas, ô menos tiene este Pueblo, un Presidio, ô Fuerza para resistir à los Moros, el que defendio con gran valor, y esfuerzo, el Ven. P. Fr. Benito de S.n Joseph, quando le asaltaron los Moros año de mil Setecientos Veinte, y dos, como se refiere en el numero 173, en honrra de la Religion, y gloria de Dios, y del Rey.

Pueblo de Baganga.

Este Pueblo, Consta de Ochenta Tributos Christianos, y treinta de Infieles Cathecuminos, y tiene como quatrocientas, y Cinquenta Almas. =

Pueblo de Caraga.

De este Pueblo toma su denominación la Prov.ª, y es el ultimo de los Dominios del Rey nrõ Señor en estas Islas. Consta de Cinquenta Tributos de Christianos, y de ciento, y diez Tributos de Infieles Cathecumenos, y de doscientas, y Cinquenta Almas Christianas, y quinientas Almas Cathecumenos. Necesita este Partido de dos Religiosos, à lo menos, para la administracion de los Pueblos Christianos, è Instruccion de los Cathecumenos. Si en este Partido de Bislig, se destinaran Missioneros, con el Estipendio Correspondiente de la Real Caxa, ni con doce Religiosos havria bastante, y tendrian todos mucho, que trabaxar, en servicio de ambas Magestades, y con mucho fruto, Espiritual, y temporal; porque son Infinitos los Infieles que habitan en los Montes de este Partido, llamados Taqubaloyes. Son Indios blancos, y de buen Cuexpo, mui dociles, y amigos de los Españoles.

Isla de Siargao, y Pueblo de Caolo.

Esta Isla esta en el Golfo, distante de la de Mindanao quatro leguas. El Pueblo principal de ella, es Cabeza de Partido, y se llama Caolo. Consta de ciento, y Veinte Tributos, y de Seis Cientas Almas, poco mas, ô menos. Tiene à su Cargo en esta misma Isla dos Visitas, que son las siguientes.

Pueblo de Cabontog.

Este Pueblo, dista como seis leguas de la Cabecera, y se vá navegando por una Silanga. Consta de doscientos Tributos, y ochocientas, y Cinquenta Almas.

Pueblo de Sapao.

Este Pueblo dista de su Cabezera quatro leguas, y se vá Embarcado por la Silanga. Consta de Ciento treinta, y Cinco Tributos, y de Seis cientas, treinta, y Cinco Almas, poco mas, ô menos. Dicha Cabecera de Caolo, tiene otros tres Pueblos de Visita, ô Anexos, en la tierra firme de la Ysla de Mindanao, que son los Síguientes.

Pueblo de Higaquet.

Dista este Pueblo de su Cabezera, quatro leguas. Consta de Cien= to, y sesenta Tributos, y como setecientas Almas.

Pueblo de Pahuntungan.

Dista este Pueblo de Higaquet, como dos leguas. Consta de Ciento, y sesenta Tributos, y Ocho cientas Almas.

Pueblo de Surigao.

Dista este Pueblo de Pahuntungan, quatro leguas, las que se nave= gan por la Silanga. Consta de Ciento treinta, y Cinco Tributos, y qui= nientas Almas.

Isla, y Pueblo de Dinagat.

Dista esta Ysla de Surigao, como tres leguas, hai en ella, un Pueblo de su mismo nombre. Consta de Ciento, y quarenta Tributos, y seis cientas Almas. Hai en esta Ysla muchos Indios fugitivos de sus Pueblos, y no cumplen con la obligacion de Christianos, ni pagan Tributo â su Mag.ᵈ Los Ministros hacen las devidas diligencias, para reducir â dhos Indios al Servicio de ambas Magestades. Este Pueblo, es tambien Visita de Cao= lo. Necesita este Partido de dos Religiosos, para la administracion de sus Pueblos, que es muy travajosa, por las muchas Corrientes, y mu= chos Temporales, Especialmente en tiempo de Brizas. Esta todo este Partido oy â Cargo del L.ᵈ Pred.ᵒʳ y Prior actual de Caolo, Fr. Mar= cos de S.ⁿ Lorenzo. Tiene un Religioso Companero, que es el L.ᵈ Fr. Antonio del Santo Christo del Desamparo.

Pueblo, y Ministerio de Butuan.

Este Pueblo, es Cabezera de Partido, y le administra, el L.ᵈ

Pred.^r, y Presid.^{te} de el Sr Lucas de la Cruz. Consta este Pueblo de Ciento, y setenta Tributos, y de setecientas, y Cinquenta Almas. Tiene el Minº de este Pueblo â su Cargo siete Visitas, ô Anexos, que son las siguientes.

Pueblo de Talacobon.

Subiendo por el Rio de Butuan, que es de los mas Caudalosos, y de mas Corrientes de estas Yslas, y navegando por el tres dias Continuos; esta â la margen de dho Rio, el Pueblo de Talacobon. Consta de Cinquenta Tributos, y doscientas, y Cinquenta Almas.

Pueblo de Hibon.

Subiendo por el mismo Rio â distancia de Cinco leguas de Talacobon, esta el Pueblo de Hibon. Que Consta de Sesenta Tributos, y de doscientas, y quarenta Almas.

Pueblo de Linao.

Subiendo por el mismo Rio, y navegando por el otros tres dias desde Hibon, se entra en la Laguna de Linao, y en su margen esta el Pueblo del mismo nombre. Consta de Setenta Tributos, y de doscientas, y ochenta Almas. Es tan penosa la administracion de estos tres Pueblos, que en el tiempo mas bonancible, desde Butuan hasta Linao, hade navegar el Ministro por el Rio, alomenos doce dias. En este Pueblo hai un Presidio, con su Cabo, y ocho Soldados Españoles. En esta Laguna de Linao hai muchos Rios, y todos poblados de muchisimos Infieles Manobos, llamados Manobos. Y desde Linao se va en una Jornada por tierra, hasta el Partido de Bislig, y toda aquella dilatada tierra, es habitada de dhos Infieles, y si se quisiera Misionar, en los Rios de dha Laguna, y en la tierra que hai hasta Bislig, ni Catorce Religiosos eran bastantes, y tendrian mucho que trabajar, y Copiosisimo fructo Espiritual, y temporal, que Coger, para Dios, y para el Rey.

Pueblo de Tubay.

Bajando por dho Rio de Butuan, y Costeando por la Mano

hasta el Río de Tubay, â distancia de quatro leguas, está el Pueblo de Tubay. Consta de Cinquenta Tributos, y dos cientas, y Cinquenta Almas.

Pueblo de Habongan.

Subiendo por dho Río, â distancia de seis leguas de Tubay, está el Pue= blo de Habongan. Consta de Ciento quaxenta, y nueve Tributos, y de seis Cientas Almas, poco mas, ô menos.

Pueblo de Mainit.

Subiendo por el mismo Río, y â distancia de otras seis leguas de Ha= bongan, se entra en la Laguna de Mainit, y en su Margen, está el Pueblo de su mismo nombre. Consta de Ciento Cinquenta, y Cinco Tributos, y de seis cientas, y diez Almas.

Fig. 24. ''Mapa de la Provincia de Caraga'' (1751) by Francisco Alegre. This map is part of a series of Recoleto documents stolen by the British during the Occupation of Manila in 1762 and afterwards brought to England. Note that the map is upside down! (With permission of the British Library, London.)

XIII

Holocaust In Caraga

Saying that the process of hispanization was the foremost influence shaping the past of Caraga, would, of course, be stating the obvious. Less obvious perhaps but just as true is the statement that another influence affected the course of that past in a very traumatic way: the devastating Moro raids against the district.

Existing documentation about Old Caraga may time and again be found wanting in many aspects, but there is no dearth of information in Recoleto chronicles and archives about the deadly reaction created by Spanish entrance into territory controlled or claimed (or coveted?) by the Moro leaders of Mindanao and Jolo.

I do not feel qualified to find out where the possible dividing line is between understandable opposition against Spanish intrusion and, say, a possible imperialism of Islam itself. This is anyway rather beyond the scope of this work. I may, however, once and for the whole rest of the following pages state that I am fully aware that there is more than the side of the coin mostly shown and deplored in Spanish reports, but these are the only ones available as far as I know. And I regret this as much as my Muslim friends might.

In those Spanish accounts it is as a general rule a clearcut drama of hatred by the "followers of the ridiculous and perfidious false prophet and the pernicious teachings of the Koran" against the salutiferous Gospel-truth to be spread by Spanish presence, or

against *"el honroso y acomodado dominio en las islas Philipinas"*:
the honorable and benign sovereignty over the Philippines. Ergo, a
simple issue from the moral point-of-view! Hatred there undoubtedly was. It had been preceded by an age-old aversion between the two
systems of belief, that had been in furious combat time and again
during the "reconquista" of Spanish soil from the "Moors" and
afterwards during the crusades into Moslem territory of the Middle
East. In Caraga the two would clash again in the new context of an
archipelago where Islam had started to get a purchase in Jolo, along
the south and west coast and up in the Polangi river of Mindanao. Its
foothold was not much more than 200 years old and still expanding
when the Spaniards appeared on the scene.

The Crescent and the Cross where both uninvited guests in the
islands of the archipelago. History has not left us much
documentation of the mode of conquest of the former, but there is
ample historical evidence of the destruction, dislocation and near
abandonment resulting even in the non-Moslem district of Caraga
when Spanish conquista clashed with Moslem reaction elsewhere in
Mindanao. The near continuous state-of-war reigning in Caraga for
nearly the whole second half of the 1700s was going to be so
traumatic for the district that it would become one of the major
reasons for lasting under-development, noticeable even up to the
first half of the 20th century.

We have already seen how as early as 1631 the Moros of
Maguindanao promised to come to the help of the Caragans if the
latter would rise up against the Spaniards, but how in the end they let
the Caragans do their own job in that undertaking.

About 1645 we see the beginning of the Dutch instigating the
leaders of both Muslim and non-Muslim areas to do a similar job for
them. This made for the kind of development described before. In
his comments Pedro de S. Francisco remarks:

> "It is not the first time in this part of the world that the
> (Dutch) heretics gave armed support to pagans and Muslims to
> oppress Christianity. What a blindness on their part! To place
> themselves, in the matter of a religious war, purely for their
> business interests, on the side of the Koran and of idolatry, both
> of which they themselves condemn, and which are both contrary
> to the Gospel which pagans and Muslims persecute with fury"
> ("Historia...," p. 153).

In the following stages, especially in the 18th century, the Moros were angry and numerous enough to wage their own wars. Montero y Vidal ("Piraterías...," 1888, p. 334) states that the outrages committed by Moro invasions all over the archipelago between 1762 and 1772 could fill whole volumes. In Caraga, this had started to apply already ten years earlier.

It is ironic to note here: once the Moro fury had methodically swept over all of Caraga for about fifty years, the Dutch in Maluku were facing their own Moro problem. On August 20, 1778, only twenty-four years after Maguindanaos and Maranaos had totally destroyed the Spanish fort of Tandag in Surigao, the Dutch Governor-General of Indonesia would inform his successor about

> "... the necessity to send soldiers, ships and war materiel to Ternate, because otherwise there is danger that it will succumb to pirates. Even if the rumors about the strength of their fleets were only partially true, it would not be very difficult for the Maguindanaos to occupy all of Maluku. It has been said that last year they had a fleet of 1000 sails at the ready. Although it seems to me that 1000 Maguindanao sails is an unbelievable number, it is nevertheless a fact that they do have ships in their fleet manned by crews of more than 200 and as tall as a two-master...Reports by boat builders from northwest Celebes (Sulawesi) who had gone there to work say that they had been continuously employed building ships for the Maguindanaos" (Lands Archief Batavia, Bundle "Ternate," no. 78, quoted in "The History of the Minahassa" by Godée Molsbergen).

Speaking about the "traumatic" effect caused by the Moro raids of the 1700s: up to as recent as the 1950s, parents in Surigao who had never read Dr. Spock but wished nevertheless to be assured of proper behavior by their children, just used the threat of "calling the Moros!" I have been told that the same is true in northern Sulawesi. One could also note how in all the early maps of Mindanao, including those of the 18th century, Punta San Agustin and the gulf of Davao look as if they had been drawn by men who were too scared to come really close to the spot and have a good look around the southeast corner of Mindanao.

When the French anthropologist Joseph Montano was traveling south to Davao along the Pacific coast in 1881, he remarked:

> "During three centuries these coastal settlements became the prey of the Moros. Till the time when the authority of the

conquistador Oyanguren was firmly established in Davao at about 1850, the Moros took to sea every year in the month of May. Their flotillas, which often counted up to fifty boats, ravaged the whole east coast of Mindanao. These exactions were not totally stopped before the subjugation of Cotabato on the Rio Grande and of the Sulu islands. The carelessness by which the Bisaya have facilitated those innumerable razzias is beyond explanation. Just a little redoubt armed with some swivel guns would have made the pueblos unconquerable. But nowhere have I seen even one suggestion of a defensive structure ("Voyages aux Philippines, ...," entry for February 10, 1881).

This adventurous Frenchman was obviously little informed about realities existing along the east coast of Mindanao during the Moro raids. In the first place, he had not been in Tandag and had not heard about the fortification once standing there, nor about its tragic end. He did not know about the little forts once established on Siargao, near Cantilan and Surigao. In the places where he did pass, Bislig, Cateel, Baganga and Caraga, there had once been "presidios," i.e., armed garrisons housed in fortifications of wooden stakes and earthwalls. Finally, he seems to have been unaware that the whole defense strategy on the east coast was determined by the Spaniards, not by the local Bisayas. As a matter of fact, the principal stronghold at Tandag had originally been built in 1609 as a protection against local tribes, as we have seen earlier. On August 31, 1797 the Recoleto parish priest of Cantilan wrote:

> "The Tandag fort was never built as a stronghold against our worst enemies, who are the Moros, but with the aim of defending the village against the pagan Manobo tribes, who were the real enemy. At that time the Moros did not yet act as enemies; they came to these villages with their merchandize and left again, just as if they were some out of many friends" (Nat. Archives Manila, Leg. 118, Pte. 1).

The Spaniards would never have trusted the coastal Bisayas for a long time with fortifications of their own armed with swivel guns! The history of Siargao, Tandag, Bislig, Cateel and Baganga shows anyway very clearly how "unconquerable" those places with their armed fortifications were, as we will see very soon. Fixed land-based forts (useful and necessary) were of no use for going after or meeting head-on the kind of enemy whose highway was the Ocean. And looking at it from the defensive viewpoint, once the (wooden, except at Tandag) strongholds were laid siege to, they could, with relative ease, by starvation and assault be taken and wiped out.

It is easy to understand that on those raids the favorite targets of the enemy were the parish priests, the churches and the convents. Much documentation material and personal, first-hand accounts must have perished on these occasions. Nevertheless, the Recoleto chronicles and manuscript archivalia at Marcilla are replete with laments about the destruction, cries for help, fear, persecution, captivity and death of missionaries and natives alike. Between 1622 and 1741 the Order lost seven missionaries at the hands of angry rebellious Caragans; in only thirty-eight years, between 1732 and 1770; five would be killed by Moros, while another became totally demented after a harrowing escape near Gigaquit.

The exact year when the first great raids on Caraga started is difficult to pinpoint. There is one indication that about 1604 Moro attacks were already quite a nuisance at Butuan. A Christian convert of Butuan, Diego Inongan, captured in a raid, and imprisoned in Cotabato, told his fellow prisoners there that it would be very easy to stop the Moros from invading Butuan: all that the people there had to do was pray to God to station a battalion of angels to guard the river entrance! (Letter of Fr. Melchor Hurtado SJ to his Provincial Fr. Lopez, 1604).

In the "Carta anua" for 1611-1612, Father Gregorio Lopez, the mission-superior, wrote to Rome that in order to protect Butuan from the attacks of the "Mindanao" (= Cotabato) natives, the government had decided to put up a military stockade in the place to be manned by a captain and some soldiers from Cebu. He adds that because of all the rumors they had heard about these Cotabato raiders, these men were not at all happy with their assignment.

There is, however, some indication that about 1670 the fear of such attacks cannot have been very prevalent at Butuan. The village, formerly located about five kilometers inland, near the present Banza, was around that time transferred to the sea coast to where now Magallanes stands. This would certainly not have occurred under conditions in which people, church and convent were seen as easy targets of regular attacks by sea-borne raiders. It was only after these attacks had become near annual disasters, that most of the seaside villages of Caraga moved to protective locations more inland. This happened to Butuan already seven years later: in 1677 it was moved back to its former location at Banza.[35] This could indicate that about that time the security situation had drastically deteriorated. If so, then it can only have been because of the menace of Moro rampages. In 1729 the people of Cateel lived either upstream or inside the mangrove swamps near the rivermouth where only small *barotos* could enter. I have not found reports about systematic and large-scale Moro invasions in Caraga between, say, 1680 and 1722. Still, some such information is implicitly contained in certain accounts, like when, as we heard earlier, (about 1670), the Tagabaloyes in the jungles behind Bislig and Cateel shared with the coastal Bisayas an implacable hatred of the Moros, and that Tagabaloyes and Bisayas had to live with their weapons close at hand all the time. As late as the early 1950s a strong aversion to the Moros was occasionally still discernible in the spontaneous vocabulary of Mandayas and Manobos in the mountains back of Lingig. We will also remember still earlier reports about "Borneans and Ternatans" who had been spreading fear and hatred — with or without Portuguese collaboration — along southern and central Philippine coasts. Also the casual references between 1680 and 1722 about fortifications existing in coastal settlements seem to betray that fear was widespread.

> It was resolved that, so far as the funds in the royal treasury would permit it, some small *armadas* should be despatched against the Moros, and that the coast dwellers should be gathered into larger villages at certain places, at the rate of at least 500 tribute-payers [ca. 2,500 persons] to each one, in order that they might be able to resist the pirates and build some little forts, which would inspire respect in the enemy. This precaution had already been taken by some of the missionaries in charge of *doctrinas*, who, not finding any other remedy, had built some fortifications around their churches, in order to guard these and enable the Indios to take refuge there when the Moros came. Others had constructed some small forts on lofty places, to protect the villages from the affronts of those robbers. At night the fathers would go to those posts, and watch lest the sentinels fall asleep, performing at the same time the duties of parish priests and of military officer. As a consequence of this order, there was no coast village which did not build some

---

[35]Butuan: in 1865 it was once more transferred from Banza to the seashore (Magallanes), from where it moved to its present site in 1877.

fortification for its defense, but no aid was given to them from the royal treasury. But the religious ministers, out of their own stipends, paid the overseers and artisans; and by dint of entreaties, persuasions and threats obliged the people to give the materials and day-laborers, expending much money and patient endeavor for the sake of building these little forts. When the Alcaldes saw these fortifications, now finished, they began to try subjecting them to their own authority, and they ensured that in every one should be stationed a warden, subject to the orders of the Alcalde, and that a certain number of men for the service of the fort should be furnished to the warden by appointment from the respective villages. The warden regularly sent these men to work in his own ricefields, or compelled them to redeem (replace) the compulsory service with money. The men had to do this, usually leaving the fort abandoned, which is, for this reason, very burdensome for the people. Here comes to be verified what Señor Solorzano[36] says, that whatever is decreed in favor of the Indians, is converted into poison for them" (Zuñiga, "Historia de Philipinas," in Blair & Robertson, 46:52 and 55).

Among the documents stolen by the British during the occupation of Manila in 1762 and now in the British Library in London, is a report of 1750 about all the mission territories of the Recoletos in the Philippines (Ms. 13973). On p. 103 ff. is the report about the "Provincia de Caraga." About Tandag it says that only very few natives *(naturales)* are living there: only "46 tributos"; this would amount to approximately 230 people. The reason given by the author of the report (the Recoleto Provincial) is: "The Indios run away from the troubles and vexations perpetrated by the Alcaldes and the Spanish and Pampango soldiers."

The latter with their families amounted to 800 souls. Juan de la Concepción, like all Recoleto authors very critical and caustic about anti-Moro policies of the government in their mission territories, wrote in his "Historia" (1784) as follows about these compulsory reductions for self-defense:

"The soldiers were more necessary for this undertaking and to prod the dodgers and the skeptics than for beating off and

---

[36] Solarzano: a Spanish jurist and member of the King's Council in 1635 when he used the quoted expression.

curtailing the Moros. They hardly minded the latter, and still less the former, with the result that everything remained in the same dire necessity and the same condition as before'' (Vol. X, p. 368).

In the Marcilla archives of the Recoletos I found a very well preserved "Travelogue to Tandag" (1730), a 34-page report about an inspection- and fact-finding trip to Surigao, Gigaquit, Cantilan, Tandag and Cateel in 1729. "Escrito humoristico" has been added to the subtitle in different penmanship. Reading the contents makes one understand the possible reason why the document is in such excellent condition: it was probably kept out of the hands of readers most of the time. If one follows "the inspector of the forts and garrisons" Don Francisco Cardenas Pacheco on that bottle-popping and bed-hopping voyage, one gets an impression of how corrupt and rotten official life could be in at least these outposts of Spanish presence in Mindanao. The preliminaries to the fateful events at Tandag in 1754 which we will presently describe, become a little more understandable after one has finished reading this "escrito humoristico!"

In 1722 Fray Benito de San Jose was parish priest of Bislig. In his biography, Francisco Sádaba ("Catalogo") mentions that already in his days the seas in the southern part of the archipelago were unsafe due to the presence of Moros from Cotabato and Jolo who "were feared everywhere as real pirates."

One day in 1722 Fray Benito happened to be in Cateel which was one of his *visitas* and where a small fort had been established about fifty years before. Just then the sound of the warning horn erupted from the lookout, and the fearful shriek "Moros, Moros!" started running through the village. Most of the people took to the safety of the hinterland, while others took shelter inside the palisade of the fort. But very soon everybody inside was becoming convinced that the situation was going to be hopeless. Fires were already raging all around; even the powder magazine ignited and blew up. The Moros besieged the fort in an ever tighter encirclement. It was the inspiration and personal courage of Fray Benito that boosted the sagging courage of the defenders, who finally did succeed in preventing the Moros from scaling the ramparts. In the end, the attackers were repelled and driven back with great loss. That night, while the soldiers were celebrating victory, Fray Benito died of a heart attack.

In 1749 the situation had considerably worsened as appears from many entries in Lib. 41 of the "Libros de Definitores" in Marcilla.

> "The year 1749 has been one of the most disastrous which the Philippines has gone through because of the multitude of Moro vessels that have been attacking everywhere, leaving behind a trail of robberies, burning and captivity...Where they delivered the worst blow of their fury was in a district that we considered very safe, namely that of Caraga. Here they burned... Gingoog, and Tubay, *visitas* of Butuan, plus Sapao and Cabuntog, which are *visitas* of Siargao. In the mentioned villages the convents, churches and all the houses were turned into ashes... Four of our Religious working in Caraga could only save their lives by escaping and running into the jungle, where they wandered around barefoot, so that the words of St. Paul applied also to them: 'They wandered around in lonely places, and went hiding in caves and holes in the ground, haunted and afflicted'." (Hebr. 11:38). (Provincial to Vicar General).

"Which we considered very safe..." Probably the Provincial was referring to trouble brewing in Jolo, Sulu and Maguindanao and thought that this would be fought out on the southern and western side of Mindanao, and not on the east coast.

In Tomo VIII of the "Historia General" of the Recoleto Order, the compiler, Gregorio Ochoa del Carmen, writes on p. 22:

> "Hardly had the Marquéz de Obando taken over the governorship of the Philippines (on July 20, 1750) when he not only declared himself decidedly a protector of the Jesuits, but he also totally conformed himself to their instructions. One of the principal reasons for the many disasters that have been recorded during the time of his fatal administration was the imprisonment for so many years of the Catholic and innocent Sultan of Jolo. The Moros swore to take revenge for that injustice and kept to that oath to their heart's content by covering the seas like corsairs as if they owned the archipelago."

A whole book could be written about the numberless intrigues (in Jolo and elsewhere) swirling around this Don Ferdinand I, born Mahomet Alimudin, the attempts at his conversion, his stay in Manila, his faked submission to baptism, the rivalry in this murky affair between Dominicans, Jesuits and Recoletos plus the Manila archbishop. A whole field for research lies waiting for a possible researcher in the Archivo General de Indias at Sevilla, but he or she must remain aware of the possibility that contemporary loyalties and antagonisms may have colored or even doctored the source material here and there. Just to cite one example: Ochoa del Carmen speaks about the "Catholic and innocent Sultan of Jolo," because the contemporary reports of the Recoleto Provincial in Manila said so. Bypassing any question of any kind of guilt or innocence of the Sultan, what about his Catholicity? To play it safe, let us listen to his own answer; it is to be found in the Sevilla archives, Legajo 706, dated July 2, 1752.

In the document, the Dean of the Cathedral Chapter *(cabildo)* of Manila, writing to the Secretary of State in Spain, informs him:

1. About the nullity of Alimudin's baptism.

2. How it had come about that he had been baptized: his seemingly Catholic and pro-Spanish attitudes in Manila had misled everybody.

3. That also his religion teachers had been struck by his suspicious questions about "the value of the Sacrament," whereas for the rest he had no problems at all with even the most difficult dogmas.

4. That even after his baptism he had shown lack of respect inside the church by remaining seated during the elevation of the Host.

The Dean adds that afterwards, when being interrogated in Fort Santiago by two Jesuits, the Sultan had stated: "I never had the intention of becoming a Christian... You should know, Father, that they induced me to sign several letters of which I did not understand the contents, and so I did not know what I was signing...."

With due respect to all parties and authors concerned, and with no more malice than they often show to each other, we may say that Alimudin clearly was a playball of local politics in Jolo, of Spanish intentions vis-à-vis the "Moro problem," and of ecclesiastical jealousies or rivalry between some religious Orders. As for the two missionary Orders concerned in Mindanao, they clearly had some deep-seated diverging opinions about how the other was failing in its missionary and administrative responsibilities. Whatsoever the truth may be, we may well say that it was not only pagans and Moros who wrote non-Christian pages into the history of Mindanao!

In all kinds of tones and undertones, contemporary Recoleto correspondence, on the local administrative level and with higher authorities in Spain and Rome, accuse the Jesuits of plotting with Governor General de Obando to deprive the Recoletos of the

Caraga mission and have it turned over to the Jesuits.

In 1753 the Recoleto Provincial wrote to the Vicar General in Spain about secret intentions of the Jesuits that had leaked out via the Jesuit school in Manila: the Jesuit Procurators Murillo Velarde and Pazuengos going to Rome were instructed to do also some strong lobbying in Madrid to move authorities there to give the whole Recoleto territory in Mindanao to the Jesuits. Meanwhile the alcaldes (of Caraga and Cagayan) were to be influenced to petition the Manila government for the same. The reasons to be given should be: that the Recoletos were not as good administrators as the Jesuits: even their own faithful had said so; the fact that there were still so many pagans in the Recoleto half of Mindanao could only be explained by their "poca aplicación": they were not working hard enough at it. One year later, on July 16, 1754 the Provincial writes again:

> "The order of the Jesuit General in Rome is to give us anything we would ask in exchange for Caraga; that is what one of them has told me under secret" (Lib. de Def. no. 41, p. 97v).

About the attitude of Governor de Obando, the Provincial complained:

> "Obando has urgently requested us that we turn over to the Jesuits the province of Caraga, Cagayan and its mission stations and also the island of Camiguin. As compensation he offers us other equally good places elsewhere that are now administered by the Jesuits. He even threatens us that, if we do not give in to his urging, he will just take away from us the administration over the mentioned places and hand it to the Jesuits without giving us any compensation; such for reasons of State as required by the service to the King in connection with the handling of the offensive war on land and sea that the Moros of Lake Lanao have announced" (loc. cit.).

The Recoletos also bitterly complained that, on instigation of the Jesuits, the troops that Manila had despatched to Mindanao, of which a part should have come to Caraga to relieve it of Moro pressure, after arriving in Cebu: 1) first drank themselves into a delirium; 2) were then coursed to the Jesuit territory instead.

Another of their gripes was that the Jesuits had been instigating the people in **Camiguin**, **Cagayan** and **Bukidnon** to petition for Jesuit missionaries, promising them, as the author scathingly states, "el oro y el Moro!" A literal translation of the expression, especially in our context, would be misleading; it means nothing more than: anything they would ask.

The complainants hoped for a better deal under the next Governor Arandia, but in the end they resolved that it would be better to meet the Jesuit requests halfway, and ceded the Bukidnon missions to them. Upon further insistence and for the sake of better relations, also Cagayan was ceded after some time. Our informer states: to comply with Matt. 5:40 "If someone asks your undergarment, gave him also your mantle!" As compensation, the Recoletos were given some Jesuit territory in Cavite. Caraga, however, "the apple of our eyes" would under no conditions be surrendered to the Jesuits.

We have digressed a little on these unsavory intramural squabbles because both the question of the imprisonment of Sultan Alimudin and the Jesuit-Recoleto animosities were very much part of the Recoletos' biggest problem in Caraga: the ever increasing devastation by Moro attacks on the whole district.

> "In vain we swamped Governor de Obando with requests and complaints, asking him to help and defend us against those robbers.In vain were the steps taken by our Provincial who, filled with anguish about the disasters of all our districts, offered him all that our poor Province possessed, to put an end to those evils; he even promised to give 1000 sacks of rice to those who would work at the construction of a fort at Surigao, plus 500 sacks for the crew of the armada that would go there for the protection of the district and of the work for the fort. It was all wasted effort. As it was said in a letter of the Provincial to the Vicar General dated February 18, 1755: the only possible explanation was that, because the Recoletos refused to surrender some missions in Mindanao to the Jesuits, the Governor had decided that all the other territory under their administration would be taken away from them. The result of that fatal policy and the consequent total absence of protection was that the Indios who paid their tribute to the King of Spain in order that his representative would protect them, once they saw themselves abandoned, went over to the Moros and paid tribute to them to avoid being killed or imprisoned. In the island of Leyte two hundred families voluntarily and at once joined the Moros and

renounced the Catholic religion. But such desertions made no
impression at all on the Governor and his mentors'' (Ochoa del
Carmen, VIII, 22-23).

There is no doubt that the two decades after 1749 belong to the
most lamentable years of the history of Caraga. In 1759 the Recoleto
Provincial would write to Spain: "All that is left of Caraga is just the
memory of the villages which we once administered in that province.
The only exception is Linao and its garrison, the sole relic that
somehow still exists.'' In the reports left behind by his successor, a
reference is found (of 1753?) stating:

> ''I have been told that the Moros have overpowered Surigao
> and that they are constructing their own fortification there. If
> that is true, what will be the extent of suffering of our
> Religious? Rather should I say: I will be grateful to God if that
> would be all, because it looks as if all the ire and the fury of the
> Moros is directed at us, because we are staying on land that is
> theirs.
>
> In the month of October of the past year 1752, the Moros
> of Jolo set upon the island of Siargao, in the province of Caraga.
> They ransacked and burned the convent and the church of the
> main village of Caolo.[37] The saddest of it all is that they have
> stolen or burned the Blessed Sacrament, because the priest who
> was there at the moment, the Lector Andres de la Santisima
> Trinidad, had barely time to save his life and he had no chance to
> remove any church ornaments, small or big; therefore,
> everything was left for the Moros to satisfy their greed with.
>
> The channel to the village of Caolo is by itself quite safe,
> but the Indios, overconfident because the Moros had never
> reached that place, had been very negligent in executing the
> protective measures ordered by the parish priest, who at the

---

[37] Caolo had more or less permanently been one of the mission stations
on Siargao, together with Cabuntog and Sapao. Already in 1631, one of
the choir boys of Bacuag came from Caolo. A few times references name it
Numancia and connect it also with Cacub, with Our Lady of Carmel as
patroness.

The map ''Isla de Mindanao'' in ''Labor Evangelica de los Padres
Agustinos Recoletos'' (1882) glaringly misplaces Caolo, Bayuyo,
Calagdan and Hibong.

moment of the disaster was in another village. His companion had reminded them several times of the order of the parish priest but they always had answered that the Father was too much afraid. As a result, such is now the situation wherein the main village of the district finds itself. The beautiful church and the nice convent, surrounded by a palisade, are now completely reduced to ashes because of the negligence of the Indios, and the church ornaments and the sacred vessels are in the hands of the Moros.

For that reason it has become necessary to order that the main station be set up in Surigao, a *visita* of this district, because in the latter village a handsome fort is under construction, at the expense of the royal government, so that in the future also the missionaries can live under its protection and will not suffer anymore such terrible robbery and burning'' (loc. cit., report of Jan. 26, 1754).

In this raid on Siargao, the mission superior, who happened to be at another station of the island, had escaped with about fifty of his people into the jungle, where the Moros finally came upon them. After a fierce hand-to-hand battle, the Moros overpowered him and cut him to pieces.

The mentioned assistant who had narrowly escaped at Caolo, fled by *baroto* to the mainland where, however, he was caught and brought to Lake Lanao as a prisoner. After unspeakable sufferings this slave of the Moros was ransomed for four hundred pesos plus...twenty slaves. The latter had been donated by a friendly Moro, who had also acted as intermediary.

The other assistant, Fray Roque, who had been only one year in the Philippines, was in Gigaquit when the Moros struck there. He still saw his chance to grab a musket and some shot and made for the mountains. For some time he was able to elude his persecutors and on one occasion he kept them at bay with his weapon. For days he wandered around without food, till he was found by some natives, totally out of his mind. Over land they brought him all the way to Linao. Eventually he was shipped to Manila, a raving madman for the rest of his life.

The parish priest of Butuan first went through the siege of the place and then escaped to Linao.

The raids of October and November 1752 are rated as the worst ever in the account of the Provincial. Cantilan (then still two separate barrios, Bayoyo and Calagdan) was burned, also Caolo,

Sapao and Cabuntog of Siargao, plus Surigao, Pahuntungan and Gigaquit on the mainland. The same happened to Butuan, Tubay, Mainit, Jabonga, Talacogon and Gingoog. "Of all these places, only the memory of what they once were is still left."

In 1752 the Recoleto Provincial reports that the Moros had occupied the goldmines of Surigao, which were now being operated by forced labor of prisoners. The newly appointed Prior of Tandag had been captured before he had even established himself in his parish. The captors took him to Malanao, where he was eventually set free after the Order had paid a ransom of five hundred pesos in cash and another five hundred in natura. During his imprisonment, when informing Manila about the conditions for his ransom, he mentioned in his letter that more than one thousand prisoners from Caraga were being kept in the Malanao region. (Marcilla archive, Provincial to Vicar General in Rome, 26 July 1752).

In his book "The Christianization of the Dioceses of Surigao and Butuan," the late Father Anthony van Odijk, MSC mentions a Canonical Book of Marriages that still existed in Surigao in the 1930s, which had this annotation:

"Fray Mateo de la Encarnación, Provincial of the San Nicolas province of the Recoletos of the holy father St. Augustin.

As the Moros have stolen and burned the Canonical Books of the village and district of Siargao, I order that this book be used to register the marriages of the main station of the aforesaid district.

Given on February 1, 1752, at the Convent of St. John the Baptist."

This Fray Mateo is the same as our reporter in many of the previous pages. The annotation is curious in more than one way: judging from its date, there must have been a previous deadly raid on Siargao, most probably the one of 1749, mentioned earlier. In January 1754 the Provincial still noted:

"From letters written in June 1753 and received in Manila in September, I am informed that many Moro boats from Malanao and Maguindanao are infesting the seas near Caraga. If again anything untoward is going to happen, the man to be blamed is no other than the Governor. I informed him about the burning of Siargao, but nothing was done, although I had asked him to send two *galeras* down for the protection of that province. He did not even deign to answer because he seems to be stupid and not to care if the Moros destroy a district of the Recoletos, as if it was not part of the King's domain like the other islands...

Of the armada of Don Pedro Zacharias two ships were lost before reaching Calapan and about 80 people were drowned. These and the other disasters show that God is on the side of the Moros because of my many faults and sins..."

"If again anything untoward is going to happen..." It would, for that very same year of 1754 was going to be the blackest in the history of the fort and the village of Tandag, a year of rivalry, treason and destruction. The fateful events in the fort are fully described by Juan de la Concepción in his "Historia General de Philipinas." First, however, a few preliminaries about the antecedents to that story.

From the previously mentioned "Travelogue to Tandag" can be gleaned that about 1720 a Don Andres Perez de Cabiedes was Alcalde of Caraga; in 1725 he was succeeded by Joseph Espino. In 1729 this Espino was deposed and condemned to prison on orders from Manila. The trip to Tandag by Captain Francisco Cardenas Pacheco was undertaken to put this order into effect and at the same time to submit the fort of Tandag and other Presidios to a thorough clean-up and re-organization. Espino had among other misdeeds been accused of engaging in excessive private business activities, for which he had been using the "for official use only" champan and its crew for buy-and-sell trips along the coasts of Caraga, Bohol and Leyte. It had always been known and whispered around that alcaldes were guilty of such abuse, but with the Moro danger becoming an ever increasing nuisance, and every vessel and crew being needed for protective coastal patrols and possible military action, this kind of corruption took on an even more aggravating aspect. And so Alcalde Espino landed in jail ("le pusieron un par de grillos"). It is, in its own way illustrative that the anonymous author of the "Travelogue" depicts the executor of the sentence (Cardenas) as indulging in the same vice, plus some. It looks as if the parish priest of Tandag shared the author's evaluation of Cardenas, whom he even suspected of having fabricated his own coat-of-arms. The pastor who hailed from the same province and knew that his real name was Guzman, at one moment could hardly control his disgust at his swaggering country-man and publicly asked him if this was really his coat-of-arms. "Of course, it is," he answered angrily. The

Recoleto stood up, turned his back and walked away to the convent, muttering to his companions: "What a country, these Philippines! People who had to flee from Spain, often with Moro or Jewish blood, flock together here, and with all their airs they try to blind even those who know them!" In Spanish "Guzman" means also nobleman.

Be that as it may have been in this particular case, coming as it does from an "escrito humoristico," it is a fact that the low moral standing of many soldiers and officers had become a real problem to the insular government. Proof for that will be found while one struggles through the Legajos 6898-6911 ("Secretaria de Guerra, Fechos y Emplejos") at the Archivo General del Reino in Simancas. The exasperating thing with the "Travelogue to Tandag" is that often one does not know where reporting ends and 'humor' takes over, and/or where both are just swimming in alcohol. That, of course, cannot be said of the "service reports" at Simancas, which are replete with cases of deportation — to Africa, America and the Philippines — of misfits who in Spain had been sentenced for various crimes, a considerable number of them for desertion. Even as late as 1794 Governor General Rafael de Aguilar bitterly complained from Manila that Madrid should stop sending to the Philippines

> "Spaniards of the lowest extraction, who all their lives have only busied themselves with the meanest and dirtiest things, because once they have been transplanted here, they consider themselves heroes and men of the first rank, purely because they have a white face" (AGS, loc. cit.).

Five years earlier, in 1789, the Provincial of the Recoletos had written to the Manila government:

> "The soldiers of Tandag who are called Spaniards, and also the Pampangos there, are actually natives of Tandag, descendants of the first Spaniards and Pampangos who were garrisoned in that Presidio and who eventually produced some white Indios" (Marcilla, Oficios y Contestaciones, Lb. 85, p. 165ff.).

This, say, intensive acculturation had brought along some other unwanted consequences that were intolerable in a military environment and at a time of national danger. This appears from the action taken by Cardenas in 1729, when he found out that most of the military had their own houses outside the fort, in Tandag and Tago.

> "All the people in Tandag and in the rest of the district are deeply disgusted because Cardenas, without concern for the poor victims who collapse from hunger, has ordered that within 15 days all the infantrists should transfer their residencies from the village to the fort; he has forbidden those poor uprooted wretches to leave the fort anymore... He himself is going out to demolish some of the houses" (Travelogue).

Some of the very few documents about Caraga in the Archivo de Simancas concern the appointments of alcaldes (Governors) to the district. Mostly (but not always) the alcalde was at the same time warden (castellano) of the fort at the capital of Tandag. In Legajo 180, fol. 217 we find the appointment paper of Gregorio Padilla y Escalante. He had been a soldier in the Philippines since 1701 and in 1738 became Alcalde Mayor of Caraga with a salary of six hundred *pesos fuertes per annum*. The appointment was for five years. Only three years later we read in Leg. 181, fol. 125, for March 1, 1741:

> "Transfer of Gregorio Padilla y Escalante. If he can not serve the whole term for the Alcaldia entrusted to him, Miguel Sanchez de Tagle should take over the post, or the person who will marry one of the daughters of Padilla in case Sanchez did not serve the remaining term out."

Clearly, the appointment had become a kind of family possession, because Sanchez was a son-in-law of Padilla; civil service rules were unknown as yet; the appointee had to pay the Crown a certain amount, and after that, who would blame him for safeguarding the return of that amount by keeping the possession in the family!

Legajo 182, fol. 148 (March 31, 1746) is about the next appointee, Fernando Miguel Lino. In the act of his appointment is provided: if he cannot serve the full term of five years, the remainder will be taken care of by either Francisco Carcanio or Cristobal Antonio de Leon.

The same Legajo, fol. 442 (December 27, 1750) reports the appointment of Juan Antonio Cebrian, with the provision that, when necessary, Ramon de Orendain or Manuel Rodriguez Pinillos will finish the five-year term.

We will meet some Tandag alcaldes again afterwards; for the moment let us interrupt this part of the story, but only to reconnect it with the previous one.

> "Already in the previous year our Province had suffered much in all its regions, but in the present one (1754) it went through even worse disasters. In the district of Butuan, with eight villages and counting all together about 800 tributes (4000 people) previously, hardly 150 are left, and these have fled to the mountains. The district of Siargao had seven villages and counted 1100 tributes; the villages have been reduced to ashes and the inhabitants have been dispersed to various provinces. The district of Bislig had five stations and there were 800 tributes; now only the garrison and fort of Cateel, consisting of a stronghold of palisades with ten soldiers, is left; with their own weapons and those of the inhabitants they have withstood the daring enemy; there are now only about 200 tributes left.
>
> In July (1754) the Moros arrived at Tandag, the capital of the province. They came in many boats, went ashore outside the range of the guns, leaving their vessels in a bay not far away. Next, they occupied the convent and started to attack the Christians who gave them a good beating. Nevertheless, they then tried to scale the walls of the fort, a reckless undertaking that would cost them dearly. Out of spite they burned the convent and a big sailboat of the parish priest that was moored nearby, after which they withdrew, leaving behind a trail of devastation in the barrios of the area" (Juan de la Concepción, "Historia General," Vol. XIII, p. 217).

That attack was only a trial-run for what was going to happen in October of that year. We have already seen that in 1746 a Fernando Lino had been appointed alcalde for Caraga for a period of five years; if necessary, Carcanio or de Leon were to fill part of that period. According to the appointment papers at Simancas, in 1750, ergo before Lino's term was ended, Juan Antonio Cebrian was appointed as his successor. Obviously, during Lino's term the positions of alcalde and castellano had been separated. Juan de la Concepción introduces the coming happenings as follows:

> "Previously, Alcalde Mayor Fernando Lino had died; in his testament he had, however, provided that a certain Rendon

would fill the vacancy upon his demise'' (XIII, 218).

In Concepción's report the resulting complications are somewhat obscure, but what is clear is that after the death of Lino (perhaps already during his life) the position of castellano, distinct from the governorship, was held by "The Lieutenant of the fort" as Concepción states, without mentioning the man's name, which was Mañaga; he had also been the vice-governor of the district. He vigorously opposed the testamentary decision of Lino, saying that the latter had no juridical faculties to make such appointments, and that he, the vice-governor and castellano, was now entitled to take over the military and political leadership. Rendon, on the other hand, insisted on his appointment by the late alcalde. Obviously, the official appointment of Cebrian was either unknown or disregarded by both parties. It came to a violent confrontation between Mañaga and Rendon, and a downright civil war situation developed at Tandag. In the previously quoted "Travelogue" we encounter this Rendon as "Don Domingo Rendon, a native of Tandag and the matchmaker *(alcaguete)* for Cardenas." Most probably he was the son of a Mexican soldier with a local woman of Tandag.

Both Rendon and Mañaga started recruiting followers. The rivalry affected even the loyalty of the local priests: the chaplain of the fort, Fray Rodrigo de los Dolores, sided with Rendon, while the parish priest joined Mañaga. The animosity grew so bitter that the chaplain, together with Rendon and his followers were forced to leave Tandag and settle in Tago. "Bien, si en esto se huviera contenido," if only it had stopped at that, sighs Juan de la Concepción. But it was not to be.

What follows is undoubtedly the most despicable thing ever to happen to Tandag. The Rendon camp sent a secret letter to Sultan Dumango of Tamontaca (Cotabato), informing him that, if he still had plans to capture the fort of Tandag, now was the opportune time because of the division in the fort and the locality. There may have been some other provisions in the communication as well, but if so, they are not known. Anyway, the invitation was not lost on the Sultan: in the shortest time possible he mustered a powerful armada, rounded Punta San Agustin of Davao and came sailing northwards. On October 9, 1754 he laid siege to Tandag on land and on sea. The armament of the fort consisted of 16 guns of calibers 12, 8 and 4, some of bronze, the rest of iron. In addition there was a good assortment of small weapons, all with an ample quantity of ammunition. Aside from the garrison of soldiers, there was a big

number of civilians, presumably the families of the soldiers who had
taken refuge in the bastion. The two military companies were not
anymore at full strength because of the split between Rendon and
Mañaga. Very soon the food supply inside the fort became as big a
problem as the enemy outside, all the more so because the refugees
from Tandag consumed more than the military defenders. A few
times some small *barotos* were able to smuggle in a limited quantity
of *camotes* and rice, but after 1 1/2 months of siege, famine forced
the beleaguered inmates to eke out their meager diet with what little
grass was still growing within the ramparts. At times guards just
collapsed at their posts from hunger, cold and rain. In case of such
sieges, one of the first things to be done was to remove all nipa
roofing to prevent it from igniting by "fire bombs" consisting of
burning resin-coated arrows or other objects hurled by the enemy.
And by now the rainy season had set in. Among the civilian inmates
there were voices suggesting surrender and hoping for the mercy of
the Moros, but Mañaga threatened to kill outright anyone spreading
defeatism. Finally, the first day of December was about to dawn over
the agonizing fort of Tandag. Under the falling rain and the last
protection of darkness, the enemy started putting ladders against the
ramparts; three Moros were able to sneak into one of the bulwarks
where they killed the guards. Then they turned the swivel-gun of that
bulwark around and started firing pointblank at the defenders inside
the fort, who by now had entrenched themselves inside the
storerooms and the chapel. The second officer of the fort killed his
own brother for saying that the fort was lost; he himself was killed
inside the occupied bulwark. Fires were already burning in various
corners and the castellano understood that the end was at hand.
Among the inmates was also his own wife. The end of the fort of
Tandag is not wanting in pathetic scenes of valor in despair. Not
wishing his wife to fall into the hands of the Moros, Mañaga told her
to put on her best clothes and jewelry and then killed her with his
own sword. Next he rushed upon the invaders who were breaking
open the main door and immediately found his own death. The
chaplain of the fort (the local parish priest) tried to save himself by a
desperate jump from the ramparts, but he was taken prisoner just
like the surviving rest of the inmates, many of them Spanish and
mestiza women. Discord and treason were paid dearly at Tandag on
that day.

When the night of December 1, 1754 fell over Tandag, it fell over
the smouldering remains of a bastion that had stood as a symbol of
Spanish presence and possession, but had now become one of

vileness and defeat.

Afraid that relief troops would be sent to Tandag, the Moros hurriedly dismantled the heavy guns and loaded them into their *pancos* together with the prisoners. However, because of the stormy December monsoon they had to throw the stolen guns over board near the bay of Lianga. Also the parish priest-chaplain, by now agonizing, was dumped into the waves "como cargo inutil."

The legitimate Alcalde Mayor Cebrian, who had been hiding in the jungles of mount Diwata during the siege, went to Iligan to petition for military assistance. A report about this can even be found in a communication by the Recoleto Provincial:

> "The Lord has consoled us with the information that a squadron of 11 ships has arrived at Tandag, the capital of Caraga. They were sent by the Governor General and were under the command of Father Joseph Ducós of the Society of Jesus, who has been charged with the re-organization of the province and the protection of the people. This expedition was successful and the said father entered in the Royal Fort St. Joseph of Tandag and unfurled there the Royal Standards of the Catholic King to the immeasurable joy and applause of the people there and of those in the other villages of the province. He rebuilt the ruins and manned it with veteran soldiers and all the armament necessary for its defense. As chaplain he appointed Fray Rodrigo de los Dolores, who all the time had remained in the area, in spite of the many hardships he had to suffer. Once he had finished these matters, he entrusted to us the administration of the parish and the chaplaincy, as it had been before, and then proceeded with his squadron southwards along the coast of Caraga to Bislig and Cateel to dislodge the Moros there. He attacked them head-on and drove them away with the loss of seven of their big boats. After that, he returned to Tandag and consulted with Fray Rodrigo about various aspects concerning the upliftment of the province and the resettlement of the people with proper security for them. Both reached complete agreement and then Father Ducós left for his station in Iligan. From there he sent his own report to Manila, and Fray Rodrigo did the same from Tandag. I have informed the governor in Manila about what Father Ducós has done. Our conversation was so ... (perhaps 'harmonious') that if we had been Jesuits, he could not have given us more information — or less. The higher government was so happy about both reports

that they sent me in the convent of San Juan all the letters they
had received and all the documents, thanking us for the way we
had done things in the province of Caraga, and promising us to
continue giving us all assistance needed to put the province of
Caraga in a better state than it ever was before'' (Marcilla. Bk.
41, p. 131r, and 131v).

An interesting document in the Archivo General de Indias should
be cited here. It is contained in Legajo 920 ("Testimonio...inrup-
ciones...Moros"), dated May 7, 1755. It is among the correspondence of Governor Pedro de Arandia with the Secretary of State; the
terminology used clearly shows that the information provided was
taken directly from Recoleto reports. After referring to the first
Moro invasion of June 1754, the author proceeds:

"On October 9 of 1754 about a thousand Moros from
Maguindanao arrived at Tandag. They said that they had already
occupied Atel (Cateel), Caraga, Baganga, Bislig, Icotuan
(Hinatuan), Liang (Lianga), Mariatag and Tago. All villages of
the jurisdiction of Cateel and those of the rest of Caraga are
totally destroyed and without people, the houses reduced to
ashes, as well as the convents, churches and statues. A great
number of Christians have been carried into captivity, and others
have been killed. Because of the shortage of food, quite a few
have died of hunger and a pestilence.... Of the eight villages
of Butuan the people, vassals of his Majesty, have been scattered
and live as fugitives along the upper reaches of the river.... The
Alcalde of the province has found people from the four regions of
Caraga in many other provinces, even as far as 100 leagues
away. The triangular fort of Tandag... is totally destroyed, and
nothing of any use is left..."

On July 15, 1756 Governor de Arandia writes again:

"Last year, on July 15, 1576 [second mailing] I wrote you
about the loss of the fort of Tandag, province of Caraga, in the
island of Mindanao. I now have the pleasure to inform you of its
reconstruction. It was not one of the biggest in this country, and
its location is in an out-of-the-way place difficult to reach, but in
spite of that it is important because it is in the middle of the
province and on the sea nearest to the Moro territory... I am
including the plan of the fort and also a certified report which I

have had printed, because it contains details of its siege and loss, and also of its restoration'' (loc. cit.).

I tried my utmost to locate the latter document in Sevilla, but in vain. Back home, while going through de la Concepción's account, I discovered that he too complains about not having found it either. But, so he adds sarcastically, this is no great loss:

> ''The siege and the fall is just as I have described it, and the restoration is not much to gloat about. After all, Father Ducós was just complying with orders when he went there with four boats full of Boholanos (eleven boats the Provincial had stated!). To get inside the fort of Tandag was by then already very easy, just as the stationing of a new garrison.
>
> As for the restoration: there was only little destruction that had to be repaired'' (XIII, 316-317).

Fray Juan was never at a loss for an anti-Jesuit dig when he needed one! No, it was far from holy peace and harmony between the Recoletos and the Jesuits in Mindanao. Perhaps Fray Juan was still irritated, possibly after reading one of his sources, a letter from the Provincial to the General in Rome, dated July 2, 1755:

> ''... I also beg your Reverence to, please, write to the Reverend Father General of the Society of Jesus, asking him to order his subjects here in the Philippines to let us live in peace and quiet, without poking their noses in any of our affairs, like we keep ours out of the business of those Reverend Fathers'' (''Cartas de Def.'' 41, p. 125v, Marcilla).

Truly, the whole story would offer enough material for a malicious piece of (non) fiction!

One of the lessons which Manila learned from the events at Tandag was the necessity to separate the position of alcalde from that of castellano. In Tandag, Father Ducós had given the latter position to Don Manuel de Espilla. However, he was granted so much authority that the still incumbent Alcalde Cebrian felt totally bypassed. Already a sickly man from the hardships endured during his escape in the jungle, he died soon afterwards, and Espilla was also given the rank of alcalde. Quite telling for those days and their antagonisms is what happened then: the first thing which the Recoletos did (with the approval of Espilla) after they had settled

again in Tandag was to send the Boholanos back to Bohol and man
the fort again with the kind of troops it had had before, *"mestizos
españoles allí patricios":* locally born mestizo Spaniards.

In 1758, three years after the restoration of the fort, the Moros
again burned Bislig and the village of Tandag, and once more they
tried to overrun the fort. But this time the defenders, having learned
their lesson, gave them a sound drubbing.

In a letter of the Vicar General to the King, dated July 1757, the
first sign of new hope for wasteland Caraga seems to be glimmering.
He writes that in Caraga ("which was the Troy and the foremost
target of the Moros") the villages of Bislig, Tandag, Siargao and
Butuan and their barrios are being repopulated. In Siargao, a new
wooden fortification with four bulwarks had been constructed,
financed by the Recoleto administration in Manila; the Alcalde
Mayor had sent a sketch of it to Madrid. For the protection of
Butuan, a large stronghold with palisades as ramparts was put up
near the mouth of the river (Marcilla, Legajo 61).

The following information is from the Provincial Chapter of
Manila (1758):

> "Of the twenty-one decisions that were approved, the
> eleventh determines that the island of Siargao with its three
> villages Caolo, Cabuntog and Sapao be separated from the
> region of Surigao, and that Caolo be the main station,
> independent from Surigao and with its own Vice-Prior"
> (Marcilla, Lb. III - de becerro -).

From the attendance list of the Chapter we glean that in 1758
there were resident parish priests in Surigao, Caolo, Butuan, Bislig
and Jabonga. The priest of Tandag was probably prevented from
going to Manila, which may be the reason why his name does not
appear. In the acts of the Chapter of 1761 we are informed:

> "Aware of the destruction caused by Moro invasions in the
> parishes of Surigao and Siargao as a result of which it has
> become impossible to maintain two priests, it is decided to make
> one parish out of the two, which will be located in Surigao"
> (ibid.).

In 1761 the new fort and its garrison were put to the test again.
Castellano Nicolas Felipe Rodriguez had left for an inspection trip to
Cateel and had entrusted the command of the fort to Fray Marcos,

the chaplain. Shortly after his departure, sixteen large Moro boats appeared before Tandag. Strong artillery fire from the fort prevented them from surrounding the bastion. However, they occupied the church and convent of Tandag and made these into their headquarters, from where they launched furious attacks for two weeks, but each time they were repulsed. In spite of that, it remained a fearful situation for the garrison and the other people who had taken refuge inside. Among the latter there were some who had gone through the siege and destruction of 1754, and some of these started talking of surrendering. It took all the vigilance of the Recoleto commander to prevent them from doing so; he threatened with severe punishment anyone who would spread such defeatism among the inmates.

The Moros outside were meanwhile engaging in their own psycho-warfare as well. From behind a wall that was still standing of the village tribunal, where they were safe from the guns, they kept calling some of the inmates by name; they repeatedly shouted that Fray Francisco — who was not inside since he had fled to the jungle — was a coward. They also called the wife of the Alcalde and her children by name, telling them that the best thing they could do was to surrender. They would be well treated and reunited with the Alcalde whom, so they said, they had captured near Marihatag.

Finally, in the third week the Moros lifted the siege. Again the church, convent and houses of Tandag were burned, and the enemy sailed away with thirty-two prisoners whom they had captured in nearby villages.

Clearly, it was still very much war in Caraga. On July 25, 1761 the Provincial noted downheartedly: "Our Province is still in a lamentable state. The Moro invasions keep going on, causing our missionaries never ending fatigue. Caraga is a district without houses, convents and churches...." In spite of the hazardous times, it was just then that a remarkable man appears for a short while in the story of the scorched province of Caraga. His name was Nicolas Norton Nicols, English by birth, turned Catholic and naturalized as a Spaniard while still in Europe.

We have seen earlier that one of the recurring gripes in Caraga was the lack of well-armed marine and land forces for the protection of the province. It appears that in 1761 Manila had once more decided to do something about it. The Recoleto Provincial wrote to Spain that he had good hope that some relief and perhaps even peace would come to Caraga soon. The Governor General had organized two relief detachments for Mindanao, one of one hundred soldiers

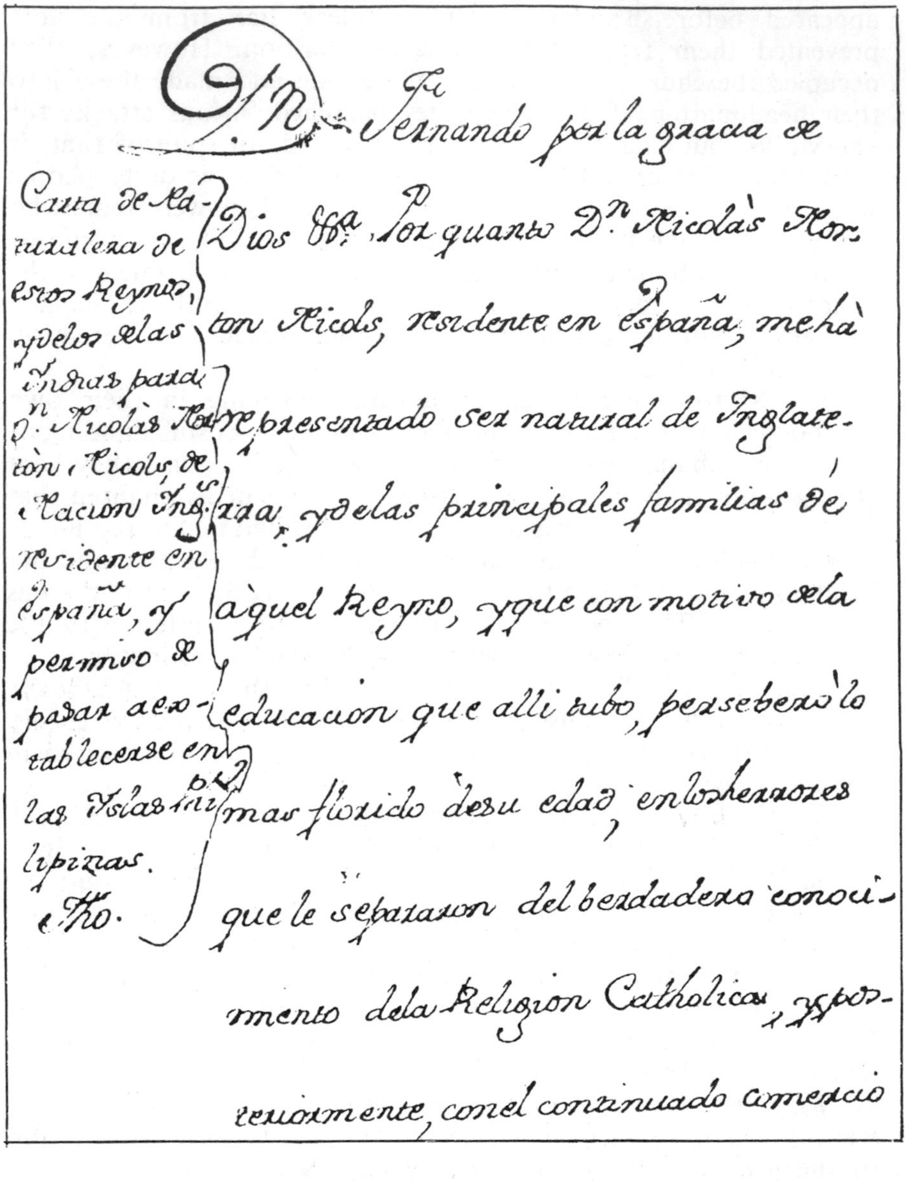

Carta de Naturaleza de estos Reynos, y de los de las Indias para Dn. Nicolàs Norton Nicols, de Nacion Ingles, residente en España, y permiso de pasar a establecerse en las Yslas Philipinas. Tho.

D. N. Fernando por la gracia de Dios &a. Por quanto Dn. Nicolàs Norton Nicols, residente en España, me hà representado ser natural de Inglaterra, y de las principales familias de aquel Reyno, y que con motivo de la educacion que alli tubo, persebero lo mas florido de su edad en los herrores que le separaron del verdadero conocimiento de la Religion Catholica, y posteriormente, con el continuado comercio

Fig. 25 First page of the naturalization documents of Nicolas Norton Nicols, signed by King Ferdinand on Aug. 3, 1758. (With permission of the Archivo General de Indias, Sevilla.)

for Zamboanga, plus another eighty soldiers destined for Caraga under the command of Don Nicolas. While still in Madrid, the latter obviously had impressed the King's Council by his concern about the lamentable lack of economic insight and commercial planning in Spanish overseas territories. Another keen-sighted man, Francisco Leandro de Viana, the Fiscal of the Royal Audiencia in Manila would write afterwards (1765):

> "Upon my arrival in these islands the inactivity and indolence of our people caused me much sorrow, for although we possessed this exceedingly rich treasure (cinnamon and other spices) there had been no one who devoted himself to its development. This I explained among other things to His Majesty in my report of June 5, 1760... In the following year came Don Nicolas Norton Nicols... and this famous and skillful Englishman began to make plantations in Caraga..." ("Viana's Memorial" in Blair & Robertson, 48, pp. 282-283).

The project, however, came to nothing, as the same Fiscal wrote, because shortly after the British occupied Manila in 1762, Don Nicolas died heartbroken "through the grief which he experienced because of the attack on us by the English from whom he could expect no favor."[38]

The mentioned project is all the more remarkable if we take into account that at the time in question most of Caraga was abandoned wasteland, open at any time to new devastations by the Moros. In the Sevilla Archives can be found the report of the sudden death of Don Nicolas (after a collapse). It mentions that he arrived in Surigao with a contingent of soldiers on 6 December 1762. Together with Captain Juan Muñoz he started immediately to draw up plans for a

---

[38] The Sevilla Archives (Filipinas, Leg. 343, fol. 226v to 229v) still contain the naturalization papers of Nicolas Norton Nicols and his authorization to depart for the Philippines, granted by King Ferdinand on August 8, 1758. It states that in the past he had lived in the error of Protestantism in England, but was now converting to the true religion after an extended stay in Spain. Out of gratitude for having found the truth here, he asks to become a Spanish citizen. He is also granted permission to engage in commerce in the Philippines, and all Spanish officials are exhorted to give him all the necessary assistance and courtesies.

fortification, but "the project could not be realized because of lack of food supplies and money for the soldiers" (AGI, Leg. 682, Exp. 14).

In March 1764 Bislig was one of the coastal villages attacked; after resisting for some time inside the local redoubt, the parish priest tried to escape to Linao via the Bislig River, but the invaders killed him while he, in the darkness of night and disguised as a native, tried to sneak onto a *baroto*.

In 1765 the Provincial, convinced, as he said, that all the reports of the last three years were insufficient to give him a proper picture of the affairs in Caraga, decided to go on a personal inspection trip, much against the advice of his counselors in Manila. He left in December, and in July of next year no news about him had reached Manila.

He returned in 1767 and wrote to the King that he had only seen ruins of villages, no people, because they were dispersed in the jungles, the missionaries being the favorite targets of the Moros time and again.

> "It is true, and I am much aware of it, that in the first years of the *conquista* some of our Religious suffered much, but at present they suffer much more, and it breaks our hearts to see it and be unable to do anything about it. Before, the only enemies were the pagans, but now they are facing pagans and Moros, and to fall in the hands of the latter is to suffer a protracted martyrdom."

Again, in July and August 1767 a fleet of more than seventy Moro boats sailed north from Cape San Agustin, first to the small fort of Cateel. This *"fuertecito"* was manned by only thirty soldiers, but was well stocked with armaments and provisions. But after a siege of eight days the local commander understood that they would be at the losing end of an eventual battle. Therefore, on a dark moonless night he and his soldiers secretly withdrew from the fort which next day was occupied and looted by the enemy.

From Cateel the armada sailed to Bislig and Hinatuan, but everywhere they found only abandoned villages. They sailed on, and reached their main target Tandag. The commander of the fort, Captain Jose Guelva y Melgarejo, was away on a business trip to Surigao and the Recoleto missionary of Tandag, Fray Valero de San Agustin, was in Cantilan, which was a part of his mission district. Aside from attending to his pastoral duties there, he was also supervising the construction of the fort and the digging of wells for sanitary drinking water in the site where the new village was going to be established out of the populations of Calagdan and Bayoyo. As soon as the Moros had been sighted, most of the people of Tandag had gone into hiding in the forest, but about one hundred able-bodied men had joined the soldiers to help defend the fort. The Moros laid siege to it, first from the seaside and next on land where they fortified themselves in two big trenches. A Spanish mestizo was able to sneak out of the fort and travel to Surigao in a *baroto* to inform Captain Guelva of the predicament at Tandag. Assisted by the priests of Surigao, the commander organized an armed flotilla, which first sailed to Cantilan. There Fray Valero joined them in his own armed sailboat with two hundred armed men from his parish. This combined armada, consisting of five sailboats plus one small vessel *("sacayanzito,"* to use the word coined by Juan de la Concepción) arrived before the besieged Tandag after some delay caused by contrary winds. Obviously, their appearance and number did not scare the Moros very much, because upon sighting the boats they shouted at those inside the fort: "Look, there comes your armada! Good for us, because now we are going to get some lunch!"

Very soon, however, they were to discover that they were going to be deprived of that. One group of Spanish and native troops under the command of Fray Valero attacked them on land and succeeded in dislodging them from their two trenches. A great number of Moro vessels were sunk on the river and the sea; very soon so many enemies were killed on land that "there was hardly a square meter that was not covered with bodies" according to Juan de la Concepción.

After the battle had lasted for about six hours, the surviving Moros fled by sea. This was the last direct attack on Fort Tandag.[39]

---

[39] Up to far into the last century Dutch colonial records of Indonesia contain many reports about Filipinos having been kidnapped in Filipino waters by either Indonesian, Sulu or Magindanao pirates who had ventured as far north as Romblon, Camarines and even Cavite. The names and the fate of these prisoners landed in Dutch reports because they had been sold as slaves in Borneo or Maluku, from where they eventually escaped and reported to Dutch authorities who returned them to the Philippines, mostly to Zamboanga. Similarly, a great number of Indonesians had been captured and sold by Maguindanao or Sulu pirates.

As late as August 13, 1851 Bishop Romualdo Jimeno of Cebu passed a circular instructing the parish priests to include in their yearly statistical

There is no need to stress that nearly one half century of fear and suffering had a very destabilizing influence on the attempts to concentrate indigenous villagers along the coast of Caraga in larger settlements. We have mentioned such attempts before, but in many Recoleto reports of those days we hear complaints about the absence of a deterring marine force in the area to give those settlements the feeling of security which they so badly needed. One complainant scathingly remarked that financial aid released in Manila, instead of being shared with Caraga, went wholly to Misamis...the district of another missionary Order, where a new fort to be named "Triunfo" was to be established. "Judging from the plans, it is going to be a second Zamboanga," one irked Recoleto reporter said!

The present town of Cantilan, or rather the way it came into existence, is one example of Spanish attempts at founding sizable villages with some provisions for self-protection. The Cantilan area appears in Spanish records from 1521 till the last quarter of the 1700s as Calagdan, Palasao or Bayoyo, after some small, still existing villages in the area. Already in 1761 a concentrated resettlement of Calagdan and Bayoyo in one place had been realized, but it was destroyed by the Moros shortly thereafter. The people fled to the mountains, where they lived in scattered clusters of houses; the parish priest was assigned to Surigao.

During the incumbency of Governor General Raon (1765-1770) a report about the condition of the fort of Tandag was made where it appears that one of its walls had collapsed and that the whole structure could only be maintained by continuous work of the

---

reports "the number of people who had the misfortune of falling into the hands of pirates ("Pastorales y demás disposiciones...", Tomo I, p. 125).

In his "The Malay Archipelago" *Alfred Russel Wallace* wrote in 1869: "...All along the coast of Batchian (N. Maluku) stretches a row of fine islands completely uninhabited. Whenever I asked the reason why no one goes to live in them, the answer always was: "For fear of the Magindanao pirates."

Every year these scourges of the archipelago wander in one direction or the other, making their rendezvous on some uninhabited island, and carrying devastation to all the small settlements around, robbing, destroying, killing or taking captive all they meet with. Their long well-manned praus escape from the pursuit of any sailing vessel by pulling away right in the wind's eye, and the warning smoke of a steamer generally enables them to hide in some shallow bay or narrow river..." (Dover Ed. 10, p. 261).

soldiers, who time and again had to prop up the walls with rocks, earth-fill and wooden supports. The main cause was erosion by the Tandag river; fear was expressed that one day a big flood would just wash the whole structure away. Meanwhile the "real" civilians of Tandag had settled elsewhere, especially in Tago, and only the families of the soldiers were left. At that time Tandag is reported as having no more than one hundred fifty indigenous civilian residents. Therefore Manila decided that the Presidio of Tandag should be transferred to Cantilan, where already many more people were living than in Tandag. A fort would be constructed on the new site, and people had already been exempted from tribute paying for two years to entice them to work on the new bastion. It would be manned by "Spanish" soldiers from Tandag (nearly all reports speak about "so called" Spaniards at Tandag!); The Pampangos would transfer to Cateel, where a better fortification was to be established. These orders were given during the time of Alcalde Zabala but were to be carried out by his successor Lasala. A report by the Recoleto provincial to Governor Berenguer de Marquina in 1789 offers a revealing flashback on the developments.

"... Alcalde Lasala was given weapons of various calibers to arm some sailboats that would function for the protection of the province. However, this new Alcalde to whom these orders were given, was not very active by character and a little slow-witted, and nothing came of the orders given by the higher authority. It was the Religious minister who started to put his shoulders to the task...For immediate needs a wooden fortification was established, to be replaced by a stone structure as soon as the Spanish soldiers arrived. But that is where everything stopped, because the Spanish soldiers refused to move out of Tandag, and the Pampangos to transfer to Cateel, and that is how things stand, Sir, up to the present. The reason is (I really cannot see any other) that the soldiers of Tandag, who are called Spaniards, and also the Pampangos are natives of Tandag, descendants of the first Spaniards and Pampangos who were garrisoned in that Presidio, who eventually produced some white Indios and some Pampangos in name. Anyway, regardless of how they were born, they as well as their parents and grandparents, do not like to abandon the place that they consider as their own village. Added to this is the laxity of the Alcalde, who even succeeded in getting permission to reside in Surigao, ostensibly because that place is a port, but in reality because he is

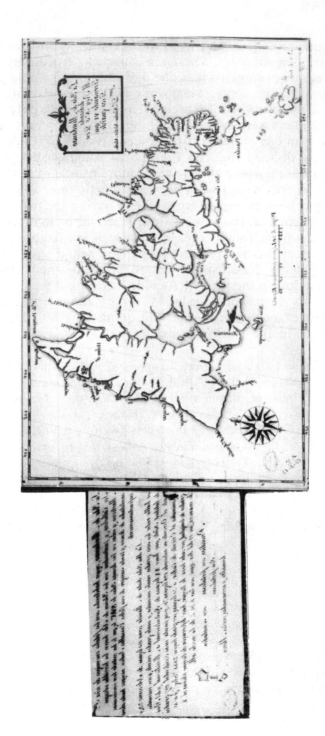

Fig. 26. Map of Mindanao by Don Nicolas Norton Nicols, 1757. (With permission of the Archivo General de Indias, Sevilla.)

after his own interest and his business... The Religious, however (Valero de San Agusan), who was Captain and Minister at the same time, made the new place his permanent residence and took care of Tandag as one of his visitas...

Sir, I conclude by saying that, what should be done is: passing a strict order to the Alcaldes of Caraga to live in the Presidio of Tandag and in the fort of which they are commanders, without leaving it longer than is necessary for a yearly visit to their province. That is the only way to make the Alcaldes execute what has been decided by the higher government, and only in that way a stone fort would soon rise at Cantilan where it is far more needed against the Moros than in Tandag'' (Marcilla, Oficios... y contestaciones,'' Lib. 85, fol. 165).

It cannot be denied that the Recoletos had their eyes on the job. The letter of the Provincial is remarkably free of the bombastic vocabulary often prevalent in the writings of contemporary churchmen. Actually, it is the answer to an accusation by the officer-in-charge at Tandag against the local parish priest for his "absentee-ism" from the fort. The retort (of which only a part has been quoted above) is a spicy example of "rubbing it in" and "giving them a dose of their own medicine!"

In addition, it gives an insight into the (second) eclipse of the Tandag fort and the painstaking rise of Cantilan as a result. The Cantilan of this context was located near the seashore, where some stone remnants and traces of water wells still recall Fray Valero de San Agustin.

Time did to Tandag what the Moros failed to do. The fort slowly decayed into an insignificant police outpost. After that it crumbled still farther until it vanished completely.

It has left behind some distinct Spanish features in the populace, traces of the *"caras blancas"* of Mexicans and Spaniards of yester-years.

It also left behind a distinct word in people's vocabulary: *"ang kota, "* just a reference to the place where once a fort had stood.

XIV

The Uneasy Foothold

In the last quarter of the 1700s the missionary apostolate in Caraga would remain a hazardous enterprise because of the unceasing Moro attacks on the coastal villages of the district. Aside from the danger which the missionaries were facing day after day, their presence and endeavors were furthermore frustrated by the fact that many of their people preferred the protection of the jungles and mountains to a risky existence along the seashore. As late as 1770, one of the priests of Surigao was attacked at sea while traveling to Siargao. Abandoned by his companions who had jumped overboard, he was overpowered and hacked to pieces in a fierce hand-to-hand fight. In 1773 the Priors of Tandag and Cebu were unable to attend the Chapter meeting in Manila because the seas of the southern Philippines were infested with hostile vintas and because they would not find suitable means of transportation. That year the Provincial sadly noted that the Order and its missionary work were *"en las ultimas agonias,"* in its death throes, because of poverty, the destruction and continuous fears in Palawan, Caraga and Mindoro, plus a series of internal problems. The poverty of the Order had reached such a degree that if one of their missionaries fell into the hands of the Moros and was carried away into captivity, it took five to six months before the money to ransom him would be available.

The statistics which the Provincial sent to the Governor in 1774 mention that the parish of Bislig had 1700 inhabitants, Tandag 2050, Surigao 2864 and Butuan 2868. The report has a note wherein the author excused himself for the incompleteness of his informations because of the unhappy situation of the Province due to never-ending Moro attacks. The parish priest, so he said, hardly had an opportunity to prepare statistics, since many of them were living as in a war zone, or had to stay in the jungle to hide from the enemy. A letter like the one wherein a Franciscan missionary in Samar poured out his heart to his superior in 1774, could have been subscribed to by many Recoletos:

> "I am writing you because my heart is deeply upset. The life which he missionaries are leading here in the Bisayas looks more like that of soldiers than of Religious. What kind of a religious life is this wherein a missionary is forced, day after day, to busy himself with cleaning cannons, muskets, rifles and pistols, with making cartridge belts, filling cartridges, making bullets, preparing fuses, constructing fortifications, being on guard day and night and watch those who have to keep watch (abantayar)? Is that the life of a minister of souls or that of a soldier (de almas, no, de armas, si)? What kind of religious life is it if, everyday or at least very often, one is obliged to fight off Moros and, if one does not kill, will be killed himself, or if one does not win, he will become a prisoner...We are crying out to heaven because we don't experience any help here on earth...Those accursed Moros are the masters of this land, and all of us, even if we are still free, are their slaves. Oh, if only the King Our Lord could see or would know what his vassals here are going through...We beg you to, please, obtain for us some direly needed help, and if that is not possible, let his Majesty himself come here and take care of this province!..." (AGI, Legajo 1052).

Then, there was another unsettling development affecting the missions of Mindanao very much. In 1768 the Jesuits had been expelled from the Philippines, "an expulsion which they had deserved" (su merecida expulsión) said one of the spontaneous Recoleto reports about the event then; the cronista Ochoa del Carmen would soften that 150 years later into la injusta expulsión! There are indeed no reports that during those days the Recoletos shed tears about the Jesuit departure in so far as it concerned Mindanao. What is clearly reported is, nonetheless, that the

Recoletos with obvious zeal gave in to the urgent requests of the
Bishop of Cebu, of the government and of the Jesuits themselves
presumably, to take over the pastoral care for the Jesuit parishes in
Mindanao and Bohol a.o. All their convents in Luzon were combed
out for priests who could somehow be spared for those vacant
places; eventually 16 were found, but in the big convent of Manila
only few residents were left. Because of the parish secularization
move in the Philippines plus the repeated attempts to subject all
parishes to the authority of the bishops instead of that of the Orders,
fewer and fewer priests volunteered for the Philippines. It is easy to
understand that very soon, with the missionaries spread so thinly, the
scarcity of personnel would acutely be felt each time a priest fell out
because of age, sickness or death. A report to the government about
the deployment in Caraga gives the following picture:

Parish	Barrios		No. of Tributes	Priests	Additional Pr. needed
Tandag	Calagdan		500	2	—
	Bayoyo				
	Marihatag				
Bislig	Hinatuan		420	1	1
	Cateel				
	Baganga				
	Caraga				
Surigao	Cabongbongan		671	1	1
	Gigaquit				
	Cacub (Siargao)				
Butuan	Mainit	Gingoog	657	1	2
	Tubay	Talacogon			
	Jabonga	Linao			

Source: (Marcilla, "Oficios ..." Lib. 85).

Population	1655	1676	1749	1778	1831	1851	1861
Surigao	3,000	3,335	4,685	5,285	9,478	16,617	17,886
Butuan	2,000	3,285	2,980	2,878	6,493	7,758	10,515
Tandag	3,000	2,500	4,330	2,747	7,929	8,229	9,680
Bislig	1,500	2,100	2,900	1,821	5,394	5,003	7,154
TOTAL	9,500	11,220	14,895	12,731	29,294	37,607	45,235

1797	Parish	Barrios	Population at 5 per tribute	Population in official register
	Surigao	Taganaan	6,187	5,311
		Gigaquit		
		Cabongbongan		
		Dinagat		
		Cacub		
		Sapao		
		Cabuntog		
	Buruan	Jabonga	3,432	3,961
		Tubay		
		Mainit		
		Talacogon		
		Linao		
		Gingoog		
	Cantilan	Tago	2,887	3,850
		Tandag		
		San Juan		
	Hinatuan	Bislig	2,837	2,835
		Cateel		
		Baganga		
		Caraga		

1749	Tributes	Population
Tandag	46	1,030
Tago	130	600
Marihatag	36	150
Lianga	80	350
Calagdan	300	1,200
Bayoyo	200	1,000
Bislig	50	250
Hinatuan	100	450
Cateel	200	1,000
Baganga	110	450
Caraga	210	750
Caolo	120	600
Cabuntog	200	850
Sapao	135	635
Gigaquit	160	700
Pahuntungan	160	800
Surigao	135	500
Dinagat	140	600
Butuan	170	750
Talacogon	50	250
Hibon	60	240
Linao	70	280
Tubay	50	250
Jabonga	149	600
Mainit	155	610
TOTAL	3,216	14,895

We might draw attention to the following:
— In the areal statistics (1655-1861) one thing is very clear: the population decrease between 1749 and 1778, caused by the unsettling events described earlier.
— In 1797 Taganaan appears for the first time in statistics.
— Cabongbongan: Like Pahuntungan one of the former locations of Bacuag, and later the predecessor of Placer.
— Cantilan has in 1797 taken over the rank formerly occupied by Tandag. San Juan is a Mandaya reduction at Punta Baculin between Hinatuan and Lianga.
— In 1797 Bislig has been replaced as *residencia* by Hinatuan. The reason is most probably the repeated destruction of Bislig by Moros; the last known attack happened in 1782. Before long, however, the missionary residence would move back to Bislig.
— The population figure for Surigao in 1778 is rather high because it includes that of Siargao. In the mid 1750s the main residency of Siargao was shifted to Surigao, which previously had been a *visita* of the former.

It is, of course, understood that very often contemporary statistics of whole regions have only a relative value. With so few resident missionaries around, it was impossible to track down all the people living in remote inland settlements. On the other hand, the very limited population could have made counting easier, too. At any rate, the figures provided are the only ones we possess, and we may assume that the enumerators tried to approximate the truth as much as possible (except when they tried to prove that they worked better than another Order!). The areal statistics and those of 1797 are from "Cuadros Estadisticos" by Toribio Minguella; those of 1749 can also be found in the British Library in the original Ms. (Add. Ms. 13973).

In 1776 the Provincial of the Recoletos wrote to the King to, please, send the priests whom he had requested in 1775 for Caraga and the other parishes in the care of the Order in the Philippines. For reasons to be dealt with more expressly afterwards, all the Religious Orders were by now handicapped by a steady decline in the number of new missionaries from Spain to staff the parishes under their responsibility.

How serious the problem was for the Recoletos, will appear from the following decision made at the intermediate Chapter of 1780:

"To inform the Governor General that we officially relin-
quish all those parishes that are vacant at the moment...because
of the non-availability of Religious to staff them" (Marcilla,
Lib. 3 -becerro-fol. 166).

In 1783 there was an alltime low in the number of priests in the
whole Caraga, as appears from a letter of Governor General Basco
to the Provincial, informing him that the Alcalde Mayor of Caraga
had written him about the death of the parish priest of Surigao, and
expressing his concern that now there were only two priests left for
the spiritual care of the whole province. The Provincial was urgently
requested to remedy that desperate situation.

To this the addressee answered that he did not have one single
priest available to fill the vacancies in Caraga, and would the
Governor, please, press the Bishop of Cebu into solving the problem
some other way.

That the government had its own worries about the uncertain
foothold of Spain on Mindanao was expressed by Governor General
Joaquin Jovellar in a report to the Ministerio de Ultramar at Madrid
in 1784.

"Our efforts at occupation are totally paralyzed. Either for
lack of means or because of poorly applied methods, 20 years
have been lost. Nothing betrays so clearly the absence of any
strong will to hold on to and, where possible, even extend
occupied territories, than the material condition of all our military
establishments in Mindanao" (see: Montero y Vidal
"Piraterias..." vol. II, p. 642).

It looks as if the urgent request of the Provincial to the King had
finally been given some attention in Spain; at least in 1776 the
personnel situation in Caraga had slightly improved: there were two
priests in Butuan, two in Surigao, one in Cantilan and one in Bislig.
Still, there were no more than two priests for the whole east coast
from Cantilan down to Bislig and Caraga.

In 1776 the Provincial informed the King about his findings. In
spite of the troublesome times and the limited number of
missionaries, progress had been made. In Butuan, for example,
about one thousand pagans living near Linao had come to ask the
parish priest that a missionary be assigned to their area, because they
all wanted to be baptized. The same was true for the district of
Cagayan. In contemporary reports to the Vicar General in Spain the

serious situation in Bohol which had led to the revolt of Dagohoy was said to be an aftermath of the misadministration by the previous missionaries, the Jesuits!

There was a lot of truth in the quoted remark of Governor General Joaquin Jovellar, however: the Hispanization process in the southern Philippines had reached a general impasse and had even come to a standstill. In eastern Mindanao this was especially true for the two southernmost villages (rather former villages) of Baganga and Caraga. While in the central and the northern part of the district some slow and hesitant recovery and repopulation was taking place, most of the residents of the deep south stayed away from the coast, preferring a miserable but relatively safe existence in the forests to living in close proximity to the Moro-dominated shores south of Bislig. In the long and ever worsening conflict between Spanish interests and Muslim resistance, they had so often been caught in the middle, where they found themselves at the receiving end of the ire of both, that they had become deaf to Spanish orders compelling them to live in controlled coastal settlements. Once the desertion had become almost general, Spanish clumsiness in dealing with those *"remontados"* often was no great help for enticing the latter to settle (again) along the shore. The Mandayas complained that there was insufficient Spanish military presence in the area to assure protection against persistent Moro claims and threats.

The documents used in the following pages are drawn from some dossiers in the National Archvives in Manila found on various occasions without any chronological or logical sequence. Since, however, they cover a relatively short period and a limited area and deal with one and the same concern, one can *(a posteriori)* discover some sequence and connection between them.

How complete the abandonment down south actually was, appears from a letter by the Recoleto parish priest of Cantilan (1796) wherein he uses the expression *"re-poblar los antiguos pueblos de Caraga y Baganga."* Obviously referring to Spanish attempts this "re-peopling" was considered very important by the Spanish government. An abandoned stretch of coast amounted to an open invitation to the datus around the Cape of San Agustin to take it. In one of the documents at hand mention is made of a Royal Order of May 8, 1790. I have been unable to find the text of that Cedula, but its contents can be guessed from the context wherein it is mentioned, and which speaks about "the resettlement, by attraction and Christianization, of former coastal inhabitants and others into a few organized littoral villages" (Letter of Alcalde M. Rivera to the

Governor General, Surigao, December 6, 1792). That indeed steps were taken and feelers put out to such effect may appear from a letter of Rivera's successor to Governor General de Aguilar:

> ... The datus of Caraga and Baganga came to see me in Cateel and offered that if a priest were assigned to their place and a garrison established there to defend them against the Moros, they would settle again in their old village of Caraga and help in the construction of a fortress or a bastion. Such a fortress could be armed with the weapons of the fort of Tandag...

> Surigao, capital of the province of Caraga, May 5, 1797.
> Juan Hipolito Gonzalez, Alcalde M.

In passing, we may point out that for the first time Surigao is mentioned as capital of Caraga instead of Tandag. The first communication dealing specifically with the pacification and resettlement of southern Caraga province is a six-page (large-size) letter to the Governor General in Manila, written at San Sebastian Convent by Fray Joseph de Santa Orocia and Fray Miguel de Salcedo. The former was at that time the Provincial of the Recoletos. The letter is obviously an answer to a preceding request by the Manila government for information and advice concerning Spanish plans for the southern Caraga district. The two authors put great stress on the necessity of government officials working together with the parish priest of the whole southern end of the province, Fray Pedro de San Blas. It is worthwhile noting that at that time there were only two priests for the whole east coast from Cantilan to Caraga! The letter continues:

> ''The biggest group of Mandayas are living in the mountains not far from the villages of Baganga and Caraga. Many, however, wanted to live more peacefully and free from the danger of the Moros, and these have withdrawn to the mountains that run from the village of Hinatuan up to Cateel. Both villages are under the spiritual administration of Fray Pedro de San Blas... He has already baptized many of the Mandayas living from Hinatuan down to Cateel, and has included them in the population register *(padron)* and incorporated them in those two old villages. Observing how this priest has unceasingly engaged in this holy labor, the whole Mandaya tribe loves him deeply, because they are by nature very docile and good. He has

decided to repopulate the old village of Caraga, as he said in a letter to the deceased Alcalde of the province; therein he mentioned that he was trying to convince the Mandayas of Caraga to work without payment on a stronghold which since then has been under construction... We hope that not only this new village will be formed, but even many others; the number of this tribe is so great that it will be impossible to settle them all in one village... The Alcalde has left Surigao with two galleys and will try to procure one or two armed tenders in the village of Cantilan so that he can proceed with more security.

He also plans to go to the land of the Moros who wish to make peace with the government, and ask the Father of Cateel, Fray Pedro de San Blas, to accompany him not just up to Caraga but even into the land of the Moros. Fray Pedro has been working not only for the resettlement of the Mandayas, but also for treaties of peace and commerce between the Moro datus and the natives of that province. His intention is that as a result the province of Caraga will suffer less persecution and that fewer of those poor people will be carried away as prisoners. Once peace will have been established, they would not need to be afraid anymore of the Moros, at least of those living near Cape San Agustin; they would only have to defend themselves against the Moros of Lake Lanao, who come via the Linapan River in the province of Misamis, and those of Ylanen and Magindanao.

The Father of Cateel is also much beloved by some of the Moro datus who ask for peace; they have come twice to visit him... Although those asking for peace are many and are among the more powerful ones, as Datu Campsa Israel, the Lord of Davao, his younger brother Alymuti, Datu Pampan, Datu Naga and many others with (part of the sentence illegible)... precaution and live always at the ready...In the whole province there is not a single armed government boat to confront the Moros of Lanao and Ylanen who frequently undertake raids and take the natives prisoner. In the district of Siargao alone they have recently taken more than 130 persons, as the Vicar Provincial of Caraga mentions in a letter of April 1, which we have recently received..."

Fray Pedro did not join the Alcalde Mayor on that trip south to Caraga, judging from a letter by the parish priest of Cantilan, Fray Francisco Marco, dated October 28, 1800. The reason is most probably that sometime between August and October 1800 he was transferred to another assignment; his pastorship of the Bislig region ended in 1800. Instead, the Alcalde took along the only other Recoleto on the east coast, the parish priest of Cantilan. In a letter to the regional superior at Surigao, he wrote that he had been in Caraga and had been deeply impressed by the reception which the people had given him and the party of the Alcalde. They had called all the people together for a meeting and both the Alcalde and the priest had extensively explained to them how good the plans were which government and church had for them. There was hardly any objection to the question of all of them living together in the village of Caraga, provided of course that proper steps would be taken for their protection against the Moros. They stressed the necessity of troops to be stationed there; on their part they had already nearly finished a strong bastion which was the best on the whole east coast.

A superficial counting showed that there were 1,753 Mandayas, but so the author states, only after the passage of a few years the exact number would be known.

They had not been able to meet with the leaders of the Davao Moros to talk about the possibility of a peace treaty, and therefore the best thing for the time being would be to rely on the existing amity. Possibly the following year a meeting with them might be arranged.

All in all it looked as if the plans for the settlement were off to a promising start. Deliberations had already been started about the assignment of missionary personnel to the region. On April 17, 1801 the Provincial of the Recoletos wrote to the Governor General in the Caraga context:

> "In the name of my province I offer you all that may be conducive to the spiritual administration of those who wish to settle in the fold of our mother the Church, since that is so much in conformity with the aims that have brought us to those remote areas."

Initially, the government had asked for only one priest, but in another communication the Provincial rightly pointed out that the work itself plus the conditions under which it had to be performed, required at least two priests. For their support he suggested to use the *"Obras Pias"* consisting of the funds derived from the properties of the expelled Jesuits, which were anyway intended for the Mindanao missions. From other sources it is known that there existed also a legacy of five thousand pesos for the Mandaya mission of Bislig, out of the testament of Juan Taboada y Salmente of Mexico.

But how about those at the business end, the Mandayas themselves? It is true that they had promised to have their children eventually baptized and that in principle they did not object to living in a settled village. But it is easy to understand that abandoning a primitive but free life in the wilderness and submitting to an organized village existence under close supervision did not come easy for our jungle dwellers. Still the impression made by the reports is that quite probably a wise policy of attraction coupled with a benevolent administration and sufficient military protection would generally have overcome those initial difficulties. Obviously, that was what an experienced man like Fray Pedro de San Blas, for ten years the parish priest of Bislig, thought too, as we may deduce from what we heard about him earlier. But on the other side, there was undoubtedly the pressure by the Moro datus of Davao, who claimed that the tribes of Caraga were their vassals and had to pay tribute to them. For the Mandayas to officially submit to Spanish authority would mean an open repudiation of the Moro rulers of Davao, who considered them their slaves. As a consequence, the Mandayas were between two fires; on the one hand the Spaniards pressing them to come down from the mountains and settle in the new pueblo, on the other hand the Moros trying to prevent them from doing so by threats and propaganda.

There was also fear among the Mandayas that once they lived together in coastal villages, they might easily become victims of abuses by Spaniards and Bisayan settlers.

There are indications that the Alcalde Mayor of the province had explained to the Governor General the problems arising from such fears. On May 13, 1801 Manila issued the following decrees:

1. Any person of whatever class who induces the Mandayas not to live in a village, under what pretext soever, will be imprisoned summarily, and after his crime has been proven, will be punished by four years incarceration in the capital, with leg-irons and chains.

2. The same punishment shall be imposed on any Spaniard, mestizo or native vassal of the King who collects tribute from the Mandayas; because nobody except the King has that right and anybody else using it flagrantly usurps his sovereign authority.

3. By this same public decree it will be forbidden to all Spaniards, mestizos or natives to make use, for domestic labor or in the

fields, of any Mandaya who is not yet living in a village and whose name has not yet been listed by the Alcalde Mayor as a vassal recognizing the dominion of our King. Such under punishment of a fine of ten pesos for the first time; if he does not have the money, he will be imprisoned for two months. This amount shall be doubled for the second offense; at the third he will summarily be put in prison, and once the delict has been verified he will be brought to the capital to suffer two years of incarceration with leg-irons and chains.

4. The Alcalde Mayor shall have these penalties publicly announced in the villages of the province, so that they come to the knowledge of all. In the same proclamation he will add that anybody who wishes to employ a Mandaya already settled in a village, must ask permission from the Alcalde Mayor, with the understanding that anybody found employing a Mandaya settled in a village without the mentioned permission, shall be sentenced to suffer the punishment imposed on him who employs a non-settled Mandaya: This is the way to stop fraud and to make it an obligation of all to contribute to the settling of the Mandayas in villages.

5. The pertinent communications shall be forwarded to the Reverend Father Provincial of the Recoletos, so that he will make available one Religious to minister to the new village: this should be a calm and prudent man with all the gentleness required to lead this new colony of Christian vassals of the King; for the increase and the solidity thereof he should strive, to learn as far as possible, the Mandaya dialect.

Between 1802 and 1804 also some further complications seem to have entered the resettlement program of Caraga. In 1803 a new Alcalde had been appointed to the province: Salvador Ximenez Rendon, probably the son or a nephew of the Rendon whom we met in Tandag in 1754. Perhaps he had been asked by Manila to give a report about what was happening at the southern end of the district. It looks as if he himself had an inkling that the situation was not very satisfactory indeed. In 1803 he made an inspection trip and returned not too happy about his findings. In October of 1804 he called before him some of the lesser political and military officials of the province who were well-informed about the situation at Caraga. Under oath and in the presence of witnesses, he made them answer the following questions:

1. Who had been the first to start this new settlement?
2. What were the motivations?

3. What promises had the Mandayas made regarding the construction of a fortification?
4. Did they know why presently the people there were so afraid that only under threat of punishment they would come down to populate the place?

The report of the first hearing goes as follows:

I, the aforementioned Alcalde Mayor and Juez Receptor ordered Don Francisco Juanillo to appear before me; I took his oath as usual and he complied, promising that under this oath he would speak the truth about what he knew and would be asked about; and aware of the contents of the preceding writ, he said:

1. That Don Juan Hipolito Gonzalez while still alive and Alcalde Mayor of this province, commissioned him to visit and supervise the elections along the whole east coast up to Baganga. While in the place of Baganga he went to the sitio of Duongan, where a Mandaya chief named Agumba was residing, and also a Capitan Mangayaay of the same tribe, with many of their subjects. They proposed to the said Captain Francisco Juanillo that as soon as a fortification was established at Caraga, they would settle there with all their subjects, because they could not stand anymore the tyranny of the Moros, and that they themselves would help in the construction of the fortification. For that purpose, the said Don Francisco Juanillo together with the defunct Commander of Cateel, Don Vicente de Castro and with Captain Don Mariano, Captain Damian, the soldiers Pedro Plaza, Culacito, Juan Alejandro and Felix Morales, made a survey of the place of Caraga. After arriving at that place, they found there a quite large plateau; it looked as if prepared by nature because of its elevation. At one point of it, quite high and close to the shore, they decided to put up the fortification. After that decision they went to the village of Baganga... (here one whole page is missing and the continuing page begins in the middle of a report about another visit to Caraga, this time by Alcalde Mayor Don Juaquin Pernia accompanied by Fray Francisco de San Basilio — we heard about that visit earlier — Juanillo is still reporting.)

... the fortification; he also found that the church, the convent and the village house had been put up and that a total of three hundred Mandayas were working at the mentioned tasks. Then it happened that the said Alcalde Mayor and Fray Francisco started to press the said chief Bundag about an idol which the chief kept in his house (they said it looked like a Santo Niño; the Mandayas gave it the name Guang-quang). Because of their insistence the said chief was forced to present to the Alcalde Mayor and Fray Francisco the idol about which they had been harassing him so much. The said Alcalde had a look at it and said that it was not the one he had asked for. To which Bundag replied that he possessed no other and that this was the one which they adored, he and his subjects.

In view of this, the said Don Joaquin Pernia overpowered the chief and declared him a prisoner. As a punishment he asked two slaves from him. At that, the wife of Bundag came and brought one of her daughters. Since Bundag did not have a second slave, he got hold of the slave of the deceased Commander and turned him over to the Alcalde, with the obligation to pay the present Commander. After this slave had been turned over, the chief was freed again, and the mentioned idol was destroyed. They divided the two Mandayas among themselves; Fray Francisco took the daughter of Bundag and the Alcalde Mayor the slave of the deceased Commander.

About this misdeed the Mandayas were deeply grieved; they went away, and the work on the fort stopped.

2. The Alcalde Mayor and Fray Francisco departed from that place, and left behind Captain Mariano with a few soldiers and the King's weapons, to proceed with the construction of the fortification without having even one grain of rice; they were forced to subsist on *camote*. And the said Captain Mariano had to go to the mountains with his soldiers in order to compel the Mandayas to come down to finish the fortification. The kidnapping of the daughter of Bundag and of the slave and the destruction of the idol which the chief kept in his house as an heirloom caused such bad feelings that they did not work their fields that year, and ran away to the mountains far away from this place.

3. On the occasion of the second visit by inspector Fausto Gabriel de la Soledad, when he arrived in this new village, he did not meet a single Mandaya. When he sent a message ordering them to come, a few appeared in a span of about two weeks.

On the occasion of the last visit by Don Joaquin Pernia, he who makes this deposition was not in this village, but he arrived shortly after the departure of the Alcalde Mayor. He was, however, informed that when the Alcalde Mayor arrived at this place, there was not a single Mandaya, and it was necessary to discharge a few artillery pieces as is customary in order to make them come down. I know for sure that there was a Mandaya woman who was with gobernadorcillo Don Nicolas Amistino, in order to be baptized. She was a daughter of the Mandaya Litig. The Alcalde took her to Surigao and when the said Litig came down to look for his daughter and heard that the Alcalde had brought her to Surigao, he said that the Spaniards had enticed them to build the fortification in order to deceive them and to take away their children to other places. And this Mandaya went back to the mountain so deeply grieved that until this moment he has not returned to the village.

4. Last year, when Señor Alcalde Mayor Don Salvador Ximenez Rendon had arrived at his first visit to the mentioned village, he found that the place had become a jungle again; in order to go up to the said place, there was a wooden stair of more than forty spans length. Since he did not encounter any Mandaya, the said Señor asked the gobernadorcillo and Sergeant Jose Bonilla, who then was in charge of the fortification, where the Mandayas were. We answered that they were in their houses in the mountains and that in order to make them come down, it would be necessary to discharge two or three artillery pieces. Indeed, after these had ben discharged, they came down and stayed here in the village to clean it and open a road to the plateau on top of the hill. After the Alcalde had left, the Mandayas went back to the mountains and did not come down anymore.

5. When Fray Marcelino de la Merced Balladares, the missionary assigned to that place, had arrived in the village, he ordered to call the Mandayas, and some came to see him. After having stayed there for about two weeks, he left again and went to the village of Baganga. Then the Mandaya Guintaopan and Captain Lindog came down, bringing along their children to be baptized. The gobernadorcillo and the Commander wrote to the Father who was then still in Baganga, informing him that the Mandayas had come down with three children to have them baptized. The said Father came, and after they had presented the three children to him for baptism, he answered that he did not intend to baptize them unless they bring him a large payment. After the Father had stayed there for about two weeks, he left; the children have

remained unbaptized until the present. Also about this deed the Mandayas were deeply grieved.

6. And this year, when the Señor Alcalde Mayor arrived at this new village, he again did not encounter any Mandaya, and it was necessary to discharge a few artillery pieces and to send some soldiers to the mountain to order them to come down. But only very few came, and with these he started again to clean the site which, as he found out, had become a jungle again.

This is what I know and can state under the oath which I have taken; this I affirm and ratify, and I declare that is the truth requested by law, and I sign it, myself and my qualified witnesses.

> Salvador Ximenez Rendon
> Francisco Juanillo
> Protacio Nepomuceno
> Eugenio Quiñones

"De que se quedaron los Mandayas muy sentidos".... Four times the sad expression returns in Juanillo's declaration; "Over this reason the Mandayas were deeply grieved"... There are four more sworn statements following the one of Juanillo. They relate, at times verbatim, the same facts. Obviously, Rendon wanted a thorough investigation of why the repopulating of Caraga and the resettlement of the Mandayas had become such a failure. Perhaps he feared that Manila would blame him for that failure.

The following document about Caraga was written one month later from Cantilan (November 19, 1804) by a Recoleto whom we met in July 1800 as Provincial of the Order: Fray Joseph de Santa Orocia. In his letter he introduces himself as "ex-Provincial, and now till his death assigned to the missions of the Mandayas." He reports that the first Mandaya mission of San Juan de Baculin was progressing very satisfactorily and that very soon hardly anybody would be left who was not baptized. One of the reasons "for the good climate" in that reduction, so he says, was that the Chinese businessmen from Cebu, Bohol and elsewhere had stayed away from the place because it hardly produced any article in which they might be interested. As a result, the Mandayas of San Juan had not been spoilt and had kept their natural goodness. In the "mission of San Salvador in the newly established village of Caraga" it is a different matter, however. The merchants from Cebu regularly came here to buy wax and other products from the natives, and the result had been much spiritual and even temporal damage.

> "Therefore I consider it necessary that certain rules be established to govern the commerce and other undertakings in this mission, for the spiritual and material good of my children, these poor Mandayas. It is out of love for their souls that I have renounced the quietude of my cloister-cell at my already advanced age. My intention is that you, as the first and principal protector of the poor Mandayas will free them from anything that could make them reluctant to join the fold of our Holy Church and the love of, and subjection to, our Sovereign."

Fray Joseph then proposes the following points to that effect:

1. With all strictness and with the necessary penal provisions steps should be taken to insure that only real natives will be allowed to live in the new mission of Caraga. At the moment there were a little over thirty families of old-time native Christians and a few settled Mandayas. With the exception of those, all the other should leave the place, because they are just vagabonds and criminals living from the sweat of the Mandayas.
2. For proper control, all merchants arriving in Caraga must present themselves immediately to the parish priest to prevent that they furtively go to the Mandayas in the mountains. Each of them must be assigned his own day for business.
3. Such business must be transacted under a shed to be put up between the convent and the fort that houses the soldiers, in order to prevent drinking sprees. After the ringing of the Angelus, all must retire to their boats till next morning.
4. They and the boat-crews must present themselves twice daily to the parish priest at nine in the morning and at five in the afternoon, "to prevent that such unwanted missionaries" will sneak away to the mountains.
5. To stamp out usury and slavery resulting from non-payment of debts, nobody is to be allowed to sell anything to a Mandaya that the latter cannot pay on the spot; such under penalty of losing the article and incurring punishment in addition.
6. It will not be permitted that anybody buy a Mandaya as slave; as far as this evil is concerned, some old-time local Christians

are even worse than outsiders.

7. The local village-head (gobernadorcillo) shall not be permitted to imprison or punish any Mandaya without the express permission of the parish priest.
8. The soldiers of the fort shall not be allowed to go to the mountain-Mandayas, except on orders of the Alcalde or of the parish priest.
9. In case of any violation of any of these provisions, the parish priest shall determine the punishment and use the local garrison commander to carry it out.

Since the village of Caraga was the most southern Spanish outpost along the Pacific coast of Mindanao, directly bordering on the Moro dominated district of Davao, it is clear that the resettlement of the village and all other Spanish efforts could never succeed without some modus vivendi with the neighboring Moro datus. Inversely, this applied for the latter too, because Caraga was going to be the southernmost spearpoint in Spanish ventures to push Muslim power back as far as possible. Lately, but only halfheartedly the datus of Davao had started to refrain from organized raids in Caraga province, but there were no guarantees that this unwritten and unspoken truce would last any length of time. Earlier we heard that attempts at friendlier relations had been made in the 1790s by the former missionary of the southern region, Fray Pedro de San Blas. Also Alcalde Rendon had met twice with the Moro leaders in question, as appears from the following report of his hand to the Governor General:

In the new village of Caraga, on August 13, 1804. I, Don Salvador Ximenez Rendon, Alcalde Mayor for his Majesty and Captain of the province of Caraga, also serving as Judge Receptor, in the presence of my qualified witnesses because of the non-availability of an Escribano Publico y Real, say: That in the village of Cateel I have met Datu Ladiamura Pampang, who said that he had come to meet me with the purpose that, right after my arrival in the new village of Caraga, he would personally go to the sitio of Davao and come back in the company of the chief datu of that place, whose name is Mucamad Amilbansa Harial, and of Datu Damuli, who is also a chief in that region, in order to make peace with them, as we had decided last year. After Datu Pampang had left, he went to the sitio of Manay where he stayed without going to Davao to inform the mentioned datus as he had promised. For that reason I was forced to order — and did order — Captain Damian to proceed to the sitio of Davao to inform the said datus of my arrival, so that they would come as had been our agreement last year, and we could conclude peace with each other. And by this write (... illegible) and sign it with my qualified witnesses.

Salvador Ximenez Rendon
Aniceto de Guzman
Regino Aguirre

Two weeks later Captain Damian returned with the answer of the datus:

Brother Alcalde,

This letter has no other purpose than to express the many memories existing among us as friends. Since it is sure that we are friends, wait for us one and a half months. During the past year we have not been able to meet, so our brother would certainly begrudge it if we would not come this year. Whether that is so or not, brother, we must have a drink together. As regards the peace question, do not worry, brother, Alcalde, because if you are also for it, there will be peace a hundred times. From the two of us; no more.

Always your brother,

Datu Damuli
Datu Mama of Davao

Obviously, as we will see presently, an official peace with all kinds of binding promises was not foremost on the mind of the Davao chiefs. Nevertheless, Alcalde Rendon waited for two months at Caraga, but none of the datus showed up, so finally he decided to return to Surigao because the northeast monsoon was about to begin. On December 8 he wrote in a report that on that day a messenger from the garrison of Caraga had arrived with letters informing him that Caraga had been mobilized and that immediately a marine force would be despatched southwards. It seems that one month earlier, on November 9, a man sent by Datu Pampang had come to Caraga with the useless information that there was no news from the datus of Davao. But he had shown more than usual interest

in the whereabouts of any Spanish navy vessels in the area. Being
told that there were none, he immediately departed. Two days later
three Mandayas arrived with the ominous information that a flotilla
of forty Moro boats had assembled in the bay of Mayo, about 60 km
south of Caraga. A reconnaissance team was despatched, but it
returned with the information that no such gathering of boats had
been seen. Probably they had meanwhile been beached and hidden or
had been moored in various rivers and creeks. Further intelligence
gathering had indeed brought to light that the Davao datus, in spite
of their "peace a hundred times," had sent two of their people to
Cotabato to ask the sultan there to come and join them for a raid on
Caraga. Once around Punta San Agustin they would be joined by
Pampang's fleet and then the armada would sail in convoy to Caraga
and occupy the place. The Mandayas living in or near the new village
had already absconded to the mountains because — so it was learned
from investigation — Datu Pampang had called some of them to
Manay and had given them a severe scolding for cooperating with the
Spaniards; he had threatened them if they settled in Caraga or
worked there on the building of houses as ordered by the Alcalde,
because so he stressed, they were his subjects. If nevertheless they
decided to live in Caraga, he had the same plans in petto for them as
he was harboring against the Spaniards!

It looks as if that raid on Caraga did not materialize after all,
because nothing about it is mentioned in Rendon's letter to Governor
Rafael de Aguilar written on January 23, 1805:

> "... The Mandayas of Caraga, Most Illustrious Sir, are
> actually more Moro than Mandaya because they have always
> lived among them and led the same kind of life as they do. The
> one who rules them is Datu Pampang who once told me that
> they are his slaves. To which I answered that the jurisdiction of
> Caraga went as far south as Punta San Agustin, and that up to
> the present there is a cross near Punta Pundaguitun, which had
> been placed there by the Spaniards at a time when the whole area
> was subject to Spain, even as far as the Hijo river where we once
> had a fortification; this can be attested by some witnesses who
> have seen it and remember the time when the whole area was
> subject to Spain. At that, he shut his mouth and did not answer
> me.
>
> I am convinced that as long as that Datu Pampang is not
> chased out of those places, the establishment of the new village
> of Caraga which is so much desired, will not be realized. Once

he is thrown out, not only the Mandayas will settle there, but even several families from Punta San Agustin will come. There are two datus, Tagunpan and Tagumanla, of the so-called Bilaan tribe who are very hostile to the Moros; they have urgently asked Captain Damian and Antonio de los Santos, whom I had ordered to explore the bay of Balete, to intercede for them, so they could have a talk with me about admitting them to this new village with more than thirty families. For that purpose they keep their *barotos* ready, so that after harvesting their rice, they can come and establish themselves in this village. There is more we can hope from them than from the Mandayas, because unlike the Mandayas they have never submitted to domination by the Moros.

With regard to the Mandayas of Cateel, Datu Olintang came to the village of Caraga and told me that they would settle in the sitio of Langaag and found a village there if his subjects and those of other datus did not come to an understanding with those of Caraga or San Juan. I had no objection to let them put up a reduction in that place, but I nevertheless consulted Father de Santa Orocia about it. He told me that he was the first person to deal with the resettlement of the Mandayas, and if they wanted to settle somewhere, they should go to Caraga or San Juan; if not, then he would chase them away. To which I replied that I had no orders from you to force them, because they always had had their differences and never wanted to live together.

From the Mandayas of the new pueblo of Our Lady of Pilar at Punta Baculin (San Juan) we can expect good results, because that group of Mandayas has always had civilized relations with the Christians of Bislig, Hinatuan and Lianga, and most of them are going to be baptized.''

In August of that year the Alcalde made another inspection trip to Caraga. From Surigao he sailed first to Cantilan to pick up Fray de Santa Orocia, who was to accompany him, and also to commission two armed *lanchas* which had been built there for coastal patrolling. There was a very special passenger aboard Rendon's vessel: a life-size statue of the "Salvador del Mundo," which was a personal gift of Don Salvador for the church of Caraga "to be venerated as Titular and Patron of the mentioned place" as stated in the deed of donation signed on August 20, 1805. Of this trip Fray Joseph sent a report to the Governor General on September 14,

1805. He was very enthusiastic about the continuing progress of the Mandaya reduction of San Juan de Baculin, but sadly mentions that he found Caraga in a wretched and run-down condition. He explains that there were several reasons for this. The first and most detrimental was that the few inhabitants were practically slaves of the Moros. It was impossible for them to shake off this yoke because there was no permanent and sufficiently strong deterrent force for their protection. The second reason was that not enough pressure had been used in the resettlement program. The Mandayas of the mountains just fooled the Alcalde with their repeated promises. The third reason was the pernicious influence of Chinese merchants from Cebu, about whom he had written already before. He strongly requests that some armed *lanchas* be permanently assigned to the region.

> "This will change the minds of the Mandayas, especially now the Moros have been driven out who formerly were living along the river near this mission. The houses of those Moros have been burned down...
>
> The Alcalde Mayor of the province has already written to you about how useful it would be for the State to construct a fort with a competent garrison in the bay of Balete, which by land is about one day travelling from the mission. The armed *lanchas* should control that point, and then the whole Mandaya tribe would be free from the Moros who would forever be forced to stay at the other side of Cape San Agustin... There are two or three pagan tribes living near that cape and near Davao who never wished to be subjects of the Moros. They would team up with us, and the Moros would be strictly confined in the area of Davao. The conquest of that area would be very easy for our arms if at any time the Moros would give us reasons to undertake it.
>
> Sir, I am saying this in the supposition that the whole coast from this mission down to Cape San Agustin does indeed belong to our Sovereign, as I have been told; my intention is not to infringe on the rights of my fellowmen..."

The last report of 1805 dealing with the problems of the repeopling of Caraga is a letter from that place dated October 13 and signed by some local leaders. It refers to the visit of the Alcalde of which we heard already, mentions also the condition of near abandonment and also the "clean-out" operation against the local

Moros. It also contains the additional information that the Alcalde went personally to the mountains to tell the Mandayas there that unless they came down and settled in the village, he "would do to them what he had done to the Moros." Only then did they begin to come to the shore with their families and started to put up their houses in the village and preparing their own ricefields. There was a no-holds-barred public meeting wherein the Alcalde told them that already for five years they had been promising him to come down and reside in the village, but that now his patience had come to an end. Everybody agreed that this was true, but that from now on, it was going to be different; before they had always been afraid of the Moros, but with the present garrison no more. Therefore, the Señor Alcalde could cut off the head of those who would not settle in the village from now on.

There has also been one event that had caused much ill-will; probably the local officials wanted to exonerate themselves by mentioning it. It concerned the very old Datu Agumba. He had asked to be baptized and the Alcalde had promised to be his godfather. They had approached Fray de Santa Orocia, but he said that he could not do it because the resident parish priest (Marcelino Balladares) was at that time in San Juan. The Alcalde had agreed to wait till the end of September, but when at the end of that month the parish priest had not yet returned, they sent the sailboat to San Juan to fetch him. However, they did not meet him there, and returned to Caraga. The Alcalde went personally to Fray Joseph with the datu, begging him to perform the baptism "because the datu was already more than one hundred years old, and everyday he came back to the village house crying for baptism *"pues el no pensaba mas que en Dios,"* he was now only thinking of God. However, so the authors and the witnesses state, the priest stuck to his refusal and "this meant a great disturbance in the new village, because everything would depend on whether or not that datu would receive the waters of baptism." Most probably, there was some canonical impediment, and Fray Joseph, being just a visitor in the place did not want to make his own decision as long as the datu was not really in immediate danger of dying *(in articulo mortis)*.

The revival of the mission of Caraga Antigua obviously needed a long incubation time. None of the combined efforts of Church and government were even remotely successful up to the first half of the 19th century. Only from memory do I know about a communication wherein even the peppy Fray Joseph de Santa Orocia sadly expressed his discouragement with Caraga; as he said: he had been able to baptize only one datu: Agumba! At least that man's problem was finally solved.

In 1807 Fray Joseph, assigned *"hasta la muerte"* to the mission of the Mandayas, died at the lonely Pacific point of Baculin.

In a letter of the Provincial of July 16, 1823 to the Archbishop of Manila, we read:

> "That the missions of San Juan (de Baculin) and San Salvador of Caraga were under the administration of my Order only up to the year 1811. This, because of lack of Religious, and also because of the few results that could be obtained from the Mandayas by such priests as Fray Santiago de San Isidro, Fray Marcelino Balladares and the reverend Father ex-provincial Joseph de Santa Orocia. These Fathers, in spite of immeasurable miseries, have labored and suffered amid want and with only very few people at hand."

XV

The Troubled 1800s

The epithet perhaps most suited to characterize the Recoleto mission in Caraga from 1622 till the last quarter of the 1800s is turbulent. In the 17th century, hardly out of the unsettling reformation period of the Augustinian Order, they were launched into the Hispanization process of the eastern half of Mindanao of which they would bear the brunt time and again. In the 18th century, while uncessantly the prime target of Moro designs, they were in addition deeply engulfed in the discordant relationship that had sprung up between them and the Jesuits. This was soon followed by government antagonism against religious Orders in general, after the Jesuits had been expelled from the country. Next, the 19th century would witness Caraga getting its share of the disturbing events which were to contribute some of the most shameful pages to Philippine Church history, events that would directly contribute to the disappearance, twice, of the Recoletos from Caraga and indirectly, elsewhere, to the hastening of revolutionary ferment.

The quotation by which we concluded the previous chapter covers actually far more historical Church drama than we might immediately think. To discover it, and to know it for what it really was, we will have to look first beyond local boundaries to Spain and the rest of Europe, and from 1800 back to the preceding century. We will remember how the Hispanization and Christianization of the archipelago had begun, we might say, with hindsight knowledge, as an idealistic venture born from a utopic faith in a sort of "hypostatic" union of the Spanish Church and the Spanish state. Under the Patronato system the state would become an apostolic state and the Church an imperial Church, a very ill-fitting set-up for both, to begin with. In spite of that, up to about 1750 the alliance struggled on in the Philippines somewhat like a marriage-of-convenience between partners of whom goodwilling neighbors would have said that, really, they were incompatible. In Spain itself that incompatibility had come into the open when an "enlightened" monarchy, inspired by secularistic philosophies, no longer evaded an open confrontation with a Church that certainly was not free of a spirit of obscurantism. It would go against the scope of this work to describe the many clashes that resulted. [40]

---

[40] See: Gustave Schnürer "Die Katholische Kirche während der Barockzeit," Bk. II. Ch. 2 (1937).

"...The outward position of the Catholic Church was in no way commensurate with her inner disposition, especially when the so-called "spirit of Enlightenment" penetrated behind the thus far tightly closed gates of the Pyrenean peninsula. At that time ecclesiastical decline became generally apparent in the Catholic countries, and as a rule it was also noticeable in Church organizations, especially in her missionary endeavors. Concern for the missions diminished, and consequently missionary vocations became fewer and fewer. The old colonial powers Portugal and Spain were totally pushed to the background by Protestant countries like Holland and England. One result was also the decrease in the means of support being made available for the Catholic missions.

The "enlightened absolutism" which found expression in Gallicanism, Josephinism and Febronianism, was in the first place interested in the suppression of the Church in their own countries, and the bishops were more concerned with the preservation of their worldly position than with their ecclesiastical duties; in the last place came their involvement with the general interests of the Church in foreign missions. As a result, the old Orders lost their idealism and enthusiasm, and everywhere narrow-mindedness and jealousies started to crop up, not the least in the missions.

The worst blow suffered by the latter was the cruel expulsion of the Jesuit missionaries by Pombal (in Portugal) in 1760, an example soon to be followed by Spain....

Efforts were indeed made to replace the expelled missionaries, but they

Repercussions were inevitably felt in the Philippines. They started with increasing state opposition against the religious Orders, culminating in the expulsion of the Jesuits from all Spanish territories. In Spain many monasteries were closed, with the result that it became impossible for the Orders to staff their overseas areas of pastoral responsibility with sufficient personnel. Obviously, this was never the foremost worry of an "enlightened ecclesiastical despot" such as Archbishop Basilio de Santa Justa y Rufina, who had been sent to Manila by Carlos III to execute the royal expulsion order against the Jesuits and make an honest-to-goodness start with the secularization of parishes in the Philippines. If successful, this would bring the local churches under control of the bishops and through them (state appointed as they were) of the government. In itself, the move was not intended as a "Filipinization" of parishes, although de facto it would lead to that in concerned parishes. The immense debacle resulting from the Archbishop's mass-production of Filipino secular priests is sufficiently known to those interested in knowing it. So is, perhaps, the on-and-off de-secularization by an alarmed government, resulting in bitter animosities between Regular and Secular clergy.

Let us return to Caraga to see how all these unfortunate developments affected the local Church of Agusan, Surigao and east Davao. It is clear that in 1811 all the plans for the settlement of coastal villages in southern Caraga of which we have spoken, were abandoned; in that year the Recoletos informed the Bishop of Cebu that they had decided to withdraw from the southern end of the province. In 1810 there had still been six priests in service; four died between 1810 and 1814, the fifth in December 1815 and the last in January 1816.

On April 25, 1809, Governor General Mariano Folgueras had sent out an alarmed communication to the Consejo de Indias in Madrid. It was printed in 1820 and circulated as a leaflet, of which a copy is in the Marcilla archives.

"'Most Excellent Sir,

The shortage of Religious being experienced in these islands by the Dominicans, Franciscans, Augustinians and Recoletos,

---

were more than ever doomed to fail when shortly afterwards the French revolution erased nearly all Church institutes for the training of missionaries.''

has forced their provincial Superiors to propose to the Vice-Patronato Real (Gov. Gen.) the abandonment of many parishes which were administered by Religious of their Orders.

Much to his regret, the Vice-Patronato had to give its approval, albeit for the time being only, till there would be a greater number of Religious, because it has been demonstrated as clearly as one could wish it that in the parishes managed by the secular clergy the results of the spiritual administration are deteriorating. There are very few individuals of this class who distinguish themselves by being outstanding parish administrators...''

Folgueras continues saying that the situation cries for more Spanish priests, secular or religious, although it would be unrealistic to expect that of the first many would ever be available. Anyway, because of their corporate discipline and organization, the Religious would undoubtedly be better qualified for the work, and thus would give more assurance that the population would remain loyal and peaceful. "...For that reason I repeat to your Excellency that it is of supreme importance that Religious will be sent to these provinces, because so many of them have died, and because many years of war and other causes have cut off the supply of missionaries..."

In 1816 the whole of Caraga was without any Recoleto. Nonetheless, that the abandonment was juridically considered only as ad interim solution appears, e.g., from all the Chapter Acts between 1815 and 1834: Parish priests were "officially" appointed to Tandag...where they never resided. No wonder that in each subsequent Chapter they are reported as "absent" in the attendance list!

In a report to the Crown in 1818 the Provincial states that he has nothing to report about Caraga because scarcity of Religious had reached such a degree that the Order had turned over to the secular clergy all its parishes in the Marianas, the town and garrison of Zamboanga, the mission stations of Pampanga Alta (Nueva Ecija) and the whole province of Caraga (Marcilla, Leg. 4, Nr. 10). The aftereffects of the Church-State separation in Spain, the persecution of the Religious, the closure of monasteries and seminaries, the suspension of state stipends to missionaries, began all to show in the Philippines.

The first secular priest assigned to an island off Caraga was Agustin D., a Spanish mestizo of thirty years, whose family name has stayed on there ever since. He and the others in Butuan, Surigao,

Siargao, Cantilan, Tandag and Bislig had, of course, to be imported from other provinces. Of at least three it is known that they came from Cebu and of one that he had been parish priest in Panay. Naturally, it would give a researcher and fellow priest joy to be able to dig up anything good about any of those who worked in Caraga parishes in eventually diminishing numbers between 1814 and approximately 1850. In case no laudatory records can be found, one would perhaps not mind too much if no information at all existed. It is a far from pleasurable experience to come only across derogatory documentation. Of course, one will try to keep aware that evil often makes for more documented history than the good or the indifferent. In many similar experiences one could take the charitable way out, entrusting such information to the sorrowful silence of one's own heart. However, those even slightly familiar with Philippine Church history know that this aspect of the fate of Philippine parishes in the past cannot just be separated from the rest of that past. It was one (repeat, one) very determining factor for future developments. As such it has to be brought up if one wishes (also local) history to receive a factual presentation. We will try to do this in our own historical context.

Of some of these priests it is on record that already prior to coming to Caraga their antecedents had not exactly been clean. One Ilongo assigned to Surigao had already caused public trouble *(motin)* in Antique; this was found out when in Surigao he antagonized the whole village by his ignorance, his stubborn refusal to preach in Bisayan instead of his Ilonggo and his objectionable personal life. People petitioned the Bishop of Cebu for "a priest who knows his job." The complaints found in the records are mainly these: absenteeism from the parish, commercialism, neglect of church and convent maintenance, gambling and immorality. Government reports repeatedly mention negligence in keeping population records for taxation purposes coupled with great zeal in collecting church stipends. The parish priest of Tandag had an armed galley of his own *"realisando su comercio con la alcaldía de Leyte."* It is very revealing (and plainly informative) to struggle through a half an inch thick dossier of his own (found in the National Archives, Manila, Leg. "Caraga") about how he tried to convince marine authorities in Manila to let the government pay for his heavy armament and boat crews ostensibly needed as protection against Moro threats on his *"viajes apostolicos"* along the Pacific coast of his farflung parish.

Of course, it is true that these priests were products of the worst times of seminary education and disciples of mentors hardly educated themselves. Still, that is an excuse only as far as it goes: one does not necessarily need any seminary training at all to be able to abstain from vices as those mentioned above. It is also not improbable that Spanish sources relished selecting at times what the records have preserved. On the other hand, many unedifying pages in Philippine Church history become at least less incomprehensible after reading preceding or contemporaneous pages concerning the Church, clergy, religious Orders of 18th to 19th century Spain itself.

From a letter of the Recoleto Provincial it appears that in that year the Alcalde Mayor of Caraga had made an urgent appeal to him and the Governor-General. The Provincial wrote:

> "...that the Order take over again the administration of the province of Caraga, because of the continuous troubles and shocking events around the clerics of this province... which was conquered for the Faith by the blood shed by our very deserving sons of the Order. In the year 1815 the administration of Caraga was totally abandoned...not because we shied away from labor and fatigue, because to be able to overcome these is part of the make-up of its members. It was the well-known scarcity of Religious which forced us to cede ad interim the administration of those parishes to the secular clergy.
>
> Since the year 1815 till the present (1827) the Order has passed through such dire circumstances that only sixteen Religious have arrived, not enough to fill the vacancies of the twenty-five who have died in the same period. For that reason it is clear why my province cannot take up again the care for those children of its very own labors; after all, at present it has nine members less than when my predecessors had to abandon it. Although we have been promised twelve to sixteen Religious to arrive in August this year, I cannot myself give any binding promise, because they still have to finish their studies, learn the dialects, and begin their pastoral work together with some older priests...
>
> With regard to the request of Father Galan (Juan Ignacio de Galan of Tandag) I have to inform your Excellency that this minister has been called to Cebu four times to see his Bishop; upon return from my visit to the Visayas he had not yet done so, because he was on a trip in his galley to engage in his business in the province of Leyte...Everybody knows that of the mission

stations only the names are left. For the rest, nothing can be found; even the church vestments, ornaments and sacred vessels which had been turned over to them (as can be proven by inventory lists) have disappeared many years ago; the only thing that could be found out is that people had seen how some of the church vestments had been converted into clothes for personal use, which they put on when yearly going to Cebu to attend the Santo Niño fiesta, on which occasion the whole province was left without priests; this happened especially after the Bishop had died.

The present Alcalde and also his predecessors, who must have seen the ruins of the churches and convents, not only in the reductions but also in the old-time parishes, could very well (and should) have prevented their total ruination by compelling the local officials and the parish priests themselves to maintain such much needed buildings.

What do you think, Excellency, how enthusiastically would any Religious take upon himself the administration of those parishes as soon as he learns about the desolate condition of the church and the convent? It goes without saying that any rational being will be overcome by disgust, when his fate will be banishment into a life that cuts him off from society and confronts him suddenly with a situation wherein he will not even have the slightest possibility to find relief from the multitude of miseries which he is facing.

Your Excellency must bring the deplorable situation of that pitiful province to the attention of the new Alcalde; he should compel those parish priests to restore things to the state in which they received them in 1815.

That is all I have to say about the matter'' (Marcilla, ''Oficios'' Bk. 86).

That government and ecclesiastical authorities were waking up to the deplorable situation will appear from the very stern words which the new Bishop of Cebu, Msgr. Santos Marañon, put in his first pastoral letter to his clergy on August 31, 1829. He mentions therein that his advanced age and his weakness is bothering him, of course, but that aside from this he is afraid

''that you, Ministers of the Lord, co-workers of Jesus Christ and of me in the salvation of souls, are not as faithfully complying with your pastoral duties as you should...

How great should not be our fear and confusion if the pastors themselves who must graze and protect the sheep from the claws of the wolf, turn into greedy wolves themselves and are even worse than the very demons?'' (Pastorales y demás Disposiciones,'' Diocesis de Cebu, Vol. I).

It seems that also the attention of the new Alcalde had been **roused by Manila. A document is extant in the National Archives,** Manila (originally coded "Patronato," Carp. 5, nr. 1) in Legajo 118: "Dossier of 1831, by the Alcalde Mayor of Caraga about the need to have the parishes and mission stations of that province occupied again by the Recoleto priests."

It contains a.o. a letter from Alcalde M. Jose Aguilar to the Governor General, wherein he actually repeats a previous communication of his predecessor Francisco X. de Velasco, who had stated that there was an urgent necessity to return the Caraga parishes to the Recoletos "because the clerics administering them now are just good for nothing and show little interest in fulfilling their spiritual and temporal obligations." The Alcalde also mentions the miserable condition of the churches "which look more like animal stables than temples of Christians; the vestments are so soiled that one could call them dirty rags."

After quoting various forms of neglect of which a parish priest could be guilty and which he had witnessed in Caraga, especially in Butuan, he stresses the need for zealous priests; in the Baganga-Caraga area alone more than one thousand Mandayas could easily be brought to the faith. "Finally, the upheavals that have occurred in this province have all been instigated and directed by the clergy, who have disturbed these poor people and caused the destruction of their families, as happened in the past uprising."

There is also another communication by Alcalde Posadas requesting that if a sufficient number of Recoletos were not available, to assign at least one each to Surigao, Butuan and Bislig, and leave the smaller parishes to the seculars, so that they could learn from the Religious.

The information about a contemporary "uprising in the province" is intriguing. I have not been able to find details about such an event. It is a known fact that in the country at large there were not a few anti-Spanish elements among the native clergy, and that for more than just one reason. On August 20, 1831 the Provincial-pro tempore wrote about "a near total separation from the obedience to the King and from the community of the

Church" which was pervasive in Caraga and was said to have been caused "by the clerics who administered it and also by the despotism of the Alcaldes." The last part of the sentence (between my quotation marks) has been omitted in the "Historia General" of Manuel Carceller. The complete text is found in Marcilla ("Oficios" Bk. 87, p. 174) and in the National Archives (Legajo 118).

Among earlier records existing in the National Archives in Manila is a "Complaint by the people of Surigao against Alcalde Felipe Arseo y Roman," (Visayan text, 1815), and an extensive "Report on the province of Caraga" by the same Alcalde (1823). The complaint is signed by the barangay head Gregorio Escalante and former village officials Thomas Apostol, Nicolas Narciso, Julio Valentin, Juan Martinez, Gregorio de la Concepción, Gregorio Francisco, Juan Francisco, Rosauro Mariano, Joaquin Abales, Protacio Nepomuceno, Mario Custodio and Vicente Rafael. I have a feeling that there should have been one more signature: that of the parish priest! It is hard to believe (though not impossible, of course) that in a contemporary village setting like that of Surigao the "Principalía" would have dared to openly accuse a Spanish alcalde, unless they had the backing of the parish priest.

The accusations voiced against Arseo were: corruption, despotism, use of government vessels and crews for private business, non-payment of salaries, suppression of private commerce, immorality, entering the church with his hat on only to insult the parish priest and the sacristan, not attending Mass, not going to confession and eating meat on forbidden days.

In his own report the (retired) Alcalde said eight years later in retrospection a.o. that "a Chinese named Sanson, son of Sanson Calamay" had accused him before the Governor General because he had curtailed the nefarious commerce of the Chinese in Caraga, which was done in accordance with a special government order to protect the mission reduction of Caraga, where the "mestizo Chinese were more destructive than a raging fire." His successors Diego Martinez and Manuel Piencenaves had encountered the same opposition for the same reason, he says. As for the qualifications needed in government officials to be sent to Caraga, he remarks that they should be

> "men imbued with patriotism, with a high understanding of the interests of the state and of their duties. All private welfare should be subordinated to the common good, because any part that is incongruous with the whole becomes something lewd and

obscene. An exaggerated egotism suffocates the more noble feelings of man, makes him forget his duties to the State and the Fatherland.''

The matter of assuming once more the administration of Caraga was taken up anew in the Chapter of 1831 and approved on April 26 in a session of the Definitores.

''...My Province had been urged and invited by the Superior Government during the last days of the Alcalde preceding Señor Velasco, and pressed with all insistence and repeatedly by the former Bishop Genovés as well as by the present Ordinary, to re-assume the administration of Caraga. My Province was also much aware of so many reports about the misfortunes inflicted by evil times upon its faithful inhabitants, who certainly deserved a better fate than that which befell them in previous days, when its authorities had left it in a state of near-anarchy. It also has not forgotten that the soil of Caraga was once moistened by the sweat caused by the fatigues of its first apostolic men and drenched with the blood of so many worthy sons who shed it at the hands of barbarious and untamed natives, and who at this price conquered the latter for the Faith and the obedience to our Sovereign. No less is my Province aware of so many and such meaningful motives calling it to cast its eyes upon its first inheritance in the vineyard of the Lord.

Despite the remoteness of the province of Caraga, the expenses incurred by the Order by each Provincial during his triennial visitation, and notwithstanding the nefarious and spoiled character of the inhabitants, the destruction of churches, convents, sacred ornaments and everything else of use left behind by our last Religious in the year 1814, when the province was turned over to the Bishop of Cebu... the Definitorio agreed on April 26 that if the Superior Government insists that we take over Caraga again, we cannot evade that obligation...Special attention should be given to the selection of the Religious to go there; only those should be elected who are considered most suited to undertake a new kind of work in villages wherein everything has to be started anew and which therefore should be handled with utmost prudence and *delicadeza*... In the name of my Province I herewith assume again the spiritual administration of Caraga from this moment on...'' (National Archives, loc. cit.).

In 1832 Bishop Santos Marañon of Cebu had gone on a visitation to part of the province of Caraga, and in October of that year he wrote to the King:

> "... I returned to Cebu much comforted after seeing that the Recoleto Fathers who had come to Mindanao upon my request... are doing their utmost to rebuild the churches, the convents, civilization and catechetical instruction in those unhappy villages, which had been completely abandoned by the Filipino secular priests..." (Jesuit Archives, Loyola, Spain). [41]

Once things had reached that stage, one of the many problems still confronting the Recoleto superiors was the fact that the new mission venture had to be entrusted to very young priests arriving from the re-opened seminary in Spain. Among the remaining veterans very few were able to work under conditions found in Caraga. Much attention is given in the remaining documentation to that aspect; from the contemporary correspondence it becomes abundantly clear that the administration of the Order was deeply concerned not only with the spiritual welfare of the people of Caraga but also with that of the young missionaries who were going to live among them. Therefore the Vice-Provincial decided that the prior of the Manila community should serve as teamleader of a group of three destined for Surigao. He was to pick up his companions in Bohol while on his way south. But then a complication arose: the leader handpicked by the Vice-Provincial had obviously been selected against his own will, and he refused the assignment on juridical and personal grounds. For a while that caused a serious internal authority crisis in Manila, and it looked as if the takeover of Surigao was going to be postponed till another mature leader could be found. In the end, the refusing candidate was judged to be

---

[41] Because of the limitation mentioned before, we cannot go deeper into the developments of the Church, the secular clergy, religious Orders and the State in Spain itself. We should, however, remain aware that in the mother country there is more to be taken into account than only the side shown by any of the four protagonists separately. This, of course, applied also in the Philippines. We refer the reader back to footnote 40: cf. o.a. also "Church, Politics and Society in Spain 1750-1874" by William J. Callahan (Harvard University Press 1984).

juridically entitled to his refusal. Still, in 1846 we find him on the appointment list as parish priest of Tandag.

In 1834 Fray Fernando Ramos is listed as the first "restored" Recoleto parish priest of Surigao. The last *"Plan de Almas"* (parish statistics) of 1833 still shows the name of the incumbent secular, Yamson, for Surigao. Of the six parishes mentioned (Surigao, Siargao, Cantilan, Tandag, Bislig and Butuan) only Butuan and Cantilan have a Recoleto parish priest, the other four still seculars.

In the following two *Planes de Almas* (1834 and 1840) available, a new item has been entered in the *informatica:* the age of the parish priests and the number of service years. The young age of the various Recoletos becomes very apparent. The puzzling difference in

YEAR	PARISH	INHABI-TANTS	PARISH PRIEST	AGE	YEARS IN SERVICE
1834	Butuan	5,671	Prospero de S. Vicente, Rec.	32	3
	Surigao	9,675	Fernando Ramos, Rec.	27	3
	Cantilan	3,200	Francisco Villas, Rec.	26	?
	Bislig	4,335	Benito de San Agustin, Rec.	30	5
1840	Butuan	6,360	Prospero de S. Vicente, Rec.	33	10
			Juan Felipe (?) Sec. (Ass.)	36	7
	Surigao	6,871	Fernando Ramos Rec.	34	10
			Macario Nepomuceno, Sec. (Asst)	?	?
	Cantilan	3,330	Joaquin de San Miguel, Rec.	29	3
	Tandag	3,680	Pedro Garcia, Rec.	28	4
	Bislig	3,500	Gregorio Henriquez, Sec.	57	27

(Condensed from Leg. 16, Marcilla)

population figures for Surigao and Bislig in 1834 and 1840 is most probably caused by respective changes in parish boundaries between those years.

Right from the outset it also emerges with absolute clarity that Caraga was still the same hardship post it had been before. Administratively neglected in the preceding years, the provincial revenues were so low and population records in such poor condition that hardly any government stipends were paid to the parish priests. Worried about the pitiful condition of his subjects in Caraga, who amid all their poverty had started to rebuild their parishes from scratch, the Provincial wrote to the Governor General on March 30, 1834 that unless their financial situation was substantially improved, some of the priests would be forced to leave the province very soon. The parish priest of Bislig had already been brought to Manila in a state of complete nervous breakdown: "totally deranged and an object of fitting compassion and tears of his confreres."

The Recoletos were by then fully aware that the Government could not do without them to carry out its plans for Mindanao, and pretty soon the pressure exerted in Manila improved the matter of financial support for the priests in Caraga.

Government plans for Mindanao: In the middle of the 1800s it becomes more and more clear that the foremost tasks in effecting the total hispanization of Mindanao were the following two:

1. the final elimination of the Moro problem;
2. the (re) population of large areas to forestall that either the Moros or even foreign powers might be tempted to come in. Intimately connected with plans for population increase was the necessity of local economic development.

On the east coast the Moro fear concerned by then nearly exclusively the Moslems of the Davao gulf area. Already in 1823 the former Alcalde Mayor Felipe Arseo, in a lecture he gave in Manila about the state of Caraga, had hammered away at the necessity of switching from the costly defensive strategy followed until then to a one-time, effective offensive attacking the Moros in their own lairs beyond Cape San Agustin.

"Why should we not attack the Moro in his own territory? Why not deprive him of all his passways, which we know very well? Why not destroy them, burn their big settlements and **force them to live in controlled villages in obeisance to our** power? In my opinion, the best defense of our pueblos is to attack that scum in their own lairs'' (''Informe sobre la Provincia de Caraga,'' National Archives, ''Erección de Pueblos'').

By the middle of the century the ability for such an undertaking had been greatly enhanced by the appearance of the first Spanish steamships in the Philippines.

> ''With the appearance of steamships a new era opened up for the Philippines, especially in connection with combating Mohammedanism and its piracies. As soon as Governor Narciso Claveria had three such vessels at his disposal, (the ''Magallanes,'' the ''Reina de Castilla'' and the ''Elcano'') he started a campaign against the pirates, attacking them in their most secret and protected hiding places...'' (Agustin de Santayana, ''La Isla de Mindanao,'' 1862, p. 66).

Claveria's name has been perpetuated in one of the main streets of Davao City, together with that of the man who would finally relieve eastern Mindanao of the perpetual fear that had paralyzed its Hispanization and development: Don Jose Oyanguren, the last conquistador of the Philippines. He was a Basque from the province of Guipuzcoa, he had come to the Philippines in 1825 in order to escape political persecution resulting from his activities as a propagandist for a Constitutional government. He settled in Surigao, where throughout the 1830s he engaged in private business. From 1839 till 1846 he functioned as Juez de Primera Instancia in Tondo, Manila. During that latter employment, an event had occurred in southern Mindanao that offered the Manila government a ready pretext for the use of force in the Davao gulf area. A peace treaty had been signed in 1838 by some Maguindanao datus and at least one from the Davao area. In 1839 some of the latter's subjects had attacked a Spanish trading vessel at Davao and killed its captain, officers and most of the crew, disregarding a recommendation from the chief Maguindanao datu ordering the Davao chiefs to extend protection and friendship to the trading party. In order to escape threatened Spanish reprisals, the Maguindanao leader publicly disowned his former allies in Davao and in doing so gave the Spaniards a free hand to punish the latter, whom they anyway hardly considered brothers in the faith because they had always lived somewhat at the periphery of Muslim orthodoxy.

Oyanguren now offered his services and knowledge of the area to the government to ''pacify'' the Davao Moros. As recompense he asked to be appointed governor of the area and to be given exclusive commercial rights therein for ten years. This idea carried the full personal approval of Governor General Claveria

> ''because it fitted perfectly in his own plans for the reduction of uncontrolled tribes and his desire to put an end, by all possible means, to any kind of piracy. Nevertheless, before giving his approval to Oyanguren, he put the plan before the Audiencia of Manila to ask for their vote, in accordance with the Code of Laws for the Indies. Here the project encountered some opposition because of the long period of authority asked by Oyanguren as well as the exclusive trading privileges all of which went against normal procedures. such had never happened anymore since the days of the early discovery, when *encomiendas* and *repartimientos* were given to deserving Spaniards, as had also been practised in the New World. But the *encomienda* system had not lasted long in the Philippines and no trace of it is found in history since the time of the intrepid Captain Esteban Rodriguez de Figueroa, to whom the area near the mouth of the Rio Grande de Mindanao had been given for two generations; however, he was killed by Moros just when coming ashore to occupy it'' (Santayana, loc. cit., pp. 68-69).

When a favorable decision was finally given about the proposed plan it was with the restriction "that it should not be considered as a contract between the government and Oyanguren, but just as a concession granted for a certain period and with proper limitations." By a decree of February 27, 1847 Governor Claveria gave to Oyanguren for ten years full authority over the territory which he would occupy in the gulf of Davao, plus exclusive trading rights for the first six years. He would be given some artillery, rifles and ammunition, with the permission to organize his own military force. It was also decided that the capital of the new province would be located at the site of the Moro village after which the gulf was named, and that it would be given the name of Nueva Vergara after the hometown of Oyanguren. Along the east coast the new province would stretch as far north as Punta Cawit. The reason given for this extension was that this area was too far away from its own capital (Surigao) and because the villages from Tandag down to Caraga were located along a coast where navigation was very difficult for a great part of the year, while overland communication was non-existent, and for such reasons it was a territory difficult to govern by the Alcalde Mayor of Surigao.

In 1848 Oyanguren took off for Davao at the head of a militia consisting of men whom he had handpicked for their initiative and courage, some of them Spaniards. Within a few months he had the whole gulf area under his control; the datus either submitted to his authority or moved out to Sarangani and Cotabato. The whole Mandaya population of Samal heartily joined the soldiers to round up those Moros living in various "rancherías" inland and near the mouth of the Hijo River. The latter point was strategically important for communication with Linao and the rest of upper Agusan. Oyanguren kept his part of the bargain, which was more than could be said of the government. Soon he found himself saddled with all the bureaucratic obligations and controls proper for provinces with an established regular government situation, administrative duties which simply did not fit the new and unorganized territory of Davao, and expenses which he could not meet. This became very soon a cause for friction between him and Manila. In addition, his exclusive trading rights caused him not a few enemies among well-positioned businessmen in Manila and Cebu, who had easy access to decision makers in the government. In 1852 Governor General Urbiztondo, the successor of Claveria, dismissed him from his position and appointed a regular governor for the province of Nueva Guipuzcoa.

Already in 1849 we find the first missionary assigned there: Fray Francisco Lopez. It throws a revealing light on the communication facilities of those days that Manila did not know that the appointee had died the previous month!

Once the Moslem territories were under control and the rest of Mindanao secure from their threat, more attention could be given to the other major problem affecting the island and its future: its economic development. In the second half of the 19th century one big factor affecting this need was underpopulation in many regions, among them the whole area then comprising the two provinces of Surigao and Nueva Guipuzcoa. It was already noted how fifty years earlier the problem of depopulation was acknowledged in the southernmost part of the east coast, but how under prevailing conditions and with contemporary methods Spanish attempts at re-peopling coastal settlements had nearly totally failed. As late as 1832 Alcalde Jose de Aguilar informed the Governor General about east Mindanao in these terms:

> "The province of Caraga is still in the same condition as it
> was two hundred years ago, because there has never been

anybody really interested in the good of the natives, for example by stimulating them to improve rice cultivation; the absence of which is an impediment to the increase of population'' (National Archives, Legajo 118).

He was just echoing what one of his predecessors, Felipe Arseo had said already in 1823. In 1850 the Recoleto Provincial Fray Jose del Carmen stated that in Surigao one factor contributing to the neglect of agriculture was the easy income derived from gold mining, but that presently, with this precious metal becoming scarcer and the competition from cheaper gold mined in California,

)   "one begins to notice more interest in the development of agricultural land; people dedicate themselves more to the cultivation of rice, *camotes* and other root crops. If they would also engage in planting cacao and abacá, a more durable kind of economy would come into existence'' (Marcilla, Legajo 61-5).

One document dated December 19, 1853 clearly shows how the government was becoming more aware that one prerequisite for speeding up economic development was a more effective administration.

        "Considering the excessive extension of the present territory known as the province of Nueva Guipuzcua and that experience has taught that it is impossible that one single governor can visit the area as often as required by its backward state; and taking into account the good results obtained from reducing the administrative boundaries to where they are indicated by the condition of the area; convinced also that presently there is an urgent necessity to pay attention to the progress and good government of the villages constituting the said province, so that agriculture, commerce and the resettlement of non-Christians can be improved, I have decreed the following after hearing the consultative vote of the Royal Fiscals:

— The alcaldia of N. Guipuzcoa will be suppressed and from its territory two military districts will be created.

— One of these districts will include the coastal area and the villages from Cape San Agustin north up to Punta Cawit (Caraga, Baganga, Cateel, Lingig, Hinatuan, Lianga, Tago and

Tandag); the other will cover all the territory known as the gulf of Davao, beginning at Cape San Agustin...

— The first will be named District of Bislig and the second, District of Davao. Both will be governed by a Politico-Military Commander...'' (Marcilla, Bk. 90, pp. 96-98).

Interesting in the context of underpopulation and under-development of east and northeast Mindanao, is a communication by Provincial Ubeda to the Government: "About the lack of population in the province of Caraga and possible means to let Cebuanos and Boholanos transmigrate to form new villages.'' He had felt heart-broken, so the writer says, when during his visitation to the coastal villages of the province, he saw so much uncultivated land and so many barrios without anybody to guide the people along the path of eternal life and to a civilized human existence with better mutual relations. As for land, there is so much of it that is suited for the best kind of abaca.

For that reason he suggests that Boholanos should be imported as has been going on in Butuan for many years and points to Gingoog bay where a new village named Palilan or Jimenez was established with its own church, by Boholanos who had started arriving there about three years ago. He adds that as an enticement they should be exempted from all taxes and personal services *(polo)* for ten years (Marcilla, Legajo 61-5).

Available contemporary documentation more than once contains noticeable government insistence that also the missionary districts and parishes should be subdivided into smaller areas and that more attention should be given to the conversion and resettlement of non-Christian tribes living in upper Agusan and the jungles facing the Pacific coast. On March 2, 1854 Governor General de Novaliches voiced his concern about upper Agusan to the Recoleto provincial in the following words:

"Every day it is becoming more urgent that a Religious be assigned to the mission of Talacogon...With his efficient help and apostolic exhortations it can be expected that the pagans living near that village, now given to idolatry and crime, can be brought to the true path of our Holy Faith and civilization...Therefore I cannot do otherwise than recommend that you appoint one religious and send him as soon as possible to the mentioned village..., in the supposition that since your answer of January last year one priest is already available.''

Five days later the Provincial answered that he was well aware of
the need for a priest in upper Agusan, but that the Governor General
should understand that not just anyone was suited for such an
assignment. This causes him a lot of worry, because also the Bishop
of Cebu kept pressuring him for the same. Recently the last secular
priest of Siargao had died, and the one at Bislig had become
demented. Also these two places needed to be attended to. Again,
one year later a communication from the Bishop of Cebu reminds
the Provincial urgently that already in 1851 the government had
insisted that one priest be assigned to Linao and one more to
Talacogon. He insistently repeats that request, stating that if two are
not available, to assign for the time being one, with extreme priority.
Finally, in February 1856 we find Fray Antonio Preciado assigned
for Linao and Talacogon.

Also the Mandaya mission stations of San Juan (Hinatuan) and
of San Salvador (Caraga) are being given renewed attention in
government communications. These missions had even been
financially adopted by an anonymous benefactress to an amount of
two hundred pesos yearly for each missionary who would establish
himself there. The Provincial informed Governor Norzagaray that
all he could do was to assign one additional priest to the District of
Bislig to take care of those reductions; that priest, however, would
have to be pulled out from Negros.

Anyone not informed about subsequent developments around
the Recoleto presence in Caraga and the rest of Mindanao might tend
to agree with the words of Fray Licinio Ruiz, one of the *cronistas* of
the Order who wrote that in 1850

> "everything was sailing before the wind; the difficulties that
> had slowed down the progress of the Recoleto Province were on
> the way to being solved. There was already a core-group of
> missionaries capable and sufficient to take care of and sustain
> that care for the extensive pastoral field under our
> administration..." ("Sinopsis Historica," 1925, p. 254).

Indeed, the dark days at the turn of the century and the
nightmares of the first quarter of the 1800s, all the despair sired by

hostile governments at home in Spain and ecclesiastical turmoil in the archipelago were beginning to look like pains of an evil past. Also the perennial problem of any missionary institute, sufficient personnel and means to support them and the needs of the apostolate, were nearing a reasonable state of Solution. In Spain the Order had been allowed to open a mission seminary again and afterwards even expand it (Monte Agudo); government awareness that without the missionaries Mindanao would be lost very soon, gave the Order a believable assurance that *patronato* stipends would keep forthcoming...

But, of course, the author of the above quotation was very well aware of "subsequent developments" around his Order in Mindanao! In fact, we did some injustice to the quotation by omitting the essential turn:

> "But then suddenly when nobody had an inkling, our Superiors were confronted with a Royal Decree ordering them to abandon forever the spiritual administration of Mindanao and turn it over to the priests of the Society of Jesus" (loc. cit.).

And here, again, we are back in the pages of Mindanao Church history wherein angels most probably have always refused to tread: the pages with the turbulent story of Jesuit-Recoleto relations vis-à-vis Caraga and the rest of Mindanao. Perhaps, for a while we can do no better than let as much as possible the pertinent documents speak for themselves.

Licinio Ruiz, op. cit. p. 255 surmises (and so does Carceller in his "Historia General" p. 439 of Vol. XI) that

> "the principal reason motivating the Royal decision was a report of the Bishop of Cebu dated November 26, 1857 wherein the prelate asked that once the Society of Jesus had been re-established (1852) in all Spanish dominions, it should be given the spiritual administration of the part of Mindanao comprising the Districts of Bislig, Davao, Polloc, the province of Zamboanga, the island of Basilan and other places located east and south of the island. The reason was that the large size of Mindanao with its one and one half million inhabitants consisting of Christians, pagans and Muslims, made it very difficult for the Recoletos to attend to all the villages and new mission stations."

> *Supuesto assi el esta-*
> *do, en que actualmte. los Pueblos de V. Magd.*
> *en las Provas. de el cargo de esta de Sn. Nicolas,*
> *y de V. Magd.: se hace indispensable á esta*
> *vra. Provª. iterar la suplica, que por su*
> *devoto Pe. Prov! á V. Magd. tiene yá re-*
> *presentada, en carta, su fha en 30. de*
> *Junio de el año passado de 54. informan-*
> *do á V. Magd. del intento del Marq. de*
> *Ovando, Govor. que fue de V. Magd. en estas*
> *Islas, de quexarnos quitar los Pueblos de*
> *Cagayan, y su Partido, y los de la isla de*
> *Camiguin, en Mindanao, solo por com-*
> *placer, y entregarse á los RR. PP. de la*
> *Compañia, que es de el año de 54. andan*
> *dhos RR. PP. en esta pretension con esta*
> *vra. Provª. de Sn. Nicolas, no solo en dhos*
> *Pueblos de Cagayan, y Camiguin, sino*
> *de todos los demas de Mindanao, y Ca-*
> *raga, de mio Cargo, y Administrazion,*
> *haciendonos recompensa dhos PP. de la*
> *Compañia, de otros Pueblos, en las Provas.*
> *de Tagalos, de los RR. PP. de la Compañia,*
> *cercanos á esta Capital; este es, y ha sido*
> *el intento de los dhos PP. el quedarse so-*
> *los en la dha Isla de Mindanao, y Caraga*
> *y*

Fig. 27. Part of a letter by Fray Benito de S. Pablo, Vicar Provincial of the Recoletos, written on July 20, 1757 to the Spanish King, about alleged plans of the Jesuits — supported by Governor General Ovando — to take over the Recoleto parishes of Mindanao. The "pueblos en las provincias de Tagalos" (a.o. Cavite Viejo and Silang) are the same as those mentioned in the chapter "The troubled 1800s." (Marcilla archives, "Comunicaciones," Bk. 41.)

Ruiz names the request of 1857 of Bishop Jimeno "the principal reason" for the Royal Decree. However, there was an earlier decision by the Crown, dated October 1852:

> "Wishing with all means at my disposal to promote the speedy reduction of all the non-Christians who still live in these islands, and since it is impossible for at least many years (with the limited number of missionaries of the four Religious Orders in existence) to do everything needed for that purpose, especially not in the new mission stations that have to be established in the islands of Mindanao and Jolo; mindful also of the important services of the Society of Jesus in the reduction and religious education of the natives in these islands as well as in the former Spanish dominions in America, I have decided that this Order shall be re-established in our dominions. To this effect, and in response to the repeated requests addressed to me by the legal Representatives of Guipuzcua and Vizcaya, the (Jesuit) house of Loyola shall be converted into a mission seminary..." (Marcilla, Bk. 90, "Comunicaciones...", p. 37).

According to Ruiz, the Recoletos were unable to guess what reasons could possibly have motivated the Bishop to make such a request in 1857. Those reasons, however, would seem to be very clear if one reads the full text of the Bishop's letter to the Queen dated November 26, 1857:

> "(The complete conquest of Mindanao, until today not feasible, becomes now possible with the help of the re-established Jesuits...) The Bishop proposes that the administration of established pueblos in the District of Bislig, and others, shall be ceded to the Jesuits, so that in the beginning the new missionaries will have a foothold where they can start their ministry; afterwards they can penetrate in various directions to the mountains in the interior and to other places inhabited by pagans or Muslims yet to be converted.
>
> Señora, such is the opinion which the Bishop of Cebu has the honor to convey to the justified attention of your Majesty...Everything is possible and even very easy if the will of all is focused on the superior interest of Church and State" (Marcilla, Legajo 62-1-).

It seems clear that the Bishop was convinced that the efforts and capabilities of the Recoletos alone were insufficient to play the role required in contemporary government plans for Mindanao. After all, in the year 1857 plans were already being readied for what in 1860 would be officially decreed: the establishment of the first politico-military government for all of Mindanao. Under this new government set-up the island would be divided in six Districts:

1. Zamboanga
2. Northern District (Cagayan/Misamis)
3. Eastern District (Surigao)
4. Davao
5. Central District
6. Basilan

Article 13 and 14 of the mentioned decree stated:

(13) — The mission of the Society of Jesus which has been sent to Mindanao will take over the spiritual care of the island and will occupy the existing parishes; this shall be done in accordance with the availability of personnel and in the form it deems convenient.

(14) — The principal task of the mission will subsequently be the conversion of non-Christian tribes; furthermore, after the parishes have been staffed, a sufficient number of missionaries shall be kept available to dedicate themselves for the first purpose. The missionaries will be supported by the Ministry of Finance to the amount of eight hundred pesos each per year.

One cannot help wondering what had really happened in Madrid...In itself it should have been possible (even more than in the final solution) to take care of government intentions for Mindanao with *both* Orders present in the island, like for example in the pre-1768 set-up, wherein the Recoletos served the eastern and the Jesuits the western half of Mindanao. Had this possibility been considered initially? After all, the first Royal Decree of 1852 did not exclude it. Therefore, who objected against it in the end: the government (on second thought), the Bishop, or the Jesuits? Still in 1857 the Bishop seemingly left the second and third Districts (Cagayan/Misamis and Surigao) open for possible Recoleto occupation.

The Recoleto Commissary in Madrid, Fray Agudo called the arguments of the Bishop "poor, very poor" and added:

"The Recoletos could come forward with strong and

convincing objections against the form, the spirit and the method of the Bishop's petition. The attention of his Excellency should loudly be drawn to the fact that he cannot just ignore the high respect which the Crown since the conquest has given to the actual possession of the *doctrinas* and parishes, so that, if some change had to be made, it was done with the procedures indicated by the law of propriety. But the Bishop of Cebu, without even talking about a possible exchange or indemnification, just simply takes the parishes away from the Recoletos, without in any way shoftening such a harsh measure..."

Already in the very first decree of 1852 it had been felt as an insult when the Jesuits were praised for their past services without those of the Recoletos (undoubtedly equally great) even being mentioned. Licinio Ruiz concludes that Agudo proved beyond doubt that the arguments of the Bishop carried no weight, but were purely motivated "by goodwill towards the Jesuits for reasons of a different kind."

It appears that all the objections of the Recoleto authorities in Madrid were unable to sway the decision of the government. On September 10, 1861 (on the very feastday of San Nicolas de Tolentino, patron of the Philippine Recoleto province!) another Royal Decree came from Madrid.

"In order to forestall any doubt that could possibly arise in connection with the implementation of article 13 of the Royal Decree of June 30, 1859 about the establishment of government in the island of Mindanao, and wherein is decided that the incumbent parish priests be replaced by missionaries of the Society of Jesus, the Queen had deigned to declare that to the latter belongs the task of the future foundation and development of the *misiones vivas* (beginning parishes) in the island, and that they should take over the administration of the parishes and *doctrinas* already organized by the Recoletos as soon as these become vacant through the death or transfer of those who presently occupy them by canonical appointment and administrative capacity.

Since, however, her Majesty wishes at the same time to grant some indemnification and show the appreciation with which she views the distinguished services of the Recoletos to the Church, she grants the Province of San Nicolas de Tolentino

the faculty to administer the parishes of Cavite or others that are
served by the indigenous clergy, as soon as these become vacant,
in the same way as indicated for those parishes in Mindanao still
administered by the Recoletos'' (L. Ruiz, op. cit., p. 264).

Confronted with the inevitable, the Recoleto Provincial finally
informed the Bishop of Cebu on February 10, 1862 that he bowed to
the wish of the Queen ''as is just and my duty.'' He added:

> ''Because the Royal Order takes effect from now on, I have
> the honor and the satisfaction to be the first to comply with it by
> respectfully informing your Excellency that the parish of Mainit
> in the third or eastern District of Mindanao is presently vacant
> because the priest who administered it has died; therefore I turn
> it over as ordered.''

In July of that same year we read that the "richest parish" of the
Philippines, Antipolo, was given to the Recoletos as compensation
for Mainit!

There was one man who foresaw complications arising from this
and similar "compensations." On May 18, 1863 the very Provincial
who accepted Antipolo wrote to the Bishop of Cebu: "The parishes
of Cavite, and especially Antipolo, are going to be fatal, and that
ill-fate will involve upheavals of incalculable dimensions..." The
Philippine revolution and its preambles would prove him right.

In another communication, dated August 14, 1862, the
Provincial informs the Governor General that aside from Mainit he
also hands over the parishes of Bislig, Lubungan (Zamboanga),
Davao, Pollok and Basilan. ("Importantisima Cuestión," 1863,
Madrid-Complemento, p.22).

In spite of all the official (Spanish) courtesy in which the
turn-over documents are dressed, one senses some hidden sarcasm
because the whole matter — so is stated several times — was a very
humiliating and hurting experience for the Recoletos. Some years
later it would turn into a debate between Father Pastells of the
Jesuits and Fray Toribio Minguella of the Recoletos; in their
respective published utterances haughtiness and anger are politely
and coolly covered up as in some Congressional debates between two
"Distinguished Gentlemen from..." In a queerly twisted way old
animosities had come full turn.

Very intriguing is also at least one other Recoleto response to the
clause of the Royal Decree stipulating that the Jesuits were to take

over Recoleto parishes as soon as these became vacant "through death or transfer of the incumbent parish priest." In the case of Tandag, care was taken that there would be neither death nor transfer; in the "Labor Evangelica de los Pp. Recoletos" by Fray Fidel de Blas, we see Fray Juan Engroba in uninterrupted possession of the parish of Tandag from 1847 till 1877! If anything, it looks like a pathetic gesture saying: "They will not get the very spot where our glory in Mindanao started in 1622." In 1877 the Provincial received a hint: the "gobernadorcillo y principales de Tandag" informed him that they would give their "gustoso consentimiento" if a Jesuit were appointed to Tandag...They received the following curt answer:

> "Tandag shall pass to the Jesuits as soon as it becomes vacant, in accordance with the regulations. Taking into account that in the thirty years wherein the present parish priest has administered the parish, no complaints against him have been made, it would not be fitting to deprive him of a position of which he has been in pacific possession for so many years" (Marcilla).

Nevertheless, it looks as if in 1884 (Engroba had by then been replaced by Fray Juan de Dios) the Recoletos officially surrendered Tandag...up to a point! The administration decided: "From now on, beginning with the next Chapter, the priory named Tandag shall carry the name "Santa Cruz de Manila," as shall also be the title of the appointee to that place, who shall attend the Provincial Chapter by virtue of being Prior of Santa Cruz de Manila."

Since 1884 Tandag was de facto occupied by a Jesuit, Father Peruga...after Fray Juan de Dios had still refused to budge in 1882! Tandag was definitely one of the places where the Recoletos made it very clear that the Jesuits were not welcome. Understandable, perhaps, because, as just stated, Tandag was the place where the Recoleto mission in Mindanao had started in 1622.

In 1871 the first Jesuit, Father Martin Luengo had sailed into the parish of Surigao. There was no Recoleto to welcome him, as can be deducted from a letter (now in Marcilla) which he wrote on September 30, 1871 to the Recoleto parish priest of Gigaquit, who obviously still considered himself the "official" caretaker of Surigao, which he had left shortly before: "I have just received a letter from you wherein you tell me that I should officially have informed you that I have taken over the parish of Surigao..."

The rest of the text clearly shows that the letter from Gigaquit had not exactly been friendly. So, for that matter, was the answer! Also the transfer of Cantilan had not been free of unpleasantness. In his biography of Father Heras, Father Saderra Mata, SJ remarks: "Cantilan was a village known to be rich, but also corrupt and anti-Jesuit." Perhaps he should rather have said that Cantilan was pro-Recoleto, because it had been founded by them in the late 1700s and still felt an understandable loyalty to the Order... At any rate, when Father Salvador Ferrer, the first Jesuit parish priest of Cantilan received his appointment letter from his superior, it read:

> "...Confiding in God and holy obedience, and with only Father Sansa as companion, you will go to Cantilan, which will become a real calvary for both of you. If they will not receive you, or if there will be a troublesome demonstration against you, then you will return to Surigao, and from here we will inform the Bishop so that he can take the necessary canonical steps" (Miguel Saderra Mata: "Noticias biograficas del R.P. Juan B. Heras, SJ, p. 56).

There were, however, no incidents when Fr. Ferrer took over Cantilan in 1880.

In the Jesuit archives at Sant Cugat, Barcelona, is a set of fourteen letters written by the same Father Luengo as a report about his exploratory trip along the whole east coast of Mindanao from Surigao down to Sigaboy in Davao. Time: June 5 till July 16, 1873. Upon arriving at Tandag he went to the convent (ill at ease, I presume) because here he had to pick up the parish books and other articles belonging to the vacant parish of Bislig. In and out of the convent — so he says — took him one hour; he was told that he could go to Bislig and pick up there what he wanted because everything had been left in that place. He did not stay overnight in the convent — he mentions giving a flimsy excuse — but slept in the cramped sailboat in which he travelled. Before daybreak next morning (Trinity Sunday) he wanted to say a very quiet Mass, "not wishing to disturb the parish priest..." In spite of his adopting a low profile, many people attended, and afterwards a big group came to the beach to see him off. Luengo explains this sympathy as follows: "so good is the fame left behind by the Jesuits in the past."

In spite of the turn-over gestures referred to earlier (Mainit 1862, Bislig 1863) the records show that the Recoletos did not abandon those places immediately. The last Recoleto parish priests left Mainit and Bislig only in 1871, Gigaquit in 1872, Bunawan and Butuan in

1875, Cantilan in 1880, Numancia in 1882 and Tandag in 1884.

Not without some peculiar feelings of sympathy I copied in Marcilla the "testament" of the last Recoleto of Bislig, Fray Pedro Sanchez; he wrote it in Hinatuan on October 27, 1871.

> In the name of the Blessed Trinity, and believing all that Our Holy Mother the Church believes and commands to believe, and in compliance with my vow of poverty, I hand over to my superiors all that I possess for my personal use. This consists in some carabaos (I do not know exactly how many) in Cateel, some fourteen cows in Bislig, and all the things in the convent of Bislig, furniture and clothing; also twenty-three sheep and twenty-two goats; in addition about six hundred pesos in cash which were left after I had paid the church accounts.
>
> If my superiors approve it, I would like that from this they will send a part (perhaps two or three hundred pesos) to my father whose name is Pablo Sanchez and who lives in Tarazona, Aragon; the rest to be used to pay my debts with the Procurator and elsewhere.

Hinatuan, October 27, 1871
Fray Pedro Sanchez.

THEY ARE REMEMBERED FOREVER IN BLESSING
+ (1 Mac. 3:7)

All in all 251 Recoletos have worked as missionaries in the Old Caraga District, for shorter or longer periods. Of these 51 died in what are now the provinces of Agusan, Surigao and Davao Oriental. They were the following:

1623	Tandag	Juan de la Madre de Dios	Murdered L E [1]
1624	Gigaquit	Juan de San Nicolas	Murdered L E
1631	Tandag	Jacinto de Jesus Maria	Murdered R

---

[1] *M* after cause of death means murdered by *Moros*.
  R after cause of death means murdered by native *rebels*.
  L E after cause of death means murdered by local *enemies*.

1631	Tandag	Alonso de San Jose	Murdered R
1631	Surigao	Pedro de San Antonio	Murdered R
1631	Tandag	Juan de Santo Tomás	Murdered R
1631	Bislig	Juan de San Agustin	Nat. death
1641	Linao	Agustin de Santa Monica	Murdered R
1647	?	Caspar de Santa Monica	Drowned at sea
1671	Butuan	Miguel de Santo Tomás	Nat. death
1702	Siargao	Jose de S. Pedro y S. Pablo	Nat. death
1707	Butuan	Domingo de San Agustin	Nat. death
1707	Butuan	Joaquin de San Nicolas	Nat. death
1722	Siargao	Roque de San Jose	Nat. death
1722	Cateel	Benito de San Jose [2]	Murdered M
1734	Siargao	Jeronimo de San Miguel	Nat. death
1738	Pahuntungan	Jose de San Nicolas	Sunstroke
1739	Tago	Jose de Copacavana	Drowned
1739	Tago	Roque de Santa Monica [3]	Drowned
1744	Butuan	Felipe de la Sma. Trinidad	Nat. death
1744	Butuan	Franco. de la V. de Moncayo	Nat. death
1750	Surigao	Tomás de la Concepción	Nat. death
1753	Siargao	Jose d.l.V. del Niño Perdido	Murdered M
1754	Tandag	Antonio del Sto. Cristo	Murdered M
1761	Butuan	Lucas de la Cruz	Nat. death
1762	Surigao	Eusebio de la Concepción	Exhaustion
1764	Jabonga	Francisco de la Concepción	Nat. death
1764	Bislig	Esteban de San Jose	Murdered M
1764	Tandag	Nicolas de la Natividad	Nat. death
1770	Siargao	Jose de Santa Theresa [4]	Murdered
1771	Butuan	Agustin de San Jose	Nat. death

---

[2] Benito de San Jose actually died of a heart-attack after helping to beat off a Moro assault on Cateel.

[3] Roque de Santa Monica is not listed in Licinio Ruiz's ''Synopsis Historica'' from where this list is partly taken.

[4] Jose de Santa Theresa: see his namesake at Tandag 1785.

1772	?	Jose de San Nicolas	drowned at sea
1781	Paniguian	Juan de Jesus	Nat. death
1784	Gigaquit	Miguel de San Mamos	Shipwrecked
1785	Bislig	Jose de Santa Theresa	Nat. death

The following all died a natural death:

1788	Cantilan	Valero de San Agustin
1805	Surigao	Juan Elorza de la Concepción
1807	Baculin	Jose de Santa Orocia
1814	Surigao	Pantaleon de la Virgen del Tremedal
1814	Hinatuan	Pascual de la Virgen del Pilar
1815	Cantilan	Miguel de la Virgen de los Arcos
1817	Butuan	Francisco de San Basilio
1844	Butuan	Prospero Bon de San Vicente
1845	Tandag	Pedro Garcia de San Jose
1861	Surigao	Romualdo Sanchez de Santo Tomás
1865	Dinagat	Dionisio Busto de San Jose
1866	Butuan	Miguel Garcia de la V. de los Martires
1872	Cateel	Pedro Sanchez de la Concepción
1878	Cantilan	Modesto Marzo de San Nicolas
1883	Tandag	Juan Engroba de las Angustias.

XVI

The Odyssey of Bunawan and Talacogon
1867 - 1879

Among the thousands of bundles of old documents in the National Archives in Manila, there are about five or six that have been catalogued under the heading "Erección de Pueblos, Caraga/Surigao." They contain what is left of all the paperwork that once accompanied the official establishment of towns, villages and barrios in the present two Surigao and two Agusan provinces in the second half of the previous century. However, going through all those browned and brittle, faded and often damaged handwritten papers, one begins discovering very soon that the heading "Erección" de Pueblos can be rather misleading. More than half of the paper-pushing between Manila and the mentioned districts is not about the first-time establishment of the localities concerned but about their transfer to some other location. It can safely be stated that of all the settlements existing at the turn of the century, hardly any was still in the same location where it had been fifty or twenty-five years earlier. And it is remarkable that in Agusan the reason given for a transfer was nearly always the ever recurring floods during the rainy season. Anybody still believing that the 20th century floods are only the evil consequences of modern logging operations, will have a surprise coming if he will take the trouble of wrestling with those 19th century documents reporting near annual floods at a time when there was no logging at all. [42]

The following pages are about the odyssey of two villages of upper Agusan to the seacoast about 80 km north, and back again to their original locations twelve years afterwards. A transfer with a history of its own, as we shall see. Its scenario unrolled during the in-between years when the Recoleto era in northeast and east Mindanao was coming to an end, and the "restored" Jesuits of the Spanish Aragon province had just begun to take over the missionary responsibility over the area.

BUTUAN, BUNAWAN, TALACOGON

In 1867 Agusan had very few settled villages aside from Butuan, Bunawan and Talacogon. To the jurisdiction of Talacogon belonged two little barrios, Suribao and San Juan de Suribao (nowadays the spelling is Solibao). Butuan, as we have seen, was a very old settlement dating from before Spanish times; between 1521 and 1865 it had been shifted to different locations three or four times. In 1865 it moved (but not without much trouble) from Banza to where Magallanes is now, and in 1877 it was finally located in its present site.

Also the Talacogon-Bunawan area must have had a population with at least some tribal organization in the late 1500s, because the on-the-spot reports of the first evangelization efforts (started in 1597) mention that "the chieftains of Layalaya, 80 km upstream from Butuan" invited the missionary of Butuan to come and preach in their district.

Bunawan has at times been identified as being the old Linao about which we heard in the chapter "With a spirit apostolically bold." Here "El Padre Capitan" had established a fort of wooden stakes and an earth-wall, named "Real Fuerte de San Juan Bautista"; its purpose was to prevent the Moros of Davao and Cotabato from penetrating Agusan via the Hijo, Polangi and Agusan river. It served simultaneously as a place of refuge for the

---

[42] See Peter Schreurs: "Agusan's Loggers, Hewers of Wood and Carriers of water?" In *Philippine Quarterly of Culture and Society*, University of San Carlos, Vol. 9, No. 4 (1981).

Also id., id. (Augmented) in "Kebar Seberang," James Cook University, Townsville, Australia, vol. 15 (1985).

newly converted Christians, who were not safe anymore from attacks by surrounding pagan Manobo and Hadgaguan tribes. As we have mentioned earlier, the original Linao was distinct from Bunawan and located a little south of that place, till the flood of 1861 destroyed the settlement, which was then moved to "San Jose de Bunawan." Some writings of the Recoleto and Jesuit missionaries of the previous century mention that prior to 1867 Bunawan was of practical importance as a stop-over place for soldiers and mail carriers on the way to Bislig and the rest of southern Surigao.

After having practically been abandoned for about one century, the Talacogon-Bunawan district was again given a resident Recoleto missionary in 1856 upon the repeated demand by the Spanish government. In April 1875 Father Domingo Bové settled in Bunawan as the first Jesuit missionary of the restored Society to work in Agusan. He travelled to his assignment via the mountain trails behind Bislig. Not much is explicitly known about Talacogon before that dramatic year of 1867. All that can be safely said is that after Butuan and Bunawan it was the third village of some importance in Agusan.

Pointing to Butuan, Bunawan and Talacogon as practically the only settled villages in 1867 does not mean to suggest that for the rest there was hardly any population in the province. There definitely was, and perhaps even more than the combined population of the just mentioned places. But the people were living in scattered huts along the Agusan river and its tributaries, near plains that were suited to rice cultivation, and in the forests along the mountain slopes. In 1875, when taking the river route from the present Magallanes (then Butuan) to middle and upper Agusan, one would have seen what the Jesuit historian Pablo Pastells speaks of in Vol. I, Ch. 17 in his "Misión de la Compañia de Jesus." He describes there the findings of the first Jesuit superior, Father Luengo, who made a reconnaissance trip through Agusan in that year:

> "From where the farmlands of Butuan come to an end, small houses of Manobos began to be seen, scattered along both banks of the river, till one reached Talacogon... At a very short distance and in amicable fellowship with the Christians lived the Manobos in several *rancherias* [i.e., scattered clusters of a few houses of pagans]. The same was the case along the upper reaches of the Agusan river beyond Bunawan; there existed the *rancherias* of Maasin, Calibon, Maondo, Pasian, Jaguimitan, Panaon, Nabo and Batuto.

In the time of Governor Salazar, since the year 1856, there were a number of other villages of about twenty houses each...The Manobos were a people with a tough character and wild customs; they killed and enslaved as if they had no humane feelings. With the Spanish authorities, however, they behaved quite differently. As soon as the Governor, Don Fernando Salazar, planned to make them live in villages in 1856 and sent his commissioners to them for that purpose, they did not object, but formed little villages on the banks of the river and paid their tribute. The same happened in 1867 when Governor Boscasa reestablished those villages that had already disappeared.''

MURDER AND SLAVERY

The Manobos may indeed have behaved peacefully with the Spaniards but that was definitely not the case with regard to the neighboring Mandayas and even their fellow Manobo tribesmen. One of the reasons why the Spaniards wanted more and easier control over the inland tribes and therefore tried to concentrate them in accessible little villages under a pattern of social and political discipline, was to put an end to the practice of murder and slavery prevailing among them. These practices were so rampant that still in 1880 the French anthropologist Joseph Montano, passing through the area, remarked: "Agusan is a land of terror; it is at the point of depopulating itself." The wars and vendetta killings had become worse after the military detachment of Linao had been moved to the Hijo rivermouth in Davao in 1850. Previously, this little garrison had given the Spanish authorities in Butuan and Surigao (then capital of the District) at least some assurance of peace and order in the interior. Now, with the situation worsening daily, at a time when Spain was busy affirming its rather weak foothold in other areas of Mindanao (some other world powers showed interest in the island) they started planning a drastic measure to control the inland natives: transferring them to the coastal area of northern Agusan and putting them together in one or two centers of population.

PROCEDURE FOR TRANSFER

The standard operating procedure of transferring a village started with a written petition signed by the local village authorities and the leading inhabitants *(principalía)* explaining the reason for the intended transfer. Via the provincial governor — who added his own observations — that petition was forwarded to the Governor of Mindanao at Zamboanga, who in turn brought it to the attention of the Governor General in Manila. Usually the papers went back and forth a few times before Manila made a definite decision. Also local parish priests and even higher prelates took part in the procedure and their findings and opinions counted heavily at the tables where the decisions were going to be made. Going through the papers of a few cases does not give one the impression that Manila took such transfers lightly. But Manila was far away and as a rule could only rely on the truth of the information given by provincial and local authorities. And, of course, both the latter could make the impression in Manila that they were representing the will of the people concerned, while in fact at times such was not the case. From later developments it is clear that this happened in 1867 in Bunawan and Talacogon.

A PETITION FOR TRANSFER

In the second half of 1867 such a petition for transfer had been sent to the office of the Governor of Surigao. I have been unable to find documents pertaining to that first step of the process (with signatures) in the National Archives. But from references to it in the rest of the dossier, it appears that the petition consisted of three parts. The first, from Talacogon, had obviously been signed "by the local gobernadorcillo (mayor) Beray and the *principalía* on June 20, 1867." The second (from Suribao) was also dated June 20 and carried the signature of Apolinario Curato. On July 2 the *principales y cabezas* (leading inhabitants and barangay heads) of Bunawan did the same. Via the Governor of Surigao the petition had gone to the Governor of Mindanao, and by the latter's comment to the Governor General we are informed about what the contents of the papers had been:

> "The Governor of the third district of Mindanao has elevated to the superior government the documents pertaining to the transfer of the villages of Talacogon, Bunawan, Suribao and San Juan de Suribao...The mentioned documents were expedited on June 20 by the gobernadorcillos and principal inhabitants of the mentioned villages...According to the explanations of those

of Talacogon, they are living in a very deplorable situation. Nearly every year they suffer from famine and misery. They have nothing wherewith to engage in commerce and consequently they can hardly meet their annual (tax) obligations. During the time of the northeast monsoon, which is from the middle of December till February, the rains keep falling. In February the lakes at a distance from the village start overflowing, inundating the village and the farmlands in the *ilayas* up to Butuan. The plantations of rootcrops, which are the only recourse for the natives, are left covered with the mud carried along by the surging waters. This situation lasts for one to one-and-a-half months. During that time the inhabitants maintain themselves by fishing, until the time when the village dries up. Then they begin again to repair their houses. They also say that the land is infertile and produces nothing; the crops which they harvest are hardly enough for three or four months. The distance between this place and Butuan amounts to four days of river travel, which is risky because of the strong current. Since they live rather far from the capital, they are deprived of the visit by the Bishop of the Diocese. For all these reasons they wish to transfer to the seacoast to a place called Guinjahon, between Butuan and Nasipit. They ask to be exempted from the payment of tribute and back taxes during the time when they are working at putting up their houses and the other buildings of the new village and also in the fields for their subsistence.

What the leading citizens of Bunawan said is identical with that given for Talacogon; in addition they say that the climate of the village is bad and that the waters inundating the place during floods are sometimes one fathom deep. Therefore they ask permission to transfer to the place Quijaoan in the bay of Butuan; in that place there is enough land, good water and a good climate because it is near the sea. The people of San Juan de Suribao base themselves on the same reasons as the previous ones and ask for a transfer to the sitio Quijaoan between Butuan and Nasipit. [Note: the spelling of the place name has been kept as in the document.]

The information given by the parish priest of Bunawan/ Talacogon agrees on the absolute necessity to transfer the above mentioned villages. They make clear that in the places where the people are residing at present, they have become a miserable lot, suffering from chronic ailments resulting from the high humidity. For that reason the population does not increase; there are years

Fig. 28. Panoramic view of the bay of Nasipit, Agusan del Norte, within box the skyline of the village as it was between 1895 and 1897 when this drawing was most probably made. It appears in "El Archipielago Filipino, colección de datos," vol. I, 1900.

when the number of deaths exceeds that of births. With regard to the transfer to more than one place, they should be obliged to live in one single place.

The Governor of the district strongly supports the allegations of those concerned; he asks, however, that the mentioned villages be transferred to the barrio of Cabadbaran, a little village along the sea, at a distance of two hours from its mother-place Butuan. There is a large plain in that area, covered with cogon and low shrubs; it has fertile lands, clean air and good drinking water, and opens possibilities for fishing. With such favorable factors they can change their starvation existence for one of abundance because food will be easy to obtain. Under the supervision of the parish priest and of the authorities, they would, in a short time, create comfortable living conditions. With the natural increase in population they would produce new revenues for the treasury, whereas at present they will pay the tribute only when forced by strictness and even then with great difficulty...

The Governor of Surigao states in addition that the transfer can be effected in thirty or thirty six hours, because he has beforehand already given the order to provide them with *barotos* by which they could cover the greater part of the distance because of the favorable current.

Although it is true that with this new setup the parish of Butuan will lose three barrios, it will still keep nineteen with the barrio of Nasipit, plus six belonging to the village of Gingoog in the second district; that makes twenty-five in all. Then there is the advantage that there will be another priest at only two hours distance. It is easy to travel on foot or on horseback over the terrain or by *baroto* along the sea coast.

The result of that transformation would be that five localities with thirteen substations would be brought together at one place; jointly with the two of Tubay, they would form a parish with the probability of expansion, which would be for the advantage of the priest and of the faithful..."

The Governor of Mindanao who had received the foregoing information from Governor Boscasa of Surigao, informs the Governor General that, as far as he is concerned, he is in agreement with the necessity of the requested transfer. His communication was signed at Zamboanga on April 29, 1868.

In Manila the dossier passed through the various bureaucratic departments of the government and finally reached the last office: that of the Royal Fiscals. There it was approved with four votes in favor, one against. However, Manila informed Mindanao that exemption from the payment of tribute for one year would have to be requested from the Royal Government in Spain, since this was beyond the powers of even the Governor General.

With that last restriction the document of approval was signed on November 10, 1868. As far as Manila was concerned, the people of Bunawan and Talacogon could start packing their things and move to the greener pastures of Cabadbaran, for which they were seemingly so deeply longing. Or were they?

FREE OR FORCED?

The whole procedure which began on June 20, 1867 and ended on November 10, 1868, gives the impression of being wholly aboveboard: a well-reasoned request coming from the grassroots, passing through proper channels to Manila and back. However, with the hindsight provided by later developments, it is obvious that the matter had been railroaded, or that the signatories had been extremely naive and did not know what they were signing for. Had the signatures been forced or bought? Governor Boscasa was a rather ruthless person. In the National Archives (in the Legajos catalogued under "Caraga") one can find a set of documents, many of them barely legible, but clearly adding up to a whole dossier of accusations against him coming from places under his jurisdiction such as Surigao, Butuan, Tandag, Lianga, Hinatuan and Bislig. During the days when the transfer of Bunawan and Talacogon was in the making, a similar process had been decided for Butuan.[43] When

---

[43] The Marcilla Archives contain three documents of 1868 that relate to this transfer. The first is a request for aid by the parish priest of Butuan, Fray Matias Villamayor, to put up a church and convent at the new site of "Baug" (= Magallanes). In another letter he accuses the Governor (Boscasa) for his abuses. The third is a letter of the mayor (gobernadorcillo) Diego Rosales, dated October 22, 1868 and addressed to the Governor of Surigao: "Don Diego Rosales, incumbent mayor of the village of Butuan, together with all the past and present village officials, and with the agreement of all the past mayors, as well as of our parish priest Fray Matias Villamayor, in answer to your kind letter of... (blank) October of this year

the latter transfer did not materialize quickly enough, (there was dissension among local leaders) Boscasa threatened to burn the old place (at Banza) down! The least that can be said is that, in spite of their convincing sounding story, the signatories completely bypassed the difficulties a great number of people would have to undergo to transfer themselves and their habitat over such a distance. And that goes obviously for the parish priest, too. And it was a brazen lie that the distance to the coast could be covered in

---

wherein you express your desire to know our opinion about the name which our village should carry because it has been transferred to sitio Baug, states,

— that the name Butuan of our village has been taken from its river Butuan, and that also after being transferred it is located at the mouth of same river;

— that the name Butuan which it carries since 1639, is connected with many honorable events that are part of Philippine history, as a result of the zeal and courage of its parish priest of those days, Fray Agustin de San Pedro, known as El Padre Capitan.

Therefore we, the signatories, desire and request that also our new village will always be called Butuan, without addition or change of any kind.''

To which we may here add the correction that the name Butuan existed already in 1521, and not only ''since 1639.'' It is also remarkable that among the famous past events connected with Butuan, nothing is said about the First Mass! The reason is, of course, that the monument claiming this event for Butuan was put up only four years later, in 1872. During its inauguration that year, Governor Carvallo in his address stressed how privileged the reluctant Butuanos were to be living on such hallowed ground! It seems that Carvallo, with the monument at Butuan-on-the-sea, intended not only to immortalize a ''historic'' event but also to give this Butuan a token of permanency in its site at Baug-Magallanes. That permanency would, however, last only five years.

Still in 1870 many Butuanos had obviously not yet moved to the new site. Legajo 103 in the National Archives at Manila contains a complaint against Governor Boscasa: 1) He had threatened to burn down the remaining houses at the old site. 2) People had been given a written request-form for transfer to be signed by them. Fray Villamayor advised not to sign, but Gobernadorcillo Rosales gave the opposite advice. Because of his attitude the Governor accused Fray Villamayor of ''subversion,'' had him arrested and imprisoned in Surigao. The documents about his arrest are in Marcilla, and also a protest letter of Diego Rosales against it (Legajo 62).

"thirty or thirty six hours." Clearly, the application for transfer did not represent the wishes of the majority of the people concerned, as appears from what happened afterwards.

SUBSEQUENT EVIDENCE

Let me insert here the following information which I found in the Archives of the Recollect Fathers at Marcilla. Legajo 62, doc. 1, contains a letter of complaint against the Spanish Governor Manuel Boscasa of Surigao. It was written on April 13, 1869 by the Recollect parish priest of Bislig, Pedro Sanchez, and addressed to his superior in Manila with the request that it be passed to higher government authorities in Manila.

The writer begins by saying that since Boscasa took office he has shown time and again, by words, deeds and in writing, his extreme disdain for the priests. He acts as a tyrant in his dealings with the natives, and as a result there is everywhere a noticeable deterioration in all the essential branches of public administration.

"The gobernadorcillos and the other administrative officials are living with the continuous fear that, as a reward for what practically is a forced service (I am convinced that nobody would voluntarily become gobernadorcillo under this gentleman) they will receive all kinds of punishment, meted out without the reasons ever being given. As a consequence they just agree to sign anything that the said gentleman wishes to put before higher authorities under the pretext that it is for the good of the province. A proof hereof is what has happened in the villages of Bunawan and Talacogon which have requested transfer to a place called Cabadbaran, not far from Butuan. They were moved to do so out of fear, because such transfer is not only inconvenient for them, but even for Butuan itself and for Bislig. Bunawan and Talacogon are, so to say, two strongholds from where Christian ideas will spread to the surrounding country, so that little by little the tribes living there will be attracted to the fold of the Church. What is happening now is tantamount to doing away with such a rich potential for peaceful development of the country. Such glorious hope will totally disappear with that transfer, because the countless pagans living along the banks of the Agusan river will be completely left to their grosser instincts and exposed to the very possible risk of falling into the hands of the Moros who live near lake Mindanao. In my opinion, this possibility should be very seriously considered, and if that transfer should be realized; it would involve an imminent and lasting danger to Butuan and Bislig. Your Reverence will believe that I am not making any unfounded statements here, if you bear in mind how in the past the Moros kept this river area in slavery, and how expeditions had to be dispatched against them from Butuan. This could easily happen all over; we must keep in mind that the Moros about whom we are talking are living not far away: after a two days travel in the direction of the said lake up river from the place where the old Linao was located, one will meet Moros who are subject to the datus of the Hijo river and of the lake just mentioned.

For these reasons, and in addition because the communication between the east coast of Mindanao and the bay of Butuan will become totally impossible except by sea, I venture to believe that, if the inhabitants of Bunawan and Talacogon have signed a petition to the superior government to transfer to another place, they have done so solely out of fear..."

In short, if established places like Bunawan and Talacogon were removed, upper Agusan would become totally pagan again. The Moros might move into the area and the overland route between Butuan and southern Surigao would be cut. In the 1600s and 1700s the Linao station with its military detachment had more than once been the last refuge for Recoleto missionaries who had escaped from Cateel, Bislig, Gigaquit and Butuan during the Moro attacks. Understandably, aside from his practical fears, Fray Pedro Sanchez of Bislig had a weak spot in his heart for an area with so much Recoleto history in its past. On the other hand, it must be considered strange that his confrere in Bunawan had originally given his approval to the transfer; unless, of course, Boscasa had lied about this, too.

CONSEQUENCES OF THE TRANSFER

A few years after Fray Pedro had written his letter, the Jesuits had begun to assume the pastoral care of Agusan and Surigao. Among the many problems inherited by them was, of course, the unhappy question of the forced transfer of Bunawan and Talacogon. Father Pablo Pastells speaks about it in his "Misión" Vol. I, Ch. 17:

> "Governor Boscasa wanted to place the villages of Bunawan, Talacogon, Suribao and San Juan de Suribao together in one locality and incorporate them into the little village of Cabarbaran, giving it the name "La Reunion." The superior government of the islands approved the transfer which, however, since it was attempted against the wishes of the inhabitants, was impossible to realize. The same happened in 1872 during Governor Carvallo's time; he even kept the leaders and the *principalia* of those villages imprisoned in Surigao; but also he could never reach his goal."

Since the great majority of the people refused to move to Cabadbaran, the newly planned village of La Reunión became an illstarred place of misery. The poor village officials of Bunawan and Talacogon who had signed the petition were forced to go to the new settlement, where they were soon leading extremely lonely lives. Nevertheless, if in our days one looks carefully into the family names of landowners in Cabadbaran, he will find not a few that clearly hail from the Bunawan-Talacogon area and belonged to the *principalia* there in 1867.

Without suggesting any anomalies on the part of the forefathers of these families, it would not be surprising if Boscasa, aside from force, had also made use of certain favors.

But meanwhile, the old places of Bunawan, Talacogon, Surigao and San Juan de Suribao in the heartland of Agusan became, in the words of the first Jesuit superior Father Luengo

> "villages where the inhabitants found themselves without church, without convent, without schools and tribunal, without private houses, streets, farmlands and domestic animals, without any industry or commerce, and what is infinitely worse, without religion and good customs, without any education and working habits, and in addition dying of hunger.
>
> Such was the situation in the valley of the Agusan river in 1874 when the missionaries of the Society of Jesus entered there" (Pastells, loc. cit.).

Afraid that the Governor would use physical force to make them join the transmigration project at Cabadbaran, many of the villagers became *"remontados,"* i.e., they absconded to the mountains and the forest.

RETRANSFER

The new missionaries were soon convinced that the dreamed-of Reunión of Cabadbaran was one of the worst nightmares to happen to the Agusan of their days and a big obstacle to their own missionary plans. Therefore, this time supervised and pushed by the Jesuits Luengo, Peruga, Bové and Heras, the tiresome procedure down from the grassroots up to the Governor General in Manila, was started all over again, to undo what had been done in 1867-1868. On February 17, 1877 Father Raymundo Peruga wrote to the Mission superior in Manila:

> "After my arrival here, I received a communication from the Governor, the contents of which was in short that he had requested the gobernadorcillo of the notorious Reunión to draw up a petition, to be signed also by the priests, wherein an explanation should be given of the difficulties which the natives were undergoing by having to transfer to the seacoast. This petition was made, and last month I presented it personally to the Governor in Surigao. He promised me that he would support it with his endorsement and send it to the Governor General.
>
> If Your Reverence has the opportunity, I believe that you would do an immense service to this Mission by seeing to it that it will be acted upon promptly by the superior government. The immediate dissolution of the historical Reunión is the first thing to be done if we wish to bring some organization and progress to these valleys" (Cartas de los Pp. de la Compañía de Jesus, Vol. II. Peruga to Mission-superior, from Bunawan).

THE PETITION FOR RETRANSFER

I have before me a photostatic copy of the petition by the *"Gobernadorcillo actual, principales y Cabezas del pueblo de la Reunión,"* the original of which is in the National Archives in Manila. A nearly identical text can be found in Pastells' "Misión" (l.c.). Both texts differ only in this: the one of Pastells is dated June 21, 1875, whereas the one in the National Archives carries the date December 1, 1876. The reason for this difference may be that the first petition was not acted upon in official circles in Manila. Pastells says that the request was acted upon "much later." Since the copy of 1876 in the National Archives carries the signatures of the petitioners (unlike the Pastells copy) I prefer to follow this text and translate it as follows:

Sir Governor,

The incumbent gobernadorcillo, the leading inhabitants and the barangay heads of the village of Reunión, with all due respect, put the following problem before you. In order to comply with the decree of the Superior Government of December 10, 1867, and in spite of the fact that it cost them deep disgust, they had abandoned their former villages of Bunawan and Talacogon, Suribao and San Juan de Suribao, and had come to live in the Reunión. But they were never able to transfer their own families, nor the rest of their subjects. The reason for this has been the feeling that comes naturally to human beings when they think about having to abandon the place where they were born and grew up and where their ancestors were born and have died. Then, there is another kind of disgust arising from the different climate and the different working habits which are part of their lifestyle. The natives of Agusan tremble when they only hear the word sea, because in their own places there are no storms, nor *baguios*, nor upheavals of the sea. Experience has come to affirm their fears, because in less than fifteen days various women and children have died who had recently come to the Reunión in the year cited above. In view thereof we ask you to, please, hear our plea and take pity on our condition, and not force us to live forever far from our wives and children, staying alone in a village which is not a village at all up to the present, after all those years since the reunión was decreed, and which can never become our abode in the future because our families will never enjoy health when they have to live here.

If the problems which our way of life causes the Government or the Department of Treasury merit that we should live together in one single village, we could agree on that, but let them not remove us from the land where we were born. Bunawan and Talacogon would be two good places for that purpose, because aside from what was stated above, they have the advantage of being barriers against the Moros of the Hijo river and a stop-over place for those who transport the mail from the region of Bislig during the rainy season. They can also be a center for the settlement of pagans who have already Christian relatives living among us. From your well-known goodness we hope to be granted this favor; it will redound to the good of your subjects and to a better administration of this province, as is also stated by the missionary Fathers of Bunawan and Talacogon.

May God keep you for many years.

La Reunión, December 1, 1876

The incumbent gobernadorcillo, Vicente Plaza

Xavier Asis
Apolinario Foncion
Catalino Pumedo
Gregorio Asis
Salomon Ayaton
Gabriel Guerrero
Apolonio Galaoran
Diego Guerrero
Hilarion Pugahan
Ap. . . (ill.) Asis

The Barangay Heads

Raymundo Aznar
Sebastian Piencenaves
Francisco Rubia
Gabriel Polintan
Casimero Curato
Tomás Asis
Santiago Nobo
Rosendo Osen
Mauricio Galaoran
Dionisio Mozo
Pascual Durango

Raymundo Peruga, SJ
Domingo Bové, SJ

To: The Politico-Military Governor of Surigao.

That petition had obviously been written with the help of Father Peruga, who earlier had already spoken of "the hellish Reunión of Cabadbaran." As can be seen from the text, the petitioners skirt the issue of whether, once allowed to go back to upper Agusan, they would wish to live in one single village, or to re-establish their separate villages as they were before 1867. But they seem to be giving a hint when saying: "Bunawan and Talacogon could be *two* good places."

In his comments, the Governor of Surigao reacts positively to the petition, but he advises the Superior Government that only one place, Talacogon, should be revived, and that the people of Bunawan should settle there. One of the papers of the dossier in question states that such was also the opinion of the "Cura Parroco of Bunawan" and the statement of the parish priest follows in quotation. The parish priest of Bunawan at that time was Father Domingo Bové, SJ, but the mentioned statement is in fact signed by Father Luengo, who was the parish priest of Surigao and the superior of the Jesuits in northeastern Mindanao. He mentions that previously he too had believed that *both* Bunawan and Talacogon should be restored to their old status but, so he says, after four visits he now feels that only Talacogon should be re-established. His reasons for the continued abandonment of Bunawan: the yearly floods *(todos los años),* the unhygienic condition of the place caused by swamps and resulting malaria fever, lack of terrain for sufficient farmlands, and, as a general consequence: "People living like lazy loafers who cannot even pay their yearly tribute"; finally, Bunawan no longer had its old importance of stop-over place for communication with or from Bislig and the rest of southeastern Surigao, because this traffic now went via the Suribao river to Hinatuan and from there to Bislig via the trail that had been opened up to the river of Bislig.

In the bureaucratic traffic of papers the matter of concentrating Bunawan and Talacogon in one single village is a point of discussion for awhile. But there was a significant number of voices warning that the people of Bunawan would never agree to living in one place with those of Talacogon. This, so it is said, had already become very clear in the Reunión of Cabadbaran. Forcing them to do so would only result in their absconding into the jungle.

Obviously, the new missionaries had no intention of waiting for official approval from Manila permitting the reestablishment and re-organization of the old settlements in their original locations, and it seems that the Governor of Surigao gave them a free hand in taking the initiatives they deemed opportune under the circumstances. Already in 1876 Father Juan Heras wrote to the superior in Manila:

"Along the banks of the Agusan, Gibong and Simulao rivers, the villages of Talacogon, San Juan Suribao and Bunawan are far apart from one another; together they form the mission station of central Agusan. These villages are deserted, they have no church, court, schools and officials, because they had to transfer to the coast near Butuan, four days traveling away. They live more like pagans than like Christians; they live at the expense of the Manobos, whom they exploit and encourage not to be converted. It will take our Fathers a lot of work to guide those people in the right path and make model Christians out of them. As soon as word of my arrival reached the village, and when it was known that I carried a letter from the Governor permitting them to return to their village and build a house for the priest, they promised to repopulate Bunawan and Talacogon, for which places two missionaries have already been appointed..." (Cartas, I, 10, 1876).

Those two missionaries were Fathers Bové (since 1875) and Peruga.

Finally, on November 19, 1878 the Government in Manila decided

1. That the so called Reunión of Cabadbaran be dissolved. The few remaining inhabitants, including the old residents of Cabadbaran, would have to join the pueblo of Tubay.
2. That Suribao and San Juan de Suribao would be returned to their old status of substations of Talacogon.
3. That Bunawan and Talacogon would be two distinct municipalities.

Only one thing was still lacking: the official approval of the King of Spain! In Madrid, on February 11, 1879 that approval was signed as Royal Decree no. 128. It arrived in Manila on April 7 of that year.

It has been believed in the region that the dissolution of the "Reunión" gave rise to the name of "Cabadbaran" from the Bisayan verb "pagbadbad," which means to dissolve, loosen, untie. It is a tempting derivation, but incorrect. The name existed already long before the attempted Reunión and its dissolution: the original spelling was "Cabarbaran," the way a true Manobo would pronounce it even today.

At any rate, Royal Decree 128 wiped this Cabarbaran from the map. Because of the increased influx of Boholano transmigrants, Tubay became a sizeable center of population, soon to be followed by Tolosa. On November 22, 1879 Father Gabino Mujica wrote from Mainit that while traveling through the location of the former Cabadbaran "he saw a nice church built of stone, but completely abandoned" (Cartas III).

XVII

Change of the Missionary Guard

"Fuimos, pues, otra vez a Filipinas..."

As was mentioned in the chapter "The Uneasy Foothold" in 1767 Carlos III expelled the Jesuits from Spain and the Spanish dominions. In 1773 Pope Clemens XIV officially suppressed the Order, very much under the pressure of contemporary European statesmen, with whom the Papacy had been continuously at odds in the 18th century. "It is practically impossible for the Church to enjoy true and lasting peace as long as the Order exists," so it is formulated in the Breve "Dominus ac Redemptor" of July 16, 1773.

In all of Europe only Russia allowed the Jesuits a relatively unimpeded existence for the time being. In 1814 Pope Pius VII revoked the ecclesiastical suspension; in 1815 Fernando VII allowed the Jesuits to re-establish themselves in Spain, and in 1816 followed the permission to take up missionary work again in South America and the Philippines. The anti-clerical measures of the preceding years had negatively affected the presence of Spanish missionaries and consequently Spain's hold on the colonies.

Nevertheless, the trials of the Order were far from over: the restoration process encountered opposition and new expulsions all over Europe, in Spain alone successively in 1820, 1835, and 1868. The suppression of 1820 was revoked in 1825, to be followed by another outburst of extreme violence in 1834, wherein seventeen

Jesuits were killed inside their own chapel in Madrid; among the survivors was Father Ignacio Guerrico, the later founder of the Tamontaca mission in Cotabato... The future superior of the first group of Jesuits to come to the Philippines in 1859, Father José Fernandez Cuevas, was one of many who were forced to go to Belgium to finish their studies for the priesthood. Another suppression order for Spain followed in 1835.

It took the insight and dedication of a Dutch Jesuit, Johan Philip Roothaan, to guide the Order to its final universal restoration and organization. This "second founder," born in 1785 in Amsterdam, had to go to Russia in 1804 to fulfill his desire to join the Order. In 1812 he was ordained there, but in 1820 one more expulsion order forced the Jesuits also out of Russia. In 1829, while in Turin, Roothaan was elected Superior General. One of the great merits of this remarkable man is that in spite of all the setbacks which the restoration of the Order was encountering in Europe, he gave the overseas missionary apostolate top-priority in his planning for the future. Many of the new members asked to be chosen for the missionary fields formerly cultivated by the old Order because Roothaan had encouraged them to do so. Roothaan's zeal for the overseas mission fields of the Church (those abandoned when the Order was suppressed and new ones to be opened) speaks very explicitly from a letter which he addressed to his confreres on 3 December 1833 (feast of St. Francis Xavier): "To promote and strengthen the desire for the foreign missions."

Their eventual return to the Philippines was in the very first place spurred by an appeal of Bishop Santos Marañon of Cebu, who after a pastoral visit to northeast Mindanao in 1832, wrote to the King how deeply shocked he was by the condition of the parishes there (see the chapter "The troubled 1800s"). Bishop Marañon informed the government that he had pressed the Recoletos to return to the Caraga district, but that much more missionary personnel from Europe would be needed to undo the harm of the past years and to assure the the Philippines would remain loyal to Spain. "I cry out to Your Majesty and beg You urgently to arrange that a great number of Religious, if possible Jesuits, will come to the Philippines."

Already in 1832 Father Roothaan and the Spanish Provincial Morey had agreed in principle to re-assume work in the Philippines, but because of the dearth of trained, mature personnel plus the vicissitudes of the seesaw restoration years, the first group could leave only in 1859, six years after the death of Roothaan. Their foremost task would have to be to step up the Christianization of

Mindanao. We have already seen how they had begun to take over the former Recoleto parishes. In 1871 it was the turn of Surigao.

In the "Boletin Eclesiastico de Filipinas," Vol. 39, (1965), p. 133 the late Father Horacio de la Costa wrote:

> "Neither the Jesuits of the Old Society, nor the Recoletos who took their places after their expulsion, did much to evangelize the pagan tribes of the rugged east coast of Mindanao, the upper reaches of the Agusan river, the Davao hinterland or the Bukidnon plateau. The Jesuits of the Restored Society did."

This statement is partly debatable and partly historically incorrect. Debatable, because the old Jesuits stayed only a very short time at Butuan (1597-1612, on but mostly off) and could consequently not "do much." As for the Recoletos, I would not really dare subscribe that "not much"; they certainly did (and at what cost at times!) what their manpower and the vexations of contemporary historical situations permitted.

As for that historical aspect: the old Jesuits were never "expelled" from the mentioned areas; therefore it cannot be said that the "Recoletos took their places there after the expulsion": these had come there in their own right. The areas where the Recoletos "took over" from the Jesuits were located elsewhere in Mindanao.

It has to be admitted that with the arrival of the restored Jesuits one notices a new élan for the Christianization and hispanization process of Mindanao. Here was a group of truly dedicated men, in a peculiar way battle-tested at home in Spain, loyal Spaniards, no doubt, but most probably also men with a tendency to relativize that loyalty somewhat against the background of what government and rabble-rousers in their own country had done to them in a not so distant past. Here are some musings of one of them standing on the beach of Mati (Davao Oriental) in 1873 and wondering if he should collect some shells to be sent to Spain:

> "What for? So that afterwards some impious and vandalic hand, out of hatred for science, will come and destroy in one moment what has cost us so much effort? What else has happened to the beautiful collections that had been sent to Spain and France from the Philippines? What has become of our Colleges where they were exposed for public admiration? It has

all disappeared like a shadow. Irreligion is a negation not only of
God and His Church, but also of society and science!'' (Luengo
letters, 1873, p. 72).

This is a series of letters specified in the archive at Sant Cugat as
written prior to the lithographed (1874-1875) and the printed (1876)
letters.

Not only were they a new breed of missionaries, they were also a
new breed of Jesuits. There are reasons to state here that in the 18th
century also the old Order had become a product of its time and
contemporary traditions, and that in the Philippines it had exhibited
many of the less desirable characteristics of the other Orders that
wrote many pages of the history of the Church missionary and the
Church sedentary of well-known yesteryears. The restored Jesuits
who came to Mindanao in the 1800s came there shorn by force of
much baroque historical heritage, of which other Orders had been
unable to unburden themselves timely. It is true that at times through
their publications in Spain they informed the homefront of their
appearance and apostolate in Mindanao in a way that evoked ill
feelings among their Recoleto predecessors... What specifically
rankled with the latter was that in their publications at home the
Jesuits hardly mentioned the pioneering work of those predecessors,
making the impression that, e.g., the Christianization of Agusan was
or was going to be their own first time enterprise. "As if they had
come to the center of Africa" a Recoleto chronicler spitefully wrote
when the first "Cartas" (letters) about Agusan and Surigao
appeared in Spain. On the other hand, the Recoletos themselves did
very little writing for a general readership. It is not so strange that,
what may be called a little "missionary braggadocio" is now and
then not absent in some of the early "Cartas." Building up an image
of he-men "roughing it" for the sake of God, Church and Madre
España made (again: now and then) for interesting reading for
benefactors at home! But all in all, the overwhelming impression is
that these letter writers were highly motivated, determined and
idealistic men, who were speaking about their apostolate and
working territory as *la Misión de nuestros amores.*"

"Esteemed and Reverend Father Superior in Christ,

Before beginning this letter I can do no less than praise God
and give Him thanks, because I have seen the fulfillment of the
delightful hope which I felt when visiting the pagan Mandayas

living in the mountains that face the Pacific Ocean and the north
of Mindanao. I have already written to Father Lluch, the
predecessor of Your Reverence, about their disposition.

Equally I thank the Lord for being able to add that the
missionaries of Mindanao, with the help from Heaven and the
support of those who are praying for the conversion of the
pagans, continue to enlarge the flock of Jesus Christ.

This letter is proof of that; may you read it with the same
contentment and happiness as I hope you will, and with which I
write it.

Please be informed, Your Reverence, that while I was in
Bislig, I received notice that holy Obedience had assigned me as
missionary of Bunawan and its three *visitas* Talacogon, Suribao
and San Juan. All I can say is, that when I received that
appointment, I felt an inexplicable contentment. Great is the zeal
and the will, granted me by Heaven, to take part, however
unworthy, in the apostolic labor entailed in the ''Go and teach''
of our beloved Jesus...'' (First published letter from Surigao-
Agusan by Father Domingo Bové to the Mission superior in
Manila, from Bunawan, August 30, 1875).

It seems not farfetched to typify them as "men in a hurry..."
making the impression that they wanted to prove something. In the
first place perhaps their own mettle as a restored Society? And why
not? Had they not clearly been made to understand by the
government that it expected them to do a better job than their
predecessors, or at least do it quicker? They would not have been
human were they not going to show the former and the latter that
indeed they did!

''I am now going to explain to Your Excellency what are the
methods followed by our missionaries in the newly organized
settlements (*''reducciones''*), the support which they have
received and the obstacles they have encountered. The answer
that Your Excellency will deign to give to my letter shall serve as
guideline for our missionaries. Once they know that their
procedure is the right one, or once their possible mistakes have
been corrected and they are assured of the powerful support of
Your Excellency, they will throw themselves with renewed zeal
on their evangelical undertaking, in the desire to give a worthy
response to the confidence which the government of His Majesty
has pleased to put in this Society for the spiritual conquest of

Mindanao and the adjoining islands'' (Father Juan Ricart, Mission superior, to Governor-general Jovellar, January 17, 1885).

For an additional understanding of the hurry of these new missionaries, we must also take into account that the Spanish Government as well as the Philippine Church were much aware of the urgency to step up the colonization of the whole archipelago in general and of Mindanao in particular. The abortive revolt at Cavite in 1872 had been a well-noted signal of growing anti-Spanish feelings, which had been building up in the second and third quarter of the previous century. Too many non-Christian spots on the map of the archipelago would add to the precariousness of the colonial hold on the islands, a fact that was not lost upon other foreign powers.

The élan shown by the new missionaries had also undoubtedly been fostered previously by the growing missionary interest noticeable in the Church of Europe of their younger days. A new apostolic spirit pervaded some of the old Orders, and many new Societies had been formed which had the overseas apostolate written on their banners. In the restored Society of the Jesuits Father Roothaan had also restored the old missionary tradition that had had such a glorious start with St. Francis Xavier. Mandated organizations like the "Society for the Propagation of the Faith" and the "Holy Infancy" had brought the missionary involvement down to the grassroots of the parishes in much of Europe, a positive development that added a new signature and dimension to the worldwide concern of the Church, which until then had belonged nearly exclusively to some Kings and higher Church echelons.

Most of the information about the development of the Christianization and hispanization of northeast Mindanao during the last quarter of the 19th century has come to us through the correspondence and other writings of the men themselves who did the job. Before being released for wider circulation, these papers went through the hands of editors who decided what was fit to print. In this way the wellknown series of "Cartas de los Padres de la Compañia de Jesus de la Misión de Filipinas" came into being. The regular correspondence of Jesuit missionaries with their superiors and with each other was also a tradition started by St. Francis Xavier and afterwards imbedded in the Constitutions of the Order.

The printing and publication of selected parts of such correspondence had started already in France and Germany in the first half of the 18th century and had also been one of the factors

Fig. 29. Father Pablo Pastells, S.J. Born in Figueras (Gerona) on June 3,
1846. Entered the Jesuit novitiate in 1866. Had to flee to France
because of the anti-religious revolution in Sept. 1868. Returned
to Spain in 1870 after being expelled also from France. Ordained
in 1871. Fled again to France in 1875, and left that same year for
the Philippines. First assignment: Caraga (1876) followed by
Bislig (1878). Worked in Mindanao till 1887. Named Mission
Superior in 1888. Returned to Spain because of illness in 1893.
Became Secretary to the Provincial of the Aragon province in
1894. Started working on collecting all documents pertaining to
the Philippine mission in 1897; his first major work: the re-
editing of Combés' "Historia de Mindanao y Jolo" (with W.
Retana). Was freed from all other work to concentrate on collecting historical documents in the Archivo General de Indias in Sevilla
in 1904, where he lived till 1930. He died on August 16, 1932.

enhancing popular missionary awareness in Europe even during the last days of the old Society.

At present, the series printed at intervals between 1877 and 1902 (which interests us here), has become very rare. In Holland there is one set (minus Cuaderno I) in the Royal Institute of Linguistics and Anthropology at the University of Leiden. Father Pablo Pastells SJ has condensed and compiled these "Cartas" and other documents, not to forget his own experiences in the field and as superior, into the three volumes of his "Misión de la Compañia de Jesus de Filipinas en el siglo XIX" (Barcelona, 1916-1917). This task was in good hands: Pastells himself had started his missionary career as parish priest of Caraga and Bislig in 1875 and 1877 respectively. Later he became the Provincial of the Jesuit Mission in the Philippines. Rizal had a lengthy correspondence with him.

What was the make-up of the missionary territory which the Jesuits inherited from the Recoletos in northeast Mindanao? Using the "Cuadros Estadisticos" (1910) of Fray Fidel de Blas OAR, we can draw up the following statistics of the parishes about the time when they were vacated by the Recoletos:

PARISHES	PEOPLE
Butuan	5,042
Bunawan (+ Talacogon)	1,807
Mainit (+ Jabonga)	3,044
Surigao	4,787
Tandag	7,571
Bislig (+ Caraga)	7,606
Gigaquit	4,643
Cantilan	5,960
Numancia	2,997
Dinagat	2,982
Cabuntog	3,354

Each of these eleven parishes was (at the time of turnover) administered by only one priest. Together they comprised, aside from their main stations, thirty-three substations, sixteen *visitas* (smaller hamlets) and thirty-six *"rancherías"* or little pagan settlements more or less in the interior.

For its civil administration the district had a Politico-military Governor residing at Surigao and a military Commander at Butuan and Bislig. Upon the arrival of the first Jesuit in Surigao (Luengo,

1871) the acting Governor was Jose Maria Carvallo (whose name appears on the "First Mass monument" at the old Butuan, erected in 1872). Of him Pastells wrote:

> "He was Catholic in his ideas, had a high concept of duty, was a protector of just causes and, although he was strict in character, he stimulated by his example (among Spaniards as well as natives) an exact fulfillment of their administrative duties. He was attentive and respectful with the priests and was used to showing them the proper consideration, even in cases wherein he deemed it necessary to go against excesses of a certain individual of that meritorious and distinguished class" ("Misión," I, p. 107).

I am not sure if Pastells is here hinting at a State vs. Church tumult in Surigao, which he relates afterwards in the "Misión" as follows:

> "The great devil of Mindanao (an expression of Combés), who did not sleep, roused a great turmoil wherein he made use of the higher authorities of the district. This happened on the occasion when the local Spaniards refused on Palm Sunday to come inside the church to accept a palm, although Father Luengo had called them two or three times. The Politico-military Governor of Surigao sent a communication to the Alcalde (here: Judge of the Court of First Instance) to inform him of the affair and asking him to prepare a summons against the missionary..." (loc. cit.).

Father Luengo refused to come to the hearing and as a result he was forbidden to celebrate any part of the Holy Week ceremonies outside the church building. However, says Pastells, the ceremonies gained in solemnity inside the church, a.o. because it was the first time that the *Siete Palabras* were preached. Finally, but only on Easter Monday, the officials "lowered their sails" and declared the case closed. On that day the Governor, the Alcalde and the other Spaniards "came to kiss the holy Relic of the *"Lignum Crucis"* which the Father held in his hands..." It seems probable that their objection concerned kissing the hands of the priest, which was part of the Palm distribution ceremony, not of the veneration of a relic! Most of the Spanish officials of those days (although in civil matters they had to cooperate with the priests) did not hide their anti-clerical feelings on other occasions. The feelings were heartily mutual! Father Luengo would soon have another experience typical for those days or rather for such compatriots in government service. He never attended the social gatherings which the local Spanish community held at nights.

> "One person, more shameless than the rest, dared to say that if the Father did not join them at night, he knew why...! To those who did not believe this manifest calumny, he said: "Would you like me to prove it to you here, before eight days will have passed?" Lifting up his right hand he exclaimed: "If within that time I will not bring the *corpus delicti* here, may they cut it off!"
>
> Before eight days — what divine judgment — a firearm exploded in the right hand of the unfortunate calumniator and shattered it to bits. He who writes this has known that calumniator without his arm and has heard the story from the mouth of Father Luengo himself" ("Misión," I, p. 112).

Like everywhere in the archipelago, the villages, barrios and *visitas* were governed by a capitan, gobernadorcillo, a *teniente absoluto* or a *teniente simple*. In the administrative matters of each locality they were assisted by the local élite *(principalía)* consisting of former capitanes, incumbent barangay heads and some bigger landowners. The rest of the titled village officials were the fiscals of the convent, the teachers, the cantores and the interpreter. All were exempted from tax payment and from the so called "polo" or personal services (public works) to be rendered for a certain number of days per year. The great rest on the community ladder were the simple *"polistas"* and *"tributos"* (tax payers). Each locality was to keep its *"padrón"* or civil registration list, in which the local population was listed by family and specified according to the just mentioned criteria. In the *padrón* was also indicated who were exempt from taxes because of age, sickness or special privilege.

At the time of the turnover the general condition of the town of Surigao left much to be desired. The predecessor of Carvallo, Boscasa, had proclaimed strict regulations about people's obligation to settle in the población instead of in the hinterland. Already on October 10, 1855 Governor Carlos de Tovaz had done the same by passing a detailed housing and zoning order for all villages of the district of Surigao (except Cantilan and Nonoc, which were in the process of being transferred). The exact size of each lot, the distance between the lots, and the classification of building materials were clearly specified, as well as the time within which the houses had to be constructed. And, of course, the punitive sanctions if either the owner or the local officials were remiss. Boscasa had enforced this order with so much severity that the people of Surigao protested against it before higher authorities. We have already seen his *modus operandi* in the transfer of Butuan to the sea coast and his role in the odyssey of Bunawan and Talacogon.

It is interesting to read how far the role of a parish priest could go during those days:

> ''Because of Father Luengo's well-considered administrative measures and his continuous vigilance, the face of the town changed nearly completely in a short time. He saw to it that the streets and houses of Surigao, which at his arrival had been completely neglected, were repaired again... The first thing to which he directed his attention was that each married couple had their own house and each house its respective various compartments. He enforced that decency be observed in the streets and that nudity be banned... In this he was so successful that not a single man, woman or child above the age of reason would dare to walk naked in the streets. He also banned all idleness... and promoted decent forms of recreation. He saw to it that his faithful spent the Sundays and feastdays in a holy way, relaxed in body but busy in spirit. He gave one sermon in the morning and a conference in the afternoon at the same hour as the cockfight. A great many did away with their fighting cock because they were a continuous temptation for them to engage in the game'' (''Misión,'' I, p. 107).

He was also an ardent promotor of public sports and games, because they kept the young men away from the *tuba* vendors, many of whom started to find themselves out of business as a result. But he had a more difficult time to eradicate the privately organized card games. Some evenings he went stealthily along the houses to catch the gamblers. More than once the culprits jumped out of the windows, leaving the money and the cards on the tables. These were then dutifully confiscated by him and he told the owner of the house that they could come to the convent to retrieve the money.

> ''But first the women used to appear in name of their husbands. He gave the money to them, but most of them

refused to accept it because it was the *corpus delicti* of their husbands. Usually it ended up in the alms box for the souls of purgatory'' (ibid.).

Having to work so hard building houses, repairing streets, no more idleness, no drinking, no gambling... no, not everyone in Surigao was convinced that happy days had come again!

> ''If some of the inhabitants, weighed down with the extra-ordinary labor, came to the missionary to unburden their afflicted hearts of its complaints, he calmed them down with the sweetness of his words and his effectful persuasive reasoning. And nearly always they went home, their wounds healed and happy with the hope of the prospective, lasting advantage which their whole family would obtain from that short labor and small sacrifice'' (ibid.).

And indeed, with all these measures, plus a stepped-up campaign to improve fishing methods, cultivate the idle lands and raising cattle (and presumably also some gentle prodding), there was soon far less famine in Surigao than in the other villages. Most of those activities had to a no mean degree been neglected because of the quick money that could be earned by gold mining. Now, "the scandalous spectacle of people swimming in gold but dying from hunger" did not occur anymore. There had been a gold rush in June 1871, when a small landslide at the foot of Mount Tirabingan near Placer had uncovered a rich vein of the precious metal. The news spread through the whole district and beyond, with the result that hundreds of fortune seekers flocked to Placer. In spite of their primitive methods the diggers were able to earn more than eighty thousand pesos in eight days.

One of the many worries of Father Luengo was the dilapidated condition of the boys and girls schools in Surigao. There was no woman to be found to teach in the latter; the boys school was nearly totally deserted. First the buildings were repaired, and the parents repeatedly reminded of punitive measures that were going to be taken if their children did not attend classes. He requested a newly graduated teacher from the Normal School of the Jesuits in Manila for the boys school; some of the more outstanding among his convent boys were enrolled at the mentioned Normal School so as to provide for future vacancies. It is interesting to know that some prominent families in the present Surigao owe their social standing to the education which some of those former convent boys received this way.

Revived schools made for more systematic catechetical instruction and the fruits hereof were visible in the regular first communion celebrations, which became big parish affairs.

News about the spiritual revival taking place in Surigao spread beyond the parish boundaries and even to other islands.

> "People braved the dangers of the sea and undertook voyages of long days to hear the word of God and confess to the missionary, especially on major feastdays. A great number of them made a general confession and then departed from Surigao with the peace of their souls and their happiness visible on their faces, to communicate the good news to their relatives in Bohol, Leyte, Misamis and Camiguin. As a result, an increasing number of people came to Surigao on all days to confess. Even those who were crippled or sick had themselves brought in *barotos* or hammocks, or they came to Surigao dragging themselves on their crutches" (op. cit., p. 109).

In the Jesuit archives at Sant Cugat near Barcelona can be found the "Historia de Surigao" in the original handwriting of Luengo himself. It is from this source that Pastells has derived most of the information about these events. Luengo's manuscript is not a "history" in the usual sense, but a *"historia domus"* of the Jesuit residence at Surigao. Parts of it are not only informative about the events themselves mentioned there, but also throw a light on other contemporary situations as, e.g., the peace-and-order problems and other social consequences of the ways in which local authority, justice and taxation were being evaded. Taganaan, which could conveniently only be reached by sea, was a case in point. Father Luengo discovered that a great many people in that village, along the mangrove channels and in the *ilayas,* were fugitives from Negros, Iloilo, Cebu, Leyte, Samar, Bohol and Camiguin, and from as near as Siargao and Dinagat. Here, in and near Taganaan, they led a completely lawless existence *"sin ley ni rey."* They had even several places for their idolatrous practices. Nearby little islets had become places of refuge for all kinds of sick and disabled people who had turned their backs on society, or more probably had been driven to do so.

"The surroundings of Taganaan at the side of the sea form a real San Lazaro, which had to be cleaned by applying to the souls the salutiferous remedy of sacramental penance, which is more efficacious than that of the healing waters of the old piscina of Siloe" (Historia).

And where formerly the dark of the nights had reverberated with the raucous merriment of *tuba* addicts and gamblers, after one intensive "mission" by Father Luengo the daily recitation of the rosary after the Angelus bells was introduced, and pious songs alternating with loud declamations of the questions and answers of the catechism filled the evening air after dusk. Then the calm of night fell "over the place and the people who had been converted to God."

In spite of all his preoccupations with the local Church of Surigao, Father Luengo and his faithful took out time to demonstrate their loyal sympathy with the center of the world Church and the Pontiff in Rome. After the forced closing of the first Vatican Council (1870), a worldwide "Jubilee" with plenary indulgence had been proclaimed for the whole Church. As has been mentioned, in the 1800s the idea of solidarity with the Church overseas had started to take roots in Europe. It is of interest to read in Luengo's "Historia de Surigao" for the first time that such awareness was also being promoted in Surigao in 1871:

"In the period granted by His Holiness for gaining the Jubilee Indulgence of the Council (which had been interrupted by the invasion of the Piedmontese troops in Rome) the people of Surigao mixed their tears with those of all the Christians of the world, and they immediately answered the voice of their missionary priest by going to confession and — as far as their poverty permitted — by putting their alms in the collection box for the St. Peter's Pence which had been placed in the church. The litany of all the saints was also prayed for the same intention on the first and the third Sunday of the month."

Events like those of the invasion of Rome undoubtedly reminded this Jesuit of the related events that in past years had led to so much persecution in Europe, and that too probably stimulated Luengo's devotion to the Pope's cause.

From the "Historia de Surigao" Pastells compiled a description of the daily life in the parish of Surigao as it was more than a century ago. That picture was still partly recognizable up to the middle of this century. I believe that such stories of the making of our local churches deserve to be preserved as part of our religious heritage.

Every day at dawn the morning bells were rung *(alba)*. At the moment of the elevation of the Host and the chalice, at noon, at sunset and at eight o'clock at night the same bells invited the people to prayer, the night bell being rung in remembrance of the dead. Daily morning Mass was at six thirty and it was attended by all the boys and girls of the two schools who would recite the rosary and other prayers in common. After the Mass the children would line up in two rows and, preceded by the Cross, walk in procession to their respective school while loudly reciting the prayers. They remained in school till ten in the morning and from two till five in the afternoon.

Monday was baptismal day, Wednesday was reserved for weddings. The Viaticum (Communion with Extreme Unction) was solemnly brought to the houses by a small procession of some people carrying lighted candles.

Processions were an important part of people's religious manifestations. The barangay heads would put up little roadside altars within their territory; in the procession one saw the Governor, the Judge, the Fiscal, the gobernadorcillo and the small Spanish community of Surigao with the *principalia* and the rest of the devotees. The brassband and a picket of the local constabulary accompanied them.

Saturdays and on some feastdays of lesser rank, as well as during the Christmas novena, a *"Misa de Reyna"* was celebrated in honor of the Blessed Virgin; this was a Low Mass at the altar while the choir sang the Kyrie, Gloria, (Credo), Sanctus and Agnus Dei, at times with instrumental accompaniment. On Saturdays the *"Salve Regina"* was sung after the Mass with the antiphons and the prayers to the Virgin and St. Joseph. This was also the day for the "churching" of mothers who had recently given birth. After the Saturday Mass the priest gave a talk to the boys and girls, after which a group of ten boys would sweep and scrub the church. On Sunday mornings there was Mass followed by a sermon; in the afternoon a *"platica"* (short conference) during Benediction with rosary. During Lent a *Via Crucis* and catechism took the place of the Rosary and the conference. Once every month there was exposition of the Blessed Sacrament. The major liturgical feasts, the month of Mary (May) and that of the Sacred Heart were surrounded by special solemnity.

One of the merits of the restored Jesuits in Mindanao has been their untiring propagation of the Sacred Heart devotion, a practice which they had brought along from Europe. For them, it was not only the passive object of a cult, but also an effective instrument for the apostolate. In one of his many letters Father Saturnino Urios explains how he considered this devotion highly instrumental in the conversion of the Manobos and Mandayas. The "Apostleship of Prayer," which is still very much alive in the devotional life of many parishes, was for the Jesuits an indispensable part of their parish organization; the feast of the Sacred Heart was a real highlight in the liturgical year.

"Many were used to attend Mass and pray the rosary daily. The women carried a scapular and the men a rosary with cross or medal around their necks. A considerable number held their novenas, read devotional books, placed little altars in their houses and decorated them as nicely as possible. During planting season they brought the seed-rice to the priest for blessing, and before harvesting they offered the first fruits of the new harvest to him. They lighted many candles and offered Masses for the intention of the souls of purgatory.

So far for the externals. With regard to the inner things, there was everything: fertile and fruitful soil; there was sterile seed and that which fell in the middle of the road to be stepped upon; there was also that which fell on stony soil, and other which produced only thorns and thistles. In these regions the missionary made himself everything for everybody in order to win everybody. He was preacher, confessor, catechist, lawyer, judge, apothecary, teacher, architect and manager. He treated everybody according to his state and condition; he instructed and ordered all with equanimity, and suffered with courage all the inconveniences inherent in his duties. He had to free himself promptly but kindly of superfluous, impertinent and inopportune dealings without giving anybody reasons for suspicion of partiality. He had to undertake with interest any work that was for the general welfare, without failing to attend to the spiritual needs of the flock. In order to deal fruitfully with people, he had very often to combine the simplicity of the dove with the shrewdness of the serpent and the obedience to his superiors with the unity and fraternal charity to his companions in the ministry" ("Misión," I, pp. 142-143).

In many of the Jesuit reports one will not fail to discover the recurring references to the rather easy response by which the people reacted to the leadership of the missionaries. Of course, one will not fail to notice certain "authoritative" features that (certainly in a colonial setting) were part of those days (in Europe as well as in Surigao), and that must have stimulated that response at times. But no less should we have an open eye for the undeniable fact that such response and the mode of presence of the local priests were at the bottom of the historical process that has produced an intensively alive Church in the Philippines of today.

> "It may lead us to the realization that the fruits of that achievement have survived the ages and are still with us, perpetuated in our institutions and embedded in our way of life — and, perhaps personified in those qualities of optimism, forbearance and orthodoxy that still sustain us amid the sordidness and confusion of the times we live in" (Ramon Echevarría, "The Philippines in 1600").

On April 12, 1873 the change of the missionary guard took place in Gigaquit: Father Juan Sansa was installed as successor to the last Recoleto pastor, Fray Juan Pablo Ruiz. Luengo himself accompanied him and personally performed the installation rites. Fray Ruiz had not exactly welcomed Luengo in Surigao in 1871, and one can easily guess his feelings now, when he had to move again for a Jesuit... who also was just doing what he was ordered to do, of course.

To the parish of Gigaquit belonged the barrios of Placer, Bacuag and Taganito; Claver did not yet exist. Already in 1873 it was decided that eventually Placer and Taganaan would be separated from Gigaquit and Surigao respectively and made into a separate parish as soon as a priest would be available to staff it. The Jesuit reports of 1873 mention a population of 4850 for the parish of Gigaquit.

That same year 1873 Luengo received a large delegation from Bislig and Caraga, who had come to Surigao to explain the need for a priest in the southernmost region of the east coast. In 1873 and again in 1875 Luengo, in his capacity as superior, made an extensive reconnaissance trip through the new Jesuit territory of Mindanao. He first went from Surigao along the east coast to Tandag, Bislig (where he installed Father Parache as parish priest), Cateel, Caraga, Manay, Sigaboy, Davao and back again. He skipped Cantilan, which would have been a logical stopping place but was still Recoleto territory; his own short report about his experiences at Tandag is slightly altered in Pastells condensation of that report.

From Luengo's personal travelogue of the journey down to Davao (in the Jesuit archives at Sant Cugat) he emerges as an ebullient observer with a deep interest in what he saw. From Tandag down to Caraga he found the parishes without any priest. Fray Pedro Sanchez, the last Recoleto parish priest of Bislig, whom we have met earlier writing his testament, had died a lonely death in Cateel one year before Luengo's visit. Twelve years before that, a similar fate had befallen the penultimate Recoleto residing in Davao (then named Nueva Vergara)...

> "Tandag is a very small village located near the seashore. It has a wide river with good water. It also has beautiful agricultural lands suited for all kinds of cultivation. The people are more civilized than those of other villages. One sees also more white faces, no doubt a result of its past history. In his "Geography of the Philippines" our learned Father Murillo (Pedro Murillo y Velarde) speaking about Mindanao, mentions Tandag as a village of some importance. Once there was a fort here (or a *baluarte*, as they say here). It was strong enough for that time when the Moros did not yet have heavy artillery pieces. In this fort, of which the ruined ramparts can still be seen, a Spanish garrison had been stationed for many years. It was predominantly composed of Mexicans under the command of an officer who was called Castellano or fort commander. When that stronghold was being built, it was intended to be just big enough to shelter the people of the village in case of a Moro attack, and the walls were quite strong. However, what had not been taken into account was that the spot was dominated by a hill, from where on a certain occasion the Moros sprayed them with cannon balls. Tradition has it that the wife of the commander, in order not to fall into the hands of the Moros, put fire to the powder magazine, with the result that not only the fort but also the few people who were still alive, were blown up."

The "tradition" about the fort being related here, is rather at variance with the Recoleto documents, as we have seen earlier; the latter were contemporary on-the-spot reports. The reality of the fort's end had been even more dramatic.

At Luengo's arrival Bislig had been without a priest for more than a year. Father Parache, the new pastor, found only a dilapidated church and convent; the latter had in addition been totally ransacked. The old church of Bislig was located about three hundred meters back of the present site; the cemetery was an annex to it.

Luengo was very much struck by the way people received him and his companion everywhere. His explanation: "This happens in all the places where we come for the first time: A Jesuit is considered as something extraordinary." Be that as it may have been, it is a fact that in the past — just like now — people who had been without a priest for a long time have always shown their happiness when one arrived, Jesuit or not. One can, however, understand his feeling when this Spanish Jesuit added: "While in Europe they look upon us as monsters, here, by the mercy of God, people have a far better opinion of us."

About the village of Caraga Luengo wrote:

> "It is the real capital of this corner of Mindanao; it is a place with a history that lives by memories and still cherishes aspirations in the midst of all its miseries... It is not even a shadow anymore of what it once was. What happened to this place is the same as what befell some noble families who have come to dire times but who, although they don't even possess a quarter anymore, don't stop thinking about their descent, and expect by all means that people acknowledge them as superior beings."

Caraga was located on a plateau on the top of a hill about thirty meters high and next to the shore. The usual method of reaching the plateau was to climb a primitive ladder of about eighty rungs from the level of the beach. Pastells mentions that afterwards (presumably when he was parish priest or shortly thereafter) an approach road to the top was built under the supervision of Brother Zumeta and Capitan Leon Balante.

Luengo entrusted also the following musings about Caraga to paper:

> "This Christian village exists already two hundred years... It sounds unbelievable that now I was in the famous capital of Caraga, where once a government post was established like in Iligan, with a garrison of Spaniards and Mexicans, from whom some of its present-day white faces originate. From here departed those fighting troops who gave the Moros such a hard time, in spite of all the latter's might. The Caragueños of those days were famous for their courage; they not only went to sea

for the defense of religion and the Spanish banner, but also accompanied their Governor up the rivers and over mountains, carrying at one time their *barotos* on their shoulders till they reached the great lake of Mindanao, an undertaking that sounds unbelievable nowadays. But in those times the people were different, like the ideas that guided them. Regardless of what has been said in some newspaper articles that have little sympathy for the work of the Religious Orders, in those days Mindanao was far better known than at present. This has undoubtedly resulted from our revolutions and politics.

In those days Caraga was the center of the mission of the Recollect Fathers, who more than once shed their blood for these regions. In our days, all that has disappeared, because from the time when it became necessary to close the fortification in order to come to the succour of Manila, which was being threatened by the notorious Chinese corsair (Coxinga) in the days of Governor Sabiniano Manrique de Lara (1653-1663), those Christians fled from the danger of the Moros and went hiding in the mountains, so that the latter occupied the territory. Only the name of Caraga remained, until the Recoletos, with much patience and perseverance, were able to settle again some people there in the beginning of this century. In this way the new village of Caraga was founded; it carries the title of Mission and is a sub-station of the parish of Bislig... Its church, which does not deserve that name anymore because it is only a dilapidated shack, has as titular the *Salvador del Mundo.*''

Obviously, Father Luengo was not taking his history books with him on his trip, and some corrections are in order here. I am not being pedantic about it, but pointing it out because oral or written local history has more than once presented a local past that never really existed. This resulted from ceaseless and repeated statements of latter-day writers or speakers that were all too readily accepted and passed on as authoritative. Butuan is very much a case in point, and I am not merely speaking about its first Mass tradition...

Luengo is clearly imputing parts of the history of the *district* of Caraga and of Tandag to that of the *village* of Caraga. And indeed, more than once writers (and oral tradition) have insinuated that the district got its name from the village of Caraga. Very probably it was the other way around. Moreover, in not a few old records ''Caraga'' refers to the present district of Cantilan, whose ''Calagan'' ''Calegan,'' ''Calagda(a)n'' occur in earlier written reports as

referring to the coastal *village* of Caraga. The latter has no
documented history of the kind of greatness which Luengo fathers
upon it. The *district* of Caraga has, and the impression is that de
facto it was the greatness of the Mandaya *race* that accounts for it.

Furthermore: the village of Caraga never had a fortification of
the importance suggested by Luengo, certainly not of the importance
of Iligan. It only had (on and off) a limited kind of military outpost
pathetically cowering at the southern limit of eastern Mindanao, the
Ultima Thule before Moroland. The "Caraga fort" at times so
named in old records was clearly the fort of Tandag. The story of
Caragans carrying their *barotos* through the jungle to the "lake of
Mindanao" is here told as if it had started from the village of
Caraga; in fact it started from Butuan in the days of *el Padre
Capitan*. Among the troops in question were indeed some
"Caragans," but these were soldiers of the fort of Tandag.

Luengo was far more right when, worrying about the extension
of the new Jesuit territory and the working conditions awaiting the
new missionaries there, he asks:

> "Where is the man of iron who would not become exhaust-
> ed after traveling for days or weeks in a *baroto* over such long
> distances, with so much deprivation and danger?... On the
> other hand, would one's heart not be moved at the thought of so
> many pagan Mandayas? According to my data (which I do not
> pretend to be exact) there are at least ten thousand of them living
> between Bislig and Caraga, including of course those who do not
> know about our government and have no contact with the
> Christian settlements. Who would not cry out: "The harvest is
> great but there are not enough laborers?"

Those are words that have rung true for many years afterwards and
to some extent still do. [44]

---

[44] In his "Historia geografica..." Agustin Cavada Mendez de Vigo,
the contemporary government statistician, remarks in 1876:

— That there is a remarkable difference between the government and the
ecclesiastical statistics of the "district of Surigao," the first reporting
29,902 people, the second 48,712. It would seem that the first number
does not include the pagan population. Afterwards Cavada specifies for the
mentioned district: 29,902 plus 10,200 pagans. That still leaves a

It could globally be said that at the arrival of the new missionaries the population of the east coast between Caraga and Tandag consisted of Mandayas who were at least nominally Christian. Only slightly more inland, away from the coast, the majority were still pagan. North of Tandag and along the coast up to Butuan (except the Mainit-Jabonga area) the population consisted predominantly of baptized Manobos. In the district of Mainit and the adjoining mountains one would find a remainder of the oldest population of the Philippines, the Negritos, here called Mamanuas. Agusan's inhabitants were again mostly Manobo, with some Mandayas in the areas touching the boundaries of the present Surigao del Sur and Davao Oriental. With the exception of Butuan and part of Bunawan-Talacogon and of Mainit-Jabonga, the Manobos were nearly all pagan.

With the takeover of Butuan (February 17, 1875) and of Bunawan (March 16, 1875), it can be said that the Jesuit mission of Agusan was on the move. The reports about the takeover of Butuan and the experiences of the new parish priest, Ramon Pamies, are still in existence in Sant Cugat; some references can be found in Pastells' "Misión" (I, Ch. 17 and 19).

Accompanied by Father Luengo and Brother Jose Zumeta, Pamies arrived at Butuan on February 17, 1875. The last Recoleto parish priest (Fray Pedro Garcia) turned the parish over to him and then left three days later. In his capacity as regional superior of the whole district of Surigao, Father Luengo then proceeded up the Agusan river and the "mission trail" via Mount Bucan to Bislig where he fetched the new parish priest for Bunawan, Domingo Bové, who had arrived there from Davao.

The village of Butuan, the new parish of Father Pamies, was then still at the river mouth (later Magallanes), where it had (again) been established in 1865 after Governor Boscasa had ordered it transferred from its location at Banza, in spite of the opposition of many inhabitants. After all there had been "a signed request",

---

difference of 8,610. If not a downright miscounting, this may be due to the fact that at the time in question not everybody took into account the shifted boundaries of the districts of Surigao, Bislig and Davao. Moreover, some parish boundaries overlapped district boundaries.

— The same statistics mention for the district of Bislig 21,076 Christians, to which 10,000 pagans are separately added.

there had been the recommendations and approvals by the parish priest, the Bishop of Cebu and the Provincial of the Recoletos... and everyone had convincing reasons. How convincing those reasons were, is told in footnote 43 to "The Odyssey of Bunawan and Talacogon." Upon the arrival of Father Pamies the place was hardly organized and settled. There was not even a convent, and Pamies had to accommodate himself in the municipal building (tribunal) till August 3 of that year. The church was just a big nipa barn. From the window of his temporary quarters he looked upon the monument claiming Butuan as the site of Magellan's arrival and of the first Mass in the Philippines; it had been put up only three years before. During the Holy Week ceremonies some weeks after his arrival he found out that on Holy Thursday the monument was decorated to serve as depository altar for the Blessed Sacrament after the Mass; on Good Friday it was brought back to the church in a solemn procession. What a beautiful symbolic ceremony... if the claim of the stones and of the books that caused it had only been true!

Father Pamies found two much older devotional practices in Butuan. The first was the fluvial procession on July 25 in honor of St. Anne, "who a long time ago had been chosen as special protectress of the village of Butuan against the voracity of the crocodiles." As for the second:

> "In a manuscript that since many years is carefully kept in the archive of this place, and which had been signed by all the notables who at that time governed this village, a promise is contained wherein they and all their subjects obliged themselves forever to celebrate with all solemnity the feast of St. Francis of Sales; in addition they had bound themselves to give one candle for each person to the incumbent parish priest. It had also been decided that this document should every year be read from the pulpit during the Mass on the Sunday preceding the feastday" (Sant Cugat archives).

Which Pamies dutifully did.

For 1877 he records that in that year once more a decision was made to re-establish the place in a new location: the site where it is at present and which formerly was called sitio Agao. One document about this transfer, which is in the National Archives in Manila, has a note inscribed in the top margin reading *"Traslado de los pueblos de Butuan, Hinatuan y Cateel."* From a letter in Cuaderno II of the "Cartas" it appears that at that time Hinatuan was moved *back* to its former location and Cateel to a new site at Dacung Banua. Hinatuan had formerly been moved higher up along the river to where now barrio Dugmanon is located. That earlier transfer had probably something to do with the Moro threats; in 1877 it was claimed that all three transfers were (again) necessitated by the yearly floods. The Butuan documents speak about floods during the rainy season and especially during the very high tides *(pleamares)* which even today occur in the months of June and October. Some of people's understandable resistance was softened by... a spiritual retreat. The antecedents had been as follows:

> "On July 25, 1876 a request for transfer was once more drawn up, signed by gobernadorcillo Diego Rosales and seventy other *"principales y cabezas del pueblo de Butuan."* The signatories state that they had called for a meeting to deliberate where to put up a provisional church [note: still at Baug/ Magallanes], because since their coming to this place there had only been a poor nipa barn.
>
> But during the meeting some had pointed out that in fact the present location of the village was not suited for a good settlement. In spite of all the work done for elevating the streets, the whole terrain was too low to prevent flooding during the extreme high tides. The speakers pointed out that during the five years of its existence in this locality, the village had continuously been threatened by the strong currents of the rivers flowing at both its sides; the riverbanks had already been badly eroded, and at the noth end the water was reaching the houses.
>
> In addition, there was the ever present danger that the village would be badly swamped by severe rainstorms, as had happened on Christmas eve 1874, when the floodwater had been one fathom deep and many houses had been destroyed by the pounding of heavy tree-trunks carried downriver by the rampaging floodwaters. On such occasions the people were totally isolated from the outside world. Moreover, there was not enough possibility for agriculture and cattle raising, so that fishing would forever remain the people's only source of income.
>
> By unanimous agreement they had therefore decided to propose that the village of Butuan be transferred about nine kilometers southwards and upriver to sitio Agao" (Document in National Archives, "Erección de Pueblos").

In mid-September 1877 a start was made with the site preparation at Agao: removal of trees and other growth, filling and laying out of streets and canals. Every week groups of men went to Jabonga to cut *"magcono"* trees to serve as posts for the new church. This went on all through 1878, but in 1879 it is reported that only few houses had been put up at the new site, although Father Pamies and his assistant Casellas were already residing in a provisional convent.

In 1880 the Governor of Surigao was coming to Agusan, and Pamies went all the way to Tubay to meet him there. Most probably the visit had to be kept a secret, because people had been made to believe that the Bishop was coming. The reason for that secrecy had to do with the military purpose of the visit: Governor Raccaj came with a detachment of soldiers, with the intention of capturing the Manobo rebel Lincuban, who lived along the Ojot river and (after initial submission) refused to allow any missionary into his area. He had even threatened to attack Butuan, as he had already done to Esperanza. People of Butuan got the surprise of their lives when suddenly, instead of the Bishop of Cebu, the Governor appeared with his armed party. They got a stiff scolding for the poor condition of the roads and the houses. Men, women and children started to work, and in a few days the whole place was clean again and like new! Pamies, in his letter remarked: "It would be a good thing if the Governor came every year!" People still living near the rivermouth at Baug/Magallanes would probably not have subscribed to that wish because:

> "The Governor went back to Surigao accompanied by Father Urios, and upon reaching the river bar and seeing that houses were still standing there and that even some new ones had been put up by Butuanos and Boholanos, he commanded to burn them down and passed a strict order forbidding to put up any house in the former village location without his permission" (Sant Cugat archives).

The first Jesuit to be assigned in the real "mission" area of upper Agusan was Father Domingo Bové. After having installed Father Pamies at Butuan,

> "Father Luengo went up the Agusan and Sumilao rivers by banca. In Bislig he notified Bové (who had come from Davao) that he had been nominated missionary parish priest of Bunawan with its three *visitas* Talacogon, Suribao and San Juan. On

March 14, 1875, accompanied by Luengo, he left Bislig for his new assignment at Bunawan. On foot they crossed the mountain (Bucan) while all the way the rain poured down on them. Time and again they sank into knee-deep mudholes; the leeches stuck to their skins and could not be removed until, fully saturated with blood, they fell off by themselves. They stayed overnight on the bank of the Miaga river, from where they took a *baroto* to Bunawan via the Sumilao river'' (Pastells, ''Misión'', I, p. 146).

Of that memorable trip (not unusual during those days: four days later Bové hiked back to Bislig to fetch a statue in Bislig) Bové has left us a few delightful letters that make up the first "Cartas" from the district of Surigao. Travelling on the Sumilao river through the forests between Bislig and Bunawan, the party passed through the territory of the feared killer-datu Malingaan. Bové relates with relish how kindly and respectfully the latter behaved when they met him and his people not far from Tudela. Six years later the "Cartas" of 1881 write about a bloody encounter between Malingaan and a punitive military expedition in which the datu and many of his family were killed.

On March 16, 1875 Father Bové took over the mission station of Bunawan. The departure of the last Recoleto missionary marked the definite end of the labor of his Order that had been began in upper Agusan as early as 1625 by the soldier-priest Fray Agustin de San Pedro, alias "el padre capitan."

The letters of Bové from Bunawan brim with the lively interest, zeal and enthusiasm rather typical for the early letters of most newly arrived missionaries anywhere. There is a touch of loveliness to his lines about the catechetical methods used by him for the first-time instruction of the pagan families: using the newly baptized children to teach the rudiments of the faith to their relatives:

> "These children, living under the same roof with their parents, brothers and sisters and other pagan relatives, recited among them in a loud voice all the prayers which they had learned. As a result, they began to listen to them, first with a certain amount of amusement, but soon because they liked it. In the end they came to do so with a holy kind of envy, which stimulated them to repeat to that new Christian what they had heard; the child would correct them when they made a mistake, and in the end the pagans of that house — without being aware

of it — were preparing themselves for receiving holy Baptism.

It could also be noticed that a certain feeling of pleasure was felt by the still pagan parents when they heard their daughters recite and answer the questions of the catechism in front of others, especially if the missionary had asked them to do so in order to show to the bystanders that it was not as difficult as they imagined it to be.

Two of these catechists engaged upon this kind of work without a particular assignment by the Father. One was a young woman, a converted *"baylan"* (sorceress), the daughter of a wellknown datu of those regions, and the other a very intelligent girl of twelve years. The Visayans called them ''the señoritas of Mambalili'' after a *rancheria* located one league distance from Bunawan'' (''Misión'', I, p. 165).

For many years catechetical instruction of the adults had by necessity to remain very rudimentary. There was little inclination and capacity for learning by rote among these primitives, and absolutely no real Christian tradition to serve as momentum or social setting for a daily learning process like, e.g., in the coastal settlements of old-time Christians, autochthonous or immigrants from Leyte, Bohol and Cebu. The arrival of the latter has been an incalculable asset for the relative ease in forming Christian communities in northern Mindanao up to quite recent times.

XVIII

A New Shape For Caraga Antigua

Perhaps the document best suited to give us an insight into the views of the missionaries on the circumstances surrounding the evangelization of north and east Mindanao in the last quarter of the previous century is the "Informe sobre la Reducción de Mindanao" by Father Juan Ricart SJ, originally written in 1883 and afterwards published in Cuaderno X (1893) of the "Cartas." Initially this report was labelled "confidential" but according to a footnote to p. 587 of the mentioned Cuaderno, in 1893 "the reasons for keeping it confidential had ceased to exist." Its purpose had been to advice the superior government of the archipelago about what would be the best procedure conducive to the final and fast colonization of Mindanao.

The author begins by pointing out that in 1881 the number of Christians in Mindanao had been 194,314. Twelve years later that number had increased to 302,173 or by 107,859. He then proceeds to indicate the factors that had caused such increase:

natural increase:	27,919
immigration plus conversion:	79,942

which makes for a (sub)total of 107,861. (The author does not mention it, but this would leave us with 2 unaccounted for!)

Under immigration is here understood: the transfer of people from other areas, especially Bohol, to Mindanao. According to the author of the report the combined number resulting from immigration and conversion deserved very special attention by the government, as had already been indicated in other reports and publications dealing with the colonization of Mindanao.

Immigration did not cost the government anything, and this, together with the work of the missionaries, leading to so many conversions to Christianity and subjection to Spain, involved relatively few expenses for the Treasury. And these two are the most important factors for the results of twelve years of colonization and pacification. Previous methods used by the government without missionary concomitant and at high costs had only a very poor outcome to show. Most pagan tribes, so the report goes on, do not present such serious obstacles to the "combined action of persuasion and mild force properly applied," in spite of the fact that as a rule they are war-like and mutually antagonistic; even their character and customs do not cause much of a problem in this respect.

The total number of pagans is estimated to be about 300,000; that of the Muslim population about 350,000. Of the latter, some could be subjected without too much difficulty, but others would be difficult to bring under Spanish control. The district of Surigao is most advanced in the reduction process of conversion and settlement under Spanish control because there are no Muslims, and as a rule the Manobos and Mandayas are rather docile people. In 1881 there were already 18 settlements that had been formed of Manobos in the Agusan valley; of the Mandayas 16 villages had been estabalished along the Pacific littoral. Twelve years later, in 1893, the Agusan valley counted 46 such reductions (comprising nearly the whole Manobo population), whereas along the east coast all the Mandayas were settled under government control, most of them Christianized.

The report reduces the reasons for the poor results in the past to three historical factors:

1. The fanatical resistance of the Moros, who were well and quite securely entrenched in their territory, and farthest away from Manila.
2. The withdrawal of the Spanish troops, notably the abandonment of the fort of Zamboanga.
3. The expulsion of the Jesuits in 1768. This would, of course, only apply to the western and southwestern parts of Mindanao, which had been mission territory of the Jesuits and counted with the highest number of Muslims.

In 1881 the following could be pointed to as the main reasons for contemporary failures in the colonization process:

1. *Wrong ideas,* such as the assumption that effective reduction would be possible by purely secular means devoid of any religious proselytism. Ricart's report clearly states that reduction and evangelization are one and the same. Especially the Muslims will never completely be subjected without preparation leading to acceptance of our religion, how much soever this had been forgotten or even denied in the past. Even the Muslims can be converted. Of course, immigration is necessary, but in itself it is not enough for the overall purpose intended, certainly not if it has only military presence to lean upon. Because of the fear which they instill in people, the military can even be an obstacle to reduction.

2. *Wrong practices:*

   The separation introduced between military occupation and evangelization. The result has very often been that the natives become aloof and eventually flee to the mountains and jungles. The Cross and the Sword should go together, says the author, and such in perfect harmony. *And let the sword precede, in case resistance is encountered.*

   "Military action at the time and places where needed will be necessary on land and sea, rivers and lakes, in order to give a good lesson to anybody daring to resist. Without causing trouble to the peace-loving inhabitants, the military should clearly show that Spain is in command, and that no jungle-lairs are beyond the reach of her arms.

   But there is a concomitant need for missionaries, who should be given a free hand and shown proper respect. They should not be restricted to parish work in the established villages, but allowed to carry the light of the Faith and of Christian morals, by word and example, to the pagan races and conquer their hearts with charity and patience."

— The military do not constitute a permanent element in the reduction process because they come and go without really settling in the areas of their assignments. The only ones who really settle among the tribal natives are the deportees and the Chinese, and both are bad liabilities. It would be far more effective to establish permanent military stations and entice the soldiers with land grants to settle there. If deportees have to be brought in, allow their families to come along, and provide them with some farming equipment.

— Attitudes: on the one hand the policy to be adopted should be one of attraction although without extreme back-bending; on the other it is also very important that government and military authorities stamp out all kinds of abuses against the natives. These authorities should not be changed too often, so that some continuity can be given to development programs once these have been started.

— In case military officials have to be assigned, it should be taken into account that the mere qualification to command a military unit is not sufficient under the circumstances; what should also be a criterion is their moral and religious attitudes.

— One more undesirable practice is that newly converted pagans are exempted for only ten years from the payment of tribute and from military conscription. This practice is counter-productive, because owing to its short-term character, it had a deterrent effect; the exemption should be for life. (This was granted eventually because of the request of the Jesuits repeated in 1884, see a.o. pp. 251-252 in "Noticias biograficas del P.J. B. Heras" by Saderra Mata).

Generally speaking, so the report states, what is needed for the effective colonization are not new theories, but just harmonizing the military-civil reduction with the conversion of the pagans, as also stipulated in the Royal Decree of July 30, 1860. In addition hereto proper attention should be given to immigration and also to agricultural development programs.

There is another report dated 1885 wherein the same Father Ricart is more specifically giving an account of the reduction process in the district of Surigao. He informs the Governor-general that the work of subjecting the Manobos and Mandayas has been successfully completed. The tribals, formerly living widely scattered, are now brought together in new settlements where they live peacefully and have their own land to cultivate. It can be expected that in the future these will form important centers of population.

The methods employed by the missionaries were the following:
1. First of all, obtaining complete information about them, their way of life, social behavior, the names of their leaders, the dialect, etc.
2. Sending some trustworthy emissaries to them to prepare them for the visit of a missionary.

"On the appointed day the latter goes there, armed with great friendliness and meekness, but also speaking with authority and dignity about his wish to be their friend and to love them; he will tell them that he has heard about such and such misfortunes suffered by them, and that out of pity he has come to help them. He mentions the name of the King and of the district governor, names which they have learned to fear and respect in their dealings with Christians. He also reminds them of misdeeds (which always exist), small or serious, committed by them or fellow-tribals against Christians, and tells them that the Governor intended to send some soldiers to punish them, but that he [the Missionary] out of love for them, has interceded for them and has obtained from the Governor the promise that if they form a village and settle there, he will not only forgive their misdeeds, but will also take them under his protection and defend them against their enemies. He will also explain the advantages of a civilized life in so far as they can grasp it, and also how benign Spanish domination is. He will talk them out of wrong ideas, answer their objections and take their fear away. He will try to soften their hearts with little gifts and treats, especially for the children.''

The next steps in the process are: selecting a site for a village, putting up houses, election of local officials, handing over the *"baston de mando"* or staff of authority to the local chief and entrusting the others with various tasks. Some old-time Christians of nearby villages will keep an eye on these fledgling communities. Eventually a visit by the Governor will strengthen their respect for authority; also the military will appear from time to time if needed for punitive purposes. The settlement should be freed from the capriciousness and at times criminal influence of some datus and from pagan and superstitious practices; people's eyes should be opened for a simple code of decent human behavior, social interaction and respect for authority. This leads unavoidably to the necessity of evangelization; one can never be sure of the stability of a reduction until they have celebrated the fiesta of the patron saint and other Christian ceremonies. On the other hand:

''The missionaries do not talk to them about baptism or religion before they are willing and interested to listen and have confidence in their words. Only when the pagans begin to like the Spaniards and appreciate their customs and the things they stand for, the missionaries begin to inform them carefully and to instruct them about the teaching of our holy Faith and show them the practices and ceremonies of our religion.''

The greatest hurdle to overcome was, of course, the reluctance of these jungle dwellers to live in a settled village, especially of the datus, who felt the loss or at least the lessening of their old authority. Those who refused baptism, e.g., because they practiced polygamy, were not to be bothered as long as they did not molest the others. Without baptism their old mentality would never really change. After baptism, a Manobo, a Mandaya or a Mamanua ceased to be such and became a Christian.

> "In 1873 and 1874 (the Jesuits) took possession of some parishes and mission stations (in the district of Surigao) to serve as bases for the reduction procedure. Up to 1877 they limited themselves to a few excursions through the pagan areas so that the people would get to know them and they the people. After 1877 till the present (1885) with the arrival of more personnel, they have been able to give themselves intensively to such an apostolic task. The result of their work, together with that of the government and the military of the district has been: 42 villages and 17,840 new converts, plus the disappearance of slavery and human sacrifices, and in addition the end of fierce warfare, vendettas and assassinations, which until then had drenched those regions in blood."

The nefarious activities of unscrupulous and abusive merchants are repeatedly mentioned as a hindrance to peaceful reduction of the pagan natives.

There is one more revealing report about the reduction process of the pagans in Mindanao. It was written by Father Pastells in 1888 and addressed to Governor-general Weyler. He stresses:

> "That reduction and colonization should not be undertaken by violent means, but by a system of peaceful attraction and persuasion.
>
> That in this country, at all times, the initiative of the missionaries should be considered as an indispensable factor, because it is guided by the law of the holy Gospel which they have to preach with their lifestyle and the word of their teaching.
>
> In Mindanao, anything that has to do with reduction and colonization, but makes abstracts from Christianity, is building air castles."

REDUCTIONS IN AGUSAN

Reduction	Race	Families	People	Part of:
S. Pablo	Mamanuas	15	85	Jabonga
S. Roque	id	21	103	id
Santiago	id	30	141	id
Santa Ana	id	25	120	Tubay
Tolosa	id. + Manobos	62	320	Tubay
Concepción	Manobos	24	76	Butuan
Tortosa	id	82	302	id
S. Ignacio	id	31	116	id
S. Vicente	id (Banuaon)	61	405	id
Amparo	Manobos	103	562	id
Las Nieves	id	109	446	id
Esperanza	id	154	702	id
Guadalupe	id	63	319	Talacogon
San Luis	id	44	223	id
Los Martires	id	15	60	id
Novele	id + Mandayas	76	441	id
Borbon	Manobos	43	219	id
Las Navas	id	41	215	id
La Paz	id	64	339	id
Sagunto	id	95	439	id
Loreto	id	184	1,004	Bunawan
S. Isidro	id	36	103	id
S. Jose	id	71	375	id
Tudela	id	84	511	id
Trento	id	39	198	id
Veruela	id	41	215	id
Patrocinio	id	38	206	id
Jativa	id + Mangulangas	166	843	id
Moncayo	id (Dibaon)	62	321	id
Pilar	Mangulangas	67	345	id
Gandia	Mandayas	85	566	id
Compostela	Mangulangas	65	344	id

Total : 2,096 10,664
(Saturnino Urios)
November 4, 1884

REDUCTIONS ALONG THE PACIFIC COAST
(All Mandayas)

Reduction	People	Part of
Loyola	396	Hinatuan
S. Nicolas	684	Cateel
S. Victor	315	Dapnan
S. Luis	589	Caraga
Sta. Fe	809	id
S. Jose	324	id
S. Pedro	482	id
Santiago	394	id
S. Ignacio	281	id
Sta. Maria	806	id
S. Francisco	310	id
Manresa	20	id
Zaragoza	209	id
Sta. Cruz	207	id
Jovellar	49	id
Tarragona	36	id
Incorporated in existing villages	1,345	
Total	7,256	

(Valentin Altimiras)
December 18, 1884

At this point, we have to draw attention to the following:
1. All the authors stress very much that past anti-religious or anti-clerical policies, in Spain and in the Philippines, are to be blamed for the failures of the former colonization attempts in Mindanao.
2. Not a few contemporary government officials were definitely anti-clerical, as is clearly stated or implied in published writings of the Jesuits. But, of course, these publications had to be circumspect and often reticent; unpublished letters in the

archives of the Jesuits in Manila and Sant Cugat de Vallés more than once speak a far clearer language. On New Year's eve 1885 the parish priest of Bislig poured out all his woes of the past year; among them the following:

> "The military commander of this place, who had given the missionaries so much to do and to suffer, has been changed for another, but what has not changed are the annoyances and the troubles that now and then stopped for a short while, but only to flare up again with more intensity and to greater embarrassment..." (Sant Cugat Archives).

Similar lines can be found in certain (also confidential) reports of such officials. There is, e.g., one by Lorenzo Moncada y Guillen from Davao, addressed to the Governor-general, dated January 2, 1878, now in the National Archives at Manila. It stresses that:

— (in the Davao district) the natives should not too soon be molested with missionary activity.

— already in 1870 Governor Sanchez had requested that no more missionaries be sent into the district to assure better reduction results.

— that it was the Jesuit mission in Samal that had destroyed the good harmony of the inhabitants with the Spanish government. (The missionary version of this incident is described by Pastells in "Misión", I, 95).

— Some tribal groups had agreed to live in settlement-villages, but they had requested that no missionaries be established among them "because these would force them to be baptized and oblige them to work on the building of churches and streets, to the detriment of their agricultural work, e.g., during the planting season."

It could even a priori be assumed that personalities like the civil authorities (anti-clerical or not) and the missionaries, also not exactly unaware of their position, role and indispensability, would rather sooner than later find themselves at odds with each other for all kinds of petty reasons. We already have cited the example of Surigao (Father Luengo). It was hardly any better in Butuan, as can be gleaned from some correspondence between the local P.-M. Commander and the missionaries which is in the Jesuit Archives at Manila. One hears of priests being forbidden to fly the official Spanish government flag on their embarcations, of a Commander being accused of forcing people out of church during the Sunday Mass, to help get his banca afloat, or, at another time, of forcing too many carriers to join him on official trips without even taking care of them underway. And if that was not enough:

> "It has upset me to see that some Reverend Fathers when they leave Butuan do not have the civil courtesy to say goodbye to the district Commandancia where I happen to be in authority, and show even less politeness to present themselves to this office upon their return. This Commandancia regrets it that they do not keep the rules of protocol and courtesy, rules to which everybody is bound. The fault lies not with me, but with the most humble sons of Saint Ignatius... If these things will not change, I will be forced to take steps against some of them because of the passive resistance with which they oppose my orders.
>
> May God keep you for many years.
>
> Butuan, March 29, 1887.
>
> Enrique Mendoza
> Commandante P.M.''

It must be remembered that at the time in question nearly all Spanish officials were appointees of anti-clerical governments at home and in the Philippines; in addition they were nearly always members of ideological organizations, in which much anti-clericalism had come together.

It is not without reason that we gave the "reduction reports" of Ricart and Pastells (there are more) some special coverage. They are found to be instructive for the understanding of theories of colonization and Christianization prevailing in those days. They do confront us repeatedly — one century later, presumably one hundred years advanced in our ways of thinking — when we wish to undertake a closer and value-added scrutiny of the processes of reduction, colonization and even Christianization of the Old Caraga district. Knowing for example how easily military power begins to lead a life of its own (and not the best), we are likely to look askance at expressions like "mild force properly applied," followed by "Let the sword precede the Cross where resistance is encountered" especially when spoken by churchmen.

I repeat: this is the benefit of a *development* (albeit often a late one) in human awareness. He who is not wholly ignorant of what could go on in probably all colonial settings of the former century (for us: in the Philippines) will feel the urge to take a fittingly critical look at some aspects of what has our attention here: the reduction of large parts of Agusan and Surigao in the last quarter of the 1800s. Critical distinction means: discerning the negative as well as the positive, and the ability not to let *ultimate goals or results* blind us to what it took at times for those at the business end of the change process.

We have all the more reason for doing this as our information has almost exclusively come to us through the writings of the change agents themselves... The Mandayas, the Manobos and the Mamanuas left no writings behind. At best (worst) some of their howling and scowling runs through the stories, as if it were, just casually, and to underline the hardships and heroism of the change agents... The patients hardly have a single line in their own right. Some awareness of this seems to be betrayed by the fact that initially the author of the first "Informe" had requested that his report remain confidential. There must have been reasons for that.

On the other hand, it is just as useful to be aware of attempts to father upon the change patients of a century ago some lines so called "their own." As recent as September 1980 there was a meeting held in Tandag (Surigao del Sur) for representatives of various cultural minorities and church-related and socio-civic organizations. In October 1980 a statement *(pamahayag)* appeared in "IGO," then a monthly publication of the secretariat of the Mindanao-Sulu Pastoral Conference (MSPC). Translated from the original Bisaya it reads:

Past and Present of the Native's Life

"In the past we lived in happiness and peace, because there were no Christians and government people to cause us trouble. Our condition was one of freedom. We had food in abundance from the wilderness and from our fields. Our children enjoyed perfect health and our sick were cured by roots, leaves and the fruits of trees. We had our own religion and our own worship. If some trouble arose in our communities, then it would be settled only by mutual agreement, and if punishment had to be meted out, the decision of the majority was followed... Although the proceeds from our products were limited, also the price of the things we had to buy, was limited... We had no problems."

Nobody will deny that presently many tribal minorities are living under undesirable conditions. And who would not like the dream of at least a past paradise to have been true? However, *all* documentation available about conditions in, e.g., Agusan one century ago (and there is a lot of documentation in existence) points to the truth of what a visiting French anthropologist, Joseph Montano wrote in 1880: *"Agusan est un pays de terreur,"* a land of terror. Shortly before Montano, one of the earliest Jesuit missionaries, Jose Canudas, wrote about upper Agusan: "No man would dare enter that wilderness unless motivated by love of God and the salvation of souls" ("Cartas," VIII, p. 256).

Of course, there is no sense (except some historical truth) in just pedantically telling the present-day tribals that their foreparents were definitely not living in a primitive paradise. But there is as little sense in making the minorities believe that, but for multinationals, or local capitalistic entrepreneurs, or even the Church of the past, they would now still be enjoying blessings like those of the primitive paradise dreamed up for them by conscienticisers of a dubious kind.

The above-mentioned Frenchman, describing the conditions prevailing in northeast Mindanao one century ago, enjoyed the privilege of the anthropologist: he did not have to offer any solution nor any effort of his own towards a solution. There were others, however, who had both to offer...and who wrote about it too. They were the Spanish missionaries who came there in the last quarter of the last century.

Montano, travelling along many of the unfinished hamlets during the torrential rainy season of 1879-1880 wrote that those hamlets looked to him *"macabre...lugubre...sepulchral,* lost in the mud under the greyness of the sky...,"* etc. They still do, one hundred years later, when huddling under torrential monsoon rains. But one important point is that most of them are still there.

It may be true that in 1880 the reduction villages were often far from what the natives would have clamored for in the first place. It is even true that for a long time many of these new villages were leading an extremely precarious existence: today they could be there and tomorrow they just disappeared, the *reducidos* had turned *remontados,* had run back to the old nomadic life of the mountains. But it is more stunningly true that today, one hundred years later, most of them still exist! They were saved from self-extermination. Nearly all those reductions are today towns and villages, etc., of the upper Agusan valley, Davao Oriental and Davao del Norte.

Montano mentions the desertion of the reduction of Amparo (then situated along the Macupahon river). So do the "Cartas" of the missionaries; they even mention that the *reducidos* of Amparo turned *remontados* not just once but four times. But of one of those four times something very moving has been reported. Back in the jungle again, the old folks — "noble savages" no doubt — could not stand any longer the crying of their own children who wanted to sing and pray the rosary in the barrio chapel of Amparo on Sunday mornings...and they went back ("Misión," II, p. 20).

What had happened there in less than twenty years? Regardless (for the moment) of the missiological vision or the philosophy of history or the sociology of development one wishes to adhere to, he will have to admit that in less than twenty years the missionary activity of the Jesuits obviously gave the warring tribes, the *"rancherías,"* the datus and the *bagani* a new sense of belonging to things that went beyond the human condition which history had allowed them thus far.

Montano's journey took him through the Jesuit-held mission territory of eastern Mindanao, and therefore his writings make very good supplementary reading after the "Cartas." From Davao he had come up the Hijo and the Sahug rivers, made an overland hike along the slopes of Hoagusan mountain, followed the Tubuan and Manat rivers, and reached the Agusan river near Moncayo. He describes the Mandayas as the "aristocracy of the Mindanao tribes," an expression also used a few times in missionary writings; Luengo even named them *"los Españoles de Mindanao."* But there was more to be said about them:

> "At all times I encounter the same fear: since Babao I am travelling in a land of terror. Going some distance from his house means for each Mandaya: encountering slavery or death... The Mandayas kill for profit, but also without even thinking of gain. They have a special word *"bagani,"* literally, murderer, but the actual meaning is *"courageous."* It refers to one who has cut off *sixty* heads. These bagani are the only ones who, after verification of their exploits, have the right to cover their head with a kind of turban made of red cloth. And all their datus are bagani!
>
> These customs, very similar to those of the Dayaks in Borneo, can sufficiently explain the depopulation along the banks of the Sahug and the misery of the inhabitants... Such a cruel regime is normal in the interior of Mindanao, and the life of the Mandayas is in no way more miserable than that of their

Fig. 30. "Kalibuhassan (Mandaya village) in 1880. From J. Montano "Le Tour du Monde," in "Globus" 1882.

neighbors. If the Mandayas are not going to get the protection of Spanish civilization, very soon only the memory of them will be left. Unceasingly suffering from the attacks of their neighbors, they wage in addition a merciless war among themselves" (Entry for November 15 and 16, 1880).

His entry for November 23 reads:

"At 5 PM we arrive at Patrocinio, a small colony of Manobos who are *"conquistados"* or *"reducidos,"* in other words, converted to Catholicism. Generally speaking, when a tribe accepts baptism and submits to Spain, the missionaries try to make them abandon their former habitat where memories of independence are still too much alive, and establish them on the banks of some river. This makes it easier to visit them. In Patrocinio the women and children do not run away at my approach. On the contrary, they come running to the river bank. One child detaches itself from the group and returns with four persons whose serious expression shows that they are notables. One of them greets me in Spanish: "Welcome, Señor, I am a Bisaya and a school teacher..."

November 26:

"The Manobos of Patrocinio tell me that I am now one hour's hiking distance from the mission of Bunawan. I send two men ahead to bring a letter to the unknown missionary who at that moment might be in Bunawan. I beg him to send me a few porters, because my *muchachos* are very tired. One and a half hours later twelve strong *nuevos cristianos* arrive at a quick pace. In a minute they put my luggage on their shoulders and bring me to the bank of a wide and fast flowing river, where two big *bancas* are moored. Fifteen minutes later I am in Bunawan. The Reverend Father Saturnino Urios of the Society of Jesus is waiting for me on the river bank and brings me to the *convento*, a very simple house but large and comfortable. "Feel at home," so this excellent missionary tells me, "you and your men need rest. You may rest here as long as you like; although our resources are limited, we will try to help you recover a little."

My *muchachos* are indeed in very poor condition and I myself am hardly better off. But I find my weariness so mediocre

in comparison with those suffered by that valiant man. Father
Urios has been in Mindanao for many years, always on the go,
visiting the *pueblos* of *infieles reducidos*, penetrating the
territories of the most feared chieftains, a life consisting entirely
of deprivations, exhaustion and danger...''

Urios told him that in one year he had baptized 5,200 pagans and,
so adds Montano, that means as many miserable people freed from
slavery and protected against violent death. Urios had cited to him
the case of one recently baptized Manobo who had told him that of
his two wives he had decided to keep the first but, so he wistfully
added, "I am making a big sacrifice, Father, in separating from the
other one. It took me so much to get her, because her father would
give her to me only in exchange for fifteen slaves. I did not have
those, so I had to start attacking some shy tribes in unknown
territory. To capture those fifteen slaves I had to do a lot of fighting
and killed more than thirty people."

In general, the *baganis* did not attack the reductions once they
were well established; they were aware that the latter enjoyed special
Spanish concern and military protection. Also the fact that the
reductions consisted of a bigger number of people was a deterring
factor. As a rule the killings committed by *baganis* and their
henchmen did not occur in "open" warfare of man-to-man fighting,
but in treacherous ambushes and raids on small helpless groups of
victims or unsuspecting individuals.

"The Mandayas crowd together in a limited number of
houses, not only because the construction of those dwellings
(ten, fifteen and even twenty meters above the ground) requires
an immense amount of effort, but also to make sure that the
defenders will always be sufficient in number to repulse an
attack. In those lofty dwellings one is never sure to see the new
day rise. In the middle of the night it can happen that the
bamboo roof will be set on fire by resin-coated arrows, and the
assailants, hiding behind their shields, will start hacking away
with their *bolos* at the tree or the posts that support the house.
In these attacks the assailant is nearly always the winner since
the arrows of the defenders are of little avail in the darkness.
Once the house has fallen down, the inhabitants — hurt or
mangled by its fall or entangled in the rubble — can no more put
up a serious resistance" (Montano, entry for November 15 and
16).

The system followed by the Jesuits for the missioneering and colonization of the pagan tribes was an imitation of an earlier undertaking of theirs in the missions of south America, especially among the Guarani Indians of Paraguay.[45] One could easily incorporate

---

[45] The "Reductions of Paraguay" (since 1654 officially called "*doctrinas*") were more or less autonomous settlements of Indians initially founded by the Franciscans and developed to great progress by the Jesuits in the Spanish colonies of South America in the 1600s and 1700s. Many laudatory but also some negative reports have been written about them, the latter often originating from the anti-clerical corners in Europe which were referred to earlier. In addition, however, more and more modern cultural anthropologists and missiologists are rather merciless with most procedures of the reduction system. The purpose of the "*reducciones/doctrinas*" was to bring the roaming Indian tribals together in fixed settlements where it would be easier to accustom them to civilization and religious life, and where they would at the same time be protected from abuses by Spanish colonists, *encomenderos* and slave-traders. These settlements were founded in the present Paraguay and adjacent areas of Argentina and Brazil along the rivers Paraná and Uruguay.

Each of the approximately thirty reductions consisted of a walled-in agricultural commune with a church, school, hospital and workshop. It also had its own militia for defense. The land and its produce were communal property: income and expenditures were centrally administered. Religion played an important part in the daily life of the reduction: common times and forms of worship and solemn celebration of religious feasts, etc.

After the expulsion of the Jesuits from South America in 1767 the reductions deteriorated and disappeared gradually, especially after 1848 when the government of Paraguay abolished all their privileges and rights resulting from their former autonomous state. Presently only a few ruins are left along the upper reaches of the Paraná river.

As for northeast Mindanao, it cannot be said that the reduction efforts of the last quarter of the 19th century were an original and first-time idea of the Jesuits. It had been in effect since the early days of the hispanization of Mindanao. (For the late 18th and early 19th century, see the chapter "The Uneasy Foothold.") Twenty years before the arrival of the Aragon Jesuits, Governor Fernando Salazar had already tried to move the scattered Manobo "*rancherias*" of upper Agusan into small villages along the banks of the Agusan river. Ten years later, when most of these hamlets had again disappeared, Governor Boscasa started the process all over, but equally

the reduction story of the restored Society in Agusan into a biography of its most outstanding promoter, Father Saturnino Urios. Arrived in the Philippines in 1874, he spent the next four years in various assignments to gather some missionary experience. In February 1879 he was entrusted with the leadership of the whole Agusan mission, then consisting of the residences of Butuan, Mainit/Jabonga and Bunawan. He was 36 years old, and Pastells says that he was assigned "to put new fire into the mission of Agusan." And that is what he most certainly did.

Two books have been written about him. The title of the first does him justice "Un Apostol de la civilización" (1920, by Ventura Pascual y Beltran), but is not much more (and could perhaps not be much more in 1920, only four years after his death) than a compilation of his letters. The other: "Ocaso del Imperio" by Adro Xavier (Alejandro Rey Stolle, 1940) differs from it only in the comments and connecting texts, which are written in the poetically romanticized (and nationalistic) language of a Spanish author who wrote it during the years of the Spanish revolution (1936-1939), perhaps with the understandable need to present to the world a paladin of another Spain: "La España de los grandes siglos, eminamente un pueblo misionero" (Pregón, p.9) [46]

---

without lasting success. The aborted "Reunión of Cabadbaran" (see chapter XVI "The Odyssey of Bunawan and Talacogon") was a clear effort along the same lines and for the same purpose. Only after the arrival of the Jesuits and under the pressure of speeding up the final colonization of Mindanao, was the reduction process resumed with greater effort and more systematically.

[46] Urios was born in 1842 into a poor family of Jativa, Valencia, eastern Spain, and grew up with relatives, who operated a barbershop. He entered the Society of Jesus when already a secular priest. Travelling along the Costa Dorada from Barcelona to Valencia and hence to Jativa, one will be struck by the names of many towns and villages; they are identical with the names which he and his confreres gave to many reduction villages of eastern Mindanao.

Back in Spain in the little historic town of Jativa (25,000 inhabitants) the name Urios does not appear in the local telephone directory, neither does that of Catayar, his mother's name. In the directory of Valencia one finds twenty-three listings under Urios (1987). In Jativa's "Oficina de Turismo" I was told that a small "plazacito" nearby had been named

Urios was assigned twice to Agusan, first from 1879 till 1891 and again from 1901 till his death in 1916. During the first period he was the leader of the whole religious, social and political reorganization of the province; in 1901 he was sent back to pull the district together again out of the shambles in which the Revolution had left it. At the beginning of the first period Urios wrote to his relatives in Spain:

> "The conquest of the territory along the Agusan river has similarities with the first conquest made by the Crown of Spain in these regions; in my opinion it is a continuation of the first. At that time there was no bloodshed, and the Spaniards sacrificed themselves for these poor people who because of their ignorance were obstacles to anything that had to do with civilization and a well-ordered life. Presently it is the same: the Manobos along the Agusan river and the Mandayas along the Pacific coast, seeing the abnegation, sacrifice and patience of the missionaries, will surrender to us body and soul, so that the day will come when we can hand them over to the government of Spain that will make them into her well-beloved sons.
>
> Let us pray that we may live to see the day, glorious for the Society and illustrious for Spain, when we can make a generous offer of them to the King, as a proof of our concern for the Faith and for the greater glory of Castilla" (Quoted in "Ocaso," p.25).

I consider it significant that, in spite of undoubtedly not a few less pleasant aspects of the reduction process, its foremost protagonist, Father Saturnino Urios, has left such a legendary name behind, not only on paper, where one could expect it, but much more among the immediate descendants of converted Manobos whom he had baptized and settled in villages. And even today, among still pagan Manobos in forlorn corners of upper Agusan, the legend is

---

"Plaza Mosen (= Rev.) Saturnino Urios." None of the several passersby whom I asked knew who the man had been whose name appeared on the signboard. Some local college students, however, told me that a few years ago some graduates had planned to visit "the place where Mosen Urios had worked," but the project had to be abandoned for reasons known to college students everywhere: lack of money.

Fig. 31. Saturnino Urios y Catayar, SJ. This picture was taken in Manila in 1916, a few months before his death. (Copied from Vol. III of ''Misión...'' by Pablo Pastells, SJ.)

kept alive that he will return some day and then they will ask him — only him — for baptism. Not to mention the several miraculous events connected with him in local oral tradition (bi-location, traveling through the air on a piece of cloth, floating down the Agusan river in a wash-basin for want of a *baroto,* etc.).

In spite of the fact that he was a stern disciplinarian who did not hesitate to personally lead a police-posse to go after wanted elements (he had been given the title of Vice-governor for the pagan districts), he is remembered not only as the "Apostle of Agusan" but also as the "Father of the Manobos." Indeed, one day he wrote: "They are my children, those poor beloved beings, and every hen believes that her chicks are beautiful!" On another occasion he referred to a notorious criminal as "he is a good-for-nothing bearded Manobo, just like me."

Not long after settling in the new Butuan together with Father Pamies, Urios announced his future plans for Agusan in a colorful way. He had invited the leading datus and other prominent Manobos living between Talacogon and Butuan. To stress also the need for reconciliation between the Christians of Butuan and the pagans of the interior, the former had been mobilized to give the Manobo delegation a grand reception. On the assigned day twenty-seven decorated *barotos,* flying the Spanish flag and carrying about one hundred fierce tribesmen and their women, all decked out in their native fineries, docked at the river pier of Butuan. Accompanied by the local brassband and a big group of curious townpeople they marched to the convent, where they were received by Urios and Pamies, who made them come up to the *sala,* where they were offered a cup of wine and a cigar. Together with that big group of pagans, one of the greatest problems of lower Agusan had marched up the convent stairs of Butuan: the fierce hatred between two leading datus named Manhumugod and Macahinlay. These two arch-enemies had waged a merciless war with each other for many years. According to Urios: "They were the terror of the area, killing people of each other's territory with treachery and cruelty."

As soon as Urios started to stress the need for reconciliation and peace, old grudges cropped up again, and calls for revenge were shouted back and forth between them.

"So I went on insisting, but nothing good could be arranged; finally, however, they gave in for a reason that may look trivial. I told them: From now on all of you are our sons; I have recently arrived here to live and die among you. You will have to celebrate my arrival in a way that will show your love for your father. All of you must unite and begin a new era. If this cannot be arranged, then it is better that I go back to where I came from. And that was the argument that closed the deliberations successfully'' (''Cartas'' III, p.34).

With the public reconciliation of these two *baganis,* now kneeling before the two priests, at least one big step had been taken towards the establishment of peace in lower Agusan. Urios immediately started to fulfill his promise to visit the Manobos in their own locations, staying at least two days in each place. The reduction of lower Agusan was off to a good start when in that same year 1879 some of the datus who had come to Butuan began to put up the first houses for a new village where they would live together; Urios named it Las Nieves, after the patron saint of his hometown of Jativa in Spain, Our Lady of the Snows. Urios must have had an enormous confidence in people's capacity for change, because as gobernadorcillo of Las Nieves he appointed a notorious former *bagani,* named Jose Domingo, a pure Manobo from the mountains near Misamis.

With a similar kind of leaders he next assembled the more than a thousand Manobos of the Ohut river into a village named *Los Remedios,* a place that would soon cause him a lot of heartache. *Esperanza* followed, but it had taken a lot of prodding before the Manobos from the Wawa and the Jauilian rivers really started to live together in that location.

Also the formation of *Guadalupe* succeeded with the settling there of the Manobos of the Maasam, Tabason and Macupahon rivers, in spite of the threats by former datus trying to prevent them from submitting to the new authority of the priest and the gobernadorcillo.

A few hours up-river, near the junction of the Agusan and Calisayan rivers, the first barrio of *San Luis* was formed; years later it would be transferred to the opposite bank of the Agusan river to be better protected against the attacks of pagans from the mountains west of the river. Not far from Talacogon *Los Martires* became the habitation for a mixture of about seventy Manobo and Mandaya families. *Gandia,* at the confluence of the Batuto and Agusan rivers, became a village of Mandayas from the Naboc and Batuto regions as well as from Cateel, Baganga and Caraga.

In 1880 *Moncayo* was formed practically from an army fieldtent pitched up near the confluence of the Manat and Agusan rivers. It started with only thirty families of one of the most feared Manobo tribes, the Dibabaon, and Urios placed it under the leadership of the (then still) pagan datu Dagojoy. This original Moncayo was abandoned in 1886 under violent circumstances and slowly rebuilt in another location. Dagojoy, baptized Luis, died in 1890.

On a beautiful plain near the Guinabutan river, Urios settled a village of mostly pagan Manobos, to which he gave the name *Jativa,* in memory of his own birthplace near Valencia. About a half-day trip from Jativa, opposite the old Maondo, rose a new village with the name *Patrocinio.* [47] Maondo had formerly been founded as a little Christian village by Father Peruga, but it had been abandoned when its captain and his family had been assassinated not long before the arrival of Urios in Bunawan. Patrocinio would soon flourish as a good Christian barrio.

Back again in Butuan Urios started giving his attention to the many Manobos living along the seacoast in the bay of Butuan. As a result, barrio *Concepción* was formed near Nasipit and Tolosa near Cabadbaran.

In order to be near to his next field of action, he now decided to put up his residence in Bunawan. Starting from there he hoped to spend a few months for the resettling of Manobos still living in many scattered places along the various tributary rivers of the Agusan. With some of those *Tudela* was expanded, while other datus and their followers joined the village of *Bunawan.* Then followed *Loreto* along the Humayan river, *La Paz* on the bank of the Argawan, *Novele* consisting of Manobos and Mandayas of the Suribao river, and *Amparo,* where the Manobos of the Maasan and Macupahon area were gathered. In January 1881 Urios reported a total of 6,055 baptisms for 1880, not including about six or seven hundred of the upper Agusan area.

Indeed, some men in a hurry, named Urios, Bové, Peruga, Heras, Canudas, Puntas had come to Agusan, and after their coming the place would never be the same anymore. But it was not appreciated by everybody. Earlier, in chapter XII "Baptize now, Evangelize later?" when speaking about the first Christianization of the Pacific littoral of Mindanao in the first half of the 1600s, we

---

[47] In 1870, after Rome had been captured by the Piedmontese troops, St. Joseph had been declared ''protector of the universal church'' with the liturgical title: *''festum Patrocinii sancti Josephi.''* It was a special devotion of Father Heras, the companion of Urios.

remarked that such a profound change (and so sudden in the case of Agusan), in order to be humanly bearable and sustainable, should not place individuals or groups before too many and too disturbing dilemmas. We also said that the new human condition being asked for, should offer the "change-patients" at least a number of new gratifications for old ones being renounced. Obviously, these prerequisites had not yet been present in the 1879-1880 situation created in Agusan. It cannot have been a mere coincidence that practically immediately after the first reduction-wave had passed over the district, there was soon hardly any area that had not risen in open rebellion, resulting in abandonment of the new settlements, and fierce fighting between Manobo *reducidos* and those preferring a wild life in the mountains to a settled existence under a controlled pattern of behavior. The old bellicose atavism of tribal warfare had found a new object: fellow tribals in the new villages, plus the new regime which the hamlets represented to them. Montano, op. cit. explains the background for the instability of the new order as follows:

> "The reduction does away with the datu and leaves him with only one wife. His authority as *capitan* or *teniente* is now precarious by nature. With regards to his *sacopes* and his slaves: only in the long run will they appreciate the benefits of the new regime. Unable to look into the future, they are not at all bothered by the hazards of a wild life; on the contrary, that condition makes it hard for them to appreciate new obligations like having to build a house for each family, a "tribunal," a chapel or a river-pier. It is true that the datu imposed on them the obligation to follow him in war, but that kind of obligation was all right with them, because they got at least some spoils out of it" (Entry January 19, 1881).

Urios himself indicates reasons that apply even today among the few remaining jungle minorities living in logging concessions or on lands that have become the object of land-speculators or land-grabbers:

> "We should not forget that the Manobos and Mandayas have their own idea of proprietory rights. Each family and each village considered as their absolute property not only the ground where their house stood, but also the mountains where they use to hunt and the rivers where they fish. No discalced friar had

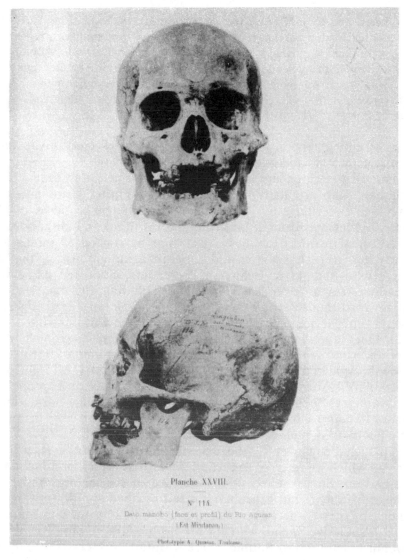

Fig. 32 The skull of Datu Lincuban. In December 1880 he was assassinated by his relative Sagud, who beheaded him in an ambush.
The head was ''brought in triumph to Butuan,'' where the French
anthropologist Montano prepared it for conservation and then
brought it to the ''Musée des Sciences Naturelles'' in Paris.
(Reproduced from Montano's ''Rapport sur une mission scienti-
fique,'' 1885). Courtesy of RITLV University Library, Leiden,
Holland.

been able to talk them out of this idea. Although they are
content with a hut that is open at all sides to wind and rain, they
want land and trails for miles around...Finally, we should
remember that prior to our arrival there was not one hamlet that
was not at war with another, and consequently, by combining
two or more villages, the old feuds might be rekindled''
(''Cartas,'' VI, pp. 153-154).

And, of course, there were again the old abuses by Visayan merchants, inspectors and interpreters.

The first serious upheaval came from the Ohut area. Datu
Lincuban, who originally had submitted to Father Urios and had
assembled the village of Remedios, where the best houses of the
whole district were found, had changed his mind and absconded to
the forest with thirty families. After that he started to molest the
nearby barrios of Las Nieves and Esperanza and ambushing the few
people who had stayed behind in Remedios. Soon his name was
spreading fear all over lower Agusan, including Butuan. He had
spread word that he would not allow any missionary in his district.
Several times Urios had tried to come to terms with him, but to no
avail. One day, when the officials of Butuan were assembled for a
meeting in the tribunal to deliberate about Lincuban's capture, he
suddenly appeared before them, alone, and shouted: "All right, you
miserable Visayans, you wish to kill me in my place and among my
own warriors? Such a plan is beyond your courage; here I am, alone,
just try to capture me." And then the proud Manobo left, throwing
them a look of contempt (Montano, o.c., December 8, 1880).

This challenge led to the expedition of Governor Raccaj of
Surigao which we referred to earlier. A surprise attack on Lincuban's
fortified dwelling resulted in the capture of his whole family and
some of his slaves, but Lincuban himself escaped and disappeared in
the nearby forest where eventually he was killed by another Manobo
rebel, his relative Sagud, who cut off his head in an ambush. It was
brought in triumph to Butuan where Montano preserved it and sent
it to a museum in Paris (see the picture on the preceding page).[48]

---

[48]Montano also relates the following poignant detail of what happened
after the attack on Lincuban's stronghold. ''His family was led away as
hostages. While the soldiers were readying to leave with the prisoners, a

That was one danger eliminated; the former settlers of Remedios presented themselves again to Urios who made them join barrio Esperanza, which had been reorganized after Lincuban had burned there the public buildings during the days of his rampage.

In that same year there was another serious upheaval in the region of Jativa as appears from a document in the Jesuit archives at Manila. It must have been quite disturbing, because the Governor took personal charge again of the soldiers sent there to quell the revolt. As a result "sixteen Manobos were taken prisoner and brought to Surigao; of these, three were shipped to the Marianas, one escaped and twelve died in jail..." (Gov. Gen. to Superior SJ, September 26, 1889).

Shortly thereafter the Manobos in the coastal villages of Butuan bay and those living close to Butuan disappeared again to their former abodes in the mountains and the forest. Father Heras wrote during those days:

> "In March, on my return trip from Bislig via Bunawan, I found that Las Nieves, Tolosa and part of San Vicente had rebelled and moved out. Hardly had they been enticed to return, when those of Esperanza rose up after killing a man from Butuan. They burned the village, including the church and the convent and threatened even Butuan; the result was that a group of Butuanos armed themselves and went after them, killing and capturing some of them."

The most bitter confrontation occurred in Tudela where datu Malingaan and his followers fortified themselves in two houses and put up a

> "fierce resistance against the soldiers who had been sent from Bunawan to subdue them. After the houses had been

---

Manobo came running to them, bolo in hand. They fired at him but missed. He threw himself at the Colonel's feet and surrendered his weapon to him. He was the fiancé of one of Lincuban's daughters.

"Don't be stupid." she shouted at him, "Can't you see that all is lost? What are you doing here?"

"Sharing your captivity," answered the heathen *caballero*, "because far from you liberty is worse than slavery" (Entry for December 8, 1880).

surrounded and one rifle-burst after the other had pierced the thin walls, those inside knew that there would be no way out for them. 'Maybe so, the wife of Malingaan shouted...but they will not get us alive. Kill me and the other women and children, so we will not fall in the hands of the Christians...'. And that is exactly what the defenders did...the soldiers being able to save only two of the women.

Guadalupe was totally abandoned after *remontados* had killed the school teacher and his son. The same happened in Jativa, where seven of its residents had been brutally assassinated on two consecutive days while working in their fields just outside the village.

In the second half of 1881 "all of lower Agusan was in rebellion" as Father Heras informed Urios. Nearly everywhere "the Manobos from the mountains near the villages, especially those of the Ohut river, prevent the new Christians of the reductions from having contact with the missionaries; they even place armed spies on the river banks to see who passes there" ("Mision" I, p.346).

At the eastern part of the mission, in the village of Caraga, Montano wrote in his travelogue on February 10, 1881:

> "At the moment this region is going through a crisis resulting from misunderstandings as well as from hatred and rival interests that lead to periodical explosions. This country is on fire, and there is a fierce war going on between the Bisayas and the Mandayas, so the *capitan* tells me. All that one hears are stories about houses being burnt and heads being cut off."

One of the promises which Urios and the Governor had made to the tribals was that they would take care of the protection of the new villages and of the administration of justice, including punishing those who should harm them. The events showed that under the circumstances this was impossible and that people were reverting to their old ways of vendetta-justice. For that reason, and on request of Urios, the Governor ordered to step up the organization of local volunteers and military units. Butuan was put under the protection of a company of fifty armed volunteers with three strongholds at their disposal. Esperanza was converted into a fortification with fifty armed policemen. Twenty riflemen were stationed at Talacogon and sixteen at Bunawan. Since Father Urios had received several death threats, he travelled now only with an escort of four soldiers and a big dog.

All in all, it seems clear that the first impact of the new order of things had been too heavy for such a primitive society to bear. By the end of 1880 the atmosphere in all the hamlets as well as in the old villages, including those close to Butuan, was very tense and worrisome enough for Urios

> "to implore the help from heaven by announcing a special afternoon prayer-ceremony with exposition of the Blessed Sacrament in honor of the Sacred Heart of Jesus to obtain the return of the *remontados*. This was done the next day, and from that day on the rebels came to present themselves day after day, and they assured that also the others would return" ("Mision" I. p.350).

The years 1880 and 1881 were certainly "years of trial and tribulation for the missionaries" as Pastells puts it. This had been their first missionary venture and they had undertaken it with much determination, courage and idealism. And now, right from the beginning, it had all the aspects of a bad failure: the greater part of Agusan was in rebellion. It was they who had taken practically all the initiatives for the reduction and pacification of Agusan, in compliance with the intentions of the Royal Decree of July 1860. It was they who had presented the government with very convincing schemes for the final *conquista* of the pagan tribes. For them, the Mindanao mission had been a splendid opportunity to prove their missionary mettle as an Order that already previously "had rendered important services in the reduction and religious education of the natives in the Philippines" as well as in South America (Royal Decree for the re-establishment of the Society in Spanish dominions, 1852). The problem of the inherent instability of the reductions and of the internecine warfare between the *reducidos ("conquistas")* and those refusing to be resettled, was going to remain a problem facing the missionaries with varying intensity for many years to come, as can be read several times in the Cartas. Still on July 30, 1886, Father Hermenegildo Jacas wrote to his friend, Dr. Leandro de Mella in Barcelona:

"In the new reductions of upper Agusan the missionaries are undergoing serious disappointments. The saddest experience for them is to see how one of their beloved reductions, established with so much sweat in the interior of Mindanao, becomes dissolved as if by magic" ("'Missiones Catolicas en el Extremo Oriente,'' 1886).

After following the establishment of the first missionary bridgeheads at Surigao, Bislig, Butuan and upper Agusan, let us also pay an exploratory visit to the southernmost outpost on the Pacific coast of Mindanao. We have a very qualified reporter about the situation there in the person of Father Pablo Pastells himself, the first Jesuit missionary to reside in Caraga in 1876 together with his companion Juan Terricabras. The area had been well reconnoitered previously, first by Father Luengo, next by Parache and Urios, who in 1875 had given a series of mission retreats in Hinatuan, Bislig, Lingig and Caraga. In September 1875 Father Heras visited the region as part of an inspection trip that took him to Surigao, Butuan, upper Agusan, Davao and Caraga. Originally, the missionary assigned to Caraga had been Father Vivero, but on September 11 he had fallen victim to the treacherous weather and waters of the Pacific coast being shipwrecked near Punta Punsan together with six convent boys.

The parish of Caraga was to comprise the area from Cateel down south to Manay. Caraga village had only slightly progressed after the settlement attempts by the Recoletos in the first decade and the third quarter of the century; Baganga counted with six little barrios, but had at most six inhabited houses in the main village. Cateel consisted of eight barrios, but would soon be transferred to a new site at Dacung Banua (the present Boston). This transfer succeeded only very slowly and reluctantly; on February 4, 1880 the Frenchman Montano, whom we met earlier, visited the new place and wrote:

"At two in the afternoon I arrived at Cateel, where I met Father Terricabras, who is on a pastoral visit. Cateel Nuevo has been established here because this stretch of coast offers a passable anchorage for bancas, while that of the old pueblo is nearly at all times unsuitable for docking. As yet the new village has only a few inhabitants. The Bisayas abandon their homesteads only reluctantly, so I am told by Father Terricabras.

In 1880 already a considerable number of converted Mandayas had started to settle on the old village-site at the mouth of the Cateel river, which kept its name and grew into the present town.

Father Pastells was clearly as much a doer-type as Urios. Hardly settled in Caraga, one week after his arrival and while still waiting for his assistant Terricabras, he called a meeting of the local *principalia* and those of the *rancherías* in the hinterland, which resulted in the definite selection of Dauan, along the Caraga river, as site for a settlement, eventually to be named San Jose.

> "He went there to trace the streets and the lots for the houses of the future reduction; according to the plan, the layout would consist of four mainstreets, intersected by six transversals; the houses would be six by three and a half fathoms, and each should have eight posts like those of the Christians that were under construction in Caraga itself. In order to prevent the spreading of fire, there would have to be a distance of six fathoms between the houses. In the middle of the village a space would be reserved for a large plaza along which the public buildings would be established: the church the tribunal, the convent and the schools for boys and girls; the remaining space would be used for the houses of the Inspector, the capitan and the principal inhabitants. The mainstreets could be lengthened indefinitely and the transversals increased in conformity with the number of people who would settle in the village. In a similar way also the other reductions of the mission would have to be laid out'' ("Misión," I, p 214)

Between Manurigao and Caraga, at the mouth of the Capanaan river, *Santa Fe* was established; *San Ignacio* came into existence southward along the coastal trail between Tubud and Manay; the latter was given a much needed sprucing up. Next followed *Santa Maria* (later *Zaragoza),* *San Estanislao, Xavier, Santiago, San Pedro, San Luis* and *Carmen.* In March 1877 he mentions a whole litany of reductions to be organized that year: *Santo Domingo, San Nicolas, San Juan, San Victor, San Manuel, Carmelo; San Vicente.* The Mandaya reduction of *Loyola* between Hinatuan and Bislig had been established the year before by Fathers Bové and Peruga.

In 1884, looking back at the eight years of his work along the Pacific coast, Pastells mentions in a letter to Provincial Cappell that "not a single one of the reductions in his working area had revolted." In the context of the times, this sounds as if he were silently making a comparison with what had happened in Agusan, or answering complaints in Manila about a too quick process of conversion and baptism of the pagans.

That did not mean, however, that south of Cateel there was only peace and harmony between 1875 and 1885. Ten years was too short a time for the natives to abandon old and deepseated animosities between Mandayas and Manobos in the hinterland between Hinatuan and Baganga. Moreover, if among Mandayas or Manobos themselves there had always been tribal customs or momentary occasions leading to killing and slavery, those customs could not that quickly be eradicated, and the occasions would keep recurring; the latter perhaps all the more because the not wholly voluntary *forzosa,* as Pastells himself said, resettlement must have brought not a few elements of additional unrest into the district. Also here, the local datus and *baganis* stood to lose much of their traditional powers. Pastells letters from Caraga and Bislig (his second parish), as well as those of his companions and neighboring priests are replete with stories of murder, arson and enslaving perpetrated by *baganis* like Bilto (the Lincuban of Caraga!), Macusang and Tilot. Several times Pastells had to request the Governor of Surigao or the military Commander of Bislig for punitive intervention, although he himself had to admit that this made matters only worse.

"Since the expedition of the Commander, all the villages were tense with fear because the enemies had become so bold that they practically entered through the very doors of the houses. While the priests were celebrating the fiesta of Dapnan, four of them sneaked into the barrio; they scared people and spread panic all around. The priests, informed about it, advised the teniente to arrest them and find out who they were, where they came from and why they had come to the village. It was found out that they were four accomplices of Bilto and Macusang, and therefore they were brought to Bislig. When Tilot and the other partners heard about this, they sent a message to Dapnan warning the people to prepare themselves, because they would make so much blood flow that the river would overflow its borders all the way from the *ilaya* to the rivermouth, Mandaya or Christian blood without distinction!....
The baganis wanted to kill all those in Baganga who had firearms; the Spaniard (Manuel Menendez) would be the first. After that it would be easy for them to do away with the rest. As

for the priest, they could capture him anytime they wished to do so by just ambushing him on his way between two villages; they would cut his head off and let it dry in the sun to remind and scare people for the future'' (''Misión'' I, p. 222).

Those threats came from the same Mandaya groups who a few years earlier had massacred one hundred seventeen Manobos of the village of Julip in upper Agusan. The Governor asked Pastells to lead a punitive expedition himself, but (unlike Urios) he refused to do so; he only insisted that the region be provided with one hundred rifles to stop the *baganis*, lift the drooping spirit of the Christians and friendly pagans, and protect the harvests and farm workers near the reductions. All this time the three Mandaya reductions near Hinatuan: the old San Juan, Loyola and the newly founded Tibay, remained quiet and progressed steadily, probably because here the people had always been living close to the old-time Christians.

All in all, the letters of Pastells, Terricabras, Peruga and Parache, filling many contemporary pages in the "Cartas," are ample testimony to the peculiar and complicated hardships encountered in a missionary venture carrying in principle a double aim on its banner: a spiritual and temporal *"conquista."* For that latter purpose, they would often be mutually instrumental. About the resulting turmoil in Agusan in 1881, Pastells would write thirty five years later:

> ''The Manobos, even those still living in dispersal, were very much aware of the difference between the missionary and the soldier or Governor; they understood that the ministry of the priest was one of peace and persuasion, while that of the government officials was one of force and sanctions; that the latter did support and promote all that was good, but also punished and suppressed what was bad. It was this understanding that accelerated the return of the rebels of lower Agusan'' (''Misión'' I, p. 346).

This was an echo of what Urios had written in 1881 ("Cartas" V, 28) but at that time it was most probably just a fervent hope, more than a reality. All the information published in the "Cartas," in spite of the selective limitation guiding their publication, explicitly mention several times or seem to imply not seldom that the capacity for such distinction did not come quickly and naturally to the tribes, certainly not to the datus and the *baganis*. But the remarkable thing is that it *did* come within the time-span of less than one generation. It bespeaks the enormous capacity for change and adaptation which these *lumadnon* must have possessed, as much as it does the inspired labor of the missionaries. Painstakingly, slowly and often after repeated failures most of the new settlements started to take root; the tribals of the *rancherías* and the *remontados,* often with a heart full of apprehensions, came down from the mountains and out of the jungle to put their present and future into the hands of the missionaries. In one decade the latter would prove to the government that all its decades-old intentions regarding the tribals and the future of Mindanao, would "remain a building of air-castles" without the element of religion being given a pre-eminent place in the endeavor. Fifteen years after the take-off of the Jesuit mission in Agusan, Father Francisco Nebot could write from Talacogon:

> "I have lived nearly the whole year in my *baroto* and have been out of Talacogon for seven and a half months, visiting one village after another. When they celebrate the feastday of their patron-saints, also our hearts are filled with joy, a joy that remains for a long time. Everywhere we see that the foundations of civilization are growing stronger and stronger, and the people, so recently snatched away from their wild customs, are not merely a promise for a great success, but they show already now the ripe fruits of religious sense and civilization" ("Cartas" IX, p.564).

But still five years later Nebot's successor at Talacogon, Father Miguel Alaix, in a long letter of May 31, 1895 addressed to his superior in Manila, warns that one should not put too much confidence in what might at times indeed look like a sincere and total conversion of the newly baptized. He was very much aware, he writes, that often — and not only in remote and inaccessible places — a lot of idolatry was secretly still practiced by the *nuevos Christianos.* Aside from other sources, "the children who always have their hearts at the tip of their tongues" had told him time and again. It is true that on New Year morning of 1887 Urios had already jubilantly claimed in his sermon: *"Nuestra conquista es cosa hecha"* (our conquest is now a *fait accompli),* but that was exuberance typical of Urios. Alaix, in his letter of 1895 extensively explains: nearly all the new settlements are still threatened by the relentless danger of sudden rebellion for all kinds of reasons, leading to total desertion by the inhabitants escaping to their former wild lives in the jungle, from where the leaders try by persuasion or by force to entice others to join them.

> "Once there will be many of them (and this will happen very soon unless strict measures will be taken) and if things will go on like at present, they will force the rest to follow them; if they refuse, they will be killed. Naturally, fear of death will force the latter to comply, and as a result the reduction-villages will dissolve like salt in water. Not only do these insurgents consider themselves free from all authority, but emboldened by the cowardice of the authorities, they also threaten the local officials like *capitanes* and village-inspectors from inside their jungle-lairs. For them there is no authority or village-life. The seriousness of this situation will become more obvious when these new *conquistas* will have to pay taxes in the near future: then all of them will rebel and pay the tax collectors with the sharp point of their *sundan* (bolo) or lance'' (Series of handcopied letters in Sant Cugat archive, obviously prepared for the printers).

Alaix then points out that the prevailing instability was leading in addition to the following:
1. An all pervading unrest in the still existing villages: day and night people have to be on guard against possible attacks of the *remontados* who have teamed up with the still pagan Manobos;
2. The teachers have become afraid and are reluctant to be assigned to a life of danger and insecurity in the villages. The loss of the teachers will have dire consequences for the work of civilization and Christianization of the natives.

The author continues that the only way to stop such unwanted developments is: a much closer cooperation between the Cross and the Sword...

The longwinded letter of Alaix has to be seen, of course, as just as illustrative of the time-colored pastoral attitudes of the author, as it is of the current events of Agusan being described! But on the other hand, the letter carries an undeniable mark of sincerity and authenticity: the deep resignation of the author in accepting the daily amount of suffering and deprivation which he and his co-missionaries had to undergo day after day and year after year.

"How often, when talking about the past, present and future tribulation and suffering, have we, priests and brothers here in Mindanao, said to encourage one another: but this is how we wish to be missionaries in Mindanao'' (loc. cit.).

   The system adhered to by the missionaries for the conversion of the pagans of Agusan is perhaps best summed up in Pastells' account of the various steps he took for the reduction and Christianization of the Mandayas along the southern east coast of Mindanao. In 1884 he wrote to the Provincial Juan Cappell:

"Once the essential public buildings have been put up, the forced reduction takes place, to make them live under a social and civil kind of authority, although they remain completely free in the matter of baptism. No other weapons are used than those of persuasion and charity coupled with the zeal shown by the missionaries for the salvation of the souls.

— The requirements for baptism are: free consent, necessary instruction, an act of supernatural faith, contrition, abandonment of proximate occasions for sin, in particular idolatry and polygamy.

— Consent has to be manifested several times, expressly and publicly before many witnesses.

— As to their instruction it is required that they know that God is one in essence and three in persons: the Father, the Son and the Holy Spirit; that He is the creator of all things and that he rewards all Christians who die in the state of grace with the eternal glory of heaven; also that He punishes the wicked who die in the state of mortal sin with the eternal pains of hell. Also, that God became man and died on the cross to save and redeem us sinners. Once they know this, they are given some visual instruction by means of pictures wherein an explication is given of the creation of the world and of our first parents, of original sin and its consequences, the promise of redemption and the fulfillment thereof in the incarnation or the birth, life and death of Jesus Christ; these pictures will also give them an overview of the other doctrines of the Creed, the ten commandments, Our

Holy Mother the Church and the sacraments, and of the necessity to preserve sanctifying grace which they have received in baptism.

— Then they are taught how to make an act of faith, hope and charity; they are induced to repent their sins and to promise not to sin anymore, and especially to abandon paganism. All this is contained in a prayer-formula which they are taught to recite before the crucifix and which is very similar to the ''Lord, Jesus Christ...''

— Finally they are asked to make a formal promise to persevere in the Christian faith. For their instruction they are placed in the care of a godfather, after which they are baptized without any further delay'' (''Misión,'' II, p. 37).

The tone of this report seems to indicate that it was intended as an answer to certain complaints that had reached Manila (from anticlerical local government officials?) about the working methods of the missionaries.

STATISTICS FOR 1890.

Main or substations	*Christians*
Butuan	3,603
Tubay	1,883
Nasipit	499
Reduction Tortosa (Buenavista)	323
Tolosa	340
Amparo	874
Las Nieves	534
Esperanza	453
Remedios	286
Milagros	570
S. Vicente	455
S. Ignacio	274
Verdú	222
Carmen	159
Santa Ana	120
Talacogon	1,454
Veruela	620

Main or substations	Christians
Prosperidad	647
Reduction Los Martires	225
La Paz	660
Sagunto	420
Novele	350
La Asunción	106
Ebro	231
Borbon	278
Las Navas	267
Azpeitia	157
Los Arcos	188
S. Luis	275
Baza	154
Santa Ines	310
Guadalupe	410
Concordia	81
S. Pedro	254
S. Jose	765
Trento	487
Reduction Tudela	425
S. Isidro	129
Loreto	588
Clavijo	118
Gracia	136
Concepción	192
Patrocinio	259
Jativa	399
Gandia	366
Compostela	334
Pilar	255
Moncayo	184
Mainit	1,670
Jabonga	1,773
Reduction S. Roque	100

Main or substations	Christians
Santiago	100
S. Pablo	50
Surigao	5,139
Visita Anaoanon	1,288
Dinagat	1,920
Nonoc	665
Loreto	1,682
Visita Libjo	824
Cagdayanao	520
Placer	4,082
Taganaan	2,382
Visita Talavera	350
Gigaquit	5,034
Bacuag	1,417
Visita Claver	1,542
Taganito	200
Dispersed Mamanuas	50
Numancia	2,347
Sapao	1,411
Visita S. Isidro	374
Pamusaingan	257
Cabuntog	1,270
Dapa	2,050
Visita Pilar	635
Cambaság	280
Socorro	137
Cantilan	6,492
Visita Lanuza	2,820
Carrascal	1,772

Main or substations		Christians
Tandag		1,998
Visita	Tago	2,393
	Tigao	897
	Cauit	482
Reduction Alba		320
Lianga		2,225
Oteiza		1,634
Marihatag		682
Visita	Gamut	319
Reduction	Barcelona	91
	Javier	420
Bislig		1,407
Hinatuan		3,272
Cateel		1,864
Visita	S. Juan	380
	Lingig	486
	Malixi	217
Reduction	Loyola	432
	S. Jose	277
	S. Nicolas	424
3 Rancherías		450
Caraga		1,174
Baganga		1,455
Dapnan		409
Quinablangan		361
Visita	Manay	364
	Manurigao	340
	Baculin	368
Reduction	Tarragona	170
	Jovellar	315
	S. Ignacio	84
	Santa Cruz	407
	Zaragoza	209
	S. Francisco	484
	Santa Maria	315
	Manresa	398
	Concepción	68
	S. Pedro	475

Main or substations	Christians
S. Jose	464
Santiago	415
Santa Fe	537
S. Luis	321
S. Victor	295

(From: "Cartas," Cuaderno IX).

Note: The data for Bunawan, Suribao and S. Juan de Suribao are missing.

XIX

The Morning-After of the Revolution

It goes without saying that a wrenching event like the Philippine Revolution and the subsequent American Occupation would hurt the Church in northern and eastern Mindanao in more than one way. That event, as far as it affected Surigao, Agusan and eastern Davao and the Benedictine and Jesuit missionaries, has been separately described in the book "Angry Days in Mindanao" by Peter Schreurs, MSC, San Carlos Publications, University of San Carlos, 1987. For the greater part of one year the Spanish missionaries disappeared nearly totally from the scene in consequence of their imprisonment and subsequent departure for the safety of Manila, if not for the home-country. This forced absence of the missionaries and the sudden confrontation with new political realities was to have a especially devastating impact on the many new Christian settlements of upper Agusan. Even during the preceding twenty-five "normal" years their existence and perseverance had often been worrisome and shaky enough, as we have seen, but nevertheless, in the 1890s most had undeniably been on the way to becoming established and rather solid assets on the map of 20th century Agusan.

Right after the disappearance of Spanish authority and of the religious mentors, who had cared more for them than the old and the new political officials ever would, the social structure of village-existence and the confidence in the guidance and protection of a provincial leadership would fall apart under the stress of new complications added to the old ones, fear, uncertainty, neglect and, of course, the old atavism of the *reducidos* themselves, which had not totally been washed out of their humanity by the water of baptism. Life had become too complicated for many of the primitive *reducidos,* who were unprepared for the turmoil that was let loose upon them, and with nobody to confide into or rely upon, many did what still came rather natural to them and turned *remontado* in the deep jungles and on the forested mountain slopes.

In April of 1900, Father Fernando Diego, the only missionary whom the revolutionary leaders of Surigao had reluctantly allowed to remain at Butuan, and who had volunteered to stay on when the others left for Manila after their liberation, made a reconnaissance trip to the villages along the Agusan river in order to size up their condition. In Amparo he found that only four or five families had remained in the village. San Mateo, on the contrary, had undergone a renovation, but in Las Nieves only very few houses were left. Esperanza was still doing all right, and so was Verdu. Estanislao at the confluence of the Libang and the Agusan rivers, had completely disappeared. Guadalupe was still in existence, and Santa Ines had been transferred to the opposite river-bank where the Maasan flowed into the Agusan, but only few of the former inhabitants had remained and even these were in danger of returning to their old *"manobismo."* San Luis was still the same as before, but Talacogon was nearly totally deserted, the grass growing more than one meter high before the convent door and the school *"en perpetua vacación."*

The forelorn appearance of the place was probably not due to real desertion but to the fact that most of the inhabitants were staying outside the village proper, near their plantations in the *ilaya;* when the news spread that a priest was in the village, they flocked to the church for baptisms, marriages and a fiesta in honor of the patron saint.

La Paz was still holding together, but Sagunto had vanished. In Loreto only six houses were still in existence, in Ausona not a single one, the same in Gracia and Concepción. Veruela, the former station of Father Diego had, however, more houses than before, and there was great rejoicing when their former parish priest was in their midst again. The villages of Borja and Vigo were gone. The inhabitants of Patrocinio had scattered to other places. Jativa had suffered rather little, unlike Compostela, Pilar, Moncayo and Gandia. In Jativa the people had collected fifty pesos which they gave to Father Diego "to

get a priest for them." San Jose and the few other villages in the area
of the Simulao river were still in their old locations.

The sad spectacle presented by so many reductions in the year
1900 was a vivid proof that after twenty-five years the habit of living
socially together in an organized village-setting had not yet become
second nature to most of the tribals. The situation had been
aggravated by the fact that right after the disappearance of Spanish
authority an uneasy and fluctuating power-vacuum had set in at
Butuan. With the arrival of the Americans in January 1901, this
gradually disappeared, and attempts were made to restore some
semblance of government and order in the interior of Agusan, but as
far as the tribals were concerned, it was now just a matter of Spanish
colonialism being replaced by colonization by "Bisaya" masters
from Butuan, who soon started to apportion the Manobo areas
among themselves, and not exactly for missionary purposes!

In February 1901 Father Urios was sent back to Butuan by his
superiors who considered him as the most qualified to guide the
Agusan mission through the *"mar de difficultades"* as he himself
qualified the prevailing conditions.

> "There is a great need here of Father Urios who, as I have
> been told, has been given the task to bring the people (of upper
> Agusan) back to the mission stations. Under the circumstances
> he could contribute a great deal to entice (the population) to
> accept the present situation instead of engaging in futile
> resistance" (Bernardino Llobera to Fr. Gregorio Parache, 2
> February 1901).

In August 1901 Urios made an extensive inspection trip to upper
Agusan. Twenty-two years ago he had made this trip for the first
time, ten years ago for the last...and now, the long hours in a
river-*baroto* he so well remembered, gave him ample time to
meditate on the great changes that had come over the Agusan valley
since the Spaniards had left.

> "The villages in the Talacogon area are very much different
> from what they were before, but I believe that with faith and
> perseverance, with zeal and patience they can be pulled together
> again, because it was a joy to see how jubilantly they received
> us....
>
> The cold village of Talacogon has thawed a little; they
> would receive a resident missionary with open arms. The captain

of the milicia here is a Butuano, who would rather have himself carried around in a sedan-chair under a *pallium*. The wise and old people shake their heads and keep sadly reminiscing about the past. They say that they would rather go to Russia and submit themselves to the Czar than be governed by their fellow Indios. They say it loudly that even thinking about independence is tantamount to not understanding the character of the local people. *Auribus meis audivi:* I have heard it with my own ears, and I more than agreed with such wisdom.

But, of course, each human being takes to loving its own, and to them (the Indios I was referring to) it is a mouthwatering prospect..." (Urios, Talacogon 6 September and Jativa 23 September 1901).

Urios complained to the American officials at Butuan about the neglect and the abuses being committed in upper Agusan and warned them that the dispersal of the settlements and the disgust felt by many natives would soon greatly frustrate their intentions for the furtherance of an efficient provincial and local administration and the peace-and-order conditions in the interior.

"I have arranged with the (American) Lt. Colonel that the new Christian villages are going to get a special administration for themselves, because these Butuanos are forcing *comandantes* and *comisionados* upon them, and these have already divided half of the area among themselves" (Urios, 2 April 1901).

As a protest, thirty two families had already moved out from Talacogon to "live freely and independently" in the Hibong (at times Gibong) district (from where the Jesuits had moved them to Talacogon before, informs Urios).

Still one decade later the disheveled and scattered condition of nearly all the former "reductions," starting with Amparo (close to Butuan) up to far into the interior of upper Agusan, is repeatedly described in a series of letters from Father Vallés (Jaime) of Butuan, published in the Spanish magazine (Misiones Catolicas en el Extremo Oriente" between 1909 and 1911.

It is hard to believe that this state of affairs at such a critical time in the history of Agusan and of the former Manobo and Mandaya settlements was not going to be one of the factors leading to what increasingly became *the problem* of the minorities in Agusan in later years when the influx of so many settlers would revive the old aversion of the tribals against the "Bisaya."

Less than a decade later the findings of Urios and Llobera would still be confirmed by the Secretary of the Interior Dean C. Worcester (who went to upper Agusan) and incorporated in his book "The Philippine Islands, past and present" (1914 and 1933). [49]

It is clear that Urios looked as askance at American intentions as he did at "Indio" leadership on the local and district level. One seems to sense his disdain and irritation when (for the first time in English) he quotes a statement of the American Commander at Butuan: "We want them to manage their own affairs." Elsewhere he writes that *"Los de la Unión"* or *"estos rubios"* (his favorite names for Americans) are like Germans: "They just go ahead, without asking advice from anybody."

It goes without saying that, so shortly after the revolution, the interference of Urios in affairs such as the organization of upper Agusan, at a time when touchy local leaders were very much in need of "proving" themselves, would mostly not be welcomed at all. When Urios practically accused the local and provincial officialdom before the American authorities of neglect and abuses of the Manobos, naming names did certainly not endear him to prominent personalities at Butuan and Cabadbaran from whose ranks the revolutionary and post-revolutionary leaders had emerged. Furthermore, once other factors (the matter of church properties, of schools and of civil-marriage procedure) entered into the existing frictions, the already soured relations at Butuan would prepare the ground for the eventual religious schism of Cabadbaran. Politico-religious elements imported from Cebu came to Agusan, sails billowing from the schismatic gale that blew from Luzon. The leading social and political elements putting that importation into motion, at a time

---

[49] "In the Agusan river valley conditions were nearly as bad. The people along the mainstream were for the most part broken-spirited Manobos. Their settlements had been parcelled out among the members of the municipal council of Butuan to be plundered. The activities of these "Christian" gentlemen had been such that a number of Manobo villages were already completely abandoned, while the people of others were gradually betaking themselves to secure hiding places in the trackless forests which stretch east and west from the banks of the Agusan river." (*Dean C. Worcester: "The Philippines, past and present,"* 1933 ed., p. 478).

when also other local controversies were brewing between priests and *principalía*, were from both Butuan and Cabadbaran.

At present it is perhaps impossible (and futile anyway) to find out how many of these were already Masons at that time or became so in the crucial years right after the revolution. Already in 1901 Urios speaks about *"los libre-pensadores de Cabadbaran."* The information that could be gathered from those who had witnessed it personally or had even been victims of the situation, plus the correspondence and other communications of the missionaries involved, clearly show that in the first ten to fifteen years of this century, the local Jesuits in Agusan, the Benedictines and later the first MSC Fathers in Surigao took the full brunt of the antagonism, the suspicion or even the hatred created by the upheaval against Spain or at least against what Spain had represented in the country at large or in the region in particular.

However, it must be made clear from the outset that the antagonism was definitely not between the great mass of the people and the missionaries, but between the latter and local government officials. Already in 1900 Father Juan B. Heras wrote about Butuan: "The attitude of the local authorities is even worse than that of Carlos III."

That gives us a lot to think if we remember that it was King Carlos III who had expelled the Jesuits from all the Spanish dominions in 1768![50]

Father Heras, then temporarily in Butuan, became involved in the first public clash between Church and State right on January 1, 1901. Municipal officials had tried to prevent him from performing the proclamation of marriage-banns, claiming that from now on this was a government prerogative. Heras announced publicly in his New Year sermon that his superior in Manila would rather abandon the parish of Butuan than permit such usurpation. But on that same occasion he wrote to Manila strongly suggesting to his superior that another priest be appointed to Butuan "who would be more flexible than he knew himself to be." The advisability to abandon Butuan for some time and put it under the care of the *Cura Bisaya* of

---

[50] It is understandable that a man like Heras whose Order had once been expelled from Spain by Carlos III, tends to depict him as an epitome of evil. However, a number of historians of good repute will not fail to describe him as a good statesman and a pious Christian.

Camiguin had, in fact, been talked about for some time.

The Church could, of course, not afford a total break, and neither could, on the other hand, the municipal, provincial and military officials. The latter obviously considered themselves in need of a little assistance from heaven, because they were preparing their army for all eventualities, and on Three Kings Day 1901 the church of Butuan was filled with "more than a thousand soldiers and their officers, all shining in new revolutionary uniforms." Good for them that the American takeover of Butuan on January 29 of that year occurred without any military confrontation! One of the military volunteers, Vicente Bustillo, perhaps unaware of what was going on at Butuan (or being a daredevil) came down from barrio Ambago on February 2nd to go to church for the feast of Candlemas. He was dressed in his military best and was wearing a dagger at his side. The Americans looked at him in astonishment, but he walked straight ahead and passed the sentinels with either a very defiant or a very innocent face...fulfilled his devotion and then walked back into the town to the gawking amusement of the Americans, who did not lift one finger to stop him!

The information about what happened in the months after the arrival of the Americans is predominantly drawn from twenty-two authentic letters of Fr. Bernardino Llobera, and another set of forty-six letters from the hand of his confrere at Butuan, Fr. Saturnino Urios. Some of the latter are incredibly hard to decipher, but when one has finally struggled through them, the collection forms a goldmine of on-the-spot documentation about the Butuan of 1901 and of events elsewhere that were either set into motion from Butuan or had been coursed to Butuan for various comtemporary reasons. It is a pity that they contain only little explicit and detailed information about developments in Surigao, because in 1901 the Jesuits had ceded all the parishes of Surigao to the Benedictines; from the hand of the latter only a limited amount of documentation exists in the archive at the Benedictine Abbey of Montserrat, Spain. The communications of the mentioned two Jesuits are among the unpublished letters in the holdings of the Jesuit archive at Sant Cugat, Spain. With few exceptions they are addressed to the superior in Manila, Father Pio Pi, and written directly from Butuan or from the field of action in some scattered other locations, which were then all administered from Butuan. These letters, already important as the only surviving primary documentation for research into contemporary local and regional history, take on added significance — and at times fascination — whenever events described at the turn of the century slowly begin to reveal the genesis and contours of recognizable local realities of our days. Family names begin appearing on paper of which until now only vague bits of oral history or of fading private memories had it that those named did not stand passively at the cradle of 20th century local history, but were instrumental in giving it course and shape...for better or for worse. Here the beginning divisions between leading families point to the party-political family-clans of the Butuan of today, and politico-religious or personal bitterness and the chicanery or opportunism of 1901 begin spelling out, vaguely at first, then clearly, the coming schism of Cabadbaran.

At the beginning of 1901 Agusan found itself between the departing twilight of the Katipunan revolution and the daybreak of the American occupation. In the second half of January 1899, when the Aguinaldo Republic had come to Surigao-Agusan in the persons of the Gonzalez brothers of Surigao and their followers, the Spanish missionaries had been imprisoned (put under house arrest) in Surigao for seventy two days. In the capital (then Surigao) the orthodox Katipunan episode came to an end already in April 1899, when Don Prudencio Garcia took over the provincial government from the Gonzalezes, who had been deposed and would soon be murdered. In May of that year Butuan separated from the joint district and (re-) imposed a Katipunan administration of its own under Valentin Calo, who in turn was deposed on 28 February 1900. An Aguinaldo-inspired guerilla-war was being waged by some straggling groups of loyalists operating up river between Amparo and San Mateo under Captain Gumersindo Flores, in the mountains near Cabadbaran under Captain Andres Atega and in the Mainit-Jabonga area under the command of General Daniel.

Even after the coming of the American occupation troops these loyalists were — in the words of Father Llobera — "still dreaming of their republic and its president." As for Butuan itself, this Spaniard to-the-bone had the following to say.

> "In Butuan an end has been put (by the Americans) to the Carnaval of the Republica Butuana and its *bal masqué*. Now Lent has come and has pulled off the masks; they are at present walking around with their shirt-tails out, their trousers ironed, faces long and heads down" (loc. cit.).

For an understanding of his attitude, we ought not to forget what this man, his own brother and his confreres had so recently gone through at the hands of the *revolucionarios,* and how at his return to Agusan he had found there a much maltreated Fr. Diego and a church and convent that had been totally ransacked...And, of course, we cannot overlook the patriotic hurt of a Spaniard spited by Filipinos and Americans alike.

Both, Llobera and Urios, had a hard time coming to terms with the new political realities and with the much diminished role left to them in the public life of their days, a role of which they were at times not even sure how much longer they would be allowed to play it, and which in any case would become considerably more complicated with the growing secularization, Protestantism and the nascent Aglipayan schism. Time and again their letters reveal the nostalgic longing of the authors for *"los tiempos de oro de nuestra dominación. "* Urios clearly had no confidence in the officialdom to which the Americans wanted to entrust self-government in local affairs; he even goes as far as to say that the abusive and scandalous behavior of the Americans at Butuan was a clear punishment meted out by God to the place, in retribution for its own misdeeds against the missionaries (and Spain, presumably): "See how God our Lord is punishing them" he writes on February 22, 1901.

At times the stress of events under which they had to live and work forced itself into the open in sermons, and this in turn created new anger among those at whom his angry words were hurled. Urios himself writes about the public disturbance created in Cabadbaran, where Fr. Llobera had allegedly thundered from the pulpit:

"Where is your republic now? Where are your soldiers and your army?" To which Urios comments: "None of the Fathers who have been victims of what happened in the second and third districts (Cagayan-Misamis and Surigao-Agusan) feels well-disposed towards them, and not all of them can control themselves enough and forget once and for all what has happened... Also Father Heras and Fr. España cannot always sufficiently restrain themselves" (Urios to Superior, 12 May 1901).

On the mentioned occasion rumors had even reached Urios that some people in Cabadbaran and Butuan were set on killing Llobera! Still, at other more relaxed moments they could look at the problems as "part of the circumstances, the times and the personalities"

(Llobera). And that was indeed the case ... at both ends of the controversies. It was all part of the post-revolutionary game, so to say, like: "having to eat only *camotes* at times, without salt, oil or any other condiment, because that too belongs to missionary life" (id. 15 January 1901).

Even Urios, at tense moments, could not keep back an occasional exasperated sigh about *"estos indios"* and: *"son indios y son nuestra cruz,"* but such remarks were at the tip of many a Spanish tongue anyway since time immemorial! It can, without any shade of doubt be said, however, that the problem of Urios was only with a limited group of people, and definitely not with their flock at large. No doubt, in many cases the problem arose from the fact that as Spanish missionaries of the old dispensation they found it hard to come to terms with the low profile demanded from them at such short notice. It may equally well be assumed that, having to deal with officials who, at similar short notice, had perforce to adopt a high profile, all the elements for conflict were at hand. Urios obviously quite realized that they would have to act calmly and with prudence:

> "We should just let things come as they may, and before doing anything, make first two steps backwards. How true it is that experience is the mother of wisdom! The trouble is that theory and practice are two different things" (Urios to Parache, 14 February 1901).

Nevertheless, at the very beginning of his second arrival at Butuan, when at a quiet moment he looked at it all dispassionately, Llobera had to admit that perhaps, everything considered, the new order had created a healthier missionary climate.

> "(what has changed is only) that now these gentlemen wish to give orders in all things that do not pertain to Church or the sacraments. All in all I consider that as a great advantage, because it frees me from a lot of work, of a great deal of trouble and a no mean amount of expenses. It does not worry me, on the contrary, I like it, because now I can disengage myself from so many irrelevant things" (15 January 1901).

As for the matter of financial support, or rather the absence of it, Urios quotes elsewhere a statement by Father Heras saying that not having to hold out his hand for money, makes him feel more independent...(Urios to Superior, 5 February 1901).

Frictions and tensions, yes there were; there was overacting at times by local officials in 1901 and thereafter, and undoubtedly Spanish stubborness too. But time and again when a bout of deep irritation or nagging pessimism was over, there would always appear the more familiar Urios with his gentle *"pobrecitos de mi alma"* for his *"indios."* And that sympathy was understood, and it was mutual, as even some of his adversaries had to admit at times. In 1903 the expropriation of cemeteries and other church properties and the usurpation of church-functions like marriages and burials had definitely spoiled Church-State relations in Butuan, Cabadbaran and (what is now) Buenavista. The municipal secretary of Butuan, with whom Llobera and Urios had been at odds since 1900 and 1901, was suspected by Urios of having been the instigator of the expropriation proceedings. When the former had heard about this suspicion he wrote a letter to Urios, explaining that as a Secretary he had only recorded the decision of the municipal Council, without taking part in the deliberations. And for the rest:

> "...With this explanation I do not intend to evoke any reaction of sympathy for me in the mind of Your Reverence, nor to create any favorable feelings for me, because, thanks be to God, my conscience is at ease, and there is nothing in me that in any way diminishes the appreciation and veneration which I owe the Society (of Jesus) in general and Your Reverence in particular. Nevertheless, I cannot deny that in my own judgment *(en me fuero interno)* I am aware of certain acts of yours that in my opinion are at variance with the real spirit of asceticism that always has stood shining like a beacon in the midst of that holy Congregation" (Simeon Trillo to Urios, Butuan 5 December 1903. Letter in Jesuit archive, Manila).

And if at times the *(ex officio* or not) clashes had been noisy indeed, and the male *principalía* felt they had (for public consumption or not) to act gruffly with the priests...there was always their womenfolk who sooner or later would intervene with weeping eyes to soften up the strained relations a bit, for the time being.

Those who best understood and appreciated the sympathy of the local missionaries with the great mass of the people, especially those with problems, were *"estos indios"* themselves. Several times the letters mention how astonished the Americans were when seeing people coming to the convent for help. In Harper's "History of the

War in the Philippines" an American journalist arriving with the first occupation troops in Davao reported in 1900 that at the grassroots the foremost concern of the people was the speedy return of their former spiritual mentor and leader, the Spanish missionary, who had been evacuated at the outbreak of the revolution.

> "The Americans have noticed that we (the missionaries) are like an oak tree and that the people come to take shelter under its canopy. At all times I intercede for them and help them if they have problems with the soldiers. I have freed three of their prisoners and serve as their interpreter when they are in difficulties...If you could see how they flock to us, big and small, you would think that we were back in the times when everything was still normal under our government" (Urios, 22 February 1901).

The coming of the Americans brought a new foreign body and another element of discontinuity into the tense and confused atmosphere of post-revolutionary Butuan. On 28 January 1901 they had steamed up the Agusan river, their big shipboard guns at the ready to flatten Butuan if any resistance were encountered. But no more than two peaceful, humble persons, Canuto Rosales and Father Llobera waved them in from the river-pier of Butuan, at which the guns were turned away from the town. Rosales was then still considered locally "Governor of Agusan," because the province had persisted in its separation from Surigao proclaimed on May 1, 1899, even after the then appointed (Katipunan) Governor Valentin Calo had been deposed and imprisoned on February 28, 1900. The Rosales administration wished to do what so many Filipino authorities all over the country were forced to do: come to terms with the inevitable and make the best of a bad situation. The remaining Calo followers, led by Valentin's son Adolfo, "tried to excite the minds of a few fools against Canuto Rosales, accusing him and some others of being traitors to the fatherland; he thought that they had made a deal with the Americans" (Llobera to Parache, 2 February 1901).

The Americans were undoubtedly the most foreign elements to settle at Butuan since the arrival of the Spaniards. All the Butuanos and their civil authorities as well as the Spanish missionaries must have been ill at ease with their coming. The few remaining Aguinaldo loyalists absconded into the forest with their weapons; for them the Americans were from then on "the enemy." Out of fear of being caught in the middle between Adolfo Calo and the Americans and Canuto Rosales, and because of the abusive behavior of the American soldiers, most people disappeared from the town, taking along with their meager belongings a great deal of panic and confusion about the meaning of it all. The same gloom was hanging over the town as Urios had noticed elsewhere during his boat trip to Mindanao three weeks earlier.

> "All the Bisayas and also the capital Cebu are desolate, sad and lifeless. They are not even a shade anymore of what they were in other days. In Ormoc and Baybay hardly a living soul could be seen. In Cagayan the people had fled, but in Balingasag and Talisayan the inhabitants were in town" (Urios, 21 January 1901).

For the incumbent municipal and quasi-provincial authorities the coming of a new colonial occupation was — from their Filipino point of view — as humiliating as it was for the Calo followers and the Aguinaldo loyalists in hiding. For Canuto Rosales it meant insult added to injury, because he lost his position as Governor of the self (Calo)-proclaimed province, which now officially returned to its status quo ante May 1899 as district of Surigao under the Governorship of General Prudencio Garcia. That development did not restore much friendship between Butuan and Surigao, in spite of the fact that Garcia had offered that friendship in a letter to Llobera and Urios. Five months later, on July 10, 1901 Garcia would pay an official visit to Butuan (a place that in the previous year had still been busy digging trenches to keep him out). He was accompanied by a new provincial Treasurer, an American captain who, writes Urios, made a very unpleasant impression.

> "Father Urios has already informed you that Mr. Garcia has come to our place in his capacity as Governor of Surigao. His purpose was to be seen and organize elections. Your Reverence will understand what a bitter experience it has been for the Butuanos to find themselves under the authority of Garcia, whom they despise as a person, and to whom they don't want to submit themselves, because he was a Filipino official and now

they have to accept him as an American authority...They did as
little as possible for his reception...Upon his departure there was
even more public coldness and fewer people. With us he showed
much respect and he promised to do everything to help us''
(Llobera to Superior, 11 July 1901).

Obviously, it was felt that the submission to American authority
was forced upon Agusan not merely as an inevitable result of
national developments, but also by Governor Garcia. The latter was
a *realpolitiker*, and furthermore, because of his weak hold on the
politico-military situation at the Surigao side, he needed the
Americans for sheer survival. It was not for nothing that he had
begged General Otis in Manila twice to hurry sending occupation
troops to Surigao. When they finally came, the Butuanos were going
to lose a double independence: that of citizens of a free nation and
that of a self-governing province!

It takes very little imagination to understand that there were some
other residents of Butuan who — for reasons of their own — had
very mixed feelings about the American occupation. They were the
Spanish missionaries, who, both for cultural and religious reasons
abhorred the Anglo-Saxon invaders in principle. The feelings were
probably not much different on the American side. What the
missionaries foresaw was 1) the total separation of Church and State
enforced and supervised by a predominantly Protestant authority; 2)
the establishment of a public irreligious school system; 3) the
sanctioning of civil marriages (already introduced anyway by the
Aguinaldo republic, just as State-Church separation); 4) Protestant
proselytizing. In short, the loss of all the privileges and the support
of the external props which the Church had enjoyed for ages. To
which we may add: the necessity to entrust the future of the tribals to
American and local officials whom Urios considered incompetent
for the task.

> ''This gentleman (the American commander at Butuan) told
> me in a letter: I hope that you will assist us in restoring civil
> government to this people...we wish them to manage their own
> affairs;...gradually the government will fall into their hands.
>
> May God guide us, we are going to be in the hands of
> children, as the gypsies are used to say'' (Urios, 2 April 1901).
>
> ''Father Heras and also Fr. Parache said that from the pulpit
> we should talk clearly to the people about Protestantism. Father
> Heras has told them already that Luther was a monk living with
> a nun'' (id. 5 February 1901).

Still, also the missionaries knew very well that they had to come
to some kind of working agreement with the Americans. The latter
no less understood that it would be doubly difficult for them to get
their pacification and organization plans off the ground without the
cooperation and some amount of personal goodwill from the
missionaries. In the first place, they knew the area and its people;
Urios had even prepared a short written history for them "about
what Agusan was, is and is going to be," and the local Commander
had accepted it with the highest appreciation. Moreover, the greatest
drawback for the Americans was that without any knowledge of the
local language and the absence of an interpreter, they could hardly
engage in any meaningful conversation or dialogue with the local
Filipino authorities and with the people at large. This handicap was
felt all the more because of the urgent questions that required
attention: the matter of the unsurrendered rebels, the disarray of the
reduction villages of upper Agusan, the behavior of the American
soldiers, the organization of schools, etc. In all these matters Urios
seemed heaven-sent, as indeed the good faithful of Butuan loudly
proclaimed. He knew a sufficient amount of English to enable him to
serve as interpreter for the Americans and the local people. There is
no doubt that without his intercession and the confidence that even
the Aguinaldo loyalists had in him, the cessation of useless hostilities
would have been delayed for a long time and probably would not
have ended peacefully.

> "After the surrenderees (from San Mateo, under
> Gumersindo Flores) had arrived, I brought them into High Mass
> and in my sermon I told them what I had to say about all the
> things which I have already mentioned to you" (Urios to
> Superior, 19 March 1901).

He must have had a large audience: it was the Patron feast of
Butuan, San Jose, then still celebrated on that date. When the
Americans were preparing for a final attack on the rebels in the
mountains of Mainit-Jabonga, it was Urios who convinced the troop
commander of the futility of such an operation. The guerillas, so he
explained, could not really present themselves as long as they were
surrounded by soldiers; they would never believe any promise of
amnesty, and so all they could do was: refuse to surrender.

> "Finally I convinced (the Commander) that he should
> withdraw the troops from the area where Daniel was holed up,

that the boat which he had at his disposal till the end of this campaign should return to Cagayan, and that the Lt. Colonel and I should again send letters to Daniel and wait once more for him. If we don't, Daniel and his men will lose their patience and will become a troop of bandits roaming around near Surigao, stealing, violating women and killing" (Urios, 15 April 1901).

"At nine in the evening Daniel and Villabrille surrendered and yesterday all the armed men from the *ilayas* of Surigao, Mainit, Jabonga, Cantilan and Claver did the same. At eight in the morning they attended Mass and I gave them an appropriate sermon with some good advice. After the Mass I went (with tears in my eyes) straight to Daniel, Commandant Mordeno, Captain Custodio, Captain Mosende and their officers Villabrille, Valdespina and Zerda. With me serving as interpreter we talked about many things, complaints and the desire for peace and prosperity. These surrenderees have in fact done more harm to their fellow-Filipinos than to the Americans because of all the crimes they have committed" (Urios to Parache 22 April 1901).[51]

The total number of surrenderees was seventy. The late Mr. Generoso Copin, who was a convent boy of Urios and Llobera and who witnessed all these events, gleefully remembered many years later that the guerillas first went to see Fr. Urios at the convent before presenting themselves to the Americans!

That indeed the rebellion of Daniel had caused much damage to the inhabitants of Jabonga and Mainit, appears from the on-the-spot findings of Urios himself. He went there shortly after the surrender of Daniel and his men.

---

[51] Although mostly just named "General Daniel," his full name was Daniel Toribio Sison. General Lukban had sent him from Leyte to Surigao in 1899 to re-conquer Surigao for the Aguinaldo republic after Prudencio Garcia had overthrown the original revolutionary government of the Gonzalezes. Garcia, however, was able to beat off this attack. After Garcia had been forced to resign by the American occupation government, General Daniel Toribio Sison was appointed Governor of Surigao. His incumbency lasted from 1904 till 1906. In that year he died after a protracted grave illness during which he entrusted himself completely to the spiritual care of the Benedictine parish priest of Surigao ("Libertas" 29 March 1906).

The present town of Sison, Surigao del Norte, is named after him.

"...Four times the people of Jabonga had to run to the
mountains because of the Americans who did not come to
capture them, but Daniel and his companions. The last time they
burned thirty-three houses..." (Urios, from Jabonga, 24 May
1901).

Mainit looked like an "open-air hospital." The village had been
completely burned down by the Americans and a typhoid epidemic
had erupted; there had been more than four hundred dead.

"...Mainit, destroyed as if the day of desolation had come over
it: without altar, without prophets, without life, as if it had
turned into a mummy...I cannot forget the fearful sight that
Mainit presented to me when I arrived there...It is without
houses, and most of the people have been attacked by typhoid;
it looked forlorn, like a place of unspeakable disaster" (Urios, 4
and 5 June 1901).

It is remarkable that all the anti-U.S. guerillas and their leaders
operating in Surigao in 1901 preferred to come all the way to Butuan
to surrender: Cortes and Pecho of Dinagat and Loreto, the not
further identified Brigido and his son Baldomero of Nonoc, as well
as the rebels of Cantilan; the latter probably had been with the
troops of Daniel in the mountains between Mainit and Cantilan. The
reason why they preferred Butuan and Urios as interpreter/mediator
is not difficult to guess: in Surigao they would have had to deal
with a merciless General Prudencio Garcia! Here a far more personal hatred and revenge had by then entered the politico-military
atmosphere after Garcia's followers had killed the original
Aguinaldo *revolucionarios* Jantoy, Simon and Wenceslao Gonzalez
in April 1899. Some anti-Garcia troops, hailing from Bacuag,
Gigaquit and Claver, had been recruited by Recaredo Gonzalez, the
surviving son of Simon; the "Capitan Custodio," whom we met
earlier as a surrenderee, was from Placer and had been a lifelong
friend of Simon Gonzalez. Cortes and Pecho (the latter no friend of
the Benedictines in Dinagat in pre-revolutionary days) had been
with the rebel forces that had chased Garcia out of Surigao in July
1899. After his return, Garcia had waged an unforgiving
extermination campaign against the Aguinaldo idealists, whether
anti-U.S. rebels or his personal enemies.

In this context it may also be noted that among the small splinter
groups of rebels who never really surrendered but stayed behind in

the hinterlands of Mainit and on Siargao, grew eventually the strange para-Christian movement(s) that a.o. led to the so called "Colorum" explosion of two decades later. One is struck by the following words written in Jabonga in 1901:

> "The human heart will at some time need religion, as a necessary consequence of our rational make-up. Therefore, in these scattered hamlets people will create their own kind of religion, with false gods and a false cult; that will be the end of the (missionary) labor of so many years. I believe that this will happen and nothing else...if they will be left without priests" (Urios, 24 May 1901).

The role played by the missionaries as mediators between the Americans, the local authorities and the people, was, of course, much appreciated by the first. And, frankly, good Father Urios was a little proud of it. Several times he mentions in his letters how well befriended he was with the Lt. Colonel in charge of the occupation troops "who hardly did anything without first consulting me." Obviously, this American knew a sincere, hardworking and experienced man when he met one...in spite, perhaps, of what he may otherwise have thought of Spaniards and Spanish priests. It may also be said here that — judging from Urios' own words — *in the given situation* the American authority and presence was in general not a total liability for the missionaries. Urios, when writing about the good reception which he had received upon arriving at Butuan, nevertheless adds:

> "We saw signs of friendliness in the Butuanos, but about this it is good to mention that the circumstance of the town being in the hands of the Americans makes the Butuanos behave in a way they would not have done if they could have acted completely on their own" (Urios, 22 February 1901).
> "The coming of the Americans has humiliated the Butuanos very much, but it has also placed us in a much more favorable position *(ha levantado a nosotros mucho tambien)*" (loc. cit.).

What Urios means to say is that people needed them now, as well as the local authorities, on all kinds of occasions, and that assured them of a relevant position and of gratitude.

There is still another aspect to be considered "under the circumstances": that of the incumbent Filipino authorities. Even if

the Americans "wanted them to manage their own affairs,"
ultimately they were back where they or their predecessors had been
in the past: in the position of underlings. At all times they had to
keep one ear cocked in the direction of the overlords. As we saw
already, collaboration with the new masters had already been
branded "treason to the fatherland" from some corner. Moreover,
not all the surrendered rebels had left their *ideological* opposition to
foreign domination behind in the jungle! The Spanish missionaries
were — in the existential reality of the moment — in quite a
complicated and vulnerable position...And they were aware of it.

> "In one of your previous letters Your Reverence praised our
> conduct of mediation between the people and the Americans,
> even when the inhabitants are not always disposed to
> appreciate the benefit of what we have been doing for them,
> and even go to the extent of misinterpreting it and calling us
> *"Americanistas."* In connection herewith I will tell you that the
> Butuanos have started a rumor among themselves that Father
> Heras had fetched the Americans, and that when they were in
> the town I had told them the hiding place of the Butuan rebels.
> Of Father Urios they say that he is a friend of the Americans and
> much more. It is a fact that this plebs *(este vulgo)* has been
> complaining, speaking ill and criticizing us far more than one
> would have believed. I know this for sure, because many have
> told me so and have asked forgiveness, although they say that
> these are only calumnies. But it is nevertheless an indication that
> if the republic returned once more, woe to us if we were still
> here!
>   What struck Father Urios most is the high degree to which
> the people, without exception, big and small, men and women
> have lost their respect, the veneration and the love for the person
> of the priest, with the result that for the slightest reason they
> begin to complain, criticize, and even curse our actions. Father
> Urios thinks that this happened because Father Diego stayed
> here behind, and so much abuse has been perpetrated against his
> authority and dignity. After that they lost their sense of shame,
> and once that has happened it is the same as when innocence has
> been lost" (Llobera to Superior, 29 June 1901).

What must have pained them most was that among those whom
the times and the local complications (and perhaps at times their own
unacceptable reaction?) had turned away from them, were some of

their former friends and helpers.

Another development (not unknown in Philippine parish life) deserves some attention, because it added to the precariousness of their position: people heaping tokens of friendship upon them under circumstances when one could not be sure that the former were not just trying to further their own cause...at least it could be understood that way. There is the peculiar case of the man who once had stood as the personification (after the Gonzalezes of Surigao) of all the evils of the Katipunan episode at Butuan: Valentin Calo. There is no harm in mentioning his name, because afterwards he did a lot of good to the priests. But that was after he had repented for having been the scourge of Father Diego during the latter's lonely vigil at Butuan from 1 May 1899 till 28 February 1900. (In memory of those days the Manila Jesuits would afterwards be ribbing the latter by calling Butuan "Villa Diego!"). But as we said, Calo repented, asked pardon from Father Diego, and afterwards he and his son Adolfo sided very much with the priests *"con calor,"* as Llobera jokingly remarked in a letter! Valentin Calo became especially active when the municipal administration (his political opponents) got into a nasty imbroglio with the parish priests because of some issues which we will deal with presently. After his deposition he had been imprisoned for some time, and so was his son when he was suspected of gun-running for rebels in the jungle. The deep devotion to the priests which both manifested afterwards might indicate that eventually both had been released from prison through the intercession of Father Llobera, although I have no written proof of that.

At any rate, I may reproduce here a letter which Llobera secretly received, which reads as follows:

"Dear Father,

According to rumors which I heard last night during a gathering in a house that I would rather not mention by name, certain elements in this town (the most prominent in the modern sense) are planning to organize a "Club" which will be open from the day of the Lord's Nativity onwards. The purpose of this Club is to launch a secret attack on the members of the Society of Jesus in order to undermine thus the principles of our Religion. When hearing about the intentions of that nefarious organization, I could not prevent indignation welling up in me against such a malicious plan. Because of the zeal which any Christian has to manifest against anything that can poison his holy faith, I hurry to inform you, so that this affair will not catch you unawares, and you may be able to take timely steps against its realization, by counteracting its deadly effect with a Catholic propaganda that will annihilate and smash the head of him who would dare to raise the banner of Lucifer.

Your Reverence knows very well the weakness of the human heart, which because of much bitterness is rather deficient in resisting the temptations of the devil. Therefore, as a Catholic as well as a friend of the Society of Jesus, which is so much different from other religious corporations, I consider it my duty to inform you so that you can take the steps which you deem best.

Your respectful and affectionate servant,
Adolfo Calo.''

Well...Adolfo seems to remember how he too had been carried away by the battle cry of the revolution. The letter is undated but is probably from November or early December 1900.

———————————

In the second half of 1901 it had become clear that the problems which the missionaries were going to face in the near future were the following: 1) the opposition against (the re-establishment of) parochial schools and the emergence of the secular public school system; 2) municipal interference with marriage procedures; 3) municipal claims on church-owned cemeteries, and even church buildings and rectories.

Such questions and the turmoil resulting from them were, of course, not typical for Butuan alone: they formed part and parcel of a political revolution, an accompanying attempt at the secularization of society, and the off-shoot of it all: the religious revolution started by Gregorio Aglipay. Just like in the nation at large, the temper of the times, heated by the clash of personalities and certain local issues, would soon leave Agusan with the lasting scar of the schism of Cabadbaran.

Up to 1899 the school for boys and girls had been a parish institute, as was the case almost everywhere. For the education of the girls the Jesuits had brought a community of "Beaterio" Sisters (now RVM) to Butuan, but after the imprisonment of the missionaries, these had returned to Manila. With all the national and local tensions, the schools had come to a standstill for nearly two years. When Urios had arrived in Surigao on his way to Butuan in February 1901, he, Father Parache and Father Heras had a conference in Surigao to assess the situation in the district and inform the Manila superior of their views.

> "We went through all the points of your letter to Fr. Parache, and these are our conclusions: The question of the parish schools should be considered as of great importance; establishing them is an urgent matter, and we should put all our efforts in arousing people to prepare the means for the return of the Sisters and to take steps to assure the subsistence of the teachers employed in both schools..." (Urios to Superior, February 5, 1901).

They were not the only ones to see the importance of re-opening the schools. It was also one of the main concerns of the American administration of the archipelago. Like in many other places of the Philippines, also in Butuan and Cabadbaran the interests of Church and State authorities would lead to very unpleasant conflicts and clashes. While it is true that by law parents were granted the freedom to enroll their children in schools of their own choice, local authorities (especially if relations with the parish priests were strained for other reasons) were easily tempted — and urged by American superintendents on orders from Manila — to favor the establishment of public schools and prevent the opening of parish schools by all means. On the national as well as on the local level in many places there was also much Protestant pressure, for obvious reasons, to undermine the potential of Catholic educational efforts. In Butuan the American Commander had promised the authorities to send them a few American teachers for English language instruction. The former head-teacher of the parochial boys school, Bayeta, had remained in Butuan, and it was hoped that he could again function as such, while the *Presidenta* of the Hijas de Maria would take care of a provisional class for girls in her own house. In spite of the primitive set-up (the boys were housed in the convent, while the public school started in a new building in a nice location), when classes started the two American teachers found themselves with an empty building; the parents had indeed made use of the legal freedom granted them. Authorities, however, did not see it that way...and reacted after two days.

"in the afternoon policemen were seen stationed under the *talisay* tree next to the convent and in some other spots, and what a spectacle it was when they started to grab our boys to bring them to the municipal building....In spite of everything we had to laugh seeing how the scared kids ran away and escaped from the hands of the policemen. There was one boy who kept running with a policeman after him, till he reached the shelter of the *bosque* (woods) next to the town. Here he concealed himself and he did not come out of his hiding place until he was sure to be safe from the claws of the policemen. Then he went home and told his parents what had happened...The next day there were fewer children, but still enough to hold classes. The boys came sneaking stealthily along, looking to all sides thinking that the soldiers were at their heels. And so they got inside, some through the sacristy, others over the fence, or in whatever way they could" (Urios to Superior, 27 October 1901).

A conspicuous beginning of the new school year it was, but it was also clear that a new and long lasting element of controversy had been injected in local Church-State relations, and Urios and Llobera could very well have done without one more. It was not any better in Cabadbaran. An undated manifest signed "Los Catolicos de Cabadbaran" can be found in the Sant Cugat archives. It witnesses to the indignation of Catholic parents who were confronting a similar battle for the Catholic education of their children. It was addressed to Governor Garcia of Surigao.

"We the Catholics of Cabadbaran inform you that since the establishment of the Catholic school here, we are being deprived of the all round freedom which the law of the United States grants us in matters of religion, as the Colonel of the Filipino *milicia* stationed here has told us.

For that reason we wish to obtain from you that all the children who out of fear of punishment or even imprisonment are at the moment in the free school against the will of their parents be allowed to return to the Catholic school where they were enrolled from the moment of the foundation of that school..."

They go on complaining that they cannot live in peace anymore in Cabadbaran, because since the foundation of the Catholic school the municipal administration, which before that time had always been on good terms with the priests, is now molesting Father Roure with all kinds of unfounded rumors, slander and threats. Also other cases of disturbed relations are mentioned; the blessing by Fr. Roure of a lot for a Catholic cemetery which the municipal administration had been eyeing for a future public burial place; also the matter of civil marriages, the formation of a *Junta Catolica* to assist the parish priests in defending the rights of the Church, and a strong sermon by Roure against the Aglipayan schism.

Understandably (for Catholics) also the matter of purely civil marriages was a very sensitive point in the daily reality of changed Church-State relations. During the imprisonment of the missionaries early in 1899, and also afterwards when very few priests were left in all of Surigao and Agusan (in 1899 and 1900 there had been only three or four — Benedictines and Jesuits — in the whole district of Surigao-Agusan and in 1901 never more than seven, eight, or nine) the civil marriage procedure had become widespread, partly out of necessity, partly as a result of strong propaganda by local civil authorities.

That propaganda was not wholly the result of secularized ideological motivations: A local administration needs money for its operations, of course, and in those grey border years between the end of the Spanish era and an organized American administration, the coffers had been virtually emptied. In April 1901 the municipal Council of Butuan had approved the following monthly payroll: for the mayor, fifteen pesos; for one male teacher, twelve pesos; for one female teacher, ten pesos; for the secretary, eight pesos; for each policeman, five pesos.

Also in Butuan, the first attempt to raise the municipal income had been the imposition of an export levy of four cents for each *picol* of abacá, much to the disgust of the local Chinese. In upper Agusan the *tributo* had been reimposed on the first generation Christians whom the law of 30 July 1860 had exempted for life. That law had earlier been revoked, but the Jesuits had pressed (as the Recoletos had done) the government to re-instate the privilege because it would be an incentive for the tribals to become Christians and settle in the reductions; in 1883 the exemption for life had been granted again. Its revocation now by the authorities at Butuan was one of the reasons why the tribal settlements could not be pulled together again after the dispersal following the revolution and the disappearance of the missionaries. From the letter of Father Alaix which we quoted earlier it appears that this revocation had been planned in 1895, during the Spanish administration.

In Jabonga and Mainit very little business tax could be levied and therefore:

> "They charge fees for baptisms, burials and marriages. Here
> in Jabonga a few clever fellows see a chance to make money by
> just invoking superior orders that marriages must be performed in
> the municipal building. All married couples now say that they
> have been married according to the law *(mandablemente)*. Last
> Sunday when I was ready to go to the altar to say Mass, I
> overheard the fiscal announcing, after performing the marriage
> banns, that anybody who knew about any impediment, should
> go to the priest...and also to the Mayor, and that the latter
> would tell them whether or not they could be married!...
> Nobody cares if this violates the Church law or if they usurpate
> the rights of the Church. They are blinded by their interest in the
> pesos which they can charge this way, because if they don't
> make them pay before the marriage, they will not give them
> even one cent after being married" (Urios, 24 May 1901).

On June 4, 1901 Urios mentions that in Mainit nearly all the recent marriages had by force been civilly performed: the *"casanderos"* were after the money which they could get out of it; he adds: "This has been introduced by authorities that impose laws, customs, manners, instructions and fees, and act as if they were priests, without bothering about us anymore."

On November 1 he requested the superior to ask the Bishop in his name to give dispensation from the marriage banns in cases where there was danger that the parents would prevent the couple from being married in church.

Another ominous development in Butuan as well as in Cabadbaran and what is now Buenavista was undoubtedly the turmoil around the ownership of cemeteries and even churches and convents. It was an echo of what had developed nationwide. In Agusan the bitterness caused by it thoroughly prepared the ground for an eventual foothold of Aglipayanism in the province.

> "The problem of church property was explained by the
> Governor of the islands, Luke E. Wright, to President Theodore
> Roosevelt in a letter dated 15 August 1904. The friars, he said,
> had been driven out of their parishes during the Revolution, or
> had fled, or had been taken prisoner; some were killed. Taking
> advantage of the vacancy thus created, some municipal

governments took possession of the churches and conventos, claiming that they belonged to the municipality since they were built on public land and with labor contributed by the people...'' (Religious Revolution in the Philippines,'' Achútegui & Bernad, I, p. 314).

The first report about trouble concerning the ownership of a cemetery is found in an undated letter of Urios, probably written in the second half of July. He writes to the superior that when he was in Tortosa (now Buenavista) ''on the 11th of this month'' (he was indeed absent from Butuan on 11 July, the second day of Garcia's visit), the barrio captain showed him a written order coming from the Fiscal of Surigao and stating that ''cemeteries, churches and other property until now in the hand of the missionaries, in case they belonged to the village, should be turned over to it.'' The captain claimed the local cemetery as property of the barrio and refused Urios permission to enter it.

Clear indications about the intentions of the authorities at Butuan appear in an official communication which Llobera received on 28 September 1901, and which he included in a letter to the superior.

Butuan, 28 September 1901

Father Bernardino Llobera,

In the Session of the Municipal Council held today, it was unanimously agreed to respectfully inform you — since you are now performing your ministry in this place — that from now on you must abstain from collecting burial fees, which belong exclusively to the municipal administration of this place, which is the sole owner of the cemetery, because until now it has shouldered the expenses for the maintenance of this holy place, together with the people.

To this effect a public announcement shall be made tonight for the information of the public, including the matter of the matrimonial — baptismal — and burial registers, which since the incumbency of the new government belong to the office of the Secretary.

Copy forwarded to you for your information and effects.

The Municipal Mayor
Pastor Atega

Urios was then on an extended visit to upper Agusan. In his absence, Llobera had to tackle the issue alone, and he wrote a letter to Governor Garcia of Surigao. Since they knew, of course, that this storm was brewing (see the July information of Urios at Tortosa), it had in essence probably been prepared in advance. Dressed in proper legal terms to impress the addressee it stated:

"My dear Sir,

I wish to inform you of something that has happened between the parish of Butuan — which I am administering at the moment — and the municipal Administration of this town.

Last Saturday, 28 September at about five in the afternoon, I received a letter from the municipal Administration, of which I am sending you an exact copy.

In my answer to this letter I have stated that, since the church of Butuan has been in peaceful proprietary possession of the cemetery up to the present and has been collecting all the burial fees and practicing acts of dominion over it with total independence, while never anything happened in it without the knowledge and approval (of the parish priest), WHEREAS moreover it is clearly and definitely determined in the official letter of the civil Governor General of the Philippines published last 21 July, stating that the municipal Council has no authority whatsoever over the church, and can therefore not deprive her of a right which she has always possessed over the cemetery and the burial fees, this church will go on, as she has always done, collecting those fees until the competent Court will pass sentence on the case.

Therefore, the terms of the law being clear, and the procedure indicated by the law for those who wish to acquire any object also being clear, I do not understand why recourse should be taken to force if the way of the law can be followed.

Therefore, Mr. Governor, I beg you kindly to make your subordinates respect the law and avoid unnecessary conflicts, because the Courts are the instances to define the terms of the right and can therefore fail (sic, not fail) where justice is employed in litigations.

There being nothing else to bring forward, I remain, with my highest respect, Yours truly,

Bernardino Llobera.''

On that same day Llobera also informed his superior in Manila about the affair and his own proceeding:

> "... Sunday morning, with the church full of people and the members of the municipal Administration sitting in their (special) pews, I explained the question and read to them the communication in Spanish; after that I explained to them in Visayan the most important paragraphs of the letter of Mr. Taft..." (Llobera, 2 October).

He went even further: to forestall a possible violent reaction of the municipal officials, he went to the American Commander and explained the problem to him. The latter promised to take the matter in hand, and next day he did indeed send a letter (translated by Llobera) to the Mayor.

Llobera also informed the superior of what had happened earlier: that the Mayor (Pastor Atega) and the Treasurer (Canuto Rosales) had been called to Surigao by Governor Garcia "to receive orders."

> "They returned early in the morning of 22 October. I did not hear anything about what these orders had been, till on the 28th I received the communication from the municipal officials; not one word, and that while Pastor Atega would like to pass as a friend of us. They have really behaved as Butuanos! But I will tell Your Reverence in all honesty that *post factum* and deep inside me, I have been extremely happy, because up to now I have not been able to give those *"ponoans"* of Butuan a piece of my mind about their excesses and all the abuse of authority which they have committed these past years. This is the first time that they have made the experience of being stopped in their disorderly appetite for giving orders without respect for law..." (loc. cit.).

Twice that Sunday Llobera put the authorities to the test by performing two burials in the customary way. Nobody interfered. He also wrote a personal letter to Governor Garcia and an urgent note to Urios in faraway upper Agusan asking him to come home as soon as possible.

The latter had meanwhile escaped an attempted assassination in Pilar, was told by the mayor of Talacogon "to limit himself to church affairs, as he did to government matters," heard in Milagros that the inspector from Butuan in charge of that area had told the people that Urios had nothing to say there, and that the people were under the orders of the municipal officials of Butuan. In Jabonga a big group of people separated from the place and went to live in Santiago. When attempts to form their own municipality in that spot were thwarted by Surigao, they joined Cabadbaran but made their own cemetery in their new place, although Surigao said that they did not need it.

Meanwhile, the loyal church faction of Butuan had started a signature campaign to vindicate church ownership of the cemetery:

"In the town of Butuan, on the 14th of December 1901, the undersigned, former *capitanes*, leading citizens and ordinary citizens *(polistas)*, born or now residing in Butuan, using the rights which the law gives us, make it known:

1) That the terrain where the cemetery and other structures owned and administered by the church are located has never belonged to the people or to the municipality, because it was wasteland ceded by the (Spanish) government for the mentioned structures;

2) That the continuation and conservation of the cemetery and other church structures were not paid for by the people but by the church, because nobody ever came there to work, unless for a daily wage or gratis, and always with the approval of the missionary parish priest, never against their will, in the knowledge that they were working for the church.

3) That this town has witnessed with dismay that the present municipal administration has tried to deprive the church, against all reason and justice, of a property of which she enjoyed peaceful possession under so many other municipal administrations that have been incumbent here in the long period of three hundred years when we were living under Spanish authority, of two years under a Filipino flag and of ten months under American government.

THEREFORE, we as Catholics, as Filipinos and as Butuanos, subjects of America, make publicly known, of our own free will that in the future the church of Butuan continue to enjoy, as she has enjoyed till the present, the ownership of its structures which are the cemetery, the convent and the church, without ever being harassed in the legitimate possession of the rights granted her by law" (Sant Cugat archive).

For sure, the manifest was finely honed, although the authors were a little carried away: the church property of the Butuan of 1901 had not been enjoyed "for three hundred" years under Spain, but only since 1876 when the terrain had been prepared for its purpose in the "new" Butuan then transferred from the river mouth.

And next Urios and Llobera had a sweet moment of revenge! The special pews for the municipal officials which the sacristan had been forced to place near the sanctuary in the days when Valentin Calo had swayed it over Father Diego were removed and demoted to the rest of the pews for the "ordinary" churchgoers!

And here we come again across that man, Valentin Calo, in the letters of both priests:

> "While I was in Nasipit, the followers of Valentin Calo (who form a bigger group than the powers that be) told me that the municipal officials were planning to proceed with a court case in the cemetery question, and that they would even go to Madrid (!), if necessary. They said furthermore that the case, aside from the cemetery, would also include the convent and the church and the priests. In order to get the court case started, they were looking for more signatures since they had gathered only a few. However, the great majority of the people would well be capable to come to our rescue and bring us to another place near the mouth of the river where they would then form a new Butuan" (Urios, 8 December 1901).

Llobera has the same information in a letter of 11 December. The irony is that, if this plan had been realized, history would have repeated itself at Magallancs: only twenty-four years earlier Butuan had (for the third time!) been moved in the opposite direction. But Urios was very reluctant to let the rights of the Church be defended too much with the weapons of a man like Valentin Calo. One of his reasons was:

> "because then we would no more be working for the good of the Church, but be engaging in a spirit of partisanship and vengeance; we would lose our status of impartiality (in local politics)" (loc. cit.)

Once the turmoil had reached that stage, the municipal officials appeared more and more in a hurry to have the litigation settled, of course, in their favor! They were convinced, says Urios:

> "that when the priests were removed (as was going to happen in
> their opinion) they would, before leaving, first sell the convent
> and the church and everything else" (loc. cit.).

Urios clearly states his fear that the "Calería" would use the
concerns of the priests and the church as a "shield" for political
intentions of their own... and for revenge. Llobera was not so sure of
that and was known to be close to the Calo family. Like in the town
at large, the complications and ramifications of the year 1901 caused
also frictions inside the convent, as Urios himself mentions to the
superior.

More and more both priests began to feel that the controversy
was putting them in an awkward and isolated position in the parish.

> "... It seldom happens that any of the prominent people
> come to see us in the convent. We are in the same condition as
> our confreres in Davao according to what we have heard about
> them: always alone and keeping ourselves occupied with
> reading. In a previous letter I wrote you already that if the Indios
> and the Americans ever came to an understanding, both would
> turn their backs on us and even begin working against us. And
> this is what has happened now" (Llobera, 11 December 1901).

What was happening in Agusan was, of course, happening in
many parishes all over the country. Still, one is tempted to believe
that municipal authorities in a district like Surigao-Agusan might not
have turned so blatantly against the priests, if it had not been for
certain political post-revolutionary developments on the national
level. It seems that such had also been the feeling of Urios. On July
30, 1901 he still wrote to Father Pastells:

> "I believe that everything will start moving again. If there is
> any place in this country where the prospects look good then it is
> our vineyard here, the third and the first districts (= Surigao-
> Agusan and Zamboanga...) I know nothing about the other
> places, but as concerns those of our region, I can assure you that
> good times will come back" ("Un apostól de la civilización,"
> Ventura Pascual y Beltran, Barcelona 1920).

We should also remember that in 1899 nearly all the places in the
district had sent petitions to the Jesuit and Benedictine superiors to
let the priests return to the parishes. Many of these petitions were

published in the contemporary "Cartas" of the Jesuits. Often they carry the signatures of the very local officials who less than two years later were agitating against them! We are given a hint as to the main reason why possible harmonious relations had now turned awry in a few lines of two letters.

> "...The present municipal administration (has turned against us) since the vice-Mayor and the Treasurer have been in Surigao, because there Garcia has infatuated them *with the ideas of the Federals*" (italics supplied) (Urios, 8 December 1901).
>
> "It would be good if Your Reverence had an article published in "Libertas" [a newspaper published by the Dominicans in Manila] about the iniquitous behavior of Garcia who, to comply with the wishes of the Federals *(por necesidades federales)* is disturbing these places" (Llobera, 15 December 1901).

At our time in question, the great agitator against the Catholic Church in the country (aside from Protestantism) was the so called "Federal party" founded by

> "Americans and leading anticlerical Filipinos, and basically hostile to the Church, [which] had been favored by the American government with almost all the provincial and local offices. Hence the municipal governments especially tended to favor the Aglipayans and harassed the Catholic Church, even though the great majority of the population did not share their sentiments, but feared to oppose those in authority. The abuse of political power was most notable in case of the possession of churches and conventos" (John N. Schumacher SJ: "Readings in Philippine Church History," p.330).

Aglipay who had done a stint in the anti-American guerilla war in Luzon, nevertheless joined the pro-American Federal Party. So, for that matter, did a good Catholic such as Benito Legarda who, however, served the Catholic cause well from inside that party.

Nearly one whole year of local commotion had shocked Urios very deeply. In great emotion he wrote, at the end of a letter to the superior in Manila:

> "Poor Philippines! I do not believe that I am writing this as an expression of a bad mood. Rather the contrary is true. In my

whole religious and missionary life I have always found myself in
conformity with the will of God, and I am doing that also now,
because I consider myself so often and so much favored by Him.
I am only upset out of sheer compassion with these people whom
I, in spite of all the burdens, love today even more than before.
Please believe me. Will you, really?'' (Urios, 19 December
1901).

It is easy to sense the painful and difficult situation in which the
revolution had left the missionaries of Surigao and Agusan... and
perhaps some of the Filipino officials no less? The first had nearly
everything against them: their being Spaniards, the mood of the
times, and their obligation in conscience to safeguard certain rights
of the Church and defend her against undeniably dangerous
developments. The local Filipino officials had no lesser sensitivities
of their own (some of them uprooted) so shortly after the upheaval
of the revolution and with the ambiguous blessing of the American
occupation.

But the former had, nevertheless, one thing still in their favor:
they were priests, and that in the midst of a basically still very
religious flock. In spite of the hostile attitude of some, the great
majority of people had no difficulty at all in letting Spanish priests
minister to them: nothing had changed for them in so far as this was
concerned, so to speak. I am saying this notwithstanding some
remarks in the style of *"o tempora, o mores"* uttered by Urios when
speaking about diminishing respect among "the people" for priests
and religious observances. He and his companion are the very ones
to contradict this time and again! Of course, among the political
leaders, many of them anti-clerical and anti-Spanish by affiliation,
there were not a few demagogues, definitely filled with contempt for
(Spanish) priests and using every available opportunity to
disseminate this attitude among their constituents. But there were
also others who, even at moments of acute confrontations and
clashes, mustered the decency to clothe their personal emotions with
the kind of dignity and grudging respect as, e.g., speaks from the
letter of Simeon Trillo which we quoted earlier.

XX

Anger: A Harbinger of Schism

Already in the early years of the presence of the Aragon Jesuits in Mindanao, there were talks going on in Spain and the Philippines about the possibility of another Order coming to the Philippines and possibly to Mindanao: the Benedictines of Montserrat, Barcelona, Spain. We will meet them in the following pages and therefore some information is in order.

The Abbey had been considering this missionary venture not solely for apostolic reasons, but also to be allowed to recruit new members in Spain and have them exempted from military conscription. Already in 1867, during the deliberations between the Order and the Spanish Crown, the following possible working areas had been considered:

— In the diocese of Nueva Caceres: the slopes of Mount Isarog, where a large part of the population was still pagan.

— In the diocese of Nueva Segovia: the central Cordillera of Luzon.

— In the diocese of Cebu: the islands of Palao and the Carolinas then administered from Cebu.

— In the diocese of Jaro: the greater part of Palawan and Mindanao.
It bespeaks the weak position of Spain in the southern Mindanao region that the government was afraid to establish an abbey in the Jolo-Sulu region, because some foreign powers might consider that

as a too outspoken Spanish gesture of authority over the area!

Anti-religious laws and attitudes in Spain were the reason why the deliberations were protracted for quite some time without any clear commitment by the Order. Only in 1895 a small group of young Benedictines had been prepared for the undertaking, and on June 6 of that year an agreement was made between Montserrat and the Spanish Jesuits that the Benedictines establish themselves in the district of Surigao. The agreement stated a.o.: "For the double aim to evangelize the natives and to establish agricultural colonies in the district of Surigao, a delegation of Benedictines consisting of as many members as deemed necessary by the superior of the Order shall come to the Philippines."

The first group to arrive consisted of eight priests and seven lay Brothers. On February 7, 1896, after a reconnaissance trip to Surigao, the leader of the group, Abbot Jose Deas, informed the Governor General that he agreed to accept the following parishes: Taganaan, Placer, Gigaquit, Cabuntog and Numancia. Exactly one thousand years after the foundation of the Abbey in Montserrat, the Order was planted in the Philippines. In that same year a second group of missionaries arrived, and the parishes of Dinagat and Cantilan could now be included in the list. In 1902 the remaining parishes of Surigao were ceded to the Benedictines, in spite of some strong objections by a few Jesuits in the district.

The Benedictines shared with the Jesuits the upsetting experiences and hardships of the revolution and imprisonment, and, of course, the post-revolutionary disturbances in Surigao.

For both Orders the year 1901 was a strong harbinger of the fury which the Church and the (foreign) priests were going to be confronted with in the first two decades of the 20th century. Looming large over these confrontations were the insidious and often violent manipulations by Aglipayan protagonists against the Church of the *"romanistas,"* for the possession not only of her influence, but even her church buildings, chapels and *conventos*. The campaign was aided and abetted by the prevailing religious ignorance of the masses, and on the part of prominent protagonists and/or those in authority, by the subservience and timidity of the common *tao*.

Cabadbaran was very much a case in point, and the developments there were typical for what Aglipayanism wanted to set in motion in Surigao and Agusan and the means employed to that effect, as soon as local conditions — especially murky ones — opened a door for its politico-religious promotors. Many of them, as it soon turned out, were hardly motivated by truly religious aims. It is not too difficult to muster a good deal of sympathy for a people's struggling for freedom and self-determination, and to view even the resulting excesses with some understanding, but I am sorry to say that I cannot sympathize with the machinations of those who tried to establish a foothold for the schism in various places of Surigao and Agusan by depriving others of that same freedom and self-determination. Earlier we have pointed out that in the multifaceted post-revolutionary turbulence the Spanish missionaries had nearly everything against them. Of Aglipayanism it may be said that nearly everything worked in their favor: the mood of the times, religious ignorance, and a set of interests closely related to those of local politicians, colored by the same sentiments and defended with the same vocabulary as used by the latter in their own opposition against former values. And we should not forget the pitiful number of Catholic priests, who could not possibly be present at all times and in all places to prevent hostile shepherds from breaking in through the backdoor. Nevertheless, Aglipayanism did have one formidable factor against it: the dogged determination of the missionaries to keep them out as long as possible, even at the expense of their own public humiliation, threats and bodily harm!

What gave the battle its peculiar degree of bitterness was that at the time when the Aglipayan onslaught and the threats of government officials (to whom the schism looked for support) were at the highest, the districts of Surigao-Agusan and of Misamis were (in the words of Dean C. Worcester, the Secretary of the Interior) "worse governed by their Filipino officials than any other" ("The Philippine Islands, past and present," 1933 ed., p.477). Worcester says that he got much of his information "from reports by the Catholic priests, teachers and other reliable persons..." and this could not be kept a secret from those concerned! In 1907 the government reacted: Agusan and the non-Christian district of Bukidnon were joined into a new "province of Agusan" and the control over it was taken away from elective local officials and entrusted to an American Governor. Only in 1914, after many of the old evils had to a great extent been corrected, did Agusan become one of the seven provinces of Mindanao, comprising the present northern and southern parts.

The documentation informing us about those black and bitter years is to be found in the archive of the Spanish Abbey of Montserrat (for Surigao), the Jesuit archives in Rome and Sant Cugat, Spain (for Agusan) and in reports for 1901-1915 in the

Manila (Dominican) daily "Libertas," of which a complete collection exists in the Dominican convent of Santo Tomás in Avila, Spain.

It is remarkable that Butuan itself has never become a stronghold of Aglipayanism like Cabadbaran, Agusan and Placer, Surigao, but it was not for lack of trying. The situation in Butuan was often critical enough to fear for the worst. On 15 April 1902 Father Llobera expressed pessimism about the future in the following words: "I will tell you in all frankness that I am of the opinion that the same Father Urios who once sang the 'Gloria in Excelsis' over his mission, will also sing the 'Requiescat in Pace' over it." What kept the great majority of the population inside the fold of the Catholic Church was most probably the fact that Butuan never was without a resident priest, even not during the dark days of the revolution and immediately thereafter. Furthermore, Butuan had a much older unifying Catholic tradition than the rather young Cabadbaran with a great part of its population consisting of uprooted inmigrants from various islands, Catholics too, but here in Cabadbaran they were without firm ties to a common local past. And a very important "saving" factor was that from 1901 till 1916 "the" priest at Butuan was Saturnino Urios! There is good reason to doubt that Cabadbaran would have turned the way it did if there had been a permanent and resident priest to watch over the place and be immediately available when and where needed. It is downright pathetic that a place like Cabadbaran, a *visita* of Butuan and once solidly Catholic, a village that even in 1900 had petitioned the Jesuit superior to give them a resident priest and begged him to get one from Spain if none was available in Manila, promising even to pay his boat fare from Spain to Cabadbaran, could not be given such a priest and the status of parish until 1913, after immeasurable damage had been done to Christian unity, persisting up to our days. Actually, events were running in a vicious circle in Cabadbaran: being without a resident priest it was an easier victim for the Aglipayan onslaught, and because of the disturbances and the division created thereby, the decision to make Cabadbaran a full-fledged parish was postponed time and again. In some reports it seems implied that the Cabadbaranons, not having a priest of their own, felt neglected especially at critical moments during the first decade of this century. This discouraged many and lessened their resistance. This was all the more the case among those who were under the dominance of a few local caciques: force and intimidation has been very much a factor in the spread of the schism in

Cabadbaran. Up to far into the century it happened time and again that good and simple barrio folk came secretly to the Catholic priest to have a child rebaptized whom they had been forced to bring to the Aglipayan minister earlier.

We mentioned "critical situations" at Butuan that could easily have turned the tide in favor of the schism. After the turbulent year 1901, there occurred another public disturbance in 1902 that set the priests and the local civil authorities again squarely against each other. On April 2, 1902 Father Llobera informed Manila: "Today I heard that the municipal government has informed the public in the town house last Sunday, that the fiesta of our holy Patron has been moved to May 15."

The long and short of an acute and violent public confrontation is that a compromise was reached just in time for May 19. But from a letter by Llobera dated May 2, 1902 it appears that one of the town councilors had meanwhile been to Cebu to look for *"un cura Bisaya para que les haga la fiesta"*: a Filipino (secular) priest to celebrate the fiesta for them. Of course, any "orthodox" secular priest would never have encroached on parish jurisdiction this way. It was from the ranks of some "borderline priests" that the ministers emerged who would lend themselves to civil authorities on such occasions. Also on April 2 Llobera writes to the superior in Manila: "The municipal councilors have gone to Surigao for the election of a Governor.[52] They have also signed a paper to ask for one or more Visayan priests. I have heard that also the councilors of Cabadbaran have signed it; not long ago they wrote to you asking for a parish priest."

By his strong resistance in the case of the fiesta date, Llobera took a great risk, but he referred to what had happened in Cebu two years before: the Bishop refused, against the request by civil authorities, to hold a commemorative funeral ceremony for Jose Rizal, so it was in the end performed by a Protestant pastor.

The newspaper "Libertas" of 25 February 1902 has some interesting information on the mentioned election meeting in Surigao. After writing that Prudencio Garcia was elected "in spite of

---

[52] Prudencio Garcia had by force taken over the governorship by overthrowing the Gonzalezes; he had been kept in this position by the Americans; this interim position would have to be submitted to an election in 1902.

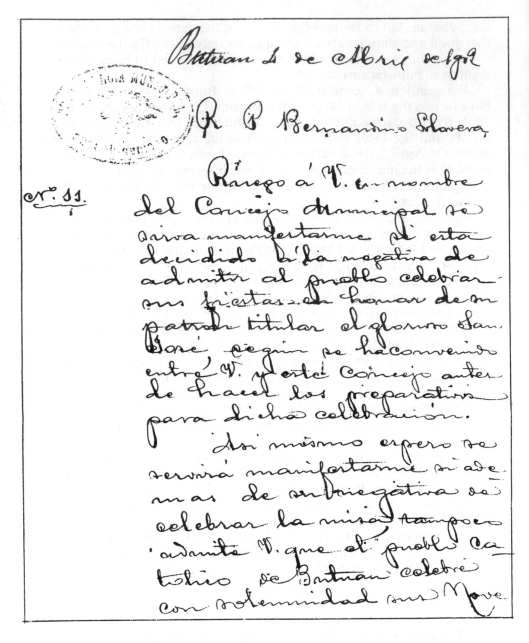

Fig. 33. Two pages of Letter from the *Presidente municipal* of Butuan asking the parish priest to reconsider his decision regarding the fiesta of 1902. (S.J. Archives, Sant Cugat, Spain.)

narios y demas funciones
dentro del templo católico
de Pontian?

Lejos de nosotros el
suponer, siquiera por un
momento, que V. fuera ca_
paz de sobreponer resenti_
mientos personales, si por
acaso existieren al interés
este pueblo que redunda en
interés y gloria de la Iglesia
y de nuestro Patron; así que
espero que su contestación
al presente sirva de medio
de conciliación entre V. y sus
hijos que son católicos de
este pueblo.

De V.R. att.º y respetuoso,

Pastor Aloya
Presidente

the fact that there was a serious criminal case pending against him,''
the paper continues:

> ''(the councilors) were unexpectedly made to sign a petition
> in the name of the whole province that the spiritual care of the
> district be entrusted to Filipino priests. Those of Placer and
> Butuan made the move to this effect, much to the surprise of the
> representatives of more than thirty civil municipalities of the
> district. Deeply astonished they listened to the proposition and
> did not know what to say or do, but finally they said that they
> had nothing against the missionaries who had not given them
> any reason to be removed in favor of Visayan priests.
> Nevertheless, out of fear of incurring the ire of the boss *(el
> cesar)*, many of them did sign; they themselves said so
> afterwards. Others did the proper thing and left the meeting
> without saying anything; there were also some who spoke up
> and said frankly what the real situation was. They stated that
> they had missionaries in their places and that they were satisfied
> with them. Any municipality wanting a Visayan priest should
> ask for one on their own account, but they for their part did not
> wish to be included in the request to be sent to the Bishop....
> We will say nothing about the sacrileges and confiscations
> committed by those very same Federals in the churches,
> cemeteries and *conventos* of some places, because that question
> is now in the hands of competent authorities.''

Already during the preceding year 1901 the relations between
government and Church had considerably worsened in Surigao itself.
On December 29, 1901 the parish priest, Eladio Alonso, OSB, wrote
to Father Urios at Butuan that the officials of Placer headed by a
nephew (sic, brother-in-law) of Governor Garcia had confiscated all
the church properties including the statue of the patron and the
latter's collection box! He testily adds that perhaps in Placer they
would now ordain one of the village councilors to the priesthood.

> ''All these orders have come from Surigao, because here one
> finds all kinds of hard-headed, rebellious and adventurous
> elements, and it is those who by their talks, shouts and
> enticements incite the others to make noise and trouble. The
> situation is very fickle and there is a lot of hypocrites around. I
> am not sure if the Fiscal belongs to the Federal party or not, but I
> have been told that he favors the confiscation of cemeteries and

that he does not like white priests...

I had the special Governor's pew removed from the church; he was mad, but there is nothing he could do about it; that pew is now locked away in my room. I knew too well what he has done and uttered against the priests'' (Letter in archive of Montserrat, Spain).

In a letter of February 22, 1902 Father Matias Roure mentions that the people of Bislig, Lianga and Hinatuan had asked insistently for a Catholic priest because the Benedictines had not yet been able to staff the southern parishes of the province. The good parishioners had said that if he came, they would even carry him there in a hammock!

That was quite unlike the officials of Jabonga and Mainit who had signed the petition for removal of the Jesuits.

After all the commotion around the town fiesta of Butuan, Father Llobera feared that the authorities would seek revenge in the near future because the outcome had been a compromise *ad hoc* only. Moreover, it had been forced upon them through a popular demonstration organized by...Valentin Calo, the zealous defender of the priests and the political opponent of the powers that were at Butuan. Was it pure coincidence that one month later Valentin and his son Adolfo were incarcerated on charges of having gone to Surigao to obtain two hundred rifles to start an uprising against the Americans...? Adolfo had also just published an article in a Manila paper about the iniquitous behavior of the Butuan authorities vis-à-vis the priests and the Church. On 13 June Father Roure mentions that also Llobera was included in the case against the Calos.

That same month of May 1902 a shocking event happened in Cabadbaran: the murder of Felix Cepeda, the former fiscal of the convent and now a school teacher. The killing had to do with the proclamation of some marriage banns. There was a new fiscal at the time, and he had certified that there was no impediment when he presented the papers to Father Llobera at Butuan. But Felix informed the latter that in one case there was a canonical impediment, and therefore Llobera refused to perform the marriage. That again caused great commotion in Cabadbaran, and threats to kill Cepeda were uttered. One month later a similar case happened, and shortly thereafter Felix Cepeda was killed in his sleep. The name of the assassin is mentioned in at least two sources, and it was still very well known among older Cabadbaranons years ago. After his release from Bilibid prison he became one of the chief agitators against the Catholic Church in Cabadbaran.

Also at the Surigao end of the district things had been boiling for some time. On January 1, 1902 Llobera writes from Tubay: "It seems that in Surigao a group of fanatical sectarians have joined together and are planning to spread discord and perturbation in the province. I have heard that the municipal officers of Placer have taken hold of the cemetery, the convent and the church, instigated by a circular from the Provincial Fiscal of Surigao. According to the jurisprudence of that man, all the churches, convents and cemeteries in the Philippines will be secularized, because everywhere people have been working on these for some time. Really, wheresoever the authority has fallen in the hands of Federalists or Masons, everything is possible."

During the years 1901 and 1902 there were three priests working in Agusan, with residence at Butuan: Saturnino Urios, Bernardino Llobera, and Matias Roure. They took turns at looking after Cabadbaran, Mainit/Jabonga and upper Agusan. In 1903 they would be joined by another veteran of Agusan: Francisco Nebot. After 1902 with its fiesta-fury, things had been relatively quiet in Butuan itself. Nevertheless, when Roure visited Esperanza in May 1903 and had noted the bad condition of the church and the convent, people told him that a certain official of Butuan had ordered them not to do any repair work on these buildings. On July 31, 1903 Roure writes to Manila: "...the peace that presently reigns up to a point between us and some leaders could still easily become disturbed, although, out of respect for Father Urios and fear that the people might not follow them, they will perhaps keep quiet and not molest us like in Cabadbaran...I mention the question of Cabadbaran, so that your Reverence will take pity on these people who — in my humble opinion — will get lost in a short time if there will not be a permanent priest among them, residing in Cabadbaran, in order to counteract, with the help of nearly all the Boholanos of Cabadbaran, the pernicious propaganda that is continuously being waged here and in other places of the district..."

In September 1903 some justice was meted out to some people in Surigao: Governor Garcia and the provincial Fiscal had been suspended, although probably for other reasons than those dealt with here. As has been mentioned (p. 421) in March 1902 he had been made Governor by election after having occupied the position ad interim since 1901. At that time he had some serious cases pending against him. Furthermore, he had not been able to improve the peace-and-order situation at all in his jurisdiction. On 16 May 1903 Urios writes that the Americans were engaged in Tubay, Santiago, Jabonga, Mainit, Placer and Bacuag in an intensive hunt for the rebels under the command of Adriano Concepción. Already one hundred fifty of them had been captured. It was known that an American judge would come from Manila to handle the court case against them. This judge was James H. Blount, who later wrote the book "The American Occupation of the Philippines" (New York, 1912). On p.414 ff. of this book he speaks about the affairs of Surigao. "In May 1903 I was sent to the province of Surigao to try some cases arising out of what has ever been known in that out of the way region as 'the affair of March 23, 1903'. In his Annual Report for 1903, pp. 29-30, in describing the Surigao affair, Governor Taft correctly states that a band of outlaws came into the town of Surigao on the day above named, killed Captain Clark, the officer in charge of the Constabulary, took the guns of the Constabularies while they were away at their midday meal, scattered about the town and departed..."

The provincial Treasurer (Luther S. Kelley) brought the seven American women living in Surigao to the safety of the townhouse, which the rebels were unable to penetrate. The court trial of the captured suspects lasted one month. Those proved guilty were hanged, including Concepción, who had held out for some time because he knew that he had nothing to lose anymore but his life: he had escaped from prison in January 1903 and from the mountains had organized the raid on Surigao.

The "Annual Report" mentioned by Blount recounts on pp. 221-223 how on 23 March 1903 a band of thirty insurgents led by Adriano Concepcion attacked the Constabulary barracks at noon while the soldiers were having their meal in a separate room. About one hundred people of the town had joined them. As booty were taken: 56 Remington shotguns; 40 Colt revolvers; 10 Springfield carbines; 20 Remington rifles; 5000 rounds of ammunition; and 5,400 pesos in cash. They stayed in the town the whole afternoon and night and departed only the next morning after the Padre of the town had warned them that a U.S. gunboat was approaching. Then they pulled out to Placer, after which they were being chased by the soldiers till June.

Various provincial and municipal officials were implicated and arrested; among those mentioned are the Presidente of Timamana and Mainit. On June 30 the military campaign was concluded. Among the town people who had joined the raid on the barracks were many Cebuano stevedores. The mentioned report has many pages of troop movements against the rebels and also a list of suspects still being hunted or already captured (Courtesy University of Leiden Library, Holland.)

As successor to Garcia was appointed a certain Hugo Salazar, from Cavite, a rabid anti-clerical. Blair & Robertson 48:27 says that he was a young Filipino, native of Luzon, educated as a pharmacist and prominent in the Federal party from 1901 till 1904. He wrote some articles under the pen-name of *"Ambot"* ("I do not know.") Salazar did not stay long in Surigao, because in February 1904 Daniel Toribio Sison, the former guerilla leader of Mainit/Jabonga, was elected successor to the Governorship of the province.

In October 1903 Urios writes that in Butuan things looked again "like in the golden era, although it cannot be more than a bronze era now." The emotions of those days had affected him very much and often he felt weak and sickly. But he was very much present that year when the cholera epidemic counted among its victims Valentin Calo and the wives of Canuto Rosales and Simeon Trillo. Father Nebot wrote about him from Talacogon on 22 January 1903: "I have to say that I would be deeply sorry if Fr. Urios would have to leave Butuan because of his health. I think that he does a lot of good and prevents a lot of evil by his presence in this place and even in other places of Agusan with his mere shadow"

On 26 August 1903 Father Roure informs: "The Mamanuas of San Roque tell me that they would agree to live again (in a village) like in the times of Father Llobera [Guillermo, the brother of Bernardino] if they were given a priest. After the storm of their aggregation with Cabadbaran, and because of the cholera and other tribulations of which they had been free before, these people now wish to have a missionary assigned to them."

In Cabadbaran, meanwhile, things had turned from bad to worse. We can read this in a letter of Fr. Roure written on 16 October 1903. "In the last session of the municipal council the proposal of Atega was unanimously approved: 1) that the church, the convent and the school belong to the people and that the priest does not even owe one nail of those structures. They will consult Surigao before answering the missionary. 2) That they should petition a priest of Aglipay and collect money for his transportation and sustenance. It pleases the council that he (Atega) has promised or given fifteen pesos to procure an Aglipayan priest; according to Atega, they are the same as we. In the meeting was also stressed that they would build a good chapel and convent for him. 3) That a lot had already been bought for twenty pesos, to serve as municipal cemetery, to be blessed by the priest of Aglipay; Atega himself wishes to be buried there...''

It seems that in Cabadbaran the question of church property and the animosities between the priests and the municipal officials, plus the threat to import an Aglipayan priest, had become more acute in 1903 because Roure had re-opened the Catholic school. This produced the same resentment as experienced in Butuan in an already soured local situation. What aggravated the bitterness and the plight of the Catholic school was the fact that the local Justice of the Peace was the same person as the Inspector of Public schools: Andres Atega!

No wonder then that Roure was accused in the Court of Surigao of inciting the people against the public schools and the local administration...Many of the Boholano inmigrants were talking about leaving Cabadbaran and settling in other places. Only the permanent presence of a priest could hold the Catholic cause together, wrote Roure to Manila. He himself was suffering from serious eye trouble, but he did not dare leave Cabadbaran for treatment in Cebu or Manila.[53]

After the authorities of Placer, led by Capitan Isidro Custodio, had taken over the local church and convent in December 1901, they started to organize opposition against the existing ownership of Catholic properties and against the Benedictines in neighboring places. Obviously with some success, because Father Romualdo Moral wrote on September 14, 1903 from Surigao that one day, when visiting Bacuag, he went ashore early in the morning, went to church and called for the local parish fiscal *("fiscalillo"* as he called him!). Immediately it became clear that certain influences had been at work also in Bacuag, because this "would-be fiscal" told him: "Father I do not like you to say Mass, because I am afraid that you are not a priest sent by Aglipay!" For that one time Father Moral was able to make him give up his resistance, however. On

---

[53] In 1938 the late Fr. Rodolfo Cabonce, SJ, born in Cabadbaran in 1906, visited some former P.I. Jesuit missionaries then staying in San Remo, Italy, because of the Spanish revolution. He related: "Father Roure was alone in the corner of a room, old and out of his mind. But when I mentioned that I was from the Philippines, his subconscious started to work, and he began to speak in Visayan, explaining that he wanted to go back to the Philippines.''

April 10, 1904 the "Libertas" carried the following report: "According to information received in this capital, the Aglipayan faction in Dinagat, Surigao, has forcefully taken over the church and the convent of that place and expelled the Catholic priest from the parish. He appealed to the provincial Governor who, however, refused to mind the conflict."

By 1903 so many complaints of illegal and forceful takeovers had reached the Insular Government from all over the country that Governor-General Taft finally passed an Executive Order, wherein all provincial Governors were directed to protect all parties who were then "in peaceable *possession*" of church-property; the real *ownership* would eventually be determined by the Supreme Court.

However, the terms employed in that Order labored under so many possibilities for selfish or opportunistic interpretation and manipulation that it only added to the problems in most dioceses. Especially in areas where the friars had moved out right after the revolution, and where a kind of parochial vacuum had come into existence when there were no Catholic priests available to hold on, municipalities and the Aglipayans had moved in, perhaps "peaceably" at the moment because there was nobody present or willing to protest.

Especially in the far-away towns and villages, enough signatures could be mustered and witnesses produced to prove that a municipal council or an Aglipayan minister were now "in peaceable" possession of church property, perhaps since three years ago!

In spite of its imperfections and open-endedness, plus its provisional character, the Order pointed already to the future Supreme Court decision of 1906 that would once and for all restore those properties to where they belonged: the Catholic Church.

In 1904, however, there was only the ambiguous Taft declaration, and in numberless places the manipulations for takeover went on as before. One such place was Bacuag, Surigao, without a resident parish priest and too close to Placer for comfort. Among the few pertinent documents extant in the Benedictine archive of Montserrat in Spain is an extensive "Relation of the attack on the convent of Bacuag, the theft of church utensils and the profanation of the church."

It had been written by Father Paulino Garcia OSB on 16 February 1904. He had come to visit Bacuag for his usual ministry on 31 January. He arrived at seven thirty in the morning and said Mass. Afterwards some people told him that the "caporal of Aglipay" had arrived in Placer. Through a letter he had invited the people of

Bacuag to visit him in Placer. He also had sent them one hundred *almanaques* "so they could learn what the duties of the Filipinos were." [54]

On February 6 some people of Bacuag had indeed gone to Placer to attend the service of the new minister. On the 7th they came back and started berating the others for not having visited the "Visayan" priest; they also started to enlist sympathizers for the new order of things as prevailing in Placer.

On February 10 the Aglipayan minister came to Bacuag. To prevent the ringing of Catholic church bells for welcoming a schismatic, Father Paulino had taken his precautions: he had removed the clappers from the bells and hidden them in the convent. The visitor from Placer was accompanied by Isidro Custodio and the Justice of the Peace. A delegation of women came to ask Father Paulino to surrender the church and convent "peaceably" to this "Visayan" successor. He told them that by what they were doing and propagating, they would incur excommunication. Obviously this did not impress them very much, because they started accusing him of being against the Filipino priest because the latter was not of his race. Presently also the municipal officials joined the women, but Fr. Paulino explained to them the Declaration of Taft concerning such matters.

Next morning he said Mass and then removed all the paraments, the crosses, candle sticks and other utensils and put them in the convent. Later that morning the visitors of the previous day came back and once more claimed the church and the convent "because these had been built by the people." Although the local *Presidente* used all his authority to prevent them from committing violence, a mob proceeded to storm the convent while Fr. Paulino was still talking to the mayor on the street. They even used force on him to get the keys out of his pockets, but did not succeed. In the end he decided to go back to Surigao, for which he had to borrow money to pay for his rowers. The mayor still gave him some breakfast. He sent a hurried letter to Fr. Bernardino Perez in Gigaquit and left.

It appears that in 1904 some people in Surigao had started to wake up to the spreading anarchy. "Libertas" of April 26, 1904 carries the following report:

---

[54] Probably the "Almanaque de Jose Rizal," which at that time was distributed all over the Philippines.

Triumph for the Catholic Church

> This is the title which our respected colleague "Ang Camatuoran" of Cebu carries over the following article. After so many intrigues and affronts caused by the Aglipayans of Placer who have taken over the church and the convent of that place where the Justice of the Peace had sided with them, the case was taken in appeal to the Court of First Instance in Surigao. After investigation, this Court declared in favor of the Catholic Church.

This decision had probably something to do with the fact that since February 1, 1904 a new Governor was in charge in Surigao: the former guerilla-leader Daniel Toribio Sison. In spite of his Masonic affiliation and revolutionary ideas, this man had never really turned his back on the Church and the priests, to whom he fully entrusted his last days when he was seriously ill.

Switching back again to Cabadbaran, we can do no better than get our information from a very involved eyewitness, Father Francisco Nebot. Tired and angry because of all the public harassment against him and the local Catholic cause, he left the place and from Butuan wrote a long letter of complaint to Governor-General Wright. It can be found in the collection "Cartas Edificantes de la asistencia de España," Bilbao, V (1905), pp. 215-224. (The document deserves to be quoted in full; we will do so at the end of this chapter.) It is important not only because of the on-the-spot information it provides about the Cabadbaran of 1904, but also because it was one of those reports to the higher government that accelerated the 1906 Supreme Court decision which would mark a turning point for contemporary developments: backwards for Aglipayanism, forward for the Catholic Church. Or to put it in less "colored" terms: it was the point at which due justice was finally done to the Catholic Church.

In his letter Nebot bitterly complains about the lawlessness prevailing in Cabadbaran, the humiliation, the harassment and raw persecution suffered by him and loyal Catholics. Repeatedly he stresses that the local authorities were not up to their duties, or more probably were themselves obstinately and deviously trying to make life for the Catholic priest impossible and prepare the way for Aglipayanism. Nebot pointedly says: this is persecution like in the times of the first Christians! Each of his major accusations or informations is accompanied by numbered Exhibits, and there are 21 of them...This is also the story of his successors, in 1905, 1906 and afterwards, not only in Cabadbaran but also in Butuan itself and elsewhere. In 1906 Urios himself was again deeply involved in the fight for survival of the Catholic school, and one day, while in Cabadbaran, the local Justice of the Peace sent him a summons on request of the authorities at Butuan for allegedly having preached there against the local American teacher (Ventura y Pascual, "Un Apostol de la civilization," p. 373). In 1906 the church of Cabadbaran was burned a second time:

> "They have again burned our church in Cabadbaran, and again we are rebuilding it in spite of all the hardships. Remember that it had a very precious retablo, and that in a village that has no priest...
>
> The municipal officials here in Butuan are very much inclined to the schism, and if it were not for our unceasing efforts to keep the good ones loyal, we would now be stuck with an Aglipayan chapel. Twice they have tried to construct one, but they were never able to get a roof on it; the work was abandoned and in the end it just collapsed..." (ibid.).

Old Butuanos remember that the place where those attempts were made, is the lot presently occupied by the "New Narra" restaurant. The Aglipayan chapel presently existing in Butuan is of a much later date.

Although in 1906 Urios speaking about Butuan speaks of "el cisma de Butuan sosegado y oculto" (slumbering and underground), the future would prove that as soon as the conditions were favorable, it could flare up. The date of the town fiesta remained an issue between the local church and the municipal authority, and it became very acute again in 1911 when the latter organized a "town fiesta" of their own: "la fiesta civica y meramente profana" as Urios typified it. It remained a familiar and welcome opportunity for the enemies of the Church to fish in murky water again.

Nevertheless, on February 5, 1910 Father Jaime Vallés would write to Spain:

> "My fellow missionaries Urios and Vila are in Cabadbaran for the fiesta celebration and to draw the plan for the future church, and also to attend to the compliance with the people's Easter duty *(katuigan)*. I believe that the Catholics of Cabadbaran could be set up as an example for the whole

Philippines. They remain steadfast in the middle of so much opposition and wish to help us in everything, even against the expressed will of their local politicians. This clearly demonstrates what faith is capable of if it is well-rooted in the heart.

Here in Butuan much public attention was given to the confession and communion of the man who had been the standard bearer of Aglipayanism. He had lost his wife at childbirth, but shortly before she died she told him: ''If you wish to live happily and in peace, go to confession and do not marry a schismatic.'' She died as a good Christian and her burial was the talk of the town. Presently he has come to confession and he is probably going to be married to a good girl of the Hijas de Maria.

Such things serve as some comfort amidst so much war as is being waged against the Church by a small group of people...'' (''Misiones catolicas en el extremo Oriente,'' vol. XVIII, no. 357, Barcelona 1910).

In 1911 the American Governor, John R. White in his annual report to the Governor General, writes:

''In March slight damage was done to the Cabadbaran Catholic convent by fire. The building is of wood and nipa and unoccupied save during the occasional visit of the Jesuit priest from Butuan or Jabonga. The President of Cabadbaran was suspended by Governor Johnson, but later re-instated by the undersigned as there was no evidence of his responsibility for the damage done to the convent'' (National Archives, Washington, Records of the Bureau of Insular Affairs, August 8, 1911 Record Group 350).

The same Governor credits Cabadbaran with a fairly efficient municipal government and the town as progressive, whereas Butuan and Talacogon ''have very poor administrations and municipal politics are an opera-bouffe.'' He also mentions that the fate of the local Chinese of Cabadbaran was hardly any better than that of the Catholic priests: they were steadfastly refused residency.

In the archive of the Jesuit Generalate in Rome is a kind of overview of the religious situation in Cabadbaran in 1912, the year before a resident priest was assigned and Cabadbaran finally became a regular parish. The paper is unsigned, and the pages incomplete. The anonymous author speaks of Cabadbaran as *''este famoso pueblo!''* According to his enumeration, the population was roughly as follows:

— Cabadbaran, Calibonan and Causwagan, together, with approximately 1000 families or 5000 people.

— "Along the road": Bayang, Sangaan and Agay, with together approximately 90 families, most of them first generation Christians.

— Along the seashore: Panlasan, Cambuayon and Rizal; the first two with old-time Christians, the last with recently converted *"conquistas"*; (no number given).

— Tubay with approximately 380 families, most of them old-timers. There is no mention of Tolosa. Total number of inhabitants is 8000 to 9000. In 1910 Governor Frederick Johnson had reported: Butuan with 5,267 inhabitants, Cabadbaran, 7,408 and Talacogon 1,543.

The author of the report then distinguishes three classes of people according to their religious affiliation:

1. Those Catholics who have resisted all heretical or schismatic influence. Of such only 60 families live in Cabadbaran proper and in Cambuayon 5 or 6.
2. Catholics "affected" by the schism, all in all numbering approximately 200 families.
3. Apostates, real or through force and deception. The "real" ones are the rich and influential families, approximately 50 or 60 of them. It is these who force or intimidate most of the rest.

Tubay is still most Catholic, although there is much religious ignorance and the *"principales"* are schismatics.

The overview also mentions that the *"apostatas originales"* are now de facto for a great part unbelievers due to their disappointing experiences with the schismatic ministers. The "ordinary" people might easily return to the Church if only there was a resident priest. When this ever should come to pass, his place of residence should be Cabadbaran proper rather than Tubay; such for "practical" reasons and also because here the Catholics have suffered most for their religion.

Many more pages could be filled with such bitter experiences related in the previous ones, but frankly, one finds no pleasure in doing so. There is another matter I can only relate with somewhat mixed feelings. After 1908, when the Dutch MSC Fathers had arrived in Surigao, one finds an occasional reference to them in

Jesuit letters from Agusan and Davao, which inevitably speak of *similar* problems encountered by those Dutchmen on the Surigao side...Urios then strongly hints more than once that these were caused because those missionaries were *"rigoristas"* or *"duros trabajadores pero sin genesis":* hard workers but (may it be translated thus?) not acculturated yet...

In 1911, when these Dutchmen were fighting in nearly all their Surigao parishes for the survival of the Catholic schools, most of the municipal presidents of Surigao signed a joint petition that the Dutchmen be sent back to Holland. It was the same story as had happened to the Jesuits and Benedictines in Surigao in 1902, and for reasons similar to those obtaining in Butuan and Cabadbaran then. Llobera (from Caraga, 18 November 1911) does not mention the similarity of circumstances, but does not forget to report that the Governor and the Doctor of Surigao had told him that "22 municipalities of Surigao had signed a petition asking for the return of the Jesuits!" The Dominican paper "Libertas" saw it slightly differently:

> "Thank God that in these islands there is no dearth of men inspired by the purest zeal for the honor of God and the wellbeing of people. These selected men have made themselves doubly meritorious for the Church and the Filipino people by their heroic perseverance and firmness, inflexibility and sturdiness with which they effectively defend the Catholic principles before the indifference of some, the biting and merciless criticism of others and the sectarian persecution of many. Likewise, by their foresight and power of observation, which they proved by pointing out the primary cause of the impending collapse of the big temple of Catholicism in these islands. Verily, all of us are saddened and complain, but not all of us do what we can do to prevent that collapse or to build a dam against the disaster that threatens us from all sides.
>
> We are referring to that group of courageous Dutch missionaries who have started a strong and decisive battle for the Catholic education of the youth in Surigao" ("Libertas," August 13, 1913).

Of course, that is very much time-colored language...What the Jesuit sources, when speaking about the contemporary difficulties of the Dutch MSC Fathers at the Surigao side of the district fail to mention is that the latter *inherited* a storm that had come into existence because of a *Spanish* past, and had already for nearly one decade been swirling around Spanish priests in Surigao as well as in Agusan.

Moreover, there were two factors that would considerably aggravate the turbulence created by the prevailing atmosphere of supercharged nationalism, suspicion and anti-clericalism in certain corners. These factors occurred practically simultaneously just at the time when the Dutch missionaries entered Surigao. One was the question of the "Arancel de Derechos" prescribed by the Diocesan Council of Cebu in 1910. This caused a problem for the priest not just with a few civil authorities or a limited number of anti-clericals at large, but with the general population, with whom he had his daily dealings. Until then the latter had been used to pay only an insignificant amount for spiritual services rendered by the parish priests; the larger expenses for the building and maintenance of churches, *conventos* and schools plus the subsistence of the parish priests were taken care of by government allotments (the "Sanctorum"). In many instances where the "Arancel" provoked resistance, an Aglipayan minister would gladly offer his services gratis or at an attractive discount, accusing the *"romanista"* priests of working for the coffers of the Pope in Rome!

The second source of much public trouble was the question of the parochial schools. Time and again this would bring the priests in conflict not only with local Filipino government officials but also with American school heads and inspectors. The question became all the more troublesome for the parish priests (by then all Dutch) after the first Provincial Council of Manila held in 1907 had put all parish priests under strict obligation to open a parochial school within two years after the publication of the Council decrees (1910). Priests who within those two years had not complied could be deposed solely for that reason! The Decrees also obliged the parish priest to use pastoral sanctions against those parents who sent their children to the public school if there was a Catholic school in the locality. ("Acta et Decreta Concilii Provincialis Manilani I," p.337).

On the other hand, local civil authorities were obliged by their own superiors to open and maintain public schools. The battle that the Jesuits had reported from Butuan in 1901 and from Cabadbaran in 1903, raged *(con brio)* in practically all the parishes of Surigao then staffed by Dutch priests since 1908. It gradually poisoned Church-State relations all over the province, with the *"brio"* undoubtedly turning *"fortissimo"* at times under the baton of sturdy Dutch reaction! Still, in 1911 when 22 mayors of Surigao, with the

support of the provincial Governor, petitioned Governor-General
Forbes to remove the Dutch missionaries—a move that had been
very much propagated by Aglipayan proselytizers—the petitioners
did not request to have the foreign missionaries replaced with
Aglipayan ministers, but either with Filipino (secular) priests, or if
none were available, to let the Jesuits return. Undoubtedly, the older
officials of Surigao, in spite of what they were or did in 1911, still
associated the latter with quieter yesteryears. At any rate, it is
worthwhile to note this "orthodox" streak coming through in the
wording of their petition. Perhaps unlike a decade earlier, the
distinction between Filipino Catholic priests and Aglipayan ministers
had become known in 1911...

To be noted is also that the Aglipayan cause, notwithstanding
that it had practically the field laid out for it, never really prospered
in places where a Catholic (foreign) priest was permanently present.
One clear and convincing example is the parish of Gigaquit, Surigao.
In Dinagat the schism only could take root after some local
rabblerousers had expelled the Spanish Benedictine parish priest
from his *convento* and taken over the parish affairs. Moreover,
Gigaquit remained a "Gonzalez place." The surviving son of Simon,
Recaredo, understandably no friend of (Spanish) priests, was also
very anti-American. Garcia, the nemesis of the family, belonged to
the pro-American, but anti-Church party of the Federalistas. His
political maneuvering facilitated the establishment of Aglipayanism
left and right. But Recaredo Gonzalez kept everything that reeked of
Garcia out of Gigaquit during the critical pre-1905 years!
Furthermore, when on a blue Monday the astonished people of
Gigaquit saw how easily two of their townmates were suddenly
promoted to the Aglipayan ministry (one assigned to Dinagat and the
other to Surigao town), they had seen everything!

The latter had previously been given a scholarship, including free
board and lodging, by the Benedictines of San Beda College in
Manila (Documentation in the OSB archive of Monstserrat, Spain,
and the MSC archive of Tilburg, Holland.)

The fact that the few imported (or locally promoted) ministers,
who had now been around a few years in Agusan and Surigao, had
not made a very favorable impression on many people, had a lot to
do with later developments. For the rest they had been roaming
ambassadors of hatred against the *"padres romanistas,"* as can be
read in contemporary letters and reports of the latter still extant in
archives. On December 25, 1910, Father Vallés, SJ, then in
Butuan as assistant to Father Urios, wrote from Cabadbaran that

most of the day he stayed inside the convent to avoid being insulted and possibly attacked on the street. As to the leading elements of the village, he adds:

> "Many have become tired of their pseudo-priests, and in the time of four years five different ones have been here. They now loudly proclaim themselves atheists, spiritists, Masons and Protestants, swearing time and again that they will not return to the Catholic Church" (Jesuit archive, Rome).

Looking back at it all 75 years later, one can, without prejudice, state that Aglipayanism has not brought much religion into the region, but has contributed considerably to an atmosphere of scepticism and indifferentism in some circles. The various Protestant denominations that started operating in the area right after the American takeover, were, of course, also often a significant nuisance to Catholic priests, but of many of them it can at least be said that they did succeed in imbuing their communities with an appreciable spirit of their interpretation of Christianity.

Finally, mindful of undeniable excesses of the Spanish Church in the Philippines in the days preceding and immediately following the revolution, we may, in spite of all the preceding lines, also point to the mitigating factors of time, persons and circumstances for a possible explanation of the excesses committed by the early leaders and followers of the schism of Cabadbaran, Placer and Bacuag.

Petition of the Rev. Father Francisco Nebot, Missionary of Cabadbaran, that with the support of the Rev. Fr. Superior of the Mission, was presented to the Governor General of the Philippines, Mr. Wright.

Sir,

The undersigned, Religious of the Society of Jesus and Catholic missionary in Cabadbaran, province of Surigao, appeals to the Higher Government asking for protection and justice.

The Catholic inhabitants of Cabadbaran and their missionary have been targets of raw persecution for more than four months, with clear indications of complicity of the local authorities and no efficient remedial steps from the part of the provincial officials. This persecution of the missionary has resulted in his departure from Cabadbaran after his church had been put on fire and after the municipal officials had made the convent inhabitable.

The municipal Presidente, the Justice of the Peace and all the members of the council except Salvador Montalban have been waging a systematical opposition against the Catholic Church, preventing the dead from being buried in the Catholic cemetery, and after a chapel has been put up for the Philippine Independent Church, by molesting the Catholics wishing to remain faithful to their religion.

I have previously been in charge of the spiritual care for Cabadbaran for eight years, without complaints from anybody; for that reason and also because one of the most conspicuous schismatics had told my superior that it was advisable that I go to this place, I was sent here as a rainbow of hope. At my arrival in Cabadbaran on August 7, 1904, I informed the municipal Presidente that my intention was exclusively to devote myself to the spiritual good of all (Exhibit No. 1). The following day he answered me and said that he was displeased with my intention to stay in the place, and without my having shown him any reason for suspicion, added that he would see to it that peace and respect for the rights of everyone would be preserved (Exhibit No. 2).

The night immediately following the receipt of his letter, a vehement stoning of my house took place, of which I informed the municipal Presidente next day (Exhibit No. 3), drawing his attention to the seriousness of this delict, because I was being maltreated as representative of Cabadbaran of the Catholic Church to which the Constitution of the United States grants complete freedom, as also to the other religions or sects. That religion was the only motive for the attack was clear from the fact that this had been the first harassment since the establishment of the P.I.C. and that also the house of my neighbor, Matias Biray, was stoned, and that another neighbor, Leon Magno, had been slapped, both being the representatives of the Catholic missionary during his absence.

When I informed the Governor of Surigao on August 11 of the misdeed committed to me on the 8th (Exhibit No. 4), I expressed my suspicion that the municipal administration would not take any efficient steps, neither to mete out punishment nor to prevent new attacks, I was basing myself on the fact that the abuse of the just mentioned two Catholics had remained unpunished and also on the hostility against the Catholics manifested in the refusal of the municipal council to return to the Catholic Church the three bells which had been confiscated under false pretexts; moreover, that he had been connected with another case (in his capacity as Justice of the

Peace) (Exhibit No. 5) wherein the Catholic Church was denied the acceptance of a statue that had been destined for her; in addition by the rigor by which the Catholics were threatened and the actual fines imposed on them for violations of municipal ordinances. I also said that this kept the Catholics in continuous fear, so that some families were planning to leave the place or had already left to live outside of the village where they believed themselves persecuted for their religious belief.

Nobody dared expose himself to the ire of the sectarians of the schism, by helping in the reparation of the church and the convent after these had been damaged in a storm, till on the 23rd Francisco Montalban with a laborer ventured to do the job with an abnegation that deserves all praise. But for that reason it happened the following night that the house of Salvador Montalban, the son of Francisco, was stoned and my own house even twice, like those of three prominent Catholics, one of them the Spaniard Don Jose Aenlle. I informed the local authorities of this new misdeed on 24th (Exhibit No. 6), and on the 26th I had to report two other cases of stoning at my convent (Exhibit No. 7). After that followed the stoning of the houses of the most prominent Catholics, but we did not report it because we considered it wasted effort or even counter-productive. As a result of my former communication a public announcement was made forbidding anybody to move around on the streets after ten o'clock at night, but nobody minded this announcement; it served only as a pretext to imprison Pedro Biray who was accosted by two policemen when he came to my house at seven o'clock.

In the question of the impossibility to find laborers for the needed repair of the church and the convent (for which I had asked the local authorities on September 10) I mentioned the well-founded fear of the people if they came to work on their own initiative or that of the missionary (Exhibit No. 8), but the answer was that also the municipality was in need of laborers for its public works (Exhibit No. 9); in the same letter he stated that the authorities were incapable of maintaining peace and order, thereby referring to my report dated the 15th (Exhibit No. 10).

This admission by the local officials that they were not capable (to keep) order and prevent the frequent evils committed against my person and other peaceful Catholics, seem (in my opinion) to constitute a very serious situation, and I had to inform the provincial authority about it, because the local authorities had not complied with their obligation to do so. I did so in a letter of October 1 (Exhibit No. 5). Either because the schismatics believed that the Catholics had been completely annihilated, or because the provincial Governor was expected any day — he is a man who, whatsoever his ideas and feelings were, was imbued with a high regard for the idea of order and justice — it is a fact that there appeared to be a pause in the persecution of the Catholics. This encouraged the latter again to come to church on Sundays, and some came also to work on the repair of the roof.

The Governor of Surigao had the kindness to come to the convent on October 16 with practically all the provincial officials. He spoke very nice words about order and freedom, and invited also me to speak. In the presence of all I repeated what I had written in my letters to the Governor. I pointed out that the greatest evil in Cabadbaran was that delicts and crimes remained unpunished, proving a high degree of negligence or weakness among the authorities, if it could not also be attributed to the ease by which the criminals could find witnesses willing to commit perjury. There is a certain individual in Cabadbaran who during the Spanish time was accused of having stoned the house of Don Angel Villanueva. He was arrested in Tubay, accused and finally held in Surigao as a presumed party also to the murder of Don Felix Cepeda. This man was also accused by Don Jose Aenlle of having stoned his house and maltreated Leon Magno in the street and even of having done so twice to an old woman; he was convicted on October 17th of that year. This individual enjoys now the full confidence of the municipal President, the Judge and the Treasurer, and to him was entrusted the delicate task to collect the fines for violations of municipal ordinances. He was also sent to my house with two policemen to force me to show my "cedula personal." In my talk I kept insisting on how serious the evil was, because I believe that it is indeed greatly so, and also since it seemed to me that the Governor was a man with a benign heart, full of patience, and that for that reason the effects of his visit might not last very long. For the same reason I brought up again the negligence committed by the municipal President in not informing the Governor of the misdeeds committed in Cabadbaran, especially since he himself had admitted that the local authority was incapable of stopping them. In the presence of all I accused him of an activity which I had not mentioned previously so as not to expose some people to worse persecution and dangers. This was the fact that he had obliged the inhabitants of Cabadbaran to appear before his council or other authorities in order to sign on a pre-prepared list if they adhered to the Catholic religion or to the P.I.C. (Exhibit No. 11). They tried to justify that disposition by saying that it was made in order to know who were Catholics so that they could work on the church without being bothered. What they did thereafter, namely stoning the houses of those who did work on the church, shows that such was not the intention. I also explained that I could not report how they had forced the *romanistas* to sign as Aglipayans, because then I would have had to prove it, and that would have exposed the signatories to terrible vengeance. They had told them that if the church would burn down, the *romanistas* would have to pay for a new one. This was not a new threat, because on September 13 a missionary who had preceded me in Cabadbaran told me: this trick of having to pay for the repair of the church is an old one and belongs to the worst evil ever invented. When a storm had damaged the church, the faithful would immediately come to repair it, but then the others would come to make them stop the work with threats and trouble-making.

Some of the Catholics who had given in to those threats saw afterwards that they had been wrong, changed their minds and were afterwards the most zealous to work for the church. Every Sunday the faithful came in greater numbers to church, until on November 1, All Saints Day, the Aglipayans got a shock because of the great multitude that attended, and it seems that they swore to keep us in continuous suspense.

I considered it my duty to inform the Governor — and I did so on November 3 — of the new era of persecution that we had entered (Exhibit No. 12). On the 11th I wrote him again (Exhibit No. 13) about new nocturnal stonings and other misdeeds. To escape from these, the people who had to work during the day, now had to stay awake the whole night to protect the lives of their wives and children. I asked him for Constabulary troops, because the incapability or the ill-will of the local authority was obvious. The following day I pointed in addition out to him that it was his obligation to inform the Governor and the Constabulary promptly of the abnormal situation in the place (Exhibit No. 14), also telling him of three new cases of stoning of my house and that since November 1 the same had happened to the houses of peaceful inhabitants.

My letter to the Governor written on the 11th was brought to him by three women, widows, who went to Surigao to seek from the Governor or the Judge the protection and the justice which they did not find in their own village, because — as I stated in my letter — ''The efforts of the guardians of justice are completely useless for various reasons, of which I have only to mention the fact that the crimes are committed in the darkness of the night, and that it is impossible to produce irrefutable witnesses.''

My letter had been given to the Governor; the bearers went to say goodbye to him after the 15th of November, before returning to Cabadbaran where they arrived on the 22nd without bringing any word of comfort or hope. Nevertheless, I found some of that comfort in the fact that the Justice of the Peace and the municipal President were at that time in Surigao, and would undoubtedly return with strict orders if not with the help of the Constabulary which I had requested.

The Justice of the Peace and the President were back in the morning of the 29th. I could not guess what orders they were carrying, because they did not tell me anything; the governor also did not give any answer.

Then there was another stoning, this time very well executed, because next to my bed dropped a piece of rock big enough to detach one board of my room. After that I gave up the little hope that was still in me. From that moment on the only thing I could tell the people (who were horrified that this still went on after the municipal President and the Justice of the Peace had returned from Surigao) was: ''Let us have patience and swallow it, because we are back in the days of the first Christians.''

Again I wrote to the municipal President informing him that also other houses had been stoned; I did so not so much to ask for protection, but to make sure that he could not claim ignorance of what was going on.

In the night of December 1 a few stones went through the nipa walls of the kitchen, forcing the convent boys who were doing the cooking, to hurry away.

Since then there was no more reason to stone the convent, because the municipal authority ordered to have its roof taken off and the staircase and the kitchen destroyed.

This event was occasioned by a fire that started at 12:45 PM and consumed the roof of the church in a little over two hours. Halfway in the afternoon the fire was nearly completely extinguished, so that the Spaniard Don Jose Aenlle suggested to return my things to the convent, because there was no more danger. But then, one of the fire-fighters became wounded and from that moment on the throwing of water stopped. A deliberation was held, and from the effects it can be deduced that they decided not to douse water anymore but let the wooden wall become a victim of the fire. It started indeed to burn, and then they agreed to take away the nipa of the adjacent part of the convent roof, to avoid its catching fire if the wind increased at night. But instead of removing the nipa closest to the church, they started with the most distant part, and when I pointed this out to the Presidente, he shouted at the workers not to remove that part, because that was not what had been agreed; but in fact he let them do it, and in addition they also removed the roof girders and destroyed the wooden staircase.

Those who witnessed these events since the middle of the afternoon, not people filled with hatred against Catholics, were deeply shocked by the procedures of the local authority, and believed that the intention was to see to it by all means that the Catholic missionary would leave the village, of which the administration had been entrusted to him. The Catholics of Cabadbaran did not dare offer me a safe place to stay that night. The Spaniard Don Jose Aenlle had a wife and children and could not take me in his house out of fear for their lives. So I had to ask the municipal President himself for a place to stay, and he indicated me an abandoned house that turned out to be uninhabitable even for one night. I owe it to the great kindness of the American teacher Mr. George Bohner that I did not have to spend the night in the open air and that my things, the properties of the convent and the church that had been saved from the fire, would not be left to the mercy of anybody.

Investigations are being made to find out if the fire had been intentional or accidental, but everybody is convinced that it was not an accident, because the time and circumstances had been carefully chosen to make the fire look like an accident, and moreover, the threats and the predictions made it probable that the hand of some schismatic had started it.

From the summary of the facts and the attached documents can clearly be gathered that the local authority of Cabadbaran has not shown the proper zeal in fulfilling its duty, and some people see manifest complicity in its behavior.

It would be ungrateful not to mention that the provincial authority and its Governor has given us some protection. They had well advised the municipal President to comply with his duty, and twice they have ordered to return the church bells. One order was given on September 6th and complied with on the 5th of October (Exhibit No. 16 and 16 bis). The other was given on the 24th but has been disregarded up to now. But the negligence of the municipal President in complying with orders of the Governor needs some comment. He had received the orders amply in time to comply with them much earlier than he in fact did. The Governor was informed of that culpable delay (Exhibit No. 5 and No. 18). Because we had no bells since May 25, it was very difficult for us to call the people to church.

I would have desired that the Governor do something against the failure of the municipal authority to inform him about the misdeeds of which the Catholics were the victims; after all, it was the Presidente himself who admitted that he was not capable to prevent them. I would also have desired that something be done to assure that some results came out of the resolution (Exhibit No. 16) that says that the criminals who stoned the houses of peaceable citizens would be punished. I would moreover have desired that, since he had become aware during his visit to Cabadbaran that the local authorities were not unconnected with the persecution, he would not have omitted to punish the forced registration of Aglipayans and *romunistas* and the threats under which it happened, and that, once informed of the protests against so many caprices passed off as ordinances but that de facto were directed at the Catholics, he would have returned the money to those who had been punished. Finally, I would have desired that some reparation or indemnization had been given for having deprived the Catholics of their church bells since May 25, and for the damage caused to the church by wind and rain when he did not allow them to work at the repair without their being exposed to grave evils. Similarly, that he would have given a proper indemnization to those who found themselves in the necessity to live outside the village and to those who had to spend many nights in the open air to keep watch, as well as to those whose houses had been stoned.

If any of these things had been done, then the people of Cabadbaran would have seen that the Governor did give some protection to his peaceful subjects and that he came out for the defense of justice...then the crimes would not have lasted that long.

When the widows Dafrosa Aznar, accusing by name a person whom she had seen stoning her house, and Marcela Doldol, still with a headwound, and also Maxima Dagani, whose son Valentin Cabonce had been attacked in the street, when these women went to Surigao in search of protection and justice, one would have expected something more than words from the Governor, but after a tiresome trip and after going into debt to pay for their fare to Surigao, these unlucky women returned here full of sorrow and became the target of ridicule by the schismatics, who once more were certain that they found protection in Surigao, while the Catholics became extremely disappointed when seeing that they had nothing to hope for than oppression here in Cabadbaran and indifference in the capital.

Still, it must be said that this is not the whole truth; the Governor *did* write to the municipal President of Cabadbaran just like on other occasions; he had even threatened him if he did not comply. He had the kindness to send me a copy of those orders (Exhibit No. 19) and also to acknowledge receipt of my last two letters; he also informed me (Exhibit No. 20) that he had told the Inspector of the Constabulary to send troops to Cabadbaran for the protection of persons and property. The truth, however, is that these letters, dated November 15, could have been sent to Cabadbaran either through the above mentioned two women who arrived here on the 22nd, or through the Justice of the Peace or the municipal President who arrived on the 29th, or in many other ways available between November 15 and 30. If they had arrived at the proper time and had been complied with, the last crimes would have been prevented, and possibly even the burning of the church and the damage done to the convent. In fact, they did not arrive in time, and were not complied with, and for that reason the Governor should have followed up the matter. Now I can only tell him that his letter and the copy dated November 15 were received by me in Butuan on December 6 while on December 3 at the time when I left Cabadbaran where I had no church and no place to stay, no Constabulary troops had arrived there (Exhibit No. 21).

I desire and ask the superior authority of the Philippines to take proper steps, so that the impunity of the crimes committed in Cabadbaran against the Catholics will not become a precedent for local and provincial authorities elsewhere.

I ask for security for the persons and the properties of the Catholics of Cabadbaran, a security which (as we learned through sad experience) can not be expected from mere words and threats.

Finally, I ask that a proper indemnization will be given to the Catholics and the church of Cabadbaran for the outrages which they have experienced during these times of unjust persecution.

These are crimes committed in contempt of the Government of the United States of America and against one of her constitutional laws, and therefore this Government should come to the defense of its honor and of justice, as she has done so often when her citizens living in other countries had been molested — for which she asked satisfactory indemnization and reparation. The Catholics of Cabadbaran although living in the province of Surigao do not thereby cease to be citizens of the United States of America; therefore they deserve equal reparation for damages incurred through the neglect or ill-will of their immediate authorities.

Basing myself on the principle of equity, and to prevent that it will be said that in municipalities of the United States there is less security for persons and their interests in time of peace than there was in semi-wild villages in the time of the revolution, the undersigned missionary of Cabadbaran has appealed to the superior Government of the Philippines.

Respectfully
Francisco Nebot SJ

CONCLUDING REMARK TO NEBOT'S LETTER

A note to the full text seems in order.
1. This (and undoubtedly other) kind of letters throw some light on the words of Dean C. Worcester about the quality of local and provincial governments in the areas mentioned by him plus the sources from where he got his information. This letter must have had a strong influence on the decision of the superior Government in 1907 to make Agusan a "special" province with appointed instead of elected officials.
2. On March 23, 1906 "Libertas" when reporting on the Christian death of Governor Daniel Toribio Sison (the Governor with whom Nebot was dealing), writes that the Manila Government did not accept his re-election "because of his sickness." That may also have been true, but the full truth is probably that factors like those mentioned in Nebot's letter had more to do with it. The decision about the "special province" was then in the making.

XXI

Epilogue

The Benedictines did not stay long in Surigao. They had come to Mindanao with a double purpose: evangelization and the organization of agricultural colonies. The latter was not even seriously attempted, and the former was a task which they might individually have accepted with idealism but for which they lacked a corporate quality. They were contemplative monks who, once uprooted from inside the protective monastery walls of Montserrat, found themselves unprepared for the tough exigencies of combining monastic rules with the pioneering apostolate required in a backyard of the archipelago such as Surigao. They had no mature overseas missionary tradition behind them, and they had applied for the task in a situation which makes one doubt if their motivations were of the kind needed to sustain their apostolate under the actual conditions they would encounter in Surigao. Right from the beginning a serious internal dissension invaded their ranks, and that again paralyzed much of the corporate or individual idealism that had brought these "displaced monks" to Mindanao. Moreover, within two years after their arrival they were caught in the upheaval of the revolution, imprisonment, cessation of Spanish authority and the kind of hostilities described in the two preceding chapters. Without the backing of the *patronato*-system they were, so to say, like babes in the woods of contemporary Surigao. Already in 1906-1907 the mother-abbey in Spain and the superior in Manila had come to the conclusion: *"missiones in Mindanao quamprimum relinquendas esse,"* that the mission stations in Mindanao should be abandoned as soon as possible, and that the missionaries should be employed in an apostolate directly connected with a community attached to the new (1902) San Beda College in Manila.

As has been stated before, the Benedictines had applied for missionary work in the Philippines in order to be allowed to accept new members and have them exempted from military service. This necessity had occurred in the days when anti-clerical governments in Spain tried to abolish the (contemplative) religious Orders. Because of the Philippine revolution and its outcome they found themselves in a Philippines free of Spanish authority, and as soon as possible they made use of the new political situation to return to their original monastic way of life. In a peculiar way, the revolution had liberated these Spaniards too!

At the same time, on November 7, 1907, the Dutch Father Henri Peeters, MSC wrote from Tilburg to the General Superior of his Society in Rome: "In the provincial Council we have been talking about the Philippines." Bishop Thomas Hendrick of Cebu had been begging all over Europe for missionaries for the parishes of Surigao that were going to be abandoned by the Benedictines. In the just mentioned Council meeting the Dutch province of the Sacred Heart Missionaries (MSC) had agreed in principle to accept the pastoral care of Surigao after many other religious corporations had. according to the Bishop, refused to do so ("Copie de lettres 1906-1909" p. 173, personal papers of Fr. Peeters).

The Generalate in Rome requested the Alsatian Father Eugene Merg, then residing in Sydney, to proceed to Surigao for an exploratory visit. In Manila the Apostolic Delegate, Msgr. Agius, himself a Benedictine, told him: "We Benedictines are not made for the missions but for the Choir."

> For the rest, the Apostolic Delegate has formally told me that by official decision of the Chapter of Montserrat, as well of the General Superior and of himself as Delegate, the Benedictines will abandon Surigao, regardless of whether we will succeed them or not (leaving the mission without priests for the moment), and would assign some of them to Manila, others to Spain.

> It is very clear that the first impression we had in Europe of the Benedictines wanting to leave Surigao to look for a better place in the archipelago is unfounded. They only wish to retire

OBISPADO

DE

CEBÚ

—=—

Pueden VV. RR.
entregar todos estos
Curatos y Misiones
á los RR. OP. del
Sag. Corazon segun
los titulos expedi-
dos en conformidad
con la comunica-
cion del P. Prior
de Benedictinos
fha. 9 del que fina-
liza, quedando satis-
fecho de la adminis-
tracion de VV. RR.
á quienes damos
gracias en nombre

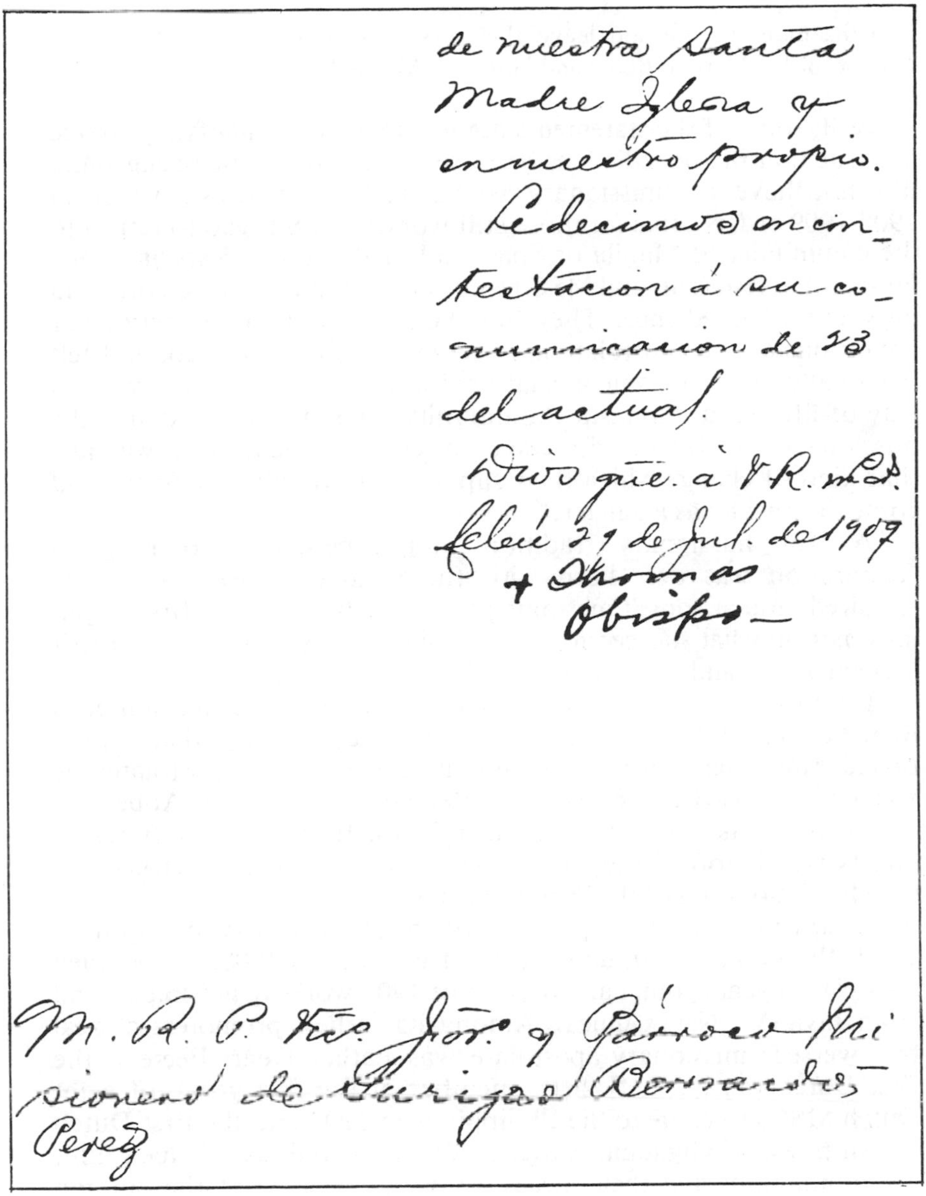

de nuestra Santa
Madre Iglesia y
en nuestro propio.
Le decimos en con-
testación á su co-
municación de 23
del actual.
Dios gue. á V R. m.s a.s
Cebú 27 de Jul. de 1907
+ Thomas
Obispo—

M. R. P. Fco. Jor. y Párroco Misionero de Surigao Bernardo
Perez

Fig. 34. Communication of Bishop Thomas Hendrick of Cebu authorizing the Benedictines to transfer the mission of Surigao to the Dutch Sacred Heart Missionaries. (Courtesy Archive Montserrat, Spain.)

into the monastic life and leave the mission field to others''
(Report of Fr. Merg to Rome and Holland, March 1908).

Still, some of the statements made above need qualifying. While
it is true that the Benedictines because of their monastic background
did not have a "missionary tradition," nevertheless, when in
1908-1909 orders came for those still working in Surigao to return to
the community of Manila or Spain, all of the nine priests and four
lay-Brothers (so OSB and MSC reports reveal) did so reluctantly and
only out of obedience. They had become used to the particular
conditions of the apostolate in post-revolutionary Surigao, and felt
personally more at home in that environment than in the restricted
way-of-life in a monastic community. To a great extent, the
missionary apostolate had made them changed men, but it was just
that kind of change which their superiors in Manila and Spain had
come to consider as a danger![55]

As for missionary tradition and experience, no religious
corporation was ever born with these values; they have to be
acquired, and at some time some persons have to be the first to put
into motion what succeeding generations of missionaries will inherit
as a corporate and moral impetus.

It may also be noted here that the Apostolic Delegate, himself a
Benedictine, was not wholly sincere when stating that "the"
Benedictines were unfit for a missionary type of apostolate; he
himself had earlier begged the Belgian Benedictine Abbey of
Aflighem to take over the Surigao mission from their confreres of
Montserrat before Bishop Hendrick of Cebu had approached the
Dutch Missionaries of the Sacred Heart!

At any rate, the Dutch province of the latter Society did not have
much "missionary" tradition behind it either in 1908. It was then
only eleven years young and only since 1903 working in Maluku and
Irian Jaya (W. New Guinea). Among its earliest promoters of zeal
for overseas missionary apostolate was Father Henri Peeters, the
first Dutchman in the Society, member of the first group of eight
Dutch MSCs to come to the Philippines in 1908 and the first Dutch
parish priest of Gigaquit, Surigao. What undoubtedly helped him,
his companions and their successors to make a go of the Surigao

---

[55] At the time of their departure from Surigao, the Benedictines were
established in the following main stations: Surigao (3 priests), Gigaquit,
Cantilan and Hinatuan, each with 2 priests.

mission and sustain it up to the present, was a goodly amount of nordic sturdiness and, say, determination, assets that, almost as certainly, may have set some charming but perhaps languid hispano-oriental sensitivities aflutter more than once... Often, under prevailing circumstances, it was perhaps the kind of hardiness needed to keep them going.

In his report, about his reconnaissance trip to Surigao, Father Merg had noted:

> "Before anything else, those who wish to undertake that mission, should be clearly aware that they will be going to a mission country pure and simple, that they will have to live the life of missionaries and accept the sacrifices and the toil inherent in such a life" (loc. cit.).

The author knew very well what a "mission country pure and simple" meant: his confreres were then already working in eastern New Guinea, he serving as their procurator in Australia; others were pioneering in the western part of the island (now Irian Jaya) and in Maluku!

Father Merg then hastens to add the following "redeeming factor" that eventual missionaries for Surigao could also take into account;

> "On the other hand, life among these people has a very interesting aspect to it, aside from the consolation which a zealous missionary always derives from the apostolic ministry. It is the fact that the inhabitants possess a naturally friendly, nice and open character. They have also a high esteem for the "Padre" whom they have always regarded, even under the former regime, as the father and leader of the people. This veneration still exists and is expressed by the prevailing custom to kiss his hand whenever they meet him, by the submission they show to him, by their fidelity to obey the Church and by the goodwill to help the priest with Mass stipends or gifts in nature, provided that he has succeeded in gaining their confidence...
>
> The faith is solidly anchored among them, although there is much ignorance among them. The great burden will be to properly instruct them, if one wishes that faith to resist the influences of the new regime of liberalism and the example of indifferentism and division shown by this new regime...

The constant experience of other missionaries recently arrived in provinces even poorer than Surigao is that the people always support the missionaries who are devoted to them; they will see to it that he will never lack what is necessary'' (loc. cit.).

Some of the first MSCs to come to Surigao thought that on certain points the report of pathfinder Merg had been relying too much on information orally supplied by the Manila superior of the Benedictines, who wished to dispose of the Surigao mission as soon as possible and therefore might have given a too rosy picture of the reality. This may have been true with regard to some needed arrangements with the Curia of Cebu and in the matter of financial security for the mission. But there has never been a Dutch successor to the Spanish Recoletos, Jesuits and Benedictines who would not have subscribed to the just quoted description of the kind of people he was going to meet in Surigao and later in Agusan.

Probably, the Dutch missionaries were intially more "foreign" to the people than their Spanish predecessors; in addition, they never enjoyed the benefits of a *patronato*-system and of a colonial context of countrymen as the latter had till quite recently been favored with. Nevertheless, they have remained longer with the people of the Old Caraga district than the Spanish Jesuits and Benedictines. History will credit them with having brought again an element of stability and reliability into a local Church which had known so much discontinuity within the time-span of the generation straddling the last quarter of the 19th and the beginning of the 20th century. History will also credit the people for having made this possible with the characteristics noticed by Father Merg.

One joy of writing local history is the opportunity one has to entrust this to paper!

Flowers on the graves of all those who walked in or between the lines of the preceding pages!

Flowers on the tables of you, children of their history, who read about them today!

Bibliography

Academia Real de la Historia: "Documentos Ineditos de Ultramar, Filipinas" Vols. I and II, Madrid, 1886-1887, Manila, 1969.

Achútegui, Pedro S. de and Miguel A. Bernad: "Religious Revolution in the Philippines" vol. 1. Manila, 1960.

Aganduro Moriz, R. de: "Historia General de las Islas Occidentales a la Asia adyacentes, llamadas Philippinas" Madrid, 1882.

Agudo, Guillermo, OAR: "Importantisima Cuestion" Madrid, 1863

Agustin, S. Gaspar de, OSA: "Conquistas de las Islas Filipinas" Madrid, 1696, new ed. Madrid, 1975.

Alcina, Francisco, SJ: "La Historia de las Islas y Indios Visayas" Madrid, 1668, new ed. Madrid, 1975.

Antonio, S., Juan de: "Chronicas de la Apostolica Provincia de San Gregorio de los Religiosos Descalzos de N. P. S. Francisco" Vol. I, Manila 1738. Picornell translation, Manila, 1977.

Argensola, Bartolomé Leonardo: "La Conquista de las Islas Malucas" 2nd. ed. Zaragoza, 1891.

Astrain, A.: "Historia de la Compañia de Jesus en la asistencia de España" 8 vols., Madrid, 1902-1925.

Ayerba, Marques de: "Sitio y Conquista de Manila por los Ingleses en 1762" Zaragoza, 1897.

Barros, Joao, de: "Historia da Asia y das Indias" Lisbon, 1552-1563, Dutch ed. Leyden, 1706.

Barrows, David: "History of the Philippines." 2nd. ed. Chicago, 1925.

Bernaldez, Emilio: "Reseña historica de la guerra al sur de Filipinas... hasta nuestros días" Madrid, 1857.

Bertrand, L.: "Philippe II et L'Escoril" Paris, 1929.

Biblioteca Hispana Missionum: I and II, Barcelona, 1930.

Blair, Emma and James Robertson: "The Philippine Islands" 55 vols. Cleveland, Ohio, 1903-1909, Manila, 1973.

Blas, Gregorio Fidel, de, OAR: "Labor Evangelica de los Padres Agustinos Recoletos en las Islas Filipinas" Manila, 1882, Zaragoza, 1910.

Brou, A., SJ: "Saint François Xavier" 2nd. ed. Paris, 1922.

Buceta, Manuel y Felipe Bravo: "Diccionario geografico-historico de las Islas Filipinas" Madrid, 1851.

Burney, James: "A Chronological History of the Discoveries in the South or Pacific Ocean" 5 vols. London, 1803.

Callahan, William J.: "Church, Politics and Society in Spain, 1750-1874" Harvard University Press, 1984.

"Cartas de los Pp. de la Compañia de Jesus de Filipinas" (1876-1902).

Census Office: "Census of the Philippine Islands" 4 vols. Manila, 1920.

Chijs, J. v.d.: "Dagh-Register van het Kasteel Batavia" Batavia, 1887-1904.

Chirino, Pedro, SJ: "Relación de las Islas Filipinas" Rome, 1604. Echevarría translation, Manila, 1969.

Colin, Francisco, SJ: "Labor Evangelica" (1663) 3 vols. Pastells ed., Barcelona, 1900-1902.

Combés, Francisco, SJ: "Historia de Mindanao y Jolo y sus adyacentes" (1667), Retana ed., Madrid, 1897.

Compañía de Jesus, Algunos padres de la misión de la: "El Archipielago Filipino" 2 vols. Washington, 1900.

Concepción, Juan de la, OAR: "Historia General de Philipinas" 14 vols. Manila, 1788-1792.

Costa, Horacio de la, SJ: "The Jesuits in the Philippines, 1581-1768." Cambridge, 1962.

Costa, Horacio de la, SJ: "Readings in Philippine History" Manila, 1973.

Crétineau-Joly, J.: "Clément XIV et les Jésuites" Paris, 1847.

Delgado, Juan José, SJ.: "Historia General...Filipinas" Manila, 1892, but originally written 1751-1754.

Desdevises, G.: "L'Eglise espagnole des Indes á la fin du 18 iéme siécle" Revue Hispanique, 39, Paris, 1917.

Dijk, L.v.: "Neerland's vroegste betrekkingen...China" Amsterdam, 1882.

Echevarría, Ramón: "The Philippines in 1600" Tr. from Pedro Chirino "Relación de las Islas Filipinas" Manila, 1969.

Fassbinder, M.: "Der Jesuitenstaat in Paraguay" (1926).

Fernandez, Pablo, OP: "History of the Church in the Philippines" Manila, 1979.

Ferrando, Juan, OP: "Historia de los Pp. Dominicos en las Islas Filipinas, y en sus misiones del Japon, China, Tungkin y Formosa" 6 vols. Madrid, 1870-1872.

Francisco, Juan R.: "The Philippines and India" Manila, 1971.

Francisco de Asis, S., Pedro de: "Historia General de los Religiosos Descalzos..." Barcelona, 1743 and Zaragoza, 1756.

Furet, Francois: The Uses of History, Solidarity 6(12):56-58(1971).

Galende, Pedro, OSA: "Apologia pro Filipinos" Manila, 1980.

Godée Molsbergen, E.: Geschiedenis van de Minahassa tot 1829" Batavia, 1928.

Herrera, Antonio de: "Historia General de las Indias Occidentales, y de los hechos Castillanos" Antwerp, 1728, 3rd. ed. Madrid, 1934.

Hulsebosch, A.: "De Reducties van Paraguay" Nijmegen, 1917.

Jacobs, Hubert, SJ: "Documenta Malucensia" 3 vols. Rome, 1974, 1980, 1984.

Jesus, Luiz de, OAR: "Historia General de los Religiosos Descalzos..." Madrid, 1681.

Joaquin, Nick: La Naval de Manila and other Essays, 1964.

Ligthart, C.J.: "De Nederlandse Jezuieten Generaal Jan Philip Roothaan" (1972).

Lopez, Rafael and Alfonso Felix: "The Christianization of the Philippines" Manila, 1965.

Marin y Morales, Valentin, OP: "Ensayo de una Sintesis de los Trabajos realizados por las Corporaciones Religiosas Españoles de Filipinas" 2 vols. Manila, 1901.

Martinez de Zuñiga, Joaquin, OSA: "Estadismo de las Islas Filipinas" Madrid, 1893.

Martinez de Zuñiga, Joaquin, OSA: "Historia de las Islas Filipinas" Manila, 1803.

Merriman, R. B.: "The Rise of the Spanish Empire" London, 1934.

Mitchell, Mairin: "Friar Andres de Urdaneta" London, 1964.

Montalban, F.: "Das Spanische Patronat und die Eroberung der Philippinen" Freiburg i.Br., 1936.

Montano, Joseph: "Voyage aux Isles Philippines et en Malaisie" Paris, 1886.

Montero y Vidal, Jose: "Historia de la piratería malayamahometana en Mindanao, Jolo y Borneo" 2 vols. Madrid, 1888.

Muratori, M. "Rélation des missions de Paraguai" Paris, 1826.

Netzorg, Morton J.: "The island of 'San Juan' off the Mindanao coast: a cartographic puzzle" *Kinaadman* 7(1):149-194 (1985).

Nicolas, Andres de, San, OAR: "Historia General de los Religiosos Descalzos..." Madrid, 1664.

Ochoa del Carmen, Gregorio, OAR and Manuel Carceller, OAR: "Historia General de los Religiosos Descalzos..." vols. VIII-XII. Madrid, 1929-1962.

Odijk, A. v., MSC: "The Christianization of the Dioceses of Surigao and Butuan" Mimeogr., Cagayan de Oro, 1973.

Oviedo: Historia General II, p. 32.

Parr, Charles McKew: "So Noble a Captain" New York, 1953.

Parrado, Gonzalez, Julian: "Memoria acerca de Mindanao" Manila, 1893.

Pascual y Beltran, Ventura: "Un Apostól de civilización" Barcelona, 1920.

Pastells, Pablo, SJ: "Misión de la Compañia de Jesus de Filipinas en el siglo XIX" 3 vols, Barcelona, 1916-1917.

Pastells, Pablo, SJ: "Historia General de Filipinas" jointly with "Catalogo ..." by Pedro Torres Lanza. Barcelona, 1925.

Pastells, Pablo, SJ and F. Mateos: "Historia de la Compañia de Jesus en... Paraguay" Barcelona, 1912-1949.

Paulus, J. et al.: "Encyclopaedie van Nederlandsch Indie" 8 vols. The Hague/Leiden, 1917-1939.

Pigafetta, Antonio: "First Voyage Around the World" Filipiniana Book Guild, Manila, 1969.

Quirino, Carlos: "Philippine Cartography" 2nd. ed. Amsterdam, 1963.

Ribadeneira, Marcelo de, OFM: "Historia del Archipielago y otros Reynos" (1598), Manila ed., 1970.

Rodriguez, Isacio, OSA: "Historia de la Provincia Agustiniana de Filipinas" 14 vols. Manila, 1965-1978.

Romero de Madridejos, Benito: "Pastorales y demas Disposiciones circuladas a los Parrocos de esta Diocesis de Cebu" Manila, 1883.

Ruiz, Licinio, OAR: "Breve Reseña de la diocesis de Cebu" 1886.

Ruiz, Licinio, OAR: "Sinopsis Historica de la Provincia de San Nicolas de Tolentino de las Islas Filipinas" Manila, 1925.

Sádaba, Francisco, OAR: "Catalogo de los Religiosos de la Provincia de San Nicolas de Tolentino de Filipinas" Madrid, 1906.

Saderra Maso, Miguel, SJ: "Misiones Jesuiticas en Filipinas" Manila, 1924.

Saderra Mata, M.: "Noticias biograficas del R.P. Juan B. Heras" Manila, 1918.

Santayana, Agustin: "La Isla de Mindanao" Madrid, 1862.

Schmidlin, J., SVD: "Katholische Missionsgeschichte" Steyl, 1925.

Schnürer, Gustav: "Die Katholische Kirche und Kultur während der Barockzeit" Dutch ed. Haarlem, 1951.

Schreurs, Peter: "Angry Days in Mindanao" University of San Carlos, Cebu City, 1987.

Schumacher, John N., SJ.: "The Propaganda Movement: 1880-1985" Manila, 1973.

Schumacher, John N., SJ: "Readings in Philippine Church History" Manila, 1979.

Schumacher, John N., SJ: "Revolutionary Clergy" Manila, 1981.

Scott, William Henry: "Why then the Butuan tradition?" Kinaadman 4:163-165 (1982).

Tiele, Pieter: "De Europeers in den Maleischen Archipel" The Hague, 1878.

Visser, B.J.J., MSC: "Onder Portugeesch-Spaansche Vlag" Amsterdam, 1925.

Wessels, C., SJ: "Geschiedenis v.d. R.K. Missie in Amboina, 1546-1605" Nijmegen, 1926.

Worcester, Dean C.: "The Philippines, Past and Present" New York, 1914, New York, 1933.

Xavier, Adro: "Ocaso del Imperio" Madrid, 1940.

INDEX

PERSONAL NAMES

PLACE-NAMES